Cardinal Manning

Cardinal Manning
An Intellectual Biography

JAMES PEREIRO

CLARENDON PRESS · OXFORD

1998

Oxford University Press, Great Clarendon Street, Oxford OX2 6DP

Oxford New York
Athens Auckland Bangkok Bogotá Bombay
Buenos Aires Calcutta Cape Town Dar es Salaam
Delhi Florence Hong Kong Istanbul Karachi
Kuala Lumpur Madras Madrid Melbourne
Mexico City Nairobi Paris Singapore
Taipei Tokyo Toronto Warsaw

and associated companies in
Berlin Ibadan

Oxford is a trade mark of Oxford University Press

Published in the United States
by Oxford University Press Inc., New York

British Library Cataloguing in Publication Data
Data available

Library of Congress Cataloging in Publication Data
Cardinal Manning : an intellectual biography / James Pereiro.
Includes bibliographical references and index.
1. Manning, Henry Edward, 1808–1892.   I. Title.
BX4705.M3P47   1998   282'.092—dc21   98-3191

ISBN 0-19-815089-X

1 3 5 7 9 10 8 6 4 2

Typeset by David Gregson Associates, Beccles, Suffolk
Printed in Great Britain on acid-free paper by
Bookcraft (Bath) Ltd., Midsomer Norton

To
M. A. Elejoste

Acknowledgements

The research for the present work was undertaken at the suggestion of Professor V. Alan McClelland. He considered that Henry Edward Manning's religious thought had been rather neglected and that, in consequence, there was a lack of proportion and perspective in the accounts of a very important area of nineteenth-century English religious history. Professor McClelland has closely followed the progress of my research, and offered me invaluable guidance and encouragement. To him I owe my greatest debt of gratitude.

During these years of research I have accumulated many other debts of gratitude. Dr David Newsome was originally a source of inspiration through his books, and was later to offer a friendly welcome to my inquiries. The Freiburg Symposia of the J. H. Newman/H. E. Manning Research Project, organized by Professors Günter Biemer and Alan McClelland over three years (1993-5), granted me the opportunity of entering into contact with Newman and Manning scholars in the friendly atmosphere of a small discussion group. I learned much from the participants at the symposia: the organizers, Dr Sheridan Gilley, the Rt. Revd Dr Geoffrey Rowell (Anglican bishop of Basingstoke), Dr Peter Nockles, Fr. Vincent Blehl, and the German contributors. In papers presented to the symposia over those three years I put forward many of the ideas contained in this book, and received invaluable help in the comments and discussions which followed them. I must thank in particular Sheridan Gilley and Peter Nockles for reading the whole manuscript and for their many suggestions. Dr Jane Garnett's Oxford Seminar on British Religious History since 1700 has enabled me to contrast the results of my research with those of scholars working in fields close to my own. Dr Garnett also read some sections of the manuscript and offered me welcome advice.

I must also thank the Revds Kenneth Macnab and William

Davage, of Pusey House (Oxford), where I spent many hours using their rich collection of printed and manuscript sources. The availability of the materials and the friendliness of the librarians made my work there very pleasant and fruitful. Many of Manning's papers are now to be found at Pitts Theological Library (Emory University, Atlanta). It was impossible for me at first to travel to the USA, but Professor Peter Erb, of Wilfrid Laurier University (Ontario), gave invaluable help by making available the edition of the Manning–Gladstone correspondence that he is preparing for publication (Manning's side of the correspondence being now at Emory). He also read, at different stages of production, the various sections of the book, and over the years we have discussed many aspects of our respective studies. I was later able to visit Pitts Theological Library, which, besides Manning's papers, also contains his library. Professor Patrick Graham, its director, and the library staff were particularly helpful and friendly. Fr. Patrick Mulhern offered me the hospitality of St Thomas More parish in Atlanta while I was working at Emory, and I greatly enjoyed my stay there.

It would be impossible for me to mention all those to whom I am indebted. I cannot conclude, however, without thanking Professor Jonathan Clark and Dr John Walsh for their suggestions and encouragement to continue my line of research, Fr. Aidan Nichols for looking at one of the chapters, as well as Fr. Ian Dickie for facilitating my work at the Westminster Diocesan Archive. Mr Andrew Hegarty was an invaluable help in checking the readability of the text, which owes much to his patience and attention to detail. Mr Jack Damian Grint gave welcome assistance in the correction of the proofs. For the faults in this work I am myself responsible.

Contents

Abbreviations

Appendix	H. E. Manning, *The Rule of Faith: Appendix to a Sermon* (London, 1838).
APUC	H. E. Manning, *The Reunion of Christendom: A Pastoral Letter* [dated Epiphany 1866] (London, 1866).
ASer	H. E. Manning, *Sermons*,
	vol. i (3rd edn., London, 1844) (1st edn. 1842)
	vol. ii (5th edn., London, 1849) (1st edn. 1843)
	vol. iii (4th edn., London, 1850) (1st edn. 1847)
	vol. iv (2nd edn., London, 1850) (1st edn. 1850).
CSer	H. E. Manning, *Sermons on Ecclesiastical Subjects,*
	vol. i (Dublin, 1869) (1st edn. 1863) [Sermons preached 1852–62]
	vol. ii (London, 1872) [Sermons preached 1859–65]
	vol. iii (London, 1873).
EC	H. E. Manning, *England and Christendom* (London, 1867).
	i. Preface
	ii. The Crown in Council, on the Essays and Reviews: A Letter to an Anglican Friend (dated 8 Mar. 1864)
	iii. The Convocation and the Crown in Council (dated 25 July 1864).
English Church	H. E. Manning, *The English Church: Its Succession and Witness for Christ* (London, 1835).
Four Evils	H. E. Manning, *The Four Great Evils of the Day* (8th edn., London, n.d.) (1st edn. 1871).
Fourfold	H. E. Manning, *The Fourfold Sovereignty of God* (London, 1871).
Grounds	H. E. Manning, *The Grounds of Faith* (new edn., London, 1856) (1st edn. 1852).
LD	*The Letters and Diaries of John Henry Newman*

vols. i–vii, eds. I. Ker, T. Gornall, and G. Tracey (Oxford, 1978–95)

vols. xi–xxxi, eds. C. S. Dessain, E. E. Kelly, T. Gornall (London, 1961–72; Oxford, 1973–77).

Manning MSS Bod.   Manning Papers at the Bodleian Library, Oxford.

Pitts   Manning Papers at Pitts Theological Library, Emory University, Atlanta (USA).

West.   Manning Papers at Westminster Diocesan Archive, London.

M   J. D. Mansi (ed.), *Sacrorum Conciliorum nova et amplissima collectio*, vols. xlix–liii (Arnhem and Leipzig, 1923–7).

Miscellanies   H. E. Manning, *Miscellanies*, i–ii (London, 1877) iii (London, 1888).

P   E. S. Purcell, *Life of Cardinal Manning, Archbishop of Westminster* (2 vols., London, 1896).

Privilegium   H. E. Manning, *Petri Privilegium: Three Pastoral Letters to the Clergy of the Diocese* (London, 1871).
i. The Centenary of Saint Peter and the General Council (8 September 1867)
ii. The Oecumenical Council and the Infallibility of the Roman Pontiff (Rosary Sunday, 1869)
iii. The Vatican Council and its Definitions (Feast of St Edward the Confessor, 1870).

Rule   H. E. Manning, *The Rule of Faith* (London, 1838).

TM   H. E. Manning, *The Temporal Mission of the Holy Ghost, or Reason and Revelation* (6th edn., London, 1909) (1st edn., 1865).

True   H. E. Manning, *The True Story of the Vatican Council* (2nd edn., London, n.d.) (1st edn., 1877).

Unity   H. E. Manning, *The Unity of the Church* (London, 1842).

VM   J. H. Newman, *The Via Media of the Anglican Church* (new ed., 2 vols., London, 1897).

Workings   H. E. Manning, *The Workings of the Holy Spirit in the Church of England: A Letter to the Revd E.B. Pusey, DD* (London, 1864).

Introduction

Henry Edward Manning (1808–92), sometime Anglican Arch-deacon of Chichester and later second Catholic Archbishop of Westminster, was one of the most influential figures in the history of the Catholic Church and in English social life during the nineteenth century. His role was not confined to the boundaries of his country, or even of the British Empire. He reached much further to play an important part in the life of the Church Universal, particularly during the First Vatican Council, and to work for the cause of the oppressed in conti-nental Europe and in the United States of America. It may therefore come as a surprise to discover the neglect into which his life and work have fallen, a neglect which fails to do justice to his historical stature.

Manning was unfortunate in having Edmund Sheridan Purcell as his first biographer.[1] The almost cloak-and-dagger drama surrounding Purcell's biography has already been told by Sheridan Gilley.[2] Wilfrid Ward, who played an important part in it, while far removed from Manning's ideas and poli-cies, was horrified when he caught glimpses of the still unpub-lished fruit of Purcell's labours. Baron von Hügel also had caught glimpses of the manuscript. Both tried to persuade Purcell to rectify his slanted presentation of the Cardinal. Their efforts were to no avail. Purcell had cast Manning in the mould of the ambitious authoritarian and unscrupulous schemer, always quick to join the dominant party for as long as it held the upper hand, and likewise prompt in cutting off any links with it when its influence was on the wane, a man

---

[1] E. S. Purcell, *Life of Cardinal Manning, Archbishop of Westminster* (2 vols., London, 1896). The biography was a tremendous success, with four editions printed between January and March 1896.

[2] S. Gilley, 'New light on an Old Scandal: Purcell's life of Cardinal Manning', in A. Bellenger (ed.), *Opening the Scrolls: Essays in Catholic History in Honour of Godfrey Anstruther* (Bath, 1987), 166–98.

ready to sweep aside every obstacle on the way to attaining his ends. Purcell acknowledged that Manning thought his ends were God's ends. But this, far from being a redeeming feature, served to condemn him even further, as an ecclesiastical Machiavelli suffering from self-delusion and self-absolving hypocrisy. Purcell, when describing what he called Manning's 'double voice', was depicting, rather, a double character: 'a sort of Jekyll and Hyde rapidly alternating between the lowest motives and the highest, between grasping personal ambition and complete self-abnegation before God'.[3] His portrait of Manning was the result of consistent misinterpretation of his subject's words and actions. Strachey turned Purcell's portrait into a masterpiece in his own *Eminent Victorians*.[4] His embittered iconoclasm found in Purcell's biography abundant materials on which to exert his powers of satire and ridicule. His elegant prose did the rest. The resulting characterization of Manning has endured to this day.

Since Purcell, there have been attempts to present a more balanced picture of the second Archbishop of Westminster, but, as Peter Erb has pointed out, most efforts to rescue Manning from Purcell's and Strachey's distortions started by accepting the general lines of their portrait.[5] The cruel caricature had superimposed itself on the real man to such an extent that he could no longer be seen except through it. Only lately, and that slowly, has it started to crumble under the combined efforts of more serious scholarship and common sense.

Manning's character, the human side of his personality, has perhaps been the first aspect to start on the slow road towards recovery. Wilfrid Ward's essay on Newman and Manning conveyed the latter's spiritual earnestness and sincerity, his example of priestly and pastoral virtue.[6] J. E. C. Bodley, the man Manning had chosen as his biographer, produced only a brief if sensitive profile of the Cardinal. In it he offered a non-

---

[3] S. Gilley, 'New Light', 178

[4] L. Strachey, *Eminent Victorians: Cardinal Manning, Florence Nightingale, Dr Arnold, General Gordon* (London, 1918).

[5] P. C. Erb, *A Question of Sovereignty: The Politics of Manning's Conversion* (Atlanta, 1996).

[6] W. Ward, 'Newman and Manning', in *Ten Personal Studies* (London, 1908), 260–98.

Catholic testimony to Manning's deep and sincere piety, his Englishness, and his profound concern for the suffering and the oppressed.[7] These appreciations did not reach a wide public, however, and, soon after they were published, Strachey's *Eminent Victorians* dealt the *coup de grâce* to the Cardinal's reputation. Shane Leslie's biography,[8] appearing a few years after Strachey's, went part way to redressing the damage caused by some of the allegations about Manning's ambition and dishonesty, and corrected a good number of Purcell's misinterpretations and errors of fact. In particular, Leslie shed new light on the Errington case. Wilfrid Ward, in his biography of Wiseman, had already done much to free Manning from Purcell's damaging misrepresentations.[9]

The combined efforts of Ward, Bodley, and Leslie, however, did little to dent the impression made by Purcell and Strachey on the general imagination. Only recently has Manning begun to receive the attention he deserves. David Newsome and Alan McClelland have played a determining role in revising the received portrait of Manning. Newsome has offered a masterly delineation of Manning's human personality, putting flesh and blood where before there had been only a mummified figure, in which only the eyes were alive with the lust for power which consumed the man.[10] McClelland, for his part, focused on Manning's stature as statesman and social reformer, his openness to contemporary social problems and needs, his sensitivity to human suffering, and his deep concern for the underprivileged.[11] Surprisingly, Manning's efforts to ameliorate the lot of the destitute, one of his most enduring claims to greatness, was misunderstood in his own day by other Catholics. His crusades in favour of Ireland and of the

---

[7] J. E. C. Bodley, *Cardinal Manning: The Decay of Idealism in France: The Institute of France* (London, 1912).

[8] S. Leslie, *Henry Edward Manning: His Life and Labours* (2nd edn. London, 1921).

[9] W. Ward, *The Life and Times of Cardinal Wiseman* (new edn. London, 1912) (1st edn., 1897).

[10] D. Newsome, *The Parting of Friends* (London, 1966; 2nd edn., 1993); idem, *The Convert Cardinals: John Henry Newman and Henry Edward Manning* (London, 1993).

[11] V. A. McClelland, *Cardinal Manning: His Public Life and Influence 1865–1892* (London, 1962). R. Gray's *Cardinal Manning: A Biography* (London, 1985), although very readable and on the whole positive in its appreciation of Manning, depends fundamentally on previous studies and secondary sources, and breaks little new ground.

poor, his support for trade unionism, and his campaigns
against drink and vivisection were attributed by Herbert
Vaughan to failing judgement or senility. Wilfrid Ward saw
them as a manifestation of the mystical element in Manning,
on a par with his apocalyptic visions about the fall of the
Pope's temporal power. Both saw them as a triumph of uncon-
trolled emotion over reason and judgement.[12]

There is, however, a facet of Manning's reputation which
has not recovered in parallel with the new perception of his
human character and social influence. History has not judged
Manning's intellectual powers very favourably. Historians
have tended, to a great extent, to conform to Gladstone's
opinion of Manning, when he wrote:

I habitually considered Manning's faculties of action, I mean in the
management and government of men, to be far in advance of his
faculties of thought. In polemical matters he was narrow and positive: he had not the power of looking all around a great subject ...
I think in short that his mind was not philosophical: ... he arrived
with extraordinary facility at broad conclusions: and he held to
them with a tenacity no less remarkable. He was not subtle, but he
was always intensely clear: if he deceived anybody, the person
taken in was alone responsible.[13]

Wilfrid Ward took a similar line. He considered that
Manning possessed superb but, in some aspects, superficial intellectual gifts. His was a ready rather than a deep mind, and
he did not possess the very highest intellectual qualities. What
intellectual powers Manning had, however, he used to full
effect. What he lacked in intellectual grasp was hidden to
many of his contemporaries by his clarity and tenacity of conviction. These gave him a power to move others with his ideas
quite disproportionate to their degree of intellectual depth.
Will-power, boundless activity, and a practical nature contributed to making Manning an effective leader of men. His influence, nevertheless, was short-lived. It resided in the power of

[12] See Gilley, 'New Light', 182, and W. Ward, 'Newman and Manning', 275.

[13] British Library, Gladstone Papers, Add. MSS 44709, fos. 177–8. Gladstone's
opinion of Manning's intellectual powers, which for a long time had been very high,
never recovered from the shock caused by the latter's conversion to Catholicism,
which Gladstone could only account for by attributing it to some intellectual deficiency on the part of his friend (cf. Newsome, *Parting of Friends*, 367).

his presence and personality, and, as a result, was destined to die with him.[14]

This assessment of Manning's mental powers has held the field for over a hundred years, and has gained in definition as time has gone by. Frederick Cwiekowski, in his study of the English bishops' contributions and reactions to the First Vatican Council, made his own Gladstone's comments, and went on to add that, as Manning 'was decidedly not a theologian, it would be an exaggeration to talk of the "sources" of his thought'.[15] He was 'far more interested in, and capable of, dealing with living men than with abstract ideas';[16] moreover, 'the limitations of his mind rarely permitted him to grasp more than the surface of the issue at hand'.[17] As a result, his positions tended to be one-sided and simplistic. Unfortunately, Cwiekowski thought, Manning's intellectual limitations were exacerbated by his psychological make-up. His intransigence made him incapable of seeing even the possibility of another position, while the fanatical zeal with which he pursued the ideas that he had at heart made him overstep frequently the boundaries of precision and discretion.[18]

Klaus Schatz, when mapping out the differences between Newman and Manning in his recent history of the First Vatican Council, has contributed to the negative picture of the latter as a thinker. In his opinion, Manning was, in almost every respect, the antithesis of Newman. As a man of action, Manning was for resoluteness and decisiveness, for clarity and certainty, as opposed to a more subtle position which would accept open-endedness, light and shadow, in the apprehension of truth.[19] Schatz is not alone in attempting to match different theological approaches to diverse psychologies. Lurking behind this assumption is at times the implication that human and intellectual maturity are marked by the ability to live with open-ended questions and uncertainty; conversely, a certain immaturity is accompanied by an inner sense of insecurity leading a person to look for certainties, and inclining

---

[14] W. Ward, 'Newman and Manning', 261–72.

[15] F. J. Cwiekowski, *The English Bishops and the First Vatican Council* (Louvain, 1971), 319.

[16] Ibid. 57.   [17] Ibid. 56.   [18] Cf. Ibid. 317–18.

[19] Cf. K. Schatz, *Vaticanum I*, 1869–1870, i (Paderborn, 1992), 50.

him to follow those who claim to offer them.[20] This, naturally, does not make for depth of thought: men of this stamp tend to accept propositions uncritically, trusting in the authority proposing them, rather than weighing in the balance an argument for their intrinsic truthfulness.

Different psychologies would not only breed different theological tempers, but would also generate different models of the Church. Those who were inclined to rest on authority would favour a monarchical and authoritarian model of society and the Church. Studies like that of Herman Joseff Pottmeyer have suggested that papal infallibility is 'the keystone of a monarchical ecclesiology based on an absolutist political ideology'.[21] The fact that many Ultramontanes, particularly in France, were in favour of absolute monarchical power seemed to confirm this assertion. The above interpretation seems to break down in Manning's case, however. His social concerns and support for the democratic process would sit uneasily, according to this theory, with his Ultramontanism. Some have attributed this paradox rather lamely to Manning's inconsistency.

There was, in fact, no inconsistency here. Manning's religious thought was the driving force of his humanitarianism. Unfortunately, there have been few and limited studies of Manning's intellectual formation and development, and those who have charged Manning with superficiality have, on the whole, done so on the basis of preconceived notions and a rather slight acquaintance with his thought. The studies of Newsome and McClelland, which went a long way to rescue Manning's image from neglect and misrepresentation, did not present a full, coherent picture of Manning's thought and intellectual development. They were engaged in filling a wider canvas, and the complexity of the subject did not allow them to devote greater attention to every aspect of the composition.

---

[20] Significantly, Keble, when considering the defections of Newman and others, thought that this urge for certainty was the temptation of the restless argumentative intellect wanting to take refuge in the calm waters protected by the defence walls of infallibility (cf. *Sermons Academical and Occasional* (Oxford, 1847), pp. lxvi–xvii).

[21] J. T. Ford, 'Infallibility: A Review of Recent Studies', *Theological Studies*, xl (1979), 289.

Newsome's works, although limited in this respect and sharing to some extent Gladstone's view of Manning's intellectual powers, are the best introduction to Manning's theological development. Before him, Y. Brilioth[22] and A. Härdelin[23] had offered, almost accidentally, a few passing glimpses into Manning's thought. The centenary of Manning's death (1992) could have been a great opportunity for a reappraisal of his life and thought. It left behind only the disappointment of a missed opportunity. David Newsome's *Convert Cardinals* (1993) and the Catholic Record Society's commemorative volume (1992)[24] were the only real contributions to a serious study of Manning. In the latter, Geoffrey Rowell and Christopher O'Gorman contributed interesting papers on some aspects of Manning's Anglican theology. More recently, Peter Erb, in his Aquinas Lecture at Emory University cited above, has produced an illuminating study of Manning's concept of the role of the will in theology and in the process of conversion.

The only comprehensive study of Manning's religious thought has been that of Ferdinand Cruz.[25] His book on Manning's concept of the Church tried to bring together in an organic whole the ideas dispersed in the sermons and books of his subject's Catholic period. Cruz identified some of the positive elements in Manning's thought as anticipating advances in ecclesiology which have become part of the common patrimony in our own century. He also remarked on the shortcomings of his approach, although the fact that he did so from the standpoint of the ecclesiology of the Second Vatican Council is hardly fair to Manning. The limitations of Cruz's book are mainly due to its unhistorical character. The study concentrates on Manning's Catholic works, and, on the whole, pays little attention to the historical circumstances in which they were written and the problems they were intended to address. Nor did Cruz consider Manning's role during the First

---

[22] Y. Brilioth, *The Anglican Revival: Studies in the Oxford Movement* (London, 1925).

[23] A. Härdelin, *The Tractarian Understanding of the Eucharist* (Uppsala, 1965).

[24] V. A. McClelland (ed.), 'Henry Edward Manning (1808–1892)', *Recusant History*, xxi 2 (Oct. 1992).

[25] F. L. Cruz, *Spiritus in Ecclesia: Las relaciones entre el Espíritu Santo y la Iglesia según el Cardenal Manning* (Pamplona, 1977).

Vatican Council. The book suffers, as a result, from a lack of perspective, and falls into some errors of interpretation.

The present work tries to follow Manning's intellectual development from the early years of his Anglican ministry till the First Vatican Council. My aim has been to link his ideas to the precise historical moment in which they were conceived and expressed, in order to gain a deeper understanding of his thought. At times, a particular incident has offered an occasion to bring together Manning's utterances on a particular subject over a longer period of time. The few cases in which this has been done are those in which Manning's thought showed a particular consistency, enduring almost unchanged despite the passing of time.

Manning was not a systematic theologian. His thought was rarely distilled into clearly conceived treatises. He developed and expressed his ideas in numerous letters, sermons, and minor works of circumstance. I made the decision, when starting out on the present study, to let Manning speak in his own words. This may at times reduce the clarity and structure of the text, but the inconvenience should be more than compensated by direct contact with Manning's way of expressing his thought. In the selection of quotations, earlier texts have been preferred to later expressions of the same or similar concepts, in order to locate chronologically, as far as possible, the emergence of his ideas.

There are some aspects of Manning's thought which I have not dealt with in detail in the present study. This is intentional. The main omission concerns Manning's ideas about the relationship between Church and State. Jeffrey von Arx has worked on this subject, concentrating on the controversy surrounding the loss of the Pope's temporal power and the polemics generated by the *Kulturkampf* and Gladstone's *Vaticanism*.[26] The forthcoming publication of the Gladstone–Manning correspondence prepared by Peter Erb will shed further light on the subject. The reader is referred to these

[26] J. P. von Arx, 'Manning's Ultramontanism and the Catholic Church in British Politics', *Recusant History*, xix 3 (May 1989), 332–47; *idem*, 'Archbishop Manning and the Kulturkampf', *Recusant History*, xxi 2 (Oct. 1992), 254–66. See also D. Quinn, *Patronage and Piety: The Politics of English Roman Catholicism, 1850–1900* (Basingstoke, 1993).

studies for detailed information. McClelland's fascinating account of Manning's involvement in social issues—education, Ireland, Trade Unions, etc.—should also be consulted to complete the picture of Manning's religious thought with the ways it translated itself into social action.

I

A Time for Building:
Manning's *Via Media*

1. *Evangelical or 'High and Dry' Anglican?*

On his arrival at Lavington in January 1833, soon after his
ordination as a deacon, H. E. Manning's theological baggage
fitted neatly into a few short sentences. He summed it up in
1850, in a letter to Samuel Wilberforce, Bishop of Oxford and
Manning's brother-in-law: 'When I came to Lavington in
1833 I believed, as I always did, in Baptismal Regeneration: I
had no view of the Sacrament of the Body and Blood of
Christ: and no idea of the Church.'[1] Years later, in the recollections of his later 'Journal' (1878–82), he described his position at this time in greater detail: 'The state of my religious
belief in 1833 was profound faith in the Holy Trinity and the
Incarnation, in the Redemption by the Passion of our Lord,
and in the work of the Holy Spirit, and the conversion of the
soul. I believed in baptismal regeneration, and in a spiritual,
but real, receiving of our Lord in Holy Communion. As to the
Church, I had no definite conception.'[2] His theological
horizon at the time of his arrival in Lavington—because of his
previous formation or because of his lack of such—bore a
certain resemblance to a mild Evangelical position or to an
ill-defined High Church stance.

Manning's words are not conclusive. The ongoing debate
about Manning's religious background and intellectual development has given rise to different interpretations of the source
and relative influence of the Evangelical and Anglican 'high
and dry' elements that are discernible in his religious make-up.
Alphonse Chapeau thought of Manning's family as being

---

[1] Manning MSS Bod., c. 656, fo. 55 (copy), letter dated 20 Oct. 1850.
[2] Quoted in *P* i, 112. This repeated plea of ignorance about the nature of the
Church in the early 1830s should not be taken too literally. Manning judged his
early views on the Church from the Catholic understanding of it which he reached
only after many years of study and development (see also H. Wilberforce's letter to
Newman in *LD* iv, 317).

strictly 'high and dry' Church of England, and did not see a contradiction in affirming that their piety was strongly Evangelical.[3] Others have tried to solve the apparent paradox by maintaining the unequivocal Evangelical character of Manning's family.[4] Shane Leslie, for his part, considered that Manning, having started from a purely 'high and dry' family religious background, had then gone through an experience of 'conversion' followed by a period of Evangelicalism, and had finally returned to his 'high and dry' roots.[5] C. O'Gorman, in a recent article, has put forward the view that the development of Manning's religious opinions only begins to make sense if 'it is portrayed ... as the waking up from a merely nominal old high churchmanship, into what became the fullness of the historical Catholic faith.'[6] His study of the sources is rather convincing, and additional evidence seems to confirm the conclusion reached.

Manning himself described his family as 'strictly Church of England of the old High school of Dr. Wordsworth, Mant, and D'Oyly. The first and the last were Rectors of Sundridge, and behold they were very dry.'[7] Although the 'Notes and Reminiscences' quoted by Purcell were written in the 1880s, they cannot be dismissed as distorted by the distance in years from the events they refer to. Much closer to the events, Serjeant Bellasis's diary recorded a meeting with Manning on 9 December 1850 during which, while describing his position in the Church of England, Manning remarked that, when he had first taken orders, 'he believed the doctrine of the Trinity, and the Incarnation, and his theological views were those of D'Oyly and Mant.'[8] Both were well-respected authors. George D'Oyly's annotated edition of the Bible had gone

---

[3] Cf. A. Chapeau, 'Manning the Anglican', in J. Fitzsimons (ed.), *Manning: Anglican and Catholic* (London, 1951), 1–2.

[4] Cf. F. K. Brown, *Fathers of the Victorians: The Age of Wilberforce* (Cambridge, 1961), 91.

[5] Cf. Leslie, *Henry Edward Manning*, ch. 4.

[6] C. O'Gorman, 'A History of Henry Manning's Religious Opinions, 1808–1832', *Recusant History*, xxi 2 (Oct. 1992), 156. The paper contains a detailed study of the Manning family's religious background.

[7] 'Notes', quoted in *P* i, 13–14.

[8] E. Bellasis, *Memorials of Mr Serjeant Bellasis* (2nd edn., London, 1895), 104. I owe this information to Dr Peter Nockels.

through several editions in the 1820s, as had the commentary on the Book of Common Prayer by Richard Mant, Bishop of Down, Connor, and Dromore. They were classic specimens of the 'high and dry school': orthodox on the credal fundamentals and baptismal regeneration, 'rational' in their evidential approach to apologetics, dry in spirituality, and stiff and rigid on Dissent and Romanism—a mixture hardly palatable to Evangelical taste.

It is difficult to determine whether Manning read D'Oyly and Mant before or during his undergraduate studies, or whether they were, rather, a pervading influence in his family which shaped his early religious views. Whatever the case may be, the course of his undergraduate reading was not designed to foster Evangelical opinions. Manning, in his later 'Reminiscences', acknowledged that Butler's *Analogy of Religion* and, in particular, his *Sermons* had exerted a powerful influence on his mind at the time. Barrow's *Sermons*, Charles Lesley on deism, Jeremy Taylor, Scott's *Force of Truth*, and the *Sermons* of Archbishop Leighton were also part of his intellectual diet. All these, if anything, would have tended to reinforce the foundations of his unconscious or dormant High Churchmanship.[9]

The Evangelical influences on Manning's intellectual make-up may be dated towards the end of his undergraduate days at Oxford. Manning himself, in a later letter to Miss Priscilla Maurice, offered a rather convincing explanation of the way in which the two traditions cohabitated within him. After saying that he had been brought up 'in the old Establishment High Church way', he added that 'at 21–22 I fell in with good Low Church friends, read Leighton which I have kept by me to this hour, and many puritan books. I never received their doctrinal opinions but embraced their devotional and practical views with all my heart.'[10] His reading of standard

---

[9] Cf. Manning's 'Notes and Reminiscences', quoted in *P* i, 67–8. For the place of Butler in the syllabus for the Greats course at Oxford see J. Garnett, 'Bishop Butler and the *Zeitgeist*: Butler and the Development of Christian Moral Philosophy in Victorian Britain', in C. J. Cunliffe (ed.), *Joseph Butler's Moral and Religious Thought* (Oxford, 1992), 63–96.

[10] Manning MSS Bod., c. 659, fo. 160, letter dated 30 Aug. 1850. The friends referred to in the letter seem to have been the Bevans and their circle. Lavington, after ordination and marriage, brought him into the devout and balanced Evangelical atmosphere of the Sargeant family. Miss Maurice was the sister-in-law of Archdeacon Hare of Lewes and younger sister of Frederick Maurice.

'Puritan' writers included works by Owen, Chandler, Howe, Flavel, and the like. They showed him a side of religion which he had not found among Anglican writers, Bishop Hall and J. Taylor excepted. The latter, Manning confessed in the same letter, had been the first to give him 'a turn to personal religion'. Meanwhile, his underlying High Church formation, although not giving him a very definite or complete set of theological views, appears to have been strong enough to keep him from accepting Evangelical dogma.

Having decided to receive Anglican Orders, Manning successfully applied for a Fellowship at Merton College. There, in his own words, he read 'the common High Church books', 'acres of Anglican writers'.[11] Certainly, his book borrowing during the months of his stay at Merton (May–December 1832) included classical Anglican divines like Bishops Hall and Bull, Hammond and Waterland. However, what is remarkable about the books he borrowed is that more were by Calvin than by any other author: Manning borrowed no fewer than seven or eight volumes of his works. All in all, his reading at Merton seems to have been intense but miscellaneous, including among other authors Grotius and Middleton, the *Sermons* of Donne and South, Bucer's *Scripta Anglicana Fere Omnia*, and the *Book of the Church* by Robert Southey.[12] On the testimony of his borrowing, and in the absence of further evidence, Manning's reading of the Fathers of the Church during his stay at Merton does not seem to have been either extensive or particularly selective. Once at Lavington, he went on reading his way into the Anglican High Church tradition, and Samuel Wilberforce seems to have encouraged him in this direction: 'you sent me to Hooker', Manning wrote in the letter to Samuel already quoted, 'to learn the real presence'.

Manning was always jealous of his independence, and reacted firmly against any attempt to identify him with a party, claiming that he had reached on his own the positions he then held: 'You mistake me', he wrote in one of his letters,

[11] 'Journal', quoted in *P* i, 89; also letter to Miss Maurice (see n. 10).
[12] Oxford, Merton College Library, MSS E-3-64. His borrowing did not include books by D'Oyly or Mant; the register of purchases shows that Merton Library had not acquired any copies of their books. About his reading at Merton see also O'Gorman, 'History', 161.

by associating me with anybody, except so far as accidental agreement warrants the putting me into the same category. Before my ordination I may say I had no intercourse with any clergy of any
kind, or class. Since that time I have lived wholly at this place, and
my views, as far as any man can say so, have been formed alone,
by the word of God; and an examination of the Christian faith before Popery corrupted it, and Protestantism wrested it aside.[13]

In the course of that reading Manning had found his own *via
media* between the two extremes of ultra-Protestantism and
Rome, which, over the centuries, had acted 'as the upper, and
nether millstones grinding truth to death'.[14]

His pastoral work urged him along that course of reading. It
presented Manning with challenges for which he was not fully
equipped, and questions which he could not answer with the
scanty theological resources at his disposal.

The first question that rose in my mind was, What right have you to
be teaching, admonishing, reforming, rebuking others? By what
authority do you lift the latch of a poor man's door and enter and
sit down and begin to instruct or to correct him? This train of
thought forced me to see that no culture or knowledge of Greek or
Latin would suffice for this. That if I was not a messenger sent
from God, I was an intruder and impertinent.[15]

Manning's train of thought also led him to confront another
puzzle: 'the necessity of a divine certainty for the message I
had to deliver became, if possible, more evident. A divine,
that is, an infallible message, by a human messenger is still the
truth of God; but a human, or fallible message, by a messenger
having a divine commission, would be the source of error, illusion, and all evil.'[16]

The pastoral implications of the answer to those two questions were momentous, and Manning felt them keenly from
the very beginning of his ministry. 'Perhaps there is none', he
wrote in 1838, 'whose anxious sense of responsibility has [not]
been sharpened by the charge of souls, and has not sometimes
felt the harassing of a doubtful mind on great and weighty
points of doctrine and interpretation.'[17] He was not alone in

---

[13] Manning MSS Bod., c. 662, fo. 2, letter to A. Hamilton, dated 10 Aug. 36.
[14] Ibid., Fol. 1.
[15] 'Journal', quoted in *P* i, 112; see also *CSer* i, 3.
[16] *CSer* i, 3.   [17] *Rule*, 12.

asking those questions. The excited theological atmosphere generated by the Oxford Movement, and the events which had stirred it up, were bringing these and other connected issues into public debate. However, it may be claimed that in Manning's early years at Lavington, these enquiries were fuelled by the demands of his pastoral work rather than by general considerations of ecclesiastical policy. None the less, the ecclesiastical statesman in him was soon to be awakened to the importance of those issues in the wider context of the relationship between Church and State.

There is no record of his reading during the early years at Lavington, but in 1840 he described to Archdeacon Julius Hare of Lewes[18] the influences which, up to that moment, had shaped his theological views. First, he mentioned Samuel Taylor Coleridge.[19] Manning added that he differed from Coleridge on many issues, but that this author had done for his mind in theology 'some of the work which Bacon did to Philosophy of nature'.[20] He did not elaborate on this point. A study of Manning's writings, however, may offer some indications as to how Coleridge's ideas influenced his thought. They seem to have complemented those he had earlier acquired from Butler's *Analogy* and *Sermons*. From Butler he had learned that the analogy of nature was useful in clearing away objections to revelation by pointing out how similar objections could also be raised against natural knowledge; that there was also a probability that the things one can see have a similarity to divine things, both being the work of God; and that moral inclination exerted a powerful influence on the mind in the search for truth. Coleridge offered what Butler had not attempted, namely, a philosophical underpinning for the Christian tradition, and an escape route from the rationalistic cul-de-sac of evidential theology. His theory of knowledge affirmed

[18] In spite of their deep theological differences—Hare's latitudinarianism versus Manning's High Church opinions—there was a deep current of sympathy running between them. As archdeacons, they shared many common concerns for Church reform.

[19] We have no record of when Manning read Coleridge, whose *Aids to Reflection* was published in 1825. Manning was not the only one among those concerned with the revival of Catholic doctrine in the Church of England who felt the appeal of Coleridge's thought.

[20] Manning MSS Bod., c. 653, fo. 22.

that scientific understanding, organizing sense perception, could not give a complete knowledge of reality, as there were aspects of it which escaped sense perception. Scientific information had to be supplemented by a knowledge above sense experience, attained by a higher faculty—reason, Coleridge called it—which provides access to truths beyond the reach of sense experience. Spiritual realities are the proper object of this faculty.

His letter to Hare went on to say: 'Next I have always said that, after the Prayer Book, Hooker best represents my mind; and Leighton except when the seams of Calvinism are yet visible.'[21] Hooker, in turn, had led him to Thorndike, 'a powerful and original intellect', who was to play an important part in the formation of his ideas. The letter was also a record of Manning's acquaintance, since before his ordination, with classic Anglican theologians such as Bramhall, Hammond, Taylor, Bull, and Beveridge, and of how, since his days at Merton, he had been familiar with Calvin's commentaries of the Scriptures, which he liked. By this time, although he does not mention it in his letters and reminiscences, his early sermons and writings show clearly that he was well versed in the Fathers of the Church, particularly Ignatius, Augustine, Irenaeus, Chrysostom, and Cyprian, and that he was acquainted with the works of modern authors like William Palmer, of Worcester College, and Newman.

High Church principles and Evangelical piety continued to coexist, awkwardly, in Manning until the late 1840s. In 1850 he would say that he had long felt 'that the low Church had no *objective truth*, the High Church little *subjective religion*. All my opinions being of what be thought the latter school, I therefore turned all my *preaching* on the former or *subjective matter*.'[22] He saw them as two parallel, not opposed, streams; he could not see where dogma and life were united and became one.

Manning's copious reading benefited from the atmosphere of Lavington which provided him with the peace required for ideas and concepts to discover their proper connections, and

---

[21] Manning MSS Bod., c. 653, fo. 22.
[22] Letter to Miss Maurice quoted in n. 10. It seems that Hare had observed and pointed this out to Manning.

to settle into a system with clear, well-defined principles. The coincidence of his views with those of the Oxford Movement should come as no surprise. At Lavington, Manning read by himself in the same direction. Besides, the Tractarians did not lay claim to originality, or to having founded a new system. On the contrary, they strove to make it clear that they were not propounding a new theory; their confessed aim, rather, was to restore the original purity of the Anglican Reformation, represented by sixteenth- and seventeenth-century Anglican divines, a purity which had been contaminated by the Protestantism imposed on it during the last 150 years.[23] Newman seemed to confirm Manning's assertion of independence from the Oxford Movement when writing to Edward Churton: 'He [Manning] is, in no conceivable sense, of the Oxford school (to use a wrong word)—Pusey knows him now, being drawn to him by congeniality of opinions—but he is Pusey's, only so far as Pusey is Truth's, and Manning also—and as you are Manning's or Pusey's, which is not at all.'[24] In one of his remonstrances to Hare, Manning would say much the same thing: 'In some things I thoroughly agree with Newman; in some things partially, in some not at all.'[25]

Manning's progress in the acquisition of definite High Church views was swift. By November 1833, Henry Wilberforce was reporting to Newman that Manning had reviewed his opinions and adopted the principle of apostolic succession, and in subsequent letters he would continue to chart—not always accurately—the development of Manning's views along Catholic lines. Apostolic succession provided an answer to the first of Manning's questions. He saw it as the origin of the divine commission that a priest receives at ordination and the source of his authority. An invitation to preach the sermon on the occasion of the Archdeacon of Chichester's 1835 visitation offered Manning the opportunity to bring before the public his ideas on the subject. In the sermon, he affirmed that the apostles were not just Christ's companions;

---

[23] Cf. J. H. Newman, 'Via Media', Tracts 38 and 41, in *Tracts for the Times*, i, no. 3 (London 1834).

[24] *LD* vi, 175, letter dated 4 Dec. 1837.

[25] Manning MSS Bod., c. 653, fo. 223, letter dated 11 Jan. 1842. See also 'Biographical Note', quoted in *P* i, 259.

they were also the witnesses of Christ's resurrection and representatives of their Master, of his personal presence. They 'were commissioned and sent by the Son, as the Son by the Father. This constituted the validity of their mission, and the value of their testimony.'[26] The priestly ministry nowadays, he continued, rests on the same foundations: forgiveness, baptism, and the sacrament of the Lord's Body and Blood can be offered only on the condition 'that the testimony we bear is a direct personal testimony, and the authority we exercise a valid commission derived to us from Himself'.[27] Christ's salvific design was clearly stated: the divine commission—the powers of teaching and sanctifying—was to be handed on, following our Lord's example, along a continuous chain which would run down the centuries. The bishops, successors to the apostles, were the links in that chain, and the validity and power of their ministry would depend on the soundness of their union with that first link, our Lord. A break in that succession would imply the end of that particular line of witness, authority, and power: 'what man [would] dare, on his own authority, renew what the authority of Christ began?'[28] The lower degrees of ministry, in their turn, derived their 'representative character from him that laid hands on us', Manning added. Thus, our 'commission to witness for Christ ... hangs upon this question:—*Are the Bishops of our Church the successors, in lineal descent, of the Lord's Apostles?*'[29] The historical argument proved it to Manning's satisfaction.

The matter was of great moment for the times he happened to live in. The circumstances, he would say, made it necessary to 'remind ourselves that we are not ministers of men, nor by men, but witnesses called and commissioned by Jesus Christ, and God the Father, who raised him from the dead'.[30] Manning's exalted vision of the episcopate was even more forcefully expressed in his letter of 1838 to the Bishop of Chichester on the principle of ecclesiastical commission: 'Our Bishop is to us

[26] *English Church*, 7. The validity of their ministry, Manning was to say later on, did not depend either on their holiness, although the example of the ordained minister has a great influence in building up the Church. Cf. H. E. Manning, *The Moral Design of the Apostolic Ministry* (London, 1841), 10 ff.

[27] *English Church*, 9.

[28] Ibid.   [29] Ibid. 10.   [30] Ibid. 22.

the source of authority and the centre of unity in order, deliberation and discipline. ... We believe that no power, spiritual
or ecclesiastical, excepting only the collective authority of the
whole Episcopal order to which supreme jurisdiction all
Bishops are severally subject, can reach us, unless it pass
through his express permission.'[31]

His second great concern also made a brief appearance in
the visitation sermon. The spiritual origin and mission of the
priestly ministry might be clear beyond any doubt, but he felt
that this was not 'sufficient security, taken alone, that our
message be according to the truth. An accredited ambassador
may pervert his message, and betray his master's charge.'[32]
The greater the authority of the witness, the more he should
be concerned not to pervert the message entrusted to him.
The temptations of false philosophy, worldly spirit, or the
desire to please might lead him to adulterate the truth revealed
by God. He should be watchful over his trust, fully aware of
the enemies threatening it.

2. *The Rule of Faith*

In his concern to promote the principle of apostolic succession,
Manning suggested to Newman the possibility of publishing a
translation of Pearson's *Vindiciae Ignatiana*. Newman agreed to
this proposal, but Manning, on second thoughts, considering
that the episcopal principle was being advanced enough by
the abundant literature on the subject, and was readily accepted by the majority of the clergy, decided to look for
another fundamental Church principle to champion. He concentrated his attention on how to find certainty for the
message he was supposed to deliver. His correspondence with
Newman and Samuel Francis Wood shows that by the
autumn of 1835 he was already studying the relationship
between Holy Scripture and Tradition. 'I have been reading',
he wrote to Newman, 'Vincentius Lirinensis; and have
thought of trying to put something together about Tradition,
its use, authority, and limits, in the Church of Christ, with an

---

[31] H. E. Manning, *The Principle of the Ecclesiastical Commission Examined, in a Letter to the Right Revd Lord Bishop of Chichester* (London, 1838), 5–6.
[32] *English Church*, 22–3.

application to the Church of England, shewing how much we necessarily and unconsciously depend on it, while we anathematize it in Popery.'[33] In November of the same year he wrote to Wood to announce that he was sending a paper on apostolic tradition. This prompted Wood to send Manning his own thoughts on the subject, including a schematic, but clear, expression of a theory of doctrinal development.[34] In his answer, which is not extant, Manning seems to have agreed in many respects with Wood's ideas but could not go along with him as far as development was concerned. Wood wrote back, minimizing their differences: 'Your paper on Tradition and your general concurrence in my view gave me very sincere delight ... Our sole difference appears to me to consist in our notions of the development of truth in the Church as stated in my 3d. proposition.' Manning had countered it, Wood recorded in his letter, with his own fourth proposition: 'Therefore the Church has no warrant to promulgate new truths.'[35] Newman, who, after his debate with the Abbé Jager, was working on the same topic in his *Lectures on the Prophetical Office of the Church*, also rejected Wood's theory of doctrinal development, and agreed in substance with Manning's answer to Wood.

Newman's *Lectures on the Prophetical Office of the Church* appeared in 1837; Manning followed with his Sermon *The Rule of Faith*, preached in June 1838.[36] In it he made his own the High Church doctrine of the rule of faith. Soon after its

[33] *LD* v. 137, letter dated 15 Sept. 1835. The first fruit of his reading on the subjects of Tradition and the rule of faith was *Tract* 78, a catena of authorities in support of the principle of Vincent of Lerins: *Quod semper, quod ubique*. The tract appeared in 1837, and served as groundwork and a readily available quarry of material for his *Sermon* and *Appendix* on the rule of faith.

[34] See J. Pereiro, 'S. F. Wood and an Early Theory of Development in the Oxford Movement', *Recusant History*, xx 4 (Oct. 1991), 524–53. Wood, brother of the first Lord Halifax, had been a disciple of Newman at Oxford. His was an original mind, and, in London and from London, he co-operated in many Tractarian ventures.

[35] Manning MSS. Bod., c. 654, fo. 442; Wood to Manning, letter dated 18 Dec. 1835. Wood's third proposition in his letter to Manning dated 19 Nov. 1835 read: 'In common with other societies the Church has the inherent power of expanding or modifying her organisation, of bringing her ideas of the truth into more distinct conciousness, or of developing the truth itself more fully' (ibid., fo. 440).

[36] Caroline Sargent, Manning's wife, had died on 24 July 1837, less than four years after their marriage. Manning was devastated by her death, and after it, immersed himself in work in an attempt to overcome his grief.

publication, the sermon came under fierce attack from the Evangelical party, and the Rector of Lavington defended his positions with a barrage of quotations from Anglican authorities, published as a long *Appendix* to *The Rule of Faith*. It was a fortunate circumstance. The need for a defence forced Manning to provide a more complete view of his ideas on the subject, and the combined *Sermon* and *Appendix* amount to a fairly complete treatise on the rule of faith.

Manning preached the sermon on a text from the Epistle to the Galatians: 'But though we, or an angel from heaven, preach any other Gospel unto you than that which we have preached unto you, let him be accursed. As we said before, so say I now again, if any man preach any other Gospel unto you than that ye have received, let him be accursed' (Gal. 1: 8–9). He considered that St Paul's words had not lost any of their original force; they were an everlasting injunction: 'We may no more swerve from the pure faith of Christ's Gospel, and be held guiltless, than the fickle Galatian, or the inflated gnostic.'[37] The dangers threatening the faith had grown more numerous from the time of the apostles: errors had multiplied since then, and to counter them, we no longer have 'the inspired servants of our Lord to bear a living and personal witness to the mind of the Holy Ghost'.[38] There was no refuge to be found behind the plea of non-wilful error. Manning rejected it as a subterfuge to pacify one's conscience: 'though *wilful* heresy be the blacker sin, yet the doctrinal errors of the cold earthly mind, of the indolent and unconcerned heart ... have their graduated measures, and those not small, of positive moral guilt'.[39] Doctrinal error had its moral root in 'a sinful temper of mind', and, in its turn, produced pernicious effects in the flock of Christ. The ordained minister bore a double responsibility for this. The charge of souls had, therefore, made Manning anxious 'to find some *rule* by which to measure the proportions of the faith'. His aim was not 'to inquire what are the specific *doctrines* of the Gospel, but what is the *rule* by which we may ascertain them'.[40] He conceived the rule of faith as a test of doctrine: 'the test by which we ascertain the

---

[37] *Rule*, 8.   [38] Ibid. 9.   [39] Ibid. 8–9.
[40] Ibid. 13.

character of revelation, the proof of the *fact* being presupposed'.[41] It was obvious to him that such a rule must exist,
'unless the knowledge of the Gospel be revealed over and over
again, from age to age, to churches and to individuals,
immediately, as in the beginning: that is, unless the faith once
delivered to the saints is, by the same supernatural communication, still being perpetually delivered to the saints'.[42] This
would amount to perpetual inspiration, which possibility
Manning rejected.

Manning's line of argument started from an assumption
which he considered generally accepted: that Scripture contains all things necessary for salvation. This, though, was not
the same as saying that Scripture needed no interpreter. That
would have been the case 'if either the Scriptures were so
clear that private Christians could not err in understanding
[them], or Churches so infallible as never to go astray in expounding the interpretation'.[43] Experience showed, according
to Manning, that Churches had erred, and that individual
Christians had produced innumerable and contradictory interpretations of the same scriptural text. He then went on to
state the obvious: the faith of the first Christian communities
did not depend on written books; the preaching of the Gospel,
and the foundation of churches built upon that faith, had preceded the writing of the scriptural books.

The original apostolic teaching had subsequently been summarized in brief formulas—symbols or creeds—for the confession of faith of the candidate for the sacrament of baptism, 'as
the condition of his entering into the Church of Christ, and
the rule of his faith afterwards'.[44] The creeds of the different
Churches, although diverse in their actual wording, were all
the same in substance. They preceded the writing of the New
Testament books, and when the latter were received by the different Christian communities, they were interpreted in light of
the faith that those communities already professed: 'each particular Church read and understood its own particular Scripture in the sense of the faith before delivered to it, and the

---

[41] *Appendix*, 1.   [42] *Rule*, 13.   [43] Ibid. 26.
[44] Ibid. 28; Keble had expressed similar ideas in his sermon at Winchester on 27
Sept. 1836: 'Primitive Tradition Recognised in Holy Scripture', in *Sermons*, 172–231.

whole Church read and understood the whole Scripture in the sense of the Apostolic teaching, which all in common had received. In each particular Church, therefore, as well as in the Church at large, there was both the Scripture and the sense.'[45] Tradition, therefore, attested both to Scripture—handing us the canon of the inspired books—and to the sense. Thus, 'the Rule of Faith, as recognised and contended by the reformed Church of England, is Scripture and antiquity, or Universal Tradition attesting both Scripture and the sense'.[46]

He described the workings of the two elements of the rule by saying that Scripture's role is to be 'the proof of the creed [which stands here for Tradition], and the creed the interpreter of Scripture'.[47] The foreword to Tract 78 had been more explicit in its description of the relationship between Scripture and Tradition: 'Catholic tradition teaches revealed truth, Scripture proves it; Scripture is the document of Faith, tradition the witness of it; the true Creed is the Catholic interpretation of Scripture, or Scripturally proved tradition; Scripture by itself teaches mediately and proves decisively; tradition by itself proves negatively and teaches positively; Scripture and tradition taken together are the joint Rule of Faith.'[48] This, Manning claimed, did not produce a circular argument; they were two witnesses attesting to the one truth, the harmony of the two being the first rule of interpretation.

This, however, did not solve all the problems, as there still remained a large body of doctrine not included in the Creed but fundamental to the faith: namely, original sin, the doctrine of justification, the Real Presence of Christ in the Eucharist, etc. The innumerable repugnant interpretations of these doctrines witnessed to Scripture's need for an expositor. The practice of the Anglican reformers, and the canons of 1571, offered welcome support here: where the creeds were silent, the Anglican Church listened to those who were presumed by their antiquity to know the truth and, by their uniform consent, neither to be mistaken themselves nor to deceive us. Manning thought that few texts of Scripture would be left without a

---

[45] *Rule*, 28.   [46] *Appendix*, 33.   [47] *Rule*, 35.
[48] H. E. Manning and C. Marriott (eds.), *Catena Patrum no. III. Testimony of Writers in the Later English Church to the Duty of Maintaining quod semper, quod ubique, quod ab omnibus traditum est*, Tracts for the Times, 78 (new edn., London, 1839), 2.

clear interpretation after having applied the above principles. That was what Bramhall had called 'the infallible rule of faith': Holy Scripture interpreted by the Catholic Church, the tradition of the Christian world united. Nothing should be put forward as a necessary article of faith except those doctrines which, in accordance with Vincent of Lerins's rule, had been believed always, everywhere, and by all.

The consent of the Christian world was, for Manning, 'a visible and perpetual miracle', and Christians knew it to be 'the voice of God, prolonged from the Apostles to themselves'.[49] It could not be otherwise, Manning said: 'nothing short of an universal cause, in all places acting alike with *one unerring uniform* operation, could bring about an *universal* effect, which like the laws of the material world, and the instincts of animate creatures, point by their universal harmony to the sole universal Agent'.[50] Thus, nowadays, universal agreement with the Church of the apostolic age was 'the *surest test of agreement with the doctrine of the Apostles of Christ*'.[51] Manning, following Palmer, went even further: 'I maintain that Christians cannot possibly admit that any doctrine, established by universal tradition can be otherwise than *divinely, infallibly, true.*'[52]

The existence—and character—of a truth belonging to that universal tradition was determined by historico-critical methods: the 'existence of such a tradition from the beginning is a matter of fact, which is to be established on the same sort of evidence as proves any other historical fact'.[53] There was a danger in this of which Manning was still unaware. The difficult task of sifting through the vast body of writings of the Fathers, and of weighing the not always concordant material, threatened to remove 'the real authority in the Church from the faithful and from their pastors into the hands of the Church historians, who could declare with expert information the teaching of the early Church'.[54]

Scripture and Tradition made up the rule of faith of the An-

[49] *Appendix*, 62.
[50] Ibid.   [51] Ibid. 3.   [52] Ibid. 112
[53] Ibid. 112, again quoting Palmer.
[54] O. Chadwick, *The Spirit of the Oxford Movement: Tractarian Essays* (Cambridge, 1990), 30.

glican Church. This was also the rule of primitive Christianity: the perfect rule which God had devised as the external channel of conveyance for his revealed truth. In conformity with His general providence, as shown in the establishment of the Church and the sacraments, God had also provided for a medium, external to the individual, to perpetuate and dispense truth.

It was a position much in need of defence. The ultra-Protestant party lost no time in attacking the Tractarians and their friends on that count, accusing them of upholding Romanist doctrines, while rejecting those of the Anglican Church. On the other side, Catholic controversialists—like Wiseman—, argued that such an idea of the rule of faith was little, if any, different, from the principle of private judgement. The Tractarians' strategy in defence was twofold. They first endeavoured to prove that the principle of *sola Scriptura* was opposed to the tenets of the Anglican Reformation, while showing that the principle of private judgement was theoretically absurd and had already proved to be unworkable in practice. Secondly, they attacked the Roman doctrine of the infallibility of the Church, in order to defend themselves against the charge of Romanism, while fighting off Catholic objections to the Anglican rule of faith.

3. *The Roman Rule of Faith: The Infallibility of the Church*

Both Manning and Newman would deal in their books with the so-called Roman doctrine of the infallibility of the Church, of which they had a rather distorted and superficial notion. They approached it from different angles, and treated it in different ways, which went some way to show their diverse intellectual frames of mind. It is easy to detect, though, their common basis in Butler's doctrine in the *Analogy*.

Newman considered that the infallibility claimed by Rome was the first principle, 'the sovereign and engrossing tenet', 'the foundation-stone, or (as it may be called) the fulcrum of its theology'.[55] In this system the living Church becomes the author and teacher of the Faith, which supersedes and makes unnecessary the appeal to Scripture and antiquity. In his

---

[55] *VM* i. 69.

opinion, the origin of the doctrine of infallibility could be traced back to an original misconception: the notion 'that any degree of doubt about religious truth is incompatible with faith, and that an external infallible assurance is necessary to exclude doubt'.[56] Otherwise, according to those who uphold the doctrine of infallibility, what is called faith would be no more than mere opinion; certainty, to be such, would require the conjunction of God's revelation and the Church's infallibility to convey it.

Newman equated infallibility with omniscience: 'to know some things in any subject infallibly, implies that we know all things'.[57] Only an absolute knowledge would exclude uncertainty. This presumption forced the Church of Rome, according to Newman, to build up a complete theology; and in developing his argument, he seemed to identify the theology of the schools with the doctrine of the Church. In this system there would be no room for doubt or obscurity; all questions would be settled. This process, according to Newman, being contrary to the divine dispensation, could only be the work of the human intellect, to which divine truth would thus be subject. To Newman's mind, the rationalistic bent of the doctrine of infallibility was obvious. He concluded his analysis of this Roman principle by declaring it defective 'in respect of *proof*, it is defective even viewed in its *theory* in two main points ... Roman theologians, though claiming for the Church the gift of Infallibility, cannot even in theory give an answer to the question *how* individuals are to know for certain that she is infallible; nor in the next place *where* the gift resides.'[58] They cannot 'complete their system [Roman theology] in its most important and essential point'.[59] The Roman rule of faith—its dogmatic system—was based on infallibility, a doctrine that had not even been defined as a dogma! Nevertheless, Rome, acting on that principle, affirmed its decrees to be irreformable, because infallible: 'she must insist on what she has once

---

[56] *VM* i. 85–6.   [57] Ibid. 89.   [58] Ibid. 122.
[59] Ibid. 125.
[60] J. H. Newman, 'Home Thoughts Abroad', *British Magazine* (1836), in *Discussions and Arguments on Various Subjects* (London, 1891), 29. Newman and Froude had been appalled by the discovery of the full import of the doctrine of infallibility, during

decreed; and when she abandons that claim she breaks the principle of her own vitality'.[60]

Manning, when studying the Roman rule of faith, concentrated his attention on whether there existed a living judge in the controversies about the Faith. To establish the principle which he was going to criticize, he quoted from a Catholic source, Berington and Kirk, affirming: *'the same spirit which dictated the writing of the Scriptures, [is] directing the Church to understand them'*.[61] The Church, thus, would be a living and infallible judge of interpretation. Manning considered that great evils followed from this principle, the chief one being that if the meaning of Scripture was 'tied to follow the utterance of a *living* voice which shall claim the supreme right of interpretation, [the interpretation] must vary with its living expositor'.[62] The Church may use Tradition, and the Roman Catholic Church called on antiquity as witness to its dogmas, but both Tradition and Scripture were made 'to follow the interpretation of the present Church. Of antiquity it [the Roman Church] accepts so much as is in accordance with its existing system; of the rest, some it explains away, some it rejects, some utterly condemns.'[63] To make matters worse, Catholics also affirmed that 'some points of *belief* ... were *not committed to writing in Holy Scripture*, but rest on *oral* tradition alone'.[64]

The Roman Church, Manning pointed out, maintained 'that there is a living infallible judge, who may, from time to time, declare, upon the sole proof of unwritten tradition, points of necessary doctrine, and add them to the Creed'.[65] This contradicted Vincentius's rule: *quod semper, quod ubique, quod ab omnibus*. Manning did not develop this point further, as Newman had done. He went beyond Vincentius, to look for support in Galatians 1: 8: 'Sed licet nos, aut angelus de caelo evangelizet vos vobis praeterquam quod evangelizavimus

---

their visit to Wiseman in Rome. They found, to their horror, that one of the corollaries of the doctrine was that the acts of the successive Councils were obligatory for ever. Cfr. R. H. Froude. *The Remains of Richard Hurrel Froude*, ed. J. Keble and J. H. Newman, Part I (London, 1838), i. 307.

[61] *Appendix*, 82.   [62] Ibid. 85.   [63] Ibid. 100–1.
[64] Ibid. 82.   [65] Ibid. 26.

vobis, anathema sit.' Taylor and Thorndike had rebutted Bellarmine's translation of *praeterquam* in this text as 'against', claiming that it stood for 'besides', in addition. According to their interpretation, the apostle was not only condemning any teaching contrary to the truths he had taught the Galatians, he was also anathematizing those who attempted to add to the Creed, as points of necessary belief, truths unknown to the primitive Church.

The doctrine of infallibility, Manning thought, presupposed the existence in the Church of an inspiration of the same kind as that which had dictated Holy Scripture. This guidance of the Holy Spirit would be *perpetual* and *immediate*. The Holy Spirit would inspire the Church with the meaning of Scripture; the Church, when reading Holy Scripture, would infallibly perceive its true interpretation, or, rather, receive it from the Holy Spirit. This would make redundant the recourse to Tradition as the interpreter of Scripture: 'The infallibility of the *living* Church absorbs all proof into itself,'[66] Manning would say, quoting Newman's *Lectures*.

Manning considered that the origin of this erroneous notion of infallibility was to be found in an a priori argument which presumed that God could not leave the Scriptures without an infallible interpreter and judge in the controversies about the Faith. The Roman doctrine then concluded: 'from our anticipations of what God would be likely to do, that therefore He has done so'.[67] He again dwelled on this point in a letter to Pusey of 7 December 1839, in which he gave advice on how to deal with someone on the verge of Popery. The a priori argument, he said, was inadmissible; if used at all, it would tell 'against infallibility on the idea of probation which includes Churches as well as men.'[68] If the infallibility of the Church were true, it should be part of 'the original Christian Revela-

---

[66] *Appendix*, 100.

[67] Ibid. 94. This assertion was supported by a long quotation (pp. 96–8) from Butler's *Analogy* against this type of argument. Manning was always alive to the danger of 'sliding from the ideas of the Reason into a priori theories of what revelation is or ought to be' (Manning MSS Bod., c. 653, fo. 22, letter to Hare dated 25 Sept. 1840); Coleridge, Butler, and even Bacon were quoted by him as witnesses for this principle.

[68] Pusey House, Oxford, Pusey Correspondence to Manning, letter 2.

tion', and thus 'capable of the same sort of proof, i.e.: 1. Scripture or 2. Catholic Tradition. But there is no proof in either. The onus is on the Romanists.'[69] Manning also dismissed the claim that infallibility—a gift granted to the apostles—was intended to be perpetual; the promises of divine guidance 'in the search after divine truth, relate rather to the *moral* than to the *intellectual nature*'.[70] God had already provided for the preservation of truth in the Church by fixing the rule of faith: Scripture and Tradition. 'The office and work of the Holy Spirit is plainly to *sanctify* us, through the truth *already understood*, by means of the outward teaching which God has appointed for that end.'[71]

Manning, like Newman, also remarked upon the lack of agreement among Catholics concerning the seat of infallibility: 'investing the pope with infallibility is the *Italian* doctrine, the *Gallican* and *British* Romanists placing it in the Church assembled in council'.[72] It made little difference, as far as Manning was concerned, whether the Pope or the Council were considered infallible: a living and, therefore, changing judge—whether an individual or a collectivity—could not avoid introducing doctrinal changes. He considered that the Roman and the Protestant rules of faith, though very different in their formulation, had something in common, and tended to produce similar fruits. Both exalted the living judge guided by the Holy Spirit: the Church collective, for Catholics; the individual person, in Protestantism. The consequences of both rules could already be seen in practice: the Roman Church— against St Paul's injunction—had introduced new doctrines, unknown to the primitive Church; Protestants, on the other hand, had excluded some of those taught by the apostles.

Both, Catholics and Protestants, undermined the foundations on which Christianity was built: the '*attack on universal tradition*'—Manning would say—'*undermines the foundation of Christianity*. It is not an *interpretation*, but *the Gospel* that is at stake.'[73] In both the Protestant and the Catholic system

---

[69] Ibid.   [70] *Appendix*, 91.   [71] Ibid. 91–2.

[72] Ibid. 87. Manning, in 1838, was reading Gallican authors, Bossuet and Dupin in particular. This reading was prompted by a double ecclesiastical concern: the rule of faith and the relationship between Church and State.

[73] Ibid. 111.

human reason was set above Scripture, thus opening the door to rationalism and subjectivism, and finally to scepticism. A return to the true rule of faith would, on the other hand, correct those inclinations. Nor would this be the only benefit consequent to its adoption: sharing in common the true rule of faith would considerably reduce the number of doctrinal differences among Christians, the source of their disputes, and strengthen the bond of brotherly love among them.

4. *An Infallible Rule or an Infallible Church?*

Bramhall's words about the infallible rule of faith were a *locus communis* among High Churchmen and those who shared their ideas. The Church as teacher of the Faith—a rallying cry for Tractarians—had been entrusted by God with its keeping, and commissioned to transmit it. Still, Catholic controversialists were to impugn the soundness of the Anglican rule of faith, likening it to private judgement. At the beginning of the century Charles Butler and Bishop Milner had entered the controversialists' arena on similar grounds; Wiseman would renew and reinforce the argument in the mid-1830s in his *Lectures on the Principal Doctrines and Practices of the Catholic Church* (1836). In them, he argued from the Thirty-Nine Articles of the Church of England. The sixth said that 'Holy Scripture containeth all things necessary to salvation; so that whatever is not read therein, nor may be proved thereby, is not to be required of any man that it should be believed as an article of faith, or be thought requisite or necessary for salvation'. It falls to the Church, according to the twentieth Article, to decide in controversies of faith what is or is not to be believed on the above basis; 'and yet', it continues, 'it is not lawful for the Church to ordain any thing contrary to God's written word; neither may it so expound any passage of Scripture, as to be repugnant to another'. Nothing contrary to Holy Scripture can be imposed as an article of faith, either by an individual on another or by the Church on its members.

These Articles, to Wiseman's mind, left open the question of the whereabouts of the authority capable of judging whether the doctrinal decisions of the Church were or were not in accordance with Holy Scripture. If there is a rule—as there must be—for determining whether the Church's decisions are in accordance with Scripture, who shall apply it? '[I]f the Church, not being infallible, may teach things contrary to Scripture, who shall judge it, and decide between it and those whose obedience it exacts?'[74] He could see only two possible answers to this question: 'if *the Church* is not to be obeyed when it teaches anything contrary to Scripture, there are only two alternatives,—either that limitation supposes an impossibility of its so doing, or it implies the possible case of the Church being lawfully disobeyed'.[75] The first possibility—that the Church will never contradict Scripture in her decisions on matters of belief—is equivalent to upholding the Catholic doctrine of the infallibility of the Church. The other possible answer would admit that the Church may err. In that case, he concluded, it was up to the individual to determine the question: 'each one has to judge for himself, whether the Church be contradicting the express doctrines of Scripture, and, consequently, each person is thus constituted judge over the decisions of his Church'.[76] This implied that the Church is not able to require belief in any particular doctrine, given that any individual may question any doctrine by pronouncing it to be contrary to Scripture, as the Presbyterians had done under Elizabeth, and others did thereafter.

Manning, in his letters to the *British Magazine*,[77] reacted angrily to what he considered to be Wiseman's wilful deformation of the Anglican rule of faith. S. F. Wood, on the other hand, while admitting that the Anglican rule of faith was as Manning had described it, concurred that the recent condition of the Church of England lent substance to Wiseman's claims, and he upbraided Manning for his intemperate language: 'it would be more wise, more humble, more truthful, and more Christianlike to confess our practical defection from our principles, and to warn and to recall men to them, than hastily to

---

[74] N. Wiseman, *Lectures on the Principal Doctrines and Practices of the Catholic Church* (2 vols., London, 1836), i. 30.
[75] Ibid.   [76] Ibid.
[77] H. E. Manning, 'The Errors or Unfairness of Dr. Wiseman', *British Magazine*, x (Nov. and Dec. 1836), 614–20 and 753–8. The two letters may have been one originally, the editor printing as two because of its length. In favour of this hypothesis may be cited the continuity of the text and the fact that while the November letter was undated, the one published a month later was dated 11 Aug. 1836.

tax him with unfairness'.[78] Newman, reviewing Wiseman's *Lectures* in the *British Critic*, reacted in a similar way, almost welcoming them as a revulsive to help the Church of England rise from her state of prostration. Manning was unrepentant, and in a long note in the sermon on the rule of faith, he again addressed Wiseman's objections, repeating his charge of unfairness. In the *Appendix*, though, he made his own Wood's point about the condition of Anglican theology in the previous century: 'Our adversaries know full well how far we have departed from the principles of that age [the seventeenth-century Anglican divines]; and they take due advantage of it.'[79]

Against Wiseman, Manning affirmed that the sixth Article did not claim that Scripture is so clear as to need no interpreter, or that every man is able to interpret it for himself. Wiseman had falsely attributed to the Church of England the ultra-Protestant rule of faith.[80] The Church, Manning continued, is the supreme authority in matters of faith, but this does not mean 'authority which admits of no limit or restriction';[81] she is bound by the Catholic traditions tested on the principle of *universitas, antiquitas, consensio*. It was not up to the individual to judge the proper application of this rule by the Church. The Anglican Church, 'far from submitting either the rule, or her decisions according to the rule, to the judgment of her individual members, will not submit them to the judgment even of particular churches, or to any tribunal less than that to which all particular churches are subject, that is, a general council, of which, either the members shall truly *represent* the Church Catholic, or the decrees be univer-

---

[78] *P* i. 119. Manning decided to inform himself about the Catholic controversy. In Feb. 1837 he told Newman that he was reading Milner's *End of Religious Controversy* (cf. *LD* vi. 33); in the *Sermon* and in the *Appendix* he also quoted Milner's *Letter to a Prebendary*, and referred to Charles Butler.

[79] *Appendix*, 130.

[80] Wiseman also thought himself justified in yoking under the same rule of faith the Anglican Church and Protestants on the grounds that the High Anglican doctrine was not received by the Anglican Church. 'Let the Church, *as a Church*, detach itself from all other sectaries in its reasoning against us, let it avow disapprobation of their principles, ... and then we will acknowledge its right to record a separate plea from the great body of Protestants' (N. Wiseman, 'The High Church Theory of Doctrinal Authority', (*Dublin Review*, July 1837, repr. in *Essays on Various Subjects* (2 vols., London, 1853), ii. 133). [81] *Rule*, 24–5.

sally *received*.[82] Manning did not realize at the time that he had only moved Wiseman's objection one step further away. Was the universal Church infallible? If not, who was to judge the correctness of the doctrinal decisions of a non-infallible universal Church? The Thirty-Nine Articles left Manning little room for manoeuvre. Article 21 clearly affirmed that General Councils 'may err, and sometimes have erred, even in things pertaining unto God; wherefore things ordained by them as necessary unto salvation have neither strength nor authority, unless it may be declared that they be taken out of Holy Scriptures'. Manning had made this doctrine his own. The Church in Council is not infallible, he wrote to Pusey; as a matter of fact, '[t]here is no more guarantee that a Council shall necessarily coincide with Catholic Tradition than an individual man'.[83] Wiseman's objection remained unanswered.

Palmer of Worcester, in his *Treatise on the Church*, offered a possible escape route out of this theological cul-de-sac. He affirmed that a 'General Synod, confirmed by the Roman Pontiff, has not, without the consent of the universal Church, any irrefragable authority'.[84] This consent or judgement of the universal Church would be shown by the acceptance and execution of the Synod's decrees by the universal Church. It could only be a moral unanimity. 'Scripture, in teaching us that heresies were to exist, shows that a judgment *absolutely unanimous* could not be expected at any time; but if the judgment be that of so great a majority of the church that there are only a very small number of opponents, then its unanimity cannot fairly be contested.'[85] Was the moral unanimity of the universal Church infallible?

The infallibility of the Church was a concept that haunted men like Newman and Manning, and many others in a similar theological position. Newman, in his *Second Lecture on*

---

[82] *Rule*, 25.

[83] Pusey House, Oxford, Pusey Correspondence, Manning to Pusey, letter 2, dated 7 Dec. 1839. Newman's Tract 90 (1841) would claim that article 21 was compatible with a belief in the infallibility of Ecumenical Councils; the conditions which fulfilled the notion of such a gathering were rather vague, though, and left ample room for the exercise of private judgement along the lines of Wiseman's objection to the Anglican rule of faith (cf. *VM* ii. 291–3).

[84] W. Palmer, *A Treatise on the Church of Christ* (3rd edn., 2 vols., London, 1842), ii. 117.

[85] Ibid. 81.

the Prophetical Office of the Church, had condemned the Roman doctrine of infallibility as a 'theory in itself extravagant', and one which—as he would try to show in Lectures III and IV— had generated innumerable evils. Still, in Lecture VIII he went on to claim for the Church almost as much. The Church Catholic, he said, is not only 'bound to teach the Truth, but she is ever divinely guided to teach it; her witness of the Christian Faith is a matter of promise as well as of duty; her discernment of it is secured by a heavenly as well as by a human rule. She is indefectible in it, and therefore not only has authority to enforce, but is of authority in declaring it. ... The Church not only transmits the faith by human means, but has a supernatural gift for that purpose; that doctrine, which is true, considered as an historical fact, is true also because she teaches it.'[86] She would have no authority if she were declaring a lie; only truth can demand the assent of conscience. The reception of the Athanasian Creed was for Newman 'another proof of our holding the infallibility of the Church, as some of our Divines express it, in matters of saving faith ... [The] Church Catholic is pronounced to have been all along, and by implication as destined ever to be, the guardian of the pure and undefiled faith, or to be indefectible in that faith.'[87] And, in another place, he claimed that the Church Catholic 'may be truly said almost infallibly to interpret Scripture aright'.[88] Having reached this point, the constraints of the Thirty-Nine Articles and the polemic with Rome made it rather difficult for Tractarian theology to determine how indefectible the indefectibility of the Church was or how infallible its *almost* infallibility was.

Newman would admit that the texts used by Roman Catholics to support the Church's infallibility could bear that interpretation; even more, 'there surely is no antecedent reason why Almighty God should not have designed to bestow on the Church that perfect purity which the Roman School claims for her'.[89] He went so far as to accept as a probability, and as

---

[86] *VM* i. 190.   [87] Ibid. 192.

[88] Ibid. 158; Keble, for his part, would speak of 'a constant and practically infallible Tradition', while rejecting infallibility in the Roman sense ('Postscript to the Sermon on Tradition', in *Sermons*, 407).

[89] Ibid. 196.

a premiss for the sake of argument, that God might have promised infallibility to his Church; but, he added, this promise
depended on man's co-operation for its fulfilment. History
showed, on the other hand, how many times the divine inten-
tions had been mysteriously frustrated by man. The scriptural
texts on which the Roman claims were based, Newman said,
attested to unity as the divinely appointed condition for the
Church to be clad in all her glory. If infallibility had been intended as a gift for the Church, it would have required the
presence in it of a superhuman charity. This was true of the
early days of the Church, but that extraordinary unity was
soon broken. Nowadays, he said, the Church is not one; it has
become many, and without unity, it has 'lost the full endowment and the attribute of Infallibility in particular, *supposing
that were ever included in it*'.[90] The gift, though, was not altogether
lost: unity is capable of degrees, and higher or lower measures
of truth would be attached to different degrees of unity.
Again, providentially, those divisions had not occurred until
after the fundamentals of the Faith had been fully enunciated
and fixed. The Church, in its three branches, had always preserved this fundamental outline of the Faith. This partly offset
Wiseman's claim, as far as the fundamental beliefs were concerned—that is, the truths necessary for salvation.

Palmer, along the same lines, asserted that it was not to be
believed 'that the whole existing church would unanimously
teach what was contrary to the articles of the faith certainly
revealed by Christ'.[91] These 'fundamentals' were made up of
the Nicene Creed, the doctrines of the Trinity and the Incarnation, and the doctrine of grace. Catholic orthodoxy rested on
them and on episcopal government, the guardian of sound doctrine. The divisions between the Churches were 'only concerning matters of opinion and practice'.[92] If that were the
case, and if the non-fundamental doctrines were of an optional
nature, what would then justify the separation from Rome?
The answer was a well-rehearsed one: Rome had added to
those fundamentals of faith, claiming that doctrines which
were only matters of opinion—sometimes true doctrines de-

[90] Ibid. 201; my emphasis.   [91] Palmer, *Treatise*, ii. 62.   [92] Ibid.

formed by abuses, at other times errors—were necessary for salvation.

The Tractarians, though, soon felt themselves smothered by the narrow limits of the doctrine of fundamentals. Antiquity, without the medium of the Anglican reformers, was to be seen, then, as normative in all matters of doctrine and practice. The preface to the second part of Froude's *Remains* spoke of the 'great principle of Catholicism, *Quod semper, quod ubique, quod ab omnibus*' as the only safe way for the Church. In the application of this principle, the Tractarians went far beyond the so-called doctrine of fundamentals. For the author of the preface to the *Remains*, a mind 'thoroughly uncompromising in its Catholicity, would feel deeply, that an Ancient Consent binds the person admitting it alike to all doctrines, interpretations, and usages, for which it can be truly alleged'.[93] The principle of Catholicity demanded recourse to antiquity. A national Church has no separate existence, being merely the presence of the Church Catholic in a particular place. It is in the measure of her union with the Church Universal that she is able to teach uncorrupted truth and administer the means of salvation; she is able to teach and sanctify in so far as she is the Church Catholic. Christian antiquity represented the paradigm of Catholicity, not as something lost in the past but as living in the present. Fidelity to antiquity, in doctrine and moral ethos, was therefore the touchstone of Catholicity for the Anglican Church. The national Church, its formularies and liturgical practices, were to stand or fall by that test. Were a national Church to insist 'as the condition of her communion on something contradictory to the known consent of Antiquity, such communion can no longer be embraced with a safe conscience'.[94] The same grounds used to legitimize the separation from Rome could be used now to refuse allegiance to the national Church. Here the Tractarians and the High Anglican tradition parted company. High Churchmen

---

[93] Froude, *Remains*, Part II (Derby, 1839), i. p. xiii.

[94] Ibid., p. xvii. The authors of the preface, perhaps unknowingly, had dealt the death-blow to the principle of apostolic succession as the guarantor of orthodox doctrine. Antiquity reigned now in its place, and although apostolic succession was still paid lip-service, antiquity had become the supreme doctrinal tribunal to which the Tractarians would time and time again appeal.

warned of the danger of subjectivism and private interpretation in access to the Fathers without the safeguards provided by the Anglican formularies, the living Church, and the
traditional theological method. It has been claimed that the
casualties of the new method soon piled high, one on top of
another: 'The old controversial method against Rome in
Tract 71 ... the existing liturgy in Tracts 75 and 86, the Reformers in Froude's *Remains*, the Thirty-Nine Articles in Tract
90, and then the Caroline Divines, were all victims of this
looking at Antiquity using "his own eyes". At length, even the
Vincentian Rule itself fell victim.'[95] It would, perhaps, be
more apt to say that the Vincentian rule was given a new
meaning and role, one which Wood had already claimed for it
in his paper on tradition.

Manning would be more resolute than Newman in his denial
of the infallibility of the Church, whether as a present endowment or even as originally intended by Christ. His conviction
that the Faith would change with the changing of the living
judge made it impossible for him to countenance—even as a
possibility—the infallibility of the Church, present or past.
The only safe path to the purity of apostolic truth left to us
was to follow the universal agreement of the Church of the
apostolic and early post-apostolic ages. Nevertheless, he did
not consider the primitive Church to be infallible. In the first
pages of the *Appendix to the Rule of Faith* Manning listed twenty
objections to the rule he described in the sermon. Objections 2
and 3 argued that it was 'identical with the principle of the
Church of Rome', and that it invested 'the Church, or the
early Christian writers, with the Romish attribute of infallibility'.[96] The main purpose of the *Appendix* was to show
how the rule of faith he contended for was the recognized principle of the Church of England, and that it was also the universal rule of the primitive Church. By page 36 he felt justified
in claiming that his explanations had made clear that this rule
of faith did not 'invest the Church or early Christian writers

---

[95] P. B. Nockles, 'Continuity and Change in Anglican High Churchmanship in
Britain 1792–1850 (D.Phil. thesis, 2 vols., Oxford, 1982), 162. For the reactions of
High Churchmen to the new method of approaching antiquity, see Idem, *The Oxford
Movement in Context* (Cambridge, 1994), 113–22.

[96] *Appendix*, 3–4.

with the Romish attribute of infallibility'.[97] The practical and
theoretical difficulties of his position, though, were obvious to
Manning. In the course of his lucubrations in search of the certainty of faith, while considering the doctrine of infallibility,
he had noted down in one of his notebooks that he was ready
to accept and believe that the Church, as far as the main
truths of the Faith were concerned, '*has* not erred: and *will* not
err: but I dare not say *can* not'.[98]

There was always an ambivalent tone in the references of the
Tractarians to the Church as teacher of doctrine and her relation to the faith of the individual Christian. This was one of
her main roles, but one in which she could only be trusted up
to a certain point. Palmer had claimed that the instruction of
the existing Church is 'in its own age, an ordinary and divi-
nely-appointed external means for the production of faith'.[99]
The doctrinal decree of the universal Church—past or
present—was '*absolutely binding on all individual Christians, from
the moment of its full manifestation*'; such a judgement was '*irrevoc-
able, irreformable, never to be altered*'.[100] For Palmer, to suppose
that the universal Church 'could determine what is contrary
to the Gospel revealed by Jesus Christ, would be inconsistent
with the promises of Christ'.[101] The Church is not infallible,
though, she is only credible. The testimony of the Church is a
human testimony, given by fallible men, but it is 'a means sufficient to produce the firmest conviction that certain doctrines
were revealed by God'.[102] Then, rather surprisingly, Palmer
added: 'human testimony is a sufficient means of conducting
us to divine faith, by assuring us infallibly of the fact that God
has revealed certain truths'.[103]

Manning, for his part, thought that it was always 'both the
right, as men speak, and the privilege of Christians to labour
out their belief by analysis and induction, by evidence and
history', but that this could never become their necessary duty
'until the Church has failed of hers'.[104] Were the Church to
cease its guidance, then individual Christians would have no
choice 'but to set their hand to the hard inverted labour of

---

[97] Appendix 36.
[98] Manning MSS Bod., MS Eng. Misc. e. 1397, fos. 15–17.
[99] Palmer, *Treatise*, ii. 57.   [100] Ibid. 82 and 86, also 84.   [101] Ibid. 83.
[102] Ibid. 60.   [103] Ibid. 61.   [104] *Rule*, 44.

first seeking for evidence, and afterwards deducing, as conclusions, what they ought to have received by intuition as axioms
of revelation'.[105] That had happened at the Reformation; it
had happened again in Manning's time, when the faith and
principles of the Anglican Church, after being purified in the
Reformation, found themselves corrupted and obscured by the
prevalent Protestantism of the previous 150 years. Men had
now to work out for themselves 'the teaching of the Church as
well by the rule of her genuine protest [of the Anglican Refor-
mation], as by the witness of antiquity'.[106] Newman, in this
context, drew from his rich reservoir of imagery: 'The Church
Catholic is our mother ... A child comes to its mother for instruction; she gives it. She does not assume infallibility, nor is
she infallible; yet it would argue a very unpleasant temper in
the child to doubt her word.'[107] Samuel Wood saw more
clearly than his two friends their predicament; he told
Manning how they should feel pained 'at being obliged,—a
caution imposed by the sad experience of past errors—to *test*
what the Church may propound to us by Scripture, instead of
yielding an implicit confidence to our holy Mother'.[108]

5. *The Unity of the Church*

The year 1838 had also seen the publication of Gladstone's
book *The State in its Relations with the Church*.[109] One of its main
theses was that the State had a corporate identity and personality, a conscience, and was, therefore, able to recognize religious truth, and thus enshrine it—as it was its duty—in the
constitution. No liberal thinker or politician would subscribe
to, or let pass without remark, such a statement. The April
issue of the *Edinburgh Review* carried a savage attack by Macaulay on Gladstone's thesis. Macaulay's salvo went directly to
the point: the Church of England lacked unity with respect to
the doctrines of faith, admitting a variety of opinions, diverse

---

[105] Ibid. 45–6.   [106] Ibid. 47.   [107] *VM* i. 257.
[108] Manning MSS Bod., c. 654, fo. 441.
[109] Gladstone seems to have drawn his inspiration from Hooker's eighth book of
The Laws of Ecclesiastical Politie; Manning's ideas on the subject owed more to those
of the non-jurors, particularly of Leslie. In 1838 Manning and Wood published an
edition of Leslie's *The Case of the Regale and of the Pontificat Stated*.

and even contradictory, on almost every doctrinal point. As unity 'is the essential condition of truth, the Church has not the truth'.[110]

Macaulay's darts, by proxy, also reached the Tractarians. Unity had for them an almost sacramental character: the 'purity of faith', Newman had written, 'depends on the *Sacramentum Unitatis*'.[111] And Manning would echo this 'unity is the sacrament of truth: by unity it is conserved and transmitted; by abruption and isolation it is exhausted and extinguished'.[112] Macaulay's contention had to be answered. The Tractarians admitted that the unity of the Church had been broken; but, they would add, unity has different aspects, and breaches of unity are susceptible of different degrees, and to each of them corresponds a higher or lower share in truth. As far as they were concerned, the unity of apostolical succession was the tenure 'on which the sacred mysteries of faith are continued to us'.[113]

Manning was to devote the following years to a detailed study of the unity of the Church, a theme to which he had referred in passing in his sermon of 1835. On Christmas Day 1840 he told Gladstone about it: 'I have all but done a book on the Unity of the Church, a poor matter, but it may be a sort of flying buttress to some of your positions.'[114] He also referred to it in his correspondence with Archdeacon Hare: 'I have many thoughts about the Church,' he wrote on 17 April 1841;[115] and three months later: 'Lately all manner of things have been coming into my head; but I have been too much taken up to write. I have noted them down.'[116] His notebooks attest to the fact: they record his thoughts, and collect ideas from different authors on the infallibility of the Church,

---

[110] T. B. Macaulay, '*The State in its Relations with the Church* by W. E. Gladstone' (review article), *Edinburgh Review*, lxix. 139 (Apr. 1839), 270. See also V. A. McClelland, 'Gladstone and Manning: A Question of Authority', in P. J. Jagger (ed.), *Gladstone, Politics and Religion* (London, 1985), 148–70.

[111] J. H. Newman, 'Tract 71', in *VM* ii. 134.

[112] *Unity*, 347. [113] *VM* i. 202.

[114] Manning MSS Pitts, box 1, folder 6; see also 'Journals' entry for 15 Nov. 1888, quoted in *P* i. 272.

[115] Manning MSS Bod., c. 653, fo. 105.

[116] Ibid., fo. 162, letter dated 17 Aug. 1841.

Peter's ministry, the unity of the Church—as contained in the Episcopate, etc.

The first fruit of his labours was the sermon *The Mind of Christ the Perfection and Bond of the Church*, preached at Brighton on 9 December 1841. In it Manning claimed that the basis of Christian unity was the result of Christ's grace impressing his mind upon the minds of his own, conforming them to his divine mind: 'so long as the mind of Christ prevailed over the diversities of individual will and character, the church was united'.[117] Unity was assailed during the first 600 years of the Church, but that uniform character promptly extinguished the sparks of division and strife. Later on, the individual mind and subjective character prevailed in the Church, and the miracle of unity was destroyed. It could not be otherwise, 'for what is the source of all strife but self-exaltation; and what the withering blight of all holier aspirations but self-sparing?'[118] Manning concluded that unity in the Church was to be restored by restoring in it the mind which was in Christ Jesus. Unity was a consequence of sanctity; all other things needful would follow in its train. Hare agreed with the sermon as a whole, but he could not see, as Manning did, 'the working of the mind of Christ in the unity of the Church during the first six centuries. It was a period of all manner of fierce and wild divisions; and the chief power that held the Church together, was the unity of the Roman Empire.'[119]

Manning's *Unity of the Church* appeared in 1842. The first pages of the book introduced the unity of the Church as an article of the Creed, confessed in all the early and later symbols. As such it should be believed by all Christians. That the Church *is* one was not under discussion. What needed to be established was *how* it is one: that is, the meaning and the reality of the article, what is the doctrine of unity as revealed by Jesus Christ. The Anglican theory of the three branches posed some problems which the Roman Catholic Church and the Orthodox Church did not have to contemplate: they both claimed to be the one and only true Church, from which the

---

[117] H. E. Manning, *The Mind of Christ the Perfection and Bond of the Church* (Chichester, 1841), 8.

[118] Ibid. 20.

[119] Manning MSS Bod., c. 653, fo. 212; letter dated 30 Dec. 1841.

rest of Christians had cut themselves off. The branch theory, on the other hand, had to reconcile the essential unity of the Church with the 'apparent' divisions between its three branches.

From his research into the Old and the New Testaments Manning concluded that the unity of the Church is twofold: 'one kind of Unity being objective, consisting in its faith, sacraments, and organised polity; the other subjective, in the peace and brotherly love of the several members'.[120] The organic or objective unity is 'the identity of the Church of any age with the church of the Apostles in the faith and sacraments, and in the commission received from Christ, and transmitted by lawful succession'.[121] The subjective or moral unity of the Church, on the other hand, consists in unity of communion at two levels: first, submission to the lawful pastor of the local church; secondly, charity in the relationships with the several Churches dispersed around the world.

The apostolic succession is the guarantee that the Church is one and the same as in apostolic times. Manning liked to speak of a personal identity with the Church of the apostles: the 'properties of this personal identity', he wrote to Hare, 'are a knowledge of the pure truth; and a power to do in Christ's name the same acts for the reconciliation of man to God'.[122] The founding of the Church, he said in *The Unity of the Church*, contained in it 'the principle of succession, as the birth of a living soul contains a continuous personal identity'.[123]

Although both the subjective and the objective unity play their part in the preservation of revealed truth, it is the objective one that is essential in this task. Manning considered that 'objective unity cannot be wholly forfeited without a forfeiture of the subjective unity', while 'subjective unity may be forfeited without a forfeiture of the objective unity'.[124] This meant that although 'the channels of communion on earth are cut

---

[120] *Unity*, 86; see also 56–7. This distinction between objective and subjective unity seems to be Manning's main contribution to the debate. I have not been able to find precedents.

[121] Ibid. 162.

[122] Manning MSS Bod., c. 653, fo. 136, letter dated 21 July 1841.

[123] *Unity*, 90.   [124] Ibid. 272–3.

asunder, yet the lines of ascent and descent from earth to heaven, by which the communion of sacrifice and grace is interchanged between the faithful and their unseen Head, are open and sure'.[125] Some Churches, according to Manning, had retained objective unity while losing subjective unity. That was the case with the three branches of the Church according to Tractarian doctrine: the Anglican, the Greek, and the Roman Church. Protestantism, on the other hand, had lost both, and was, as a consequence, marked by schism and heresy.

Manning insisted that the unity of the Church is an article of faith; it has its origin and foundation on an explicit will of God, which cannot fail. It is not based on sharing in common with other Christians some vague, pious, and charitable feelings and endeavours, as Arnold propounded; it is founded on an objective system of doctrine and discipline. Manning wanted to prove that the unity of the Church existed, against all appearances to the contrary. It was recognizable and visible, and men had an obligation to submit to it if they were to achieve salvation. They could not use the existing divisions, subjective and moral, as an excuse to follow their own opinions without regard for objective truth. The divisions and differences among the branches of the Church were to be deplored. Objective unity was preserved in spite of them, but subjective unity, the final end of objective unity, was missing.

Manning studied at great length the principle of unity of discipline under a duly ordained bishop as the foundational element of the unity of the Church; orthodox doctrine depending on episcopal rule for its preservation. Möhler's *Unity in the Church* (1825) also dedicates many pages to the treatment of this subject, and his treatment of the subject is similar to that of Manning.[126] He did not lack sources in this respect.

---

[125] Ibid. 274.

[126] Manning had a copy of the 1839 translation into French of this work (J. A. Möhler, *De l'unité de l'Eglise ou du principe du Catholicisme d'après l'espirit des Pères des trois premiers siècles de l'Eglise* (Brussels, 1839). It is difficult to say whether he had read it while writing his own *Unity of the Church* or not. His copy of Möhler's work has many pencil marks in the margins of the sections he had found of interest, and the marks correspond to some of Manning's main points. On the other hand, whereas Manning introduced quotations from Möhler's *Symbolik* in the second edition of his work (1845), there are no references to *De l'unité*. Did he read it after 1845, when,

The Anglican tradition, in its controversy with Rome and with Puritanism, had developed an elaborate doctrine of the role of the bishop in the Church. Manning, in accordance with High Church doctrine, asserted that doctrinal orthodoxy and episcopacy were the terms of unity among the three branches of the Church, and among the several Churches within each branch. None of the branches had fallen into formal heresy or schism such as would cut them off 'from the one visible Church, and from communion with the one Head of the Church in heaven'.[127] Unity subsisted on the foundation of the apostolic succession and in the preservation of the essentials of the Faith. Unfortunately, the communion of charity between the Churches which made up the Catholic Church had been broken, but this had not touched the essentials of unity. Gladstone, naturally, was delighted with Manning's book, particularly with the section in which Manning dealt with the Gordian knot of whether there is unity in the Church at present.[128]

6. *Manning's Philosophy of Religion*

Manning's mind had a strong inclination, and an evident power, for synthesis. He may have preached his sermons on apostolic succession and the rule of faith urged by the questions raised by his pastoral ministry; his ideas on education may have been elucidated, at the instigation of his bishop, by the need to defend the role of the Established Church in the education of the country, under attack from prevalent political or cultural prejudices; his book on the unity of the Church might not have seen the light of day had Gladstone not been subject to the unmerciful criticism of Macaulay. This granted, it has

on his own confession, his thoughts were thrown back to the subjects of unity and infallibility? This seems most likely to be the case. The internal evidence of his writings favour this interpretation, and it is also about this time that his references to Möhler's *Unity* begin to appear in his letters. For the influence of Möhler on English readers see P. C. Erb's introduction to his edition of Möhler's *Unity* (cf. J. A. Möhler, *Unity in the Church, or the Principle of Catholicism* (Washington, 1996).

[127] *Unity*, 359.
[128] Cf. Gladstone to Manning, letter dated 30 June 1842, British Library, Gladstone Papers, Add. MSS 44257, fos. 140–1.

to be added, however, that while addressing those particular questions, he was working the knowledge he acquired into a general scheme, always looking for the connections between ideas, trying to integrate principles and concepts into a coherent general vision of reality.

Underlying his early writings, up to 1842, one can find an increasingly distinct conception of man, his end and the means by which he is to achieve it. Man's end is eternal life, Manning said, and he attains it by growing into the image and likeness of God, which he originally received, seed-like, from his Creator. Around 1838, Manning brought this idea to bear on the contemporary debate on education. As far as he was concerned, education could not be merely the intellectual process of instruction or even the means to form good citizens. Christianity had added a deeper dimension to it: 'The one predominant idea of Christian education is a remoulding of the whole nature, a rooting out of evil, a ripening of good, and a shaping of the inward character after an heavenly example. Christ is both the author, and the exemplar of the whole process.'[129] The proper character of education is thus 'moral and spiritual: and its importance not temporal alone, but eternal; involving the everlasting welfare of souls for whom Christ died'.[130] Years later, by that time a Catholic, he would describe the aim of education in similar terms: the 'formation of the will and heart and character, the formation of a man, is education, and not the reading and the writing and the spelling and the summing'.[131] Therefore, a proper understanding of man's nature and present condition, of his destiny and of the means to achieve it, was essential to carry out that task. All this, he would say, can only be found in the Church: the Church knows that the perfect model of humanity is Jesus Christ, perfect God and perfect Man; she is aware of man's fallen nature; she also has the divine remedies for his present condition.

---

[129] H. E. Manning, *National Education: A Sermon Preached in the Cathedral Church of Chichester in Behalf of the Chichester Central Schools* (London, 1838), 17.
[130] Ibid. 10.
[131] *Four Evils*, 140.

Probably the first developed exposition of Manning's ideas on the subject of the nature of man's regeneration is to be found in his book *The Unity of the Church* (1842) and in the contemporary volume of sermons. In the former, he described man's fall from the original state in which he had been created, the consequences of original sin, and how the Church helps him to recover his lost dignity. In man, created in the image and likeness of God, there was originally a moral unity, within the multiplicity of elements of which he is composed. The bond which made man one was the union of his will with God's will, the image within himself of the unity of will of the Three Persons of the Trinity. Original sin, man's disobedience, had broken the union between the creature and the Creator, the unity of man's mind with the mind of God and of man's will with God's will; it had weakened the inclination of his heart towards good, and clouded his intellect. Sin had disfigured the image of God in man because it destroyed man's unity—the external unity of man with God and of man with other men; it had also destroyed man's internal oneness. When man sins, he becomes 'manyfold', Manning said, quoting Origen. 'His one will becomes a multiplicity of wills (...). This inward anarchy is the moral opposite and conscious antagonist of the Divine image.'[132] The Church helps man recover his lost dignity by enabling him to restore internal and external unity. This is the mission that Christ entrusted to her, after having accomplished the work of redemption. With the mission, he entrusted her with the means to carry it out: the true knowledge of God and his grace.

True knowledge of God, he wrote in 1842, is 'a necessary condition to man's restoration to the Divine image'.[133] Ten years later he was to express the same idea in more explicit terms: 'Truth [particularly revealed truth] bears the stamp of God, and truth changes man to the likeness of God.'[134] Not any knowledge, but only the knowledge of the truth, effects that change. 'Opinion', he would write to Miss Stanley in 1851, 'cannot unite the soul with the eternal world; but Faith does.'[135] It was from that standpoint that Manning had

---

[132] *Unity*, 250.   [133] Ibid. 236–7; see also 177.   [134] *Grounds*, 19.
[135] Manning MSS Bod., c. 660, fo. 70, letter dated 27 July 1851.

written to Hare in 1840: 'I am too much of a Platonist to hold truth moderately—I should as soon think of holding the multiplication table in moderation.'[136] And a couple of years later, writing again to the same correspondent: 'From my heart I can say that I desire peace before all things but truth.'[137] And 'Truth before peace' would be the title of one of his later sermons; by then, Manning had undergone a long pilgrimage and suffered a considerable amount of heartache in his search for truth.

The perfection of true knowledge is to be found in Jesus Christ: nobody knows the Father except the Son, and those to whom the Son chooses to reveal Him. In Christ is also found the type of man's perfect nature. He exhibits the complete ideal of moral unity in his obedience to the will of his Father, and in his unity of charity with all mankind. Consequently, the knowledge of Christ is a revelation for man, dispelling the blindness of his mind and attracting his will towards God. Years later, during the debates around the 1870 Education Act, Manning would say that the 'knowledge of God in Christ has developed the reason and the will of man'.[138]

Manning did not overlook the importance of the will in the process of conversion. He considered that man had fallen by the will, in rebelling against God, and by the will he would be restored to his original condition. Our will is ourself, he would say, and as the will chooses, so the person is. What had brought about man's downfall had been a sin of self-exaltation, which had led him to set personal opinion before truth, and his own will before God's will. Now, the means to free him from the chains of human error and of his passions was to be found also in the will. The rebel will must submit itself to God, a submission which involves a denial of man's self-will. Manning would not fall into Pelagianism at this point: the change in man cannot be the fruit of his unaided effort, an act of wilfulness; it is brought about in us by God. But he who created us without our concourse will not work his salvation

---

[136] Ibid., c. 653, fo. 18, letter dated 24 Aug. 1840.
[137] Ibid., fo. 214, letter dated 2 Jan. 1842.
[138] H. E. Manning, *Denominational Education: A Pastoral Letter* (London, 1869), 4.

without us: the individual's will is to become consciously and energetically attached to God's will.[139]

The Church was the means which God had devised to tame the pride of man's rebellious will. She did so, on the one hand, by re-establishing two fundamental relationships: one, of *subordination* to God, expressed in obedience to an authority standing in God's place; the other, of *equality*, by uniting man with his fellow men in charity. The intellectual nature would also be tamed and restrained from its wild excesses by the Church. Man has a tendency 'to put subjective opinion in the place of objective truth'.[140] This had become a widely accepted modern-day dogma: it was 'commonly thought, and roundly asserted now-a-days', Manning said in 1838, 'that a man's opinions in religion are worth little, if he do not form them for himself, first doubting, then gathering arguments, weighing, comparing, deducing, concluding'.[141] This intellectual pride found its corrective in men's submission to the Church, 'as learners to an order of men who are divinely commissioned to teach'.[142] The principle of private judgement was the radical tergiversation of God's plan for man's redemption, fostering precisely those inclinations which were in need of correction in fallen man. In the Church, ignorance and pride, the eldest daughters of sin, would be healed: by 'the illumination of the intellectual nature through the one objective doctrine, and by the purifying of the moral nature through the one objective discipline, the will is once more enthroned supreme, and its energies united with the will of God'.[143]

Conversion, in Manning's terminology, is the life-long process by which man grows into God's likeness, through a progressive change of heart and will. In this change, God is the main agent. The powers to effect this sort of change in man 'can be found nowhere but in His truth, which is the key of the human intellect, and in His grace, which is the only hand that can touch the heart in man'.[144] He had handed

---

[139] Peter Erb, in this study of Manning's concept of the will, has shown how Manning did not conceive conversion as a purely intellectual process. For the idea of conversion as a life-long process see also P. C. Erb's *Question of Sovereignty*.

[140] *Unity*, 268.

[141] Manning, *National Education*, 23–4.

[142] *Unity*, 268.   [143] Ibid. 251.   [144] *Four Evils*, 138.

down to the Church both truth and grace, and thus Christianity was the only power which could shape man into the perfect image of God which he is supposed to be. God has his times and ways of working in each man. Manning always insisted on the priority of the divine initiative in the soul's pursuit of holiness and in the life of the Church. What is 'operative in the process [of conversion] are not sterile dogmatic principles, but the living, unifying love of God, and "[e]very light which reveals God's love leads on towards conversion." ... The powers of truth are at one with divine love, itself a sovereign life working passionately in the individual and corporate body.'[145]

7. *The First Clouds*

The book on the unity of the Church closed a circle of study for Manning. He could feel that he had established on solid foundations the principles of his belief and action. Unfortunately for him, he was not going to rest for long in the peaceful possession of the intellectual ground he had conquered so laboriously. While he was putting the finishing touches to his book on unity, the Oxford Movement was being buffeted by the storm which followed the publication of Tract 90, and which threatened to shipwreck not only its author, but also the principles which had been the banner under which so many had rallied.

That was not Manning's only source of concern. He conceived holiness, the growth of man into the likeness of God, as the aim of the work of redemption, and the purpose for which Christ had established the Church and endowed it with his gifts. This meant that, though firmly anchored intellectually in the Anglican Church, he had felt for some time the need to develop the devotional life within it. His exalted idea of the Christian vocation—a call to sanctity, to identification with Christ—found expression in his early sermons, in which he encouraged his listeners to commit themselves 'to the great movement of His mysterious providence, by which He is working out the change and transfiguration of His saints'.[146] Truth played an important part in that process by which God

---

[145] Erb, *Question of Sovereignty*, 21.   [146] *ASer* i. 60.

changes us 'into the likeness of His Son',[147] but it is not the only means he uses: 'It is by His holy word and sacraments, by acts of homage and adoration, by a life of obedience, and by a wisely tempered discipline of chastisement and peace, that He wins and conforms us to Himself.'[148]

Sanctity, beside its individual dimension, had an ecclesiological one. Manning considered it the chief and most distinctive of the properties of the Church, being as well its end. An effect implies and witnesses to the presence of the cause: sanctity witnesses to the presence of that truth and grace which are the inheritance of the true Church.[149] It was a common theme in Tractarian circles. Manning soon found himself perplexed by the limitations which the Anglican system presented to the longings awakened in the faithful by the ideals of Christian life presented to them. He expressed his perplexities to Newman as early as 1839. The response made clear their predicament: 'our blanket is too small for our bed. ... I am conscious that we are raising longings and tastes which we are not allowed to supply—and till our Bishops and others give scope to the development of Catholicism externally and wisely, we *do* tend to make impatient minds seek it where it has ever been, in Rome.'[150] The danger did not escape only those connected with the Oxford Movement; it was perceived by many a High Churchman.

Manning felt the full force of Newman's words. He considered that Rome had preserved more purely the Catholic devotional element. Roman ritual appealed to the whole man, intellect and feeling, and attracted to Rome many of the most serious minds in the Church of England. Conversions to Rome were on the increase, he wrote to Gladstone in 1840, and they would go on growing until the Catholic element of the English Church was developed so as to meet and satisfy the legitimate cravings of man's regenerate nature.[151] He was fully conscious of the importance of confession and other ascetical practices, going as far as to identify the lack of proper penitential discipline in the Church of England as the reason why God per-

---

[147] *ASer* i. 61.   [148] Ibid. 60.
[149] Cf. Manning MSS Bod., Eng. misc. e. 1396, fos. 58–60.
[150] Ibid., c. 654, fo. 36, letter dated 1 Sept. 1839.
[151] Cf. Manning MSS Pitts, box 1, folder 6, letter dated 2 Apr. 1840.

mitted it to be so afflicted, and its restoration as the only hope of doing great and abiding work for God in England.[152] He also lamented the lack of a proper ascetical theology in the Church of England. In his mind, he blamed its present deficiencies in this area on the reaction against the abuses which she had rejected at the Reformation. Some customs and devotions, though legitimate in themselves, had led to abuses, and the reformers had been forced to discard them altogether. In 1840 he complained to Archdeacon Hare: 'The Romanist errors have bereft us of our inheritance of blessed contemplation.'[153] The English Church, he confessed to Gladstone, was 'Catholic in dogma, and in polity, that is in all the objective being of a Church. But the subjective, the internal, ascetic, contemplative, devotional, moral, penitential elements are wasted down to a meagreness which is nigh unto death.'[154] These deficiencies did not worry him unduly, though. The English Church had to develop those Catholic elements she had rejected at the Reformation, after having purified them from deforming corruptions. This she would do. She was 'a real substantial Catholic body capable of development and all perfection—able to lick up and absorb all that is true and beautiful in all Christendom into itself—and this is our problem'.[155]

[152] Cf. ibid., Manning to Gladstone, letter dated 13 Dec. 1841.
[153] Manning MSS Bod., c. 653, fo. 51, letter dated 20 Nov. 1840.
[154] Manning MSS Pitts, box 1, folder 6, letter dated 11 Nov. 1841.
[155] Ibid., letter dated 17 Apr. 1841.

II
Calling First Principles into Question

A. A Time of Crisis

1. *The Events of 1843–1845*

Manning was able to appreciate the Catholic elements present in the Church of Rome and sadly missing in the English Church, the virtues of the one and the deficiencies of the other; a contrast which was to be raised to fever pitch by the younger Tractarians. Many thought that the furore created by the publication of Tract 90 called for a period of prudence and consolidation; Catholic principles and practices needed a trouble-free time to settle in the minds and hearts of people. The *British Critic* of Ward and Oakeley would not hear that advice of prudence, and its tone of almost unqualified praise for the Roman elements and system often went hand in hand with repeated criticisms of the Church of England.

High Churchmen could not but look with apprehension on these developments. Palmer, who had taken Newman's part in the Tract 90 crisis, would now publish his *Narrative of Events* (1843) designed 'to clear those who uphold Church principles from the imputation of approving certain recent tendencies to Romanism'.[1] It was a manifesto for High Churchmen, fixing the principles to be defended and the pitfalls to be avoided, and intending to prove that High Church principles did not lead to Rome. To illustrate this last point, Palmer listed the names of well-known public figures who upheld High Church principles while showing support for the English Reformation and denouncing in clear terms the errors of the Roman Church. Manning's name was included in this list. Palmer

---

[1] W. Palmer, *A Narrative of Events Connected with the Publication of the Tracts for the Times, with Reflections on Existing Tendencies to Romanism* (2nd edn., Oxford, 1843), p. v. The preface is dated 4 Oct. 1843.

denounced in clear terms the tendency to Romanism of the *British Critic*:

Within the last two or three years ... a new School has made its appearance. The Church has unhappily had reason to feel the existence of a spirit of dissatisfaction with her principles, of enmity to her Reformers, of recklessness for her interests. We have seen in the same quarter a spirit of—almost *servility* and *adulation* to Rome, and enthusiastic and exaggerated praise of its merits ... a disposition to acknowledge the supremacy of the See of Rome, to give way to *all its claims* however extreme ... The Gallican and the Greek churches are considered unsound in their opposition to the claims of Rome. The latter is held to be separated from *Catholic* unity. The 'See of Peter' is described as the centre of that unity; while our state of separation from it is regarded, not merely as an evil, but a sin ... The blame of separation, of *schism*, is openly and unscrupulously laid on the English church! Her reformers are denounced in the most vehement terms. ... Displeasure is felt and expressed if any attempts are made to expose the errors, corruptions, and idolatries, approved in the Roman communion.[2]

The men of the *British Critic* held that the Church of England was in need of being un-Protestantized. Their identification of Roman doctrines and practices with Catholicism meant that the legitimate conclusion of their principles appeared to be that 'Rome *as she is* should be our actual model in religion'.[3] Palmer went on to show that the deprecatory manner of speaking of the English Church and its reformers, together with the desire to assimilate its doctrine and practical system to that of Rome, were antagonistic to the great body of those who adhered to Church principles. He also gave clear norms of conduct for those who were unsettled in their opinions and in doubt about the Church of England's grounds. Someone in that situation was bound in conscience 'to seek silently for the solution of those doubts; to cease from writing or speaking on subjects in which his own opinions are *unsettled*'. Those who, on the other hand, were convinced of the duty of uniting to Rome should not labour, while still in the Anglican communion, 'to insinuate their own persuasion amongst the duped and blinded members of the English Church'.[4]

---

[2] W. Palmer, *A Narrative of Events*, 44–5.   [3] Ibid. 65.   [4] Ibid. 67 and 68.

Manning could not have failed to be impressed by the tone
and the content of Palmer's *Narrative*, an impression which
was to be reinforced and confirmed by certain events that
took place in late October 1843. The change in tone which
marked Manning's correspondence around this time, and his
altered state of mind, can be clearly traced to the quick exchange of letters with Newman at the end of October, after
the latter's resignation from St Mary's. What had originally
started as an expression of sympathy by Manning led to the
subsequent disclosure of Newman's true condition. 'Your
letter is a most kind one,' Newman wrote on 25 October, 'but
you have engaged in a dangerous correspondence.' And,
indeed, it was! 'I must tell you then frankly,' Newman added,
'lest I combat arguments which to me, alas, are shadows, that
it is from no disappointment, irritation, or impatience, that I
have, whether rightly or wrongly, resigned St Mary's—but
because I think the Church of Rome the Catholic Church,
and ours not a part of the Catholic Church, because not in
communion with Rome, and feel that I could not honestly be
a teacher in it any longer.' The letter went on to map in
detail the steps which had led to that conviction: the passing
flashes of light, the hesitations, the counter-arguments. It was
still an ongoing process; he felt that the events of those years
were 'confirmations of a conviction forced on me, while
engaged *in the course of duty*, viz. the theological reading to
which I had given myself. And this last mentioned circumstance is a fact which has never, I think, come before me till
now that I write to you.'[5]

It was an unexpected bolt from the blue for Manning. He
was horrified; he had now become party to a secret which
only a few friends, Henry and Robert Wilberforce among
them, knew. On 27 October Manning wrote to Gladstone
with a heavy heart: ' "The clouds return after the rain" and
they are heavy indeed. The enclosed letter fulfils all. ... What
a history is Newman's—And now what must we do each in
our place for the Church? The trust seems now to fall into the
hands of us—men younger, weaker, less learned, *every way*.'[6]

[5] Manning MSS Bod., c. 654, fos. 52 and 53.
[6] Manning MSS Pitts, box 1, folder 7, Manning to Gladstone, letter dated 27 Oct.
1843.

Many had denounced the dangers inherent in the Tractarian Movement, and he perceived now the full force of their arguments. It was a revelation which filled him with revulsion. The intensity of his feelings found outward vent in his letter to Pusey later that year. 'I can no longer deny', he wrote, 'that a tendency against which my whole soul turns has shown itself. It has precipitated those that are impelled by it into a position remote from that in which they stood, and from that in which I am.' Newman's letter had been a sudden revelation of the wrong turn which the Movement had taken.

I feel to have been for four years on the brink of I know not what; all the while persuading myself and others that all was well; and more—that none were so true and steadfast to the English Church; none so safe as guides. . . . Day after day I have been pledging myself to clergymen and laymen all about me that all was safe and sure. I have been using his books, defending and endeavouring to spread the system which carried this dreadful secret at its heart. There remains for me nothing but to be plain henceforward on points where hitherto I have almost resented, or ridiculed the suspicion. I did so because I knew myself to be heartily true to the English Church, both affirmatively in her positive teaching, and negatively in her rejection of the Roman system and its differential points. I can do this no more. I am reduced to the painful, saddening, sickening necessity of saying what I feel about Rome.[7]

Indeed, he spoke of Rome, in vehement terms, in his university sermon of 5 November. Manning had been apprehensive, at first, when he heard in September that the preaching rota had him down to preach on that day, wondering whether the distribution of preachers aimed at placing him in an embarrassing position.[8] Now, however, he saw it as an opportunity to defend vital principles. His language, when speaking about the Church, had never left any room for ambiguity: he had always expressed his rejection of Romanism clearly and, on the other hand, had manifested his faithfulness to the English Church and his trust in her title-deeds. Now, more than ever

---

[7] Manning to Pusey, 22nd Sunday after Trinity 1843, Pusey House, Oxford, Pusey Correspondence, letter 13a.

[8] Cf. Manning MSS Pitts, box 1, folder 7, Manning to Gladstone, letter dated 5 Sept. 1843. See also letter dated 27 Oct. 1843.

before, the times called urgently for clear principles and plain speech.

Newman's words had thrown a cloud over Manning's recently expressed theory about the unity of the Church: the Church of England was not a part of the Catholic Church because it was not in communion with Rome! These were as yet words which were confined to the narrow circle of a few close friends, but Manning could foresee their effect in time: a mine was being driven under the main battlements of the Anglican Church, and he felt called to strengthen its positions. The university sermon shows plainly its hurried composition and the turbulence in Manning's mind. It contains much accusation against the Church of Rome, her inordinate claims to supremacy and her efforts to justify the horrors with which some tried to impose it. More important, although obscured by the anti-Roman rhetoric, was the positive affirmation of the principles on which the Church of England based its existence.

Manning had already dealt with these topics in his book *The Unity of the Church*, published the previous year, and previously in his first letter to the *British Magazine* in November 1836. He had imbibed his ideas about the relationship between Rome and Canterbury from the writings of Thorndike and Bramhall, and he quoted them frequently. From the traditional High Church perspective, he conceived the Church as being made up of local (or particular) Churches, under the jurisdiction of their respective bishops, without subordination or dependence of one on another. As he had written in 1838, the local bishop is in his diocese the source of authority and the centre of unity, subordinate only to the collective authority of the whole episcopal order to which supreme jurisdiction all bishops are subject. Around this time, there is also a significant and subtle change in Manning's terminology, aimed at reinforcing the Catholicity of the Anglican Church; the expression 'the Church *in* England' tending now to replace frequently in his writings the rather more common one of 'the Church *of* England'.[9]

---

[9]   Cf. H. E. Manning, *A Charge Delivered at the Ordinary Visitation of the Archdeaconry of Chichester, in July 1845* (London, 1845), 46, 47; *A Charge Delivered at the Ordinary Visitation of the Archdeaconry of Chichester, in July 1846* (London, 1846), 27; etc. In 1850 he

Manning, with Thorndike and Bramhall, admitted that the Church of Rome had a primacy of honour among the Churches, based originally on the political pre-eminence of Rome, as capital of the Empire, and he would not object to 'a patriarchal power limited by the Canons of the Church, and exercised in conformity with them'.[10] However, no particular Church, not even a patriarchal see, could claim a supremacy of jurisdiction over other local Churches. Their power descended upon each one of them directly from the divine Head of the Church in heaven. Each particular Church was competent to reform itself in those areas which were its own concern; when it came to doctrines of faith and discipline which affected the whole Church, the whole Church should be consulted, Rome first because of its primacy of honour. What a local Church could not do was to impose its own practices or decisions on all other Churches, as if exercising a universal jurisdiction of divine origin. The above, according to Manning, was the doctrine of Holy Scripture and the Fathers on the unity of the Church.

Self-exaltation, Manning thought, was the source of all strife, and had been the source of most of the evils of the Church. Rome's claim of a supremacy of jurisdiction over all other Churches had been the main cause of the divisions within the Church. The blame for the divisions between the Eastern and Western Churches was to be laid at the doors of both of them, although the fault of the Greek was never so great as the usurpation of the supreme pontificate by the Bishop of Rome: 'if a more petulant temper be found among the Greeks, yet the formal and positive causes of division are to be laid to the charge of the Roman Church'.[11] The separa-

---

was to repeat similar ideas, adding that the Church in every land is the Church Universal sojourning in a particular place, and there teaching and ruling with the whole authority and power of the Divine Office committed to it (cf. H. E. Manning, *The Appellate Jurisdiction of the Crown in Matters Spiritual: A Letter to the Right Reverend Ashurst-Turner, Bishop of Chichester* (London, 1850), 4 ff., where he also uses the expression 'the Church in England'). The expression 'the Church in England' was criticized by some as removing the focus of allegiance from the national Church to the universal Church.

[10] *Unity*, 363. In this book Manning included some long notes discussing the nature of the precedence of the Church of Rome (notes on pp. 98–9 and 152–4).

[11] *Unity*, 359.

tion, having deprived them of 'the mutual check and mitigating influence of each on the other', had given rise to corruptions in discipline and doctrine in both. Still, Manning
concluded, 'on neither side is there either formal heresy or
schism of such a kind as to cut either of them off from the one
visible Church, and from communion with the one Head of
the Church in heaven'.[12]

The divisions within the Western Church, particularly that
of the Church of England from Rome, had had the same
cause: the Roman claim to universal jurisdiction. This time it
was compounded by the temporal claims of the Popes, the de-
posing power among them, over sovereigns and princes.[13]
Manning, in his university sermon, considered that the

> act of the sixteenth century was the last and the successful effort in a
> long series of ineffectual struggles against the secular encroachment
> of the Roman court. ... And the principle on which they rested
> their act, and on which our relation to the Roman Church is still
> amply to be defended, is this—that there is no one supreme prince
> or power in things temporal from whom the civil rulers of this
> realm derive their sovereign authority: neither by Divine right any
> one supreme spiritual head on earth from whom the pastors of this
> Church derive their apostolical commission: that both the Spiritual-
> ity and Temporality of this Church and Realm severally possess
> full authority and jurisdiction derived to them by succession and de-
> volution; and that both, under Christ alone, are within their respec-
> tive spheres perfect and complete.[14]

The independence of the separate Churches no more contra-
vened the obligations to Catholic unity than the independence
of the separate States clashed with the principles of inter-
national law and relations.

He defended the separation of the Anglican Church from
Rome on the principles of Bramhall's *Just Vindication of the
Church of England*, and cleared it from the charges of both
schism and heresy. There was no schism in rejecting the pre-
tence of universal jurisdiction of divine right; neither was
there heresy. As a matter of fact, the aim of the Anglican reformers had been to restore the evangelical purity of doctrine,
which had been compromised by Roman 'corruptions'. They

---

[12] *Unity*, 360 and 359.   [13] Cf. ibid. 360–6.
[14] H. E. Manning, 'Christ's Kingdom not of this World', in *Sermons Preached before
the University of Oxford* (Oxford, 1844), 91–2.

had returned to the faith of the primitive Church. In doing so they had had to remove also some true doctrines which had become contaminated and deformed by error. The Anglican Church accepted the canonical Scriptures, the Catholic creeds, the Ecumenical Councils (there had been only six truly ecumenical ones, according to Manning), the apostolic traditions, and it was ready to submit to the decisions of any future free and lawful Ecumenical Council—but to be truly ecumenical, it must bring together the three branches of the Church. In the meantime, each branch retained the power to reform itself in those questions affecting only that part of the Church.

Manning felt that the generous acknowledgement on the part of the Church of England of the Roman Church as one of the branches of the Church Universal, 'in spite of the corrupt traditions and ensnaring doctrines with which it is darkened and disfigured',[15] was not reciprocated. He considered this a sign of schismatic temper on the Roman side. Wiseman, in his polemical writings, had introduced the famous reference to the Donatists; Manning brought them in at this point in the sermon, although from a different perspective. He thought that, in the disputes between the Roman Church and the Church of England, the latter occupied the Catholic ground—acknowledging Rome as a sister Church, accepting the validity of her orders and sacraments, the possession of true faith in essentials, etc.—while Rome, like the Donatists, denied the Church of England everything, including its reality as a Church. Manning resented that rejection, and also the fact that Rome used Catholic and Roman as interconvertible terms. According to the principles of the branch theory, Rome was promoting schism both in the East and in England by setting 'altar against altar, and succession against succession. In the formation of sects in diocesan churches, in the exclusive assumption of the name Catholic, in the reordination of priests, and in restricting the One Church to their own communion, there has been no such example of division since the schism of Donatus.'[16]

[15] *Unity*, 365–6.
[16] Ibid. 364. The Jerusalem bishopric was seen by Manning as an act which undermined the first principles of the Church of England. It was an unwarranted

In his Oxford sermon on 5 November, he also directed his fire at William George Ward's[17] and Frederick Oakeley's[18] presentation of Rome as the ideal Church, on whose pattern the Anglican Church should be reformed. In fact, Manning would later say, they were subverting the Church's very foundations: they turned High Church principles upside-down by maintaining that the Roman Church was the standard of Catholic doctrine and spirit.[19] The Church of England, according to High Church principles, was the true representative of primitive Christianity, and the model on which the other Catholic Churches should reform themselves, before reunion could be achieved.[20] The events of the sixteenth century might have been the stern but necessary preparation for this mission. The aim of the separation from Rome was to restore and preserve true primitive doctrine, impaired not only by the Roman but also by the Greek Church. God's providence, however, had preserved a faithful remnant from among his erring people; those who, by God's help, had not bent their knees to Baal, were intended by him as the nucleus and leaven for the restoration of the whole to faithfulness to God. Manning's endorsement of the above principles was not unqualified.[21] Manning accepted Newman's contention, in Tract 71 and in 'Home Thoughts Abroad',[22] that the shattering of the *Sacramentum Unitatis*—guarantee of the purity of

act of intrusion: the Anglican Church could not 'by any fiction treat as void, and under our jurisdiction, sees which if they belong to any certainly do not belong to us'; this act would only 'add another to the number of contending claimants' (Manning MSS Bod., c. 653, fo. 177, letter dated 28 Oct. 1841).

[17] W. G. Ward was at the time a Fellow of Balliol. He was deprived of his degree in 1845 after the publication of *The Ideal of a Christian Church* (London, 1844), and he became a Catholic in 1845.

[18] F. Oakeley had been Chaplain-Fellow of Balliol College, and, since 1839, was incumbent of Margaret Chapel, the main centre of Tractarian ideas and activity in London. He became a Catholic in 1845.

[19] They could not be agents in the growth of Catholic principles and practice within the Church of England. As Manning wrote to Oakeley, 21 Dec. 1844: 'To those who believe that Catholic and Roman are not convertible terms, the unprotestantizing of the English Church does not signify the Romanizing of it' (Manning MSS Bod., c. 654, fo. 71).

[20] Cf. Nockles, *Oxford Movement*, 162 ff.

[21] Cf. Manning's letter to Newman, 25 Jan. 1839, in *LD* vii. 29–30.

[22] Cf. *VM* ii. 134, and *British Magazine*, Mar. 1836, repr. in *Discussions and Arguments*, 1–43. See Manning to Newman, 25 Jan. 1839, *LD* vii. 29–30.

faith—by the great schisms had meant that, since then, truth did not dwell simply and securely in any branch of the Church. The Church of England had also suffered because of the separation, and Manning's correspondence repeats the common Tractarian theme of the decline of Anglicanism in the previous century and a half. The recovery had started only recently, and its future was uncertain. But he could still defend those principles in their general outline. Within the spirit of that tradition, he added in the sermon a note of guarded optimism, which, with hindsight, looks more like defiance: the Church of England, purified by her trials, might still be 'a principle of reconciliation between east and west, and a law of unity and peace to mankind'.[23] The special dispensation of divine providence which, since the sixteenth century, had protected the Church of England and the realm from falling under the secular dominion of Rome, while at the same time preserving in the Anglican Church the purity of ecclesiastical principles, had imposed on it the responsibility of being faithful to its trust, for the good of the universal Church.[24]

Reports of the sermon were soon abroad, and Manning was genuinely surprised by the response to it in some quarters. On James Anthony Froude's authority, we have it that Manning walked to Littlemore on 6 November to visit Newman, who, to Manning's confusion, would not receive him.[25] He also heard from Charles Marriott that the sermon had set some people against him, particularly at Oxford; William Dodsworth reported similar reactions in London from his observation point of Christ Church, St Pancras. Manning was hurt by what he considered the partiality of those who had not examined what he had said but only the side he seemed to have

---

[23] Manning, *University Sermons*, 95.

[24] A year later, in a letter to Oakeley, 21 Dec. 1844, Manning's tone sounded less assured and positive about the Reformation in general, and the English one in particular. He believed that 'its moral and theological character to be in great measure evil', but he believed with equal conviction that 'the position in which it has placed us to be tenable; and that we have cause to be thankful to God for great, and extraordinary mercies in the over-ruling and result' of it (Manning MSS Bod., c. 654, fo. 68).

[25] J. H. Newman's *Correspondence of John Henry Newman with John Keble and Others, 1839–1845*, ed. J. Bacchus (London, 1917), 280. Manning wrote to Newman on 21 Dec. 1843, renewing his professions of friendship, while standing by his sermon; his letter, and Newman's response, seem to have closed the Littlemore incident (see ibid. 290–3).

taken. He did not consider himself a party man, and did not
believe that the only choice was between the line of the *British
Critic* and stark Protestantism. The sermon did not represent a
change of sides, leaving his old friends for the world. He remained on the side of the principles of the Anglican Church,
now compromised by the line and intemperate tone of Ward
and Oakeley, against whom the main force of the argument
was directed. Those who thought he was abandoning his
friends in the hour of difficulty, did so on a mistaken expectation that Manning was what he was not.[26] He was partly com-
forted, however, by the acquiescence of some of those who
read the actual sermon: more impartial readers who, like
Hope and Gladstone, did not find in it any departure from
commonly held principles.[27]

Pusey and others tried to restrain Manning's anti-Roman
rhetoric, but their efforts seem to have served little purpose
except that of forcing Manning to express his thoughts on
Rome more explicitly. Manning answered Dodsworth's remonstrances with a series of long letters in which he fully dis-
closed his thoughts; he also sent Dodsworth Newman's letter
and, apparently, a copy of his sermon. The men at Oxford, he
wrote on 6 December 1843, were making 'our position untenable; and leave us at the mercy of Roman controversialists'.[28]
They did not know the principles of the Church of England.
It was true, he wrote two days later, that her faith and practice
had to be raised to a more Catholic standard, but this could
not be done 'if we make our affirmative principles dubious,
tame, or halfhearted ... I cannot consent nor endure to be
going back in the midst of work to root up first principles to
see if they [are] alive, like children gardening ... I distinctly
and strongly feel that the prevalent tone of many of our

---

[26] Cf. Manning MSS Bod., c. 658, fo. 17, Manning to Dodsworth, letter dated 8
Dec. 1843. Manning wrote to Newman on 21 Dec., enclosing the text of his sermon.
He knew that Newman would find much to censure in it, but, repeating the phrase
he had used in his letter to Dodsworth, he did not wish Newman to think him other
than he was [cf. Newman, *Correspondence*, 290–1].

[27] Cf. Manning MSS Pitts, box 1, folder 7, letters to Gladstone dated 15 Nov. 1843
and Second Sunday of Advent 1843. See also *P* i. 235 ff.

[28] Manning MSS Bod., c. 658, fo. 6. The Roman corruptions were the justification
for the break with Rome. If they were denied, and Roman doctrine and practice
exalted, there was no escaping from the charge of schism levelled by Catholic controversialists against the Church of England.

friends does call our first principles in question.'[29] Their position was untenable: the Catholicism 'we hear of distinct from
both [Anglicanism and Romanism] is an antiquarian conceit,
a sham, and a delusion';[30] a vision born of selectiveness and
private judgement. Having dissociated himself from the *British
Critic* ideas, Manning went on to confess his conviction that
Anglicanism and Romanism were 'the only tenable and
logical systems; each on their own principles'.[31] And he felt
'fully persuaded that if the position of Thorndike and Bramhall
is not tenable the Roman Church is right; I believe their position to be tenable, and I know that it is the only alternative
to entering the Roman Communion. ... Be sure of this that
the day I cease to be Anglican I shall be Roman. Nothing in
the world could induce me to take up with the fanciful, half
and half, intermediate system which embodies the reality of
neither; and forfeits the strength of both.'[32]

He would admit to Gladstone that a tendency to Romanism
was a risk to which the restoration of Catholic principles was
liable, but it was 'something parasitical', 'a specific error by
excess and defect', alien to Catholic truth.[33] In his 1845
Charge, he would dwell briefly on the fact that the Oxford
Movement was 'alike our safety and our danger'. It was an
awakening of the Church to its dormant laws, but this had
partly led to 'an overactive, and therefore morbid self-intro-
spection, by which individual minds have suffered, and some
have been lost to us'.[34] The final issue was still undecided, but
Manning was full of foreboding thoughts.

The printed text of his sermon of 5 November did not appear
until 1844. Pusey, after reading it, wrote to Manning marvel-
ling at how he could preach such a one-sided sermon, judging
and condemning in severe words the Church of Rome, as
though he 'were not a member and Minister of a Church suffering deeply from the very same sin, in another form'.[35] For

---

[29] Ibid., fos. 12–13, letter dated 8 Dec. 1843.
[30] Ibid., fo. 24, letter dated 13 June 1844.   [31] Ibid.   [32] Ibid., fos. 26–7.
[33] Cf. Manning MSS Pitts, box 1, folder 7, Manning to Gladstone, letter dated 19
Nov. 1843. Palmer had also made this point in his *Narrative of Events* (cf. p. 72).
[34] Manning, *Charge 1845*, 49.
[35] Manning MSS Bod., c. 654, fos. 234–5, Pusey to Manning, letter dated 9 July
1844. Manning had indicated in his letter to Newman of 21 Dec. 1843 that he had
omitted 'the adverse and counter view of our state' by design, because it seemed to

Pusey, Ward's and Oakeley's writings had the virtue of calling
to the Church of England's mind its own deficiencies, and in
so doing they paid it a signal service. The 1845 *Charge* did
make some amends in this direction. Manning acknowledged
that there were threatening signs in the Anglican Church; but
more in number and much more threatening were the
dangers hanging over other Churches, particularly the
Roman one. The Church of England had already passed
through the worst of it. The branch had to be pruned to give
more fruit, and every adverse event, Manning thought, might
'be regarded as a chastisement for some failure in our steward-
ship. When we so read it, adversity becomes our strength.'[36]

Pusey, however, found the 1845 *Charge* lacking in brotherly
love for Rome. To his appeals to show charity towards the
Roman Church, Manning answered by defining the principles
on which, as he saw it, the Anglican Church's relationship
with the Church of Rome should be based. Charity, indeed,
was due to the whole Church, including the Roman, but that
should not make Anglicans forget that they owed the largest
and tenderest charity to their own Church. They should
express that charity and act on it, aware of the fact that, for
300 years, the Church of Rome had desired the extinction of
the Anglican Church, and looked for ways to undermine and
destroy it. He added: 'We owe it in charity to the whole
Church and to the Roman inclusively to do all we can to
deepen and perfect the spiritual life of the English Church; ...
I believe that the best hope of building up the spiritual life of
the English Church, and so of bringing about a reconciliation
of our Church with those from whom we are unhappily es-
tranged is a clear, firm, unambiguous tone as regards the
points at issue.'[37] Again, unrestrained praise of Roman doc-

---

him that 'many were labouring that side', and few alluding to the errors of Rome
(Newman, *Correspondence*, 290–1).

[36] Manning, *Charge 1845*, 54.
[37] Pusey House, Oxford, Pusey Correspondence, Manning to Pusey, letter 22,
dated 8 Aug. 1845. Pusey felt that he could not take any offensive ground against
Rome. He even hoped at the time 'that it may prove that the Council of Trent may
become the basis of union, that those assembled there, were kept providentially free
from error', and that it 'might, by subsequent reception, become a General Council'
(Pusey to Manning, letter 47, dated 20/22 July 1845 (copy)).

trine and practices had a negative effect: it pushed people towards Protestantism and rationalism, weakened the Catholic elements in the Anglican Church, and strengthened the un-Catholic elements in the Roman Church.[38]

A chapter of his life was now closing, and he noted in his journal: 'I have taken my last act with those who are moving in Oxford. Henceforth I shall endeavour by God's help to act by myself without any alliance. My duty is to live and die striving to edify the Church in my own sphere.'[39] Happily, as he wrote to Dodsworth, he was not troubled about 'the reality of the English Church',[40] and he could still defend it on the basis of the principles he had described in *The Unity of the Church*. His 5 November sermon had been a declaration against the Romanizing tendencies of the *British Critic*, and he would now lend his support to the *English Review*, founded by Palmer, to counteract the line of Ward and Oakeley. He was soon disappointed by its lack of life and strength, compared with the rival periodical. It did not answer the needs of the Church, and, in Manning's estimation, it was unlikely to do so in the future.[41]

The year 1844 brought little relief to the general condition of the Tractarian Party or to Manning's mind. Ward, partly in answer to Palmer's *Narrative*, delivered to the world in June of this year his *Ideal of a Christian Church*. The ultimate end of religion, he wrote in it, is personal sanctification and salvation. And, he added, there is a close connection between the highest form of holiness and the purest knowledge of the entire Christian doctrine. The ideal Church was that which would satisfy man's aspirations for truth and sanctity. He then went on to describe in detail how much the Anglican Church fell short of that ideal, as teacher of moral discipline and orthodox doctrine. On this last count he would say: 'We cannot learn doctrine from the English Church, if we would; for she *teaches* no uniform doctrine to be learned.'[42] She tolerated heterodoxy

[38] Cf. Pusey House, Oxford. Pusey Correspondence, Manning to Pusey, letter 22.

[39] Quoted by Chapeau, 'Manning the Anglican', 17. Chapeau dates it to 1845.

[40] Cf. Manning MSS Bod., c. 658, fos. 24 ff., letter dated 13 Jan. 1844.

[41] Cf. Manning MSS Pitts, box 1, folder 8, Manning to Gladstone, letter dated Easter Tuesday 1844.

[42] W. G. Ward, *Ideal of a Christian Church*, 409.

within herself and the contradictory opinions of the several parties which composed her, while omitting to make a clear affirmation of orthodox truth. The remedy for these shortcomings was to be found in a reformation carried out on the model of the Roman Church. High Church principles led in that direction, Ward affirmed, and he called on High Churchmen to join forces with the men of the *British Critic* in working for the good of the Church.

Manning expressed his frustrations and fears in his correspondence with Gladstone. He was puzzled by Ward's affirmation that he could hold the whole corpus of Roman doctrine while subscribing to the Thirty-Nine Articles, on the grounds that the latter did not condemn Roman doctrine but only abuses which Rome itself had condemned. Could the controversies of the last 300 years be reduced to mere verbal differences? The controversialists on both sides did not think so, and neither did Manning. Still, Ward's book made him reflect that the point in question was 'whether the Church of England has rightly understood, and stated the doctrine of the Roman Church'. He 'heartily wish[ed] Ward or any man would prove that we had nothing but a delusion of our own to condemn'. That man would have all Manning's help in the undertaking: 'I would not cross it with a straw,' he added.[43]

In his private utterances he acknowledged the accuracy of Ward's diagnosis of the ills of the Church of England: the lack of a proper theological science, the shortcomings in discipline and practice, etc. The greatest problem, though, was that the Church of England could not bear the knowledge of the disease, and consequently would not hear of applying the re-

---

[43] Manning MSS Pitts, box 1, folder 8, Manning to Gladstone, letter dated 28 Dec. 1844. Did Manning take upon himself the task of finding out what doctrines Rome actually held? We may probably date from this time Manning's systematic reading of Catholic theologians. Until then, his reading of Catholic authors seems to have been on the whole confined to the works of controversialists like Milner, Butler, Bellarmine, etc., or of Gallican authors. His *University Sermons* (1844) quote Thomas Aquinas's *Summa contra Gentiles*, and the second edition of *The Unity of the Church* (London, 1845) also shows traces of his Catholic reading in the introduction of quotations from Möhler's *Symbolik* and Döllinger's *History of the Church*. In time, he became, among those connected with the Catholic revival in the Anglican Church, the man best read in Catholic theology.

medies for it. [44] To Pusey he wrote in a different tone, speaking
of his disgust at Ward's behaviour during the ensuing controversy and degradation. Manning decided to wait until the full
consequences of the moment could be clearly discerned. It
was an anxious time, one in which his convictions about the
rule of faith were being tested, as he confessed a year later to
Robert Wilberforce. One thing was clear: following Palmer's
advice, he would never act or speak doubtfully. In his own
words: 'if I doubted I would cease to speak and act till I was
decided for England or Rome'. [45]

He was worried by the unsettled condition of many minds,
and, having lost confidence in Pusey, he began increasingly to
look to Robert Wilberforce for support, 'because some of the
ablest and dearest of those round us fail to satisfy me in some
of the conditions necessary for dealing fairly and solidly with
the realities of our relation to the Roman Church'. [46] The
events of the last years had raised many hard questions, and
they demanded plain answers. In October he wrote deploring
the condition of theological studies in the Anglican Church:
'our theology is a chaos, we have no principles, no form, no
order, or structure, or science'. [47] His anxiety, though, did not
extend to doubts, 'for nothing can shake my belief of the presence of Christ in our Church, and Sacraments. I feel incapable
of doubting it.' [48] Years later, he confessed to Robert to
having been more unsettled than he had admitted at the time:
he adhered to his previous intellectual convictions until 1845,
although with increasing difficulty. [49]

2. *The Development of Doctrine*

November 1845 saw the publication of Newman's *Development
of Christian Doctrine*; in it he announced publicly his conversion

[44] Cf. Manning MSS Pitts, Manning to Gladstone, letters dated 14 Oct. and 20
Nov. 1844.
[45] Manning MSS Bod., c. 658, fo. 28, letter to Dodsworth, 13 June 1844.
[46] Ibid., c. 655, fo. 27, letter dated 30 June 1845.
[47] Ibid., fo. 29, letter dated 6 Oct. 1845. A few months later (30 Dec. 1845) he
wrote again to Robert about the need for a foundation to systematic theology such
as laid by St Thomas and Melchor Cano, and confessed himself surprised at how little
he knew theology in its principles (cf. ibid., fo. 37).
[48] Ibid., fos. 28–9.
[49] Cf. ibid., c. 656, fo. 107, letter dated 22 Jan. 1851.

to Roman Catholicism. Manning at first treated Newman's book almost dismissively, as a wonderful intellectual work, subtle even to excess. The arguments, though, did not impress him: 'After reading the book', he wrote to Robert Wilberforce, 'I am left where I was found by it.'[50] Development was the refuge of the destitute—Romanist and Protestant alike—who could find no shelter in antiquity. The Faith was perfected at Pentecost, and existed 'ideally' perfect in the Church from then till the present. The only developments which had taken place had been logical and verbal, 'not ideal or conceptual'. He judged the odds against Newman's principle being true a thousand to one!

Gladstone encouraged Manning to address Newman's argument. He did not need encouragement: the book had to be answered. As he told Gladstone, he needed to find the 'ultimate positions in which I can stand and work for life'.[51] Later, in September 1846, he wrote to Hare in a similar vein: 'I feel the only rest and solid base of the Soul is Truth, and my prayer is that I may count all loss for Truth's sake.'[52] In the crisis they were going through, what was at stake was the foundation of the Faith, and the Anglican and the Roman Church were in the same predicament. He rejected the idea of development, and felt that 'the Tridentine Doctors would have severely censured the modern theories of development, or gradual rise as false, and dangerous'.[53] He upheld their principle, for who was to judge which developments were right and which wrong? 'Quo judice?', he asked in his letter to Robert Wilberforce of 30 December 1845. Manning did not read infallibility in Newman's book, but he did read in it the end of the Anglican rule of faith. The *Development of Christian Doctrine*, he would confess years later, 'opened my eyes to one fact, namely that I had laid down only half the subject. I had found the *Rule*, but not the *Judge*. It was evident that to put Scripture and Antiquity into the hands of the individual is as much

---

[50] Manning MSS Bod., c. 655, fo. 34, letter dated 30 Dec. 1845.

[51] Manning MSS Pitts, box 1, folder 8, Manning to Gladstone, letter dated 26 Dec. 1845.

[52] Manning MSS Bod., c. 653, fos. 328–9.

[53] Ibid., c. 662, fo. 68, letter to unknown correspondent, dated 10 Mar. 1846 (copy).

Private judgment as to put Scripture alone.'[54] This conviction was still some way off in 1845. For the time being the book forced him again into the same subjects as his previous studies: it compelled him 'to examine into the nature of faith and the principles of divine certainty',[55] and to review his notions of unity and infallibility.[56]

The whole question arose progressively and in order before him. The matter to be ascertained was the revelation of the day of Pentecost. This was to be done by means of a recourse to the Tradition of the Church, in which he included Sacred Scripture. This process of discernment was to be carried out by the Church. She was to achieve the deepest insights into revealed truth by contemplation, the devout reflection on the object of faith which is primarily blended with worship. In it reason pierces into the causes and relations of revealed truths, finding their mutual dependence and the order that makes them into a harmonious whole.[57] At this point, Manning arrived at an obstacle that would halt his progress: if the process of discernment by which the Church was to identify truth were to be 'only the intellectual powers of its members taken collectively, [it] would be no more than natural and fallible, and therefore could afford no basis of divine certainty for faith'.[58]

Newman, indirectly, had sown seeds of doubt in Manning's mind. Applying the Anglican rule of faith, he had reached conclusions Manning could not accept; it seemed obvious to him that the rule, as it stood, was not self-sufficient. The following years marked a time of perplexity. The clear signposts were no longer there; questions and answers were both too vague even to be formulated. It was also a time of silence, in which he started to feel the pull of Rome. The office of sub-almoner

[54] Ibid., c. 656, fo. 107, Manning to R. Wilberforce, letter dated 22 Jan. 1851.

[55] *CSer* i. 5.

[56] Cf. Manning to Laprimaudaye, letter dated June 1847, quoted in *P* i. 470; see also *CSer* i. 5.

[57] Erb has studied this question, pointing out how this conception does not lay the ground for the 'sterile scholastic rationalism which simplistically set down "truths" to be accepted in humble obediential piety and which Manning is sometimes later in his life accused of supporting' (*Question of Sovereignty*, 10). See also the letter to R. Wilberforce of 30 Dec. 1845 quoted above.

[58] *CSer* i. 5–6.

to the Archbishop of York, vacated by Samuel Wilberforce, was offered to him. He declined it. To the anxious enquiry of Robert Wilberforce he answered that the refusal meant 'no *unsettlement*, I thank God, which makes me wish to avoid new bonds'.[59] He felt this course of action to be the safest one for his soul, helping him to have a clearer perception of truth. He feared, as he confessed later to Robert, 'lest the sphere of attraction should bias me in weighing the great doubts which had then fully opened themselves to me'.[60]

Manning, his protestations notwithstanding, was certainly unsettled, and this spiritual and intellectual unsettlement grew more intense throughout 1846. 'I am conscious to myself', he recorded in his diary in May, 'of an extensively changed feeling towards the Church of Rome.' She seemed to him nearer to the truth than the Church of England. 'There seems about the Church of England a want of antiquity, system, fullness, intelligibleness, order, strength, unity; we have dogmas on paper; a ritual almost universally abandoned; no discipline, a divided episcopate, priesthood, and laity.' And in August, he added: 'wherever it [the Church of England] seems healthy it approximates the system of Rome, e.g. Roman Catholic Catechism, Confession, Guidance, Discipline'.[61] His ties with the Church of England were loosening: 'Tho'' not therefore Roman, I cease to be Anglican,' he wrote on 15 May. He went further as the months wore on: 'I believe the Bishop of Rome to be Primate and by devolution Chief,' he recorded in his diary on 5 July. And about a month later: 'Now I see that St Peter has a Primacy among the Apostles. That the Church of Rome inherits what St Peter had among the Apostles. That the Church of Rome is therefore heir of Infallibility.'[62] These, at the time, were not firm convictions. He hesitated, and he still felt that the Church of England was part of the universal Church, distinct from all Protestant bodies. Manning seems to have asked Keble for assistance in his perplexities about the rule of faith. He received a disappointing answer. Keble could

---

[59] Manning MSS Bod., c. 655, fo. 32, letter dated 30 Dec. 1845.
[60] Ibid., fo. 62, letter dated Second Sunday after Christmas 1848.
[61] *P* i. 484.   [62] Quoted in Leslie, *Henry Edward Manning*, 77–8.

only reiterate what Newman had said in his *Lectures on the Prophetical Office.*[63]

3. *Is Conversion to Rome Morally Defensible?*

Was Manning considering conversion to Rome? The subject of conversion, understood as abandoning a particular Confession or Church to give one's allegiance to another, had been considered by him before at a theoretical level. According to the branch theory, the means of salvation—doctrine and discipline, apostolic succession and valid sacraments—were available in each of the branches of the universal Church. From this perspective, conversion from one branch to another made little or no sense; even more, in most cases, it involved a denial of the reality of the Church of one's baptism, an act of schism. Manning's strategy to keep in the Anglican fold those who were 'on the verge of Popery' was outlined in some of his letters, when dealing with particular cases. As he wrote to Pusey in 1839, he would first describe, from a doctrinal point of view, the 'Roman errors'—infallibility of the Church, transubstantiation, the supremacy of the Pope, devotion to the Blessed Virgin Mary, etc.—making use of books like George Stanley Faber's *The Difficulties of Romanism* (1826) or William Palmer's *Treatise on the Church* (1838). However, these 'errors' did not touch the essentials of the Faith. Consequently, the main thrust of Manning's argument to remain in the Anglican Church was moral. Leaving for Rome involved the sin of schism; it also implied 'the deliberate and formal incurring of all the abuses of Romanism'. Moreover, it meant 'ingratitude to God who has ordained our second birth through the English Church; and given all things necessary for salvation'.[64] The safest path was to remain in the Church of England: 'A man sins heavily who leaves us, above all if he goes to Rome which is at variance with Catholic Tradition; is Schismatical in England, and idolatrous in its tendencies.'[65] Roman errors

---

[63] Cf. Manning MSS Bod., c. 654, fos. 138–9, Keble to Manning, letter dated 10 Sept. 1846.

[64] Pusey House, Oxford, Pusey Correspondence, Manning to Pusey, letter 2, dated 7 Dec. 1839.

[65] Ibid.

made him fear for the safety of those within the Roman
Church.[66]

Manning's approach to the question of conversion changed
slightly as years went by. In 1846, writing to Dodsworth, his
main suggestion was to impress on the mind of the waverer
that the bonds established by baptism to a particular Church
could not be undone lightly: 'No preference for the Roman or
any other Church on the grounds of its order, definiteness, doctrinal system and the like can cancel the filial duty springing
from our regeneration.'[67] As he saw it, the 'question of for-
saking or of abiding in the Church of England simply stands
thus: It is a sin to forsake it if it be not sin to abide in it. That
it is a sin to abide in it involves the assumption that it is either
no Church at all, or a Church in heresy, or in schism.'[68] In a
letter to Pusey of 1845 he had pointed out that it was not for
the individual to decide the above; that would be an unacceptable exercise of private judgement, a transit from faith to
reason. It was a question between branches of the Church. He
wrote:

I know of only two suppositions on which a person can be justified in
leaving the Church of England while it continues on its present
basis:

1 A judgment of the whole Church justly and truly taken condemning our position, a thing next to impossible, and therefore
   confirming our case provisionally and ad interim, or

2 A belief of an individual mind that it cannot stay in it without
   mortal sin. Which latter case precludes all arguments or
   persuasion.[69]

Manning's words encapsulated the dilemma of many who,
like him, after having journeyed along the road towards more

---

[66] In 1842 he had not wanted 'to go into the question of the comparative openness
of the way to life in the two Churches, of the means of knowledge and grace, and
the fostering and disposing causes which tend towards salvation' (*Unity*, 365). However, in 1844, writing to Oakeley, he expressed his misgivings and fears for the reality,
life, and safety of the Roman Church (cf. Manning MSS Bod., c. 654, fo. 70, letter
dated Third Sunday in Advent 1844).

[67] Manning MSS Bod., c. 658, fo. 60, letter dated 29 Aug. 1846.

[68] Ibid., fo. 59.

[69] Pusey House, Oxford, Pusey Correspondence, Manning to Pusey, letter 20,
dated 25 July 1845.

Catholic principles, felt attracted by Rome. Intellectually, and sometimes emotionally, they might incline towards the Catholic Church, but they were pulled back from the brink by the fear of suffering from a delusion. In that state they remained, at times for many years, before taking the final step. Manning felt that intellectual convictions were not entirely trustworthy, and by themselves were not enough to warrant a move: they were '*logical,* and eminently liable to mislead from their very clearness: the error being in the subject matter: in the premises, not in the reasoning'.[70] Distrust for their conclusions and fear of private judgement were usually accompanied by the painful awareness of one's own moral limitations: others, more learned and better, had abided unperturbed in the Anglican Church. All this told against haste in coming to a final decision. The issue had tremendous consequences for both time and eternity! Such people looked for guidance, and waited for the voice of God to make itself clearly heard, as in Samuel's case, by means of three divine calls, a common practice among those on the brink of Rome.[71]

Manning's conduct in those years exemplifies the working of the rule that he had prescribed for others: namely, that it would be a sin to leave the Church of England if it were no sin to remain in it. At the beginning of 1848, when writing to Robert Wilberforce of the consolidation of his conviction about the unreality of the Church of England, and of his changed disposition towards the Church of Rome, he added: 'Still I can say I have never felt the fear of safety, or pressure of conscience, which alone justifies a change.'[72] And some time later, less than a year before his actual conversion, he could write: 'I have not yet heard Him in my conscience saying, "Flee for thy life". Till then, I will die rather than run the risk of crossing His will. I fear haste, and I fear to offend God, but I fear nothing else; and in that faith by His grace I will wait upon Him, humbling and chastening my own soul.'[73]

---

[70] Manning MSS Bod., c. 655, fo. 137, letter to Mary Wilberforce, dated 2 Dec. 1849.

[71] Cf. Newsome, *Parting of Friends*, 329 and 366.

[72] Manning MSS Bod., c. 655, fo. 62, letter dated 2nd Sunday after Christmas.

[73] Quoted in *P* i. 474, letter to unknown correspondent, dated 6 May 1850.

Manning—with Keble, Pusey, and Newman[74]—felt that the safest course was to remain in the Church of one's baptism for as long as was morally defensible. Their commonly held opinion was based on the fact that conversion, particularly to Rome, involved a rejection of the presence of the means of salvation in the Church *a quo*, and a judgement on the ecclesiastical character of that communion. It was a morally dangerous step, involving an unjustifiable exercise of private judgement. Keble even maintained that English Roman Catholics should remain in their Church. He did not rule out conversion entirely, however. It would be justified, in certain circumstances, to move from one branch of the Church to another, and, in the case of a move from Rome to Canterbury, the 'migration' involved a lesser moral danger, given that the rejection of that Church in becoming an Anglican would not be as absolute as if the move were the other way round.[75]

Manning, in *The Unity of the Church* (1842), had put forward his vision for Church reunion: visible and external unity was to be achieved by corporate reunion of the branches of the Church. The best way of achieving this would be by means of a truly ecumenical Council, in which the three branches of the Church would be properly represented. While waiting for such a Council to resolve the differences between Orthodox, Anglican, and Roman, we 'go on', Keble wrote, 'appealing to it, and in the meantime submitting our judgment to that portion of the apparent visible Church, wherewith, by God's appointment, we are in communion'.[76] The imperatives of the individual conscience would soon make clear to Manning that personal convictions could not be sacrificed on the altar of corporate reunion.

---

[74] On 4 May 1844, Newman, by now 'personally' convinced that the Church of Rome was the true Church, could still write in his diary: '1. There is more responsibility in changing to a new communion than remaining where you are placed. 2. One ought to have some clear proof to outweigh the misery it would occasion to others. 3. One ought not go by private judgment but with others (quoted by M. Peterburs, 'Newman and Development', in V. A. McClelland (ed.), *By Whose Authority? Newman, Manning and the Magisterium* (Bath, 1996), 69).

[75] Cf. Keble, *Sermons*, pp. xxxi and lxix, particularly note *m* on the last page mentioned.

[76] Ibid., p. xlii.

B. A Time for Change: A Book on Infallibility

The year 1847 marked a turning-point for Manning. In February he discovered the first symptoms of the illness, suspected to be consumption, which would keep him at death's door for three months. Overwork, and his prolonged spiritual and intellectual crisis, were no doubt at the root of this breakdown of health. The enforced inactivity offered him the possibility of quiet study and reflection, and it was during those months of illness and convalescence that he found the key to unlock the answers to his many questions. He described it years afterwards, a Catholic by then:

During the long illness I read S. Leo through—and much of S. Gregory, S. Aug. and S. Optatus. All brought me in great doubt as to the tenableness of 'moral unity'. It showed me the nature of the Primacy of S. Peter. And at the same time I wrote the IVth Vol. of Sermons which was published the year after ... In that volume for the first time I began to find and to express the truth which afterwards brought me to the Church: and has filled my mind with increasing light to this day: I mean the Personal coming, abiding and office of the Holy Ghost ...

I had seen human certainty rising up to the summit of intellectual discernment and the *communis sensus* of mankind, but here it could rise no higher. The coming of the Holy Ghost from above to rest upon the intellect of the Church and to elevate it to a supernatural consciousness of faith was the first sight I got of the Infallibility of the Church. It was suggested to me by Melchior Canus' '*Loci Theol.*'.[77]

Manning was reading Cano's treatise as early as the end of 1845, but it was not till 1847 that it suggested to him the answer to his uncertainties: 'I remember how the words of Melchior Canus used to return upon me "consensus sanctorum omnium sensus Spiritus Sancti est" (De Locis Theol., lib viii [vii], c. 3). And I saw that the "consent of the Fathers" was

---

[77] Quoted by Chapeau, 'Manning the Anglican', 23. *De Locis Theologicis*, published in 1563, had soon become a classical treatise about the theological method. In *De Locis*, Cano tried to establish the study of theology on a more rigorous foundation than hitherto through a detailed study of the sources (Scripture, Tradition, etc.) of the theological arguments and their respective authority.

an inadequate and human conception of a higher and divine fact, namely, of the unity of illumination that flows from the Presence of the Holy Ghost in the Universal Church and inundates it with the perpetual light of the day of Pentecost.' That truth came upon him 'gradually, slowly, and at first dubiously'. Soon it was to become a firm conviction: 'that the Holy Ghost perpetually and infallibly guides the Church, and speaks by its voice'.[78] The words of the *Appendix* to his sermon *The Rule of Faith* then acquired a new significance for him: 'the universal tradition of all ages is no less than the voice of God'.[79]

The discovery may have taken place towards the end of his illness. The entry in his diary for 20 April 1847 described the questions then in his mind as follows: '1. Is it the will of our Lord Jesus Christ that His flock should be subject to Saint Peter and his successors? 2. Is it part of the mystery of Pentecost that the Church should be infallible?'[80] The answers were not yet fully formed in his mind; there were some intellectual difficulties to be ironed out, but he was on the road to solving them.

In later years he was not slow to acknowledge his debt to Cano. Just before his conversion, in a letter to his barrister-friend James Hope-Scott, he made a reference to it: 'The subject which has brought me to my present convictions is the perpetual office of the Church, under Divine guidance, in expounding the truth and deciding controversies. And the book which forced this on me was Melchior Canus' "Loci Theologici".'[81] Manning had previously rejected the idea of a living judge, as he felt that doctrine would change as the judge was replaced by a new one. Now he had seen that the living voice speaking in the Church, the judge in matters of doctrine, was not a perishable man but someone unchange-

---

[78] *CSer* i. 6–7.

[79] *Appendix*, 133; in 1850 he would tell Miss Mary Stanley, sister of Dean Stanley of Westminster, that sermons V and IX of his fourth volume of sermons were 'an expansion and continuation of the last paragraph of the book' (Manning MSS Bod., c. 660, fo. 11).

[80] *P* i. 487.

[81] Letter dated 11 Dec. 1850, in R. Ornsby, *Memoirs of James Hope-Scott* (2 vols., London, 1884), ii. 83; also letter to Robert Wilberforce, 22 Jan. 1851, Manning MSS Bod., c. 656, fo. 108.

able, permanent, and divine: the Holy Spirit, perpetually present in the Church.

On 11 May he was able to go out of doors for the first time for months, into the fresh air and the sun. His intellectual vision was already acquiring consistency, and soon his discovery found its way into his correspondence: 'What you say', he wrote to Robert Wilberforce on 9 June 1847, 'is my feeling, that the Presence, and Office of the Holy Spirit in the Church is the true foundation of certainty and perpetuity in doctrine. And that this is an object of *Faith*. Everything below this seems to me to be in principle purely rationalistic, whether the judge of Doctrine and Tradition be an individual or a Synod.'[82]

He also wrote to Laprimaudaye in similar, though more explicit, terms. He had found the answers to the questions he had asked himself, but they were not yet firm enough to rest on them:

First.—Is not the infallibility of the Church a necessary consequence of the Presence of the third Person of the Blessed Trinity; and of His perpetual office, beginning from the Day of Pentecost? This seems to me revealed in Scripture.

A perpetual presence, perpetual office, and perpetual *infall-ibility*—that is, a living voice witnessing for truth and against error under the guidance of the Spirit of Christ—seem inseparable.

Secondly.—Is it not a part of the revealed will and ordinance of our Lord Jesus Christ, that the Church should be under an episcopate united with a visible head, as the apostles were united with St Peter?[83]

Manning was not thinking of the primacy of the Roman Pontiff, as understood by Roman theologians: 'It is not the question of primacy with me so much as *unity of the episcopate*. *"Episcopatus unus est"*', he would say quoting St Cyprian's *De Unitate*. 'I take St Peter to have been the first of apostles, as the Primate of Christendom is the first of bishops; in spiritual order or power all being equal.'[84] It was as yet a theory of his own, and he mistrusted his conclusions. 'In this state of self-

---

[82] Manning MSS Bod., c. 655, fo. 55.
[83] Letter dated 16 June 1847, quoted in *P* i. 471.
[84] Ibid.

mistrust and fear of going wrong, I went abroad.'[85] He did not want to proceed alone. His intention was to consult and test his thoughts with Robert Wilberforce and Dr W. H. Mill, Regius Professor of Hebrew at Cambridge.

The ensuing months marked a rapid progress in the development and consolidation of Manning's ideas. 'Things seem to me clearer,' he wrote to Robert Wilberforce in January 1848, 'plainer, shapelier and more harmonious; things which were only in the head have got down into the heart; hiatuses and gaps have bridged themselves over by obvious second thoughts, and I feel a sort of *processus* and expansion going on which consolidates all old convictions and keeps throwing out the premises of new ones.'[86] Internal development and external events contributed to hammering Manning's ideas into more definite form. 'There are truths so primary and despotic that I cannot elude them', he wrote on 5 February 1848:

Such is the Infallibility of the Mystical Body of Christ on earth, through the Indwelling of the Holy Spirit. I could as soon disbelieve the Canon of Scripture, or the perpetuity of the Church. Infallibility is not an accident, it is a property as inseparable by the Divine Will as perpetuity. This is evident to me from Holy Scripture, from Catholic Tradition, from internal and necessary relations of Divine Truth and Divine acts, as well as from reasons which alone would prove nothing.[87]

It was a process that did not only affect Manning's idea of the rule of faith. It also implied a new vision of the Church. The difference between his fourth volume of sermons and the previous ones is illuminating in this respect: it shows a new reading of Holy Scripture and the Fathers, mainly St Augustine, in the light revealed to him by Cano's work.

In his recollections, quoted above, Manning said that he had written the fourth volume of sermons in 1847. His memory failed him, however, when he added that it had been published the following year: it actually appeared in 1850. It seems likely, though, that he was right about their composition. In his letters to Robert Wilberforce and T. W. Allies he repeated

[85] 'Autobiographical Note', quoted by Chapeau, 'Manning the Anglican', 23.

[86] Manning MSS Bod., c. 655, fo. 62.

[87] Ibid., fo. 63.

that the sermon 'The Analogy of Nature' was written in 1847;
the latter showed his surprise when reading it: 'Surely no. 9
was not written three years ago.'[88]

The volume of sermons was intended, Manning confessed to
Mary Wilberforce, as a manifesto of his beliefs on the Church
and infallibility: 'I read you that Sermon because I intended
to put it out as a statement of my belief. And my purpose is,
by the will of God, to publish as full a book on the subject of infallibility as I have a light to make. And by that book to take
my path.'[89]

At first glance, though, the fourth volume of sermons reads
more like a study of the nature of the Church, and of the role
of the sacraments in its life and in the life of the individual
Christian, than a treatise on infallibility. This is understand-
able, because Manning was aiming to present the topic of infallibility within its proper setting: that is, in the work of
redemption and the nature and mission of the Church. He
also dealt at length with the nature of the virtue of faith, a
topic intimately connected with infallibility.

It has been said that no Tractarian—with the exception of
Robert Wilberforce—'ever worked out a systematic and thor-
ough ecclesiology, not to speak of an entire theological
system'.[90] It could be argued, however, that Manning's fourth
volume of sermons is the expression, in a form that tends to disguise the systematic aspect of his thought, of a fairly complete
conception of the Church as the Mystical Body of Christ. Manning's attachment to the literary genre of the sermon as a
means to convey ideas continued well into his Catholic period.
In 1865, in his introduction to *The Temporal Mission of the Holy
Ghost*, he mentioned how he had tried to publish a volume of
sermons on reason and revelation; but, he added, 'when I
began to write I found it impossible to throw the matter into
the form of sermons. ... I was therefore compelled to write
this volume in the form of a short treatise.'[91]

The fourth volume of sermons also signalled the resolution of
the old dichotomy in Manning's mind between *objective truth*

---

[88] Ibid., c. 657, fo. 197, letter dated 29 Jan. 1850.
[89] Ibid., c. 655, fo. 136, letter dated 2 Dec. 1849.
[90] Härdelin, *Tractarian Understanding*, 84.
[91] *TM* 1–2.

and *subjective religion*. The Council of Trent had helped him to find the answer. He could now see how they became one: the nature of God, and of the Church, defined the laws of the spiritual life of the Christian. 'God and man', he wrote to Miss Maurice, 'are one by Incarnation; we are reunited with God through the Word made Flesh; we are joined to the Word made Flesh by Regeneration; and the support of this union is the Real presence.'[92] Archdeacon Hare had captured the new drift in Manning's thought when he told Miss Maurice that these sermons 'were more Roman and more Evangelical than the other three volumes'.[93]

1. *The Church as the Mystical Body of Christ*

The sermons unfolded Manning's conception of the Church as the Mystical Body of Christ within the general context of God's plan for man. The whole economy of creation and of grace, he said, is the manifestation of God's love for man, and the greatest sign of that love is his desire that men may be called, and actually be, sons of God. This is not a static condition, but one in which man was to grow by developing and bringing into further perfection the original likeness that had been granted to him.

Original sin frustrated God's plan for man. Humanity's subsequent fallen condition made necessary a work of restoration, amounting to a true new creation. In God's providence, Christ, the Creator of all things, was now to be also the principle of their restoration. 'The mystery of the incarnation [therefore] is not a mere isolated fact,' Manning said, 'terminating in the personality of the Word made Flesh, but the beginning and productive cause of a new creation of mankind.'[94]

Christ is the Son, the perfect image of God the Father, and he will be the one to restore the image of God in man, and return to him his lost sonship. The Incarnation 'is the restoration of our manhood to God in the Person of Jesus Christ'. In the mystery of the Incarnation is contained and effected 'the mystery of our renewal, in body, soul, and spirit, to the image

[92] Manning MSS Bod., c. 659, fo. 161, letter dated 30 Aug. 1850.
[93] Ibid.
[94] *ASer* iv. 92; see also 180.

of God'.[95] By sharing in our humanity, he has redeemed man's nature. This is the foundation on which the new humanity is built: the 'mystery of the Incarnation is, indeed, a humanising of God, as it is also a deifying of man; for in Him the Godhead and the manhood are alike perfect and indivisible'.[96]

Manning described the nature of this deifying procedure even further when he said that it 'does not mean that we are made partakers of the incommunicable Godhead, but that we are made partakers of the manhood of the incarnate Word'. In so doing, he added, our nature is made divine. 'We partake of Him: of His very flesh, of His mind, of His will, and of His spirit.'[97] Christ's human nature was divinized—without losing any of its human characteristics—by his contact with the divine nature in the one Person; similarly, we are divinized by entering into contact with the divinity through our union with Christ's human nature. The 'Word, who is by eternal genera-tion of one substance with the Father, by the mystery of the In-carnation became of one substance with us'.[98] Then, as the Son lives by the Father, 'so we, distinct in person, but par-taking of His substance, live by the Son'.[99]

The union in Christ of the divine and human natures is not something accidental; it is, rather, a 'substantial' union. Manning conceived man's union with Christ to be of a similar character: 'our union with the Word made flesh', he would say, 'is not figurative or metaphorical, by affinity and relation of will, or love only, but in substance, spirit, and reality. ... How can there be any living union which is not real? or [a] real union which is not substantial? ... Branches do not derive their life by a figurative engrafting, neither is the union of the trunk and the root a metaphor. The Incarnation is a real and substantial partaking of our manhood; and our union with Christ is a real, substantial partaking of His.'[100]

---

[95] Ibid. 181.   [96] Ibid. 52.   [97] Ibid. 203.

[98] Ibid. 184. Manning used the terms 'substance' and 'nature' indistinctly. This may be a source of confusion at times, although the actual meaning of the terms is clarified by the context in which they are found. His insistence on using the expression 'of one substance' may be due to the fact that this is the Prayer Book's rendering of the credal word *consubstantialem*, or *homoöusion*.

[99] Ibid. 186.   [100] Ibid. 187; see also *TM* 63.

This sharing in Christ's manhood was not possible for man while he was still on earth. His presence then was local, and men's relation to it external. St Paul showed Manning the first step in understanding the process through which man was to become united with Christ. In the Epistle to the Ephesians he had written: 'He that descended is the same also that ascended up far above all heavens, that he might fill all things' (Eph. 4:10). Manning considered Jesus' departure from this earth as the necessary prelude to His return in a new mode of presence; by it, 'His local presence was changed into an universal presence.'[101] He is now present on earth in his mystical body. Through it he reaches the whole world and is able to embrace all men. The words of Hebrews 10:5 (quoting Ps. 40:6), 'You wanted no sacrifice or cereal offering, but you gave me a body', are taken by Manning as referring not only to the physical body of Christ but also to the mystical one; the Father granted Jesus a body—physical and mystical—in which and through which he carries out the work of redemption.

The living principle of the mystical body is the Holy Spirit. His coming, as announced by Christ, was dependent on Jesus' departure to the Father. From there he would send his Spirit. 'If He had tarried with us, He had abode alone; the Comforter had not come; His mystical body had not been knit together; His truth and spirit had not dwelt in us.' He went to the Father, though, and the Holy Spirit descended on the Church. Christ's presence and action, as far as man was concerned, had been beforehand 'local, exterior, and imperfect'; after the coming of the Holy Spirit, they became 'universal, inward, and divine'.[102] The Holy Spirit, who was the agent of the union of the divine and the human nature in Christ, was the agent of man's union with Christ. Christ partook of our nature 'by the operation of the Holy Ghost, and we of His by the power of the same Spirit. The miraculous Agent in the Incarnation and in the holy Sacraments is the same third Person.'[103]

Man joins Christ, being incorporated into his mystical body through baptism, the sacrament of man's regeneration by

---

[101] *ASer* iv. 89.   [102] Ibid. 103.   [103] Ibid. 187.

water and the Holy Spirit. This new birth is a free gift from
God. Man can only be the recipient of it, and in no way the
agent: 'the dust of the ground [was not] more passive when
the first man was made in God's likeness, than we, when,
through baptism, we were born again as sons of God'.[104]
Christ through his holy sacraments began a new line of spiritual generation. His Mystical Body is 'the whole fellowship of
all who are united to Him by the Spirit'.[105] Baptism,
however, like our natural birth, is only the beginning of life:
'The work of our renewal, indeed, is not perfected in regeneration [baptism], but only begun.'[106]

The mystical and the physical body of Christ are not independent, unconnected realities in Manning's thought. 'The
glorious Body of the Word made flesh is the centre of His mystical body, and to it He joins us one by one.'[107] Manning considered the parable of the vine and the branches an almost
perfect image of the mystical body. In it, he said, 'we see the
perfect outline of the Incarnation, or Christ mystical in all fullness: the root, the stem, the branches ... It describes by antici-
pation the life, growth, and fruitage of the Church, and
reveals also the source and channels through which the quickening life passes into all its structure and farthest sprays.'[108]
The sacraments are those channels through which the grace of
Christ's sacrifice flows to us, one by one.[109]

Manning affirmed that the natural body of Christ is, as it
were, 'the root out of which, by the power of the Holy Ghost,
His mystical body is produced' and kept alive. Men 'were engrafted into the stock of the Word made flesh. ... Then began
the growth and expansion of the mystical vine.'[110]

2. The Unity of Life of the Mystical Body of Christ

Christ and Christians become a unity of life; the many
members become one body and share in one life. The Church
is 'the production and overflow of His life and substance—the
fruit and fulfilment of His incarnation,—the complement and
perfection of His mystical body. What is the Church but

---

[104] Ibid. 27.   [105] Ibid. 201.   [106] Ibid. 182.
[107] Ibid. 275.   [108] Ibid. 190.   [109] Cf. ibid. 220.
[110] Ibid. 198–9.

Christ's invisible presence openly manifested by a visible organisation? The Church is Christ mystical,—the presence of
Christ, by the creative power of His incarnation, produced
and prolonged on earth.'[111]

St Paul had written that Christ is the 'head over all things to
the church, which is his body, the fullness of him that filleth
all in all' (Eph. 1 : 22–3). Manning understood his words as implying that the prerogatives of the head had now become the
prerogatives of the body: 'When He ascended up on high, the
virtues of His glorified manhood were shed abroad upon His
Church.'[112] Therefore, he added, 'the Church is one, because
He is one; holy, because He is holy; catholic, because His presence is local no more; apostolic, because He still sends His
own servants; indefectible, because He is the Life; unerring,
because He is the Truth'.[113]

A community of life is thus established between Christ and
Christians, whereby the whole Mystical Body, and each individual within it, share Christ's life. 'As His Godhead and
manhood are united in one divine person, so we and the Lord
of the resurrection are united in one mystical body. A living
head must needs have living members; and a Head that is
risen must raise His members in due season.'[114] Our Lord's
words 'I am the Resurrection and the Life' did not only mean
' "I will quicken and raise mankind from the dead", but "I
am the Resurrection, and all rise in Me: I *am* 'the Life', and
all live in Me" '.[115] Christ is the Mystical Body's own inward
principle of life and growth.

If the natural body of Jesus is the stock on to which the
Christian is engrafted, his sacramental body is the means by
which Christ's life is communicated to all members of the Mystical Body, and sustains them. It is by his presence in every
part of the Mystical Body that he keeps all and each alive: 'as
the life and substance of the first creation are sustained and
perpetuated until now, so in the second, which is the mystical
Vine, He is root and trunk, branch and fruit; wholly in us,
and we in Him'.[116] Manning uses an analogy to expand on
the character of that presence by saying:

---

[111] *ASer* iv. 93.   [112] Ibid. 181–2.   [113] Ibid. 103.
[114] Ibid. 345.   [115] Ibid. 287.   [116] Ibid. 198.

the humanity of the second Adam is the immediate and substantial instrument of our regeneration and renewal. It has, therefore, a supernatural presence throughout the whole mystical body of Christ. As the substance of the first man is the productive cause of the whole human race, so the Manhood of the second, in its reality and presence, is extended throughout the Church. It is the presence of God which upholds all the creation of nature: it is the presence of the incarnate Word which upholds all the creation of grace.[117]

Manning apparently did not wish to develop further this theme which was dear to Tractarian thought. Robert Wilberforce, only two years earlier, had described this concept in great detail in his book on the Incarnation, and Manning did not probably feel it necessary to reiterate the argument. It may be useful, though, to describe here, briefly, Robert Wilberforce's line of argument, so as to clarify the background to Manning's thought. The first Adam, Wilberforce had written, is not only the originating generative principle of human life, but also the original in which all his descendants are generated. The unity of form is a consequence of the law of descent from a single parent. This guarantees a perpetual succession of beings, in each one of whom the original type reappears. Analogically, Christ is the originating principle and the original of the new creation of the sons of God. 'The necessity then of Christ's Presence according to His humanity, rests upon His being that Pattern Man, in whom renewed manhood shone forth in its brightest colours, by reason of those supernatural endowments with which it was invested. So that it is essential that we should be as truly united to Him by grace, as we were to the first Adam by nature.'[118]

Manning pulls together the threads of his thought by saying: 'In one sense the Church is called the body of Christ, by metaphor and analogy to the members and unity of a natural body: in another sense mystically, because of its true and vital union with Him.' The image of the vine has a similar representative value. It describes 'the intense inwardness and spirituality of the body of Christ, [it] expresses equally its visible unity and organisation. It is as visible, sensible, and local as was the

---

[117] Ibid. 92–3.
[118] R. Wilberforce, *The Doctrine of the Incarnation of our Lord Jesus Christ, in its Relation to Mankind and to the Church* (London, 1848), 308.

natural body of Christ Himself. In all the world it is visibly manifest as the presence of its unseen Head. It speaks, witnesses, acts, binds, and looses in His name, and as Himself.'[119] The unity of life and 'personality' of the Mystical Body imply therefore a unity of action, the highest manifestation of which is to be found in the sacrifice of Christ in the Eucharist, the first foundation of the Church. In the Eucharist Manning discovered the Church's 'perfect unity of life and act with Christ its Head'. Christ's priesthood, like his other prerogatives, descends from the Head to the body. As a result, in the sacrifice of the Eucharist, 'He offers the body in Himself, and the body, in and for itself, offers Him unto the Father'.[120]

After speaking of the physical, mystical, and sacramental bodies of Christ, Manning makes clear that there are not three different bodies of Christ, but only one, 'one in nature, truth, and glory. But there are three manners, three miracles of divine omnipotence, by which that one body has been and is present; the first, as mortal and natural; the second, supernatural, real, and substantial; the third, mystical by our incorporation. The presence is one, the manner threefold; the substance one in all three: all three one in Him.'[121]

Love is the bond which holds together the Mystical Body of Christ. And this unity of love is a divine gift: the oneness and expansion of God's love, flowing down from heaven and spreading in the Church, is 'the cause and the law of unity and communion to the visible Church'. That love 'had its beginning upon earth in Him who is Love incarnate; from Him it spread and embraced His disciples, binding them into one visible fellowship'.[122] The resulting unity has a mystical and testimonial significance. The 'unity of love is a type of the unity of nature',[123] Manning would say somewhat cryptically, implying that, although the members of the Mystical Body cannot achieve the unity of the three Divine Persons in the oneness of God's nature, they reflect it in the unity of love and its corollaries. Christ's visible body, physical as well as mystical, 'is the earthly clothing, the mystical impersonation of the love of God'.[124] His Mystical Body is a revelation of the

---

[119] *ASer* iv. 201. [120] Ibid. 223–4. [121] Ibid. 202.
[122] Ibid. 296. [123] Ibid. 290. [124] Ibid.

love which unites the Divine Persons, and it also reveals the love of God for man. After the Ascension, the 'Love of the Father and of the Son was thenceforward manifest, not in a natural, but in a mystical body, which, from age to age, perfects itself by the inward working of its own principle of life'.[125]

Manning, from the publication of his fourth volume of sermons, affirmed unequivocally that the communion of charity is an essential element of the unity of the Church. This meant a departure from his previous position. He had until then maintained that 'the unity of the Church is organic and moral—that the organic unity consists in succession, hierarchy, and valid sacraments, and the moral in the communion of charity among all the members of particular Churches, and all the Churches of the Catholic unity'. He had also affirmed 'that moral unity might be permanently suspended, and even lost, while the organic unity remained intact, and that unity of communion belongs only to the perfection, not to the intrinsic essence of the Church'.[126] In his third volume of Anglican sermons he had still spoken of the theory of the three branches, though separate, making up the one Church. By the time he wrote the fourth volume, he had come to realize that the unity of charity and communion is an integral element of the unity of the Church; that visible unity, following from the law of charity, is an essential characteristic of the visible Church.

The Church is

therefore, by its very nature and law, one and indivisible, ever enlarging, all-embracing; gathering in all nations, fusing all races, harmonising all tongues, blending all thoughts, uniting all spirits: making the earth once more of 'one lip', of one speech, of one heart, and of one will. ... 'There is one body and one spirit, even as ye are called in one hope of your calling: one Lord, one faith, one baptism' (Eph. 4: 4–5), one altar, one holy sacrifice, one divine tradition of corporate identity and living consciousness, sustaining the illumination of truth, seen by love alone, and itself sustained by the Holy Ghost.[127]

Schism is a most grievous sin, but it does not rend the unity of the Church: 'it is a sin against the indivisible love of God. To

---

[125] Ibid. 296.   [126] *TM* 28.   [127] *ASer* iv. 297.

separate from the Church is to forfeit love; for love cannot be divided. Schisms do not rend it, but are rent from it. As the life retires into the living trunk when branches are cut away, so love still dwells undivided in the life of the Church when members fall from its communion.'[128]

Manning was conscious of this change in his way of thinking, and he later offered an explicit retraction of the ideas he had previously expounded in his book *The Unity of the Church* (1842). In *The Temporal Mission of the Holy Ghost* (1865) he pointed out the three errors into which he 'unconsciously fell' in his Anglican books and sermons. He confessed that he had

not understood from whence the principle of unity is derived. It had seemed to be a constitutional law, springing from external organisa- tion, highly beneficial, but not a vital necessity to the Church. ... I had not as yet perceived that the unity of the Church is the external expression of the intrinsic and necessary law of its existence; that it flows from the unity of its Head, of its Life, of its mind, and of its will; or, in other words, from the unity of the Person of the Incar- nate Son, who reigns in it, and of the Holy Ghost, who organises it by His inhabitation, sustains it by His presence, and speaks through it by His voice.[129]

3. The Infallibility of the Mystical Body of Christ

Manning then described how Christ, beside his life-giving and sanctifying work, also continues his teaching action in and through the Church. The imperfect knowledge of the apostles was to become full illumination in the Church at Pentecost, by the working of the Holy Spirit. Since then, the same Holy Spirit has sustained and unfolded Christ's revelation. In Man- ning's own words:

When He departed, the Spirit of Truth took up all that He had re- vealed, and unfolded it with great accessions of divine illumination. He then opened a ministry of interior and perfect faith, which has guided His Church in all ages and in all lands unto this day. His own teaching [Christ's] was partial and local: the guidance of the Holy Spirit is plenary and universal. And our Teacher departs not, but abides with us for ever: a guide ever present, though invisible; ever presiding, though in silence; unerring, though teaching

[128]   *ASer* iv. 297-8.   [129]   *TM* 30; see also *CSer* i. 17-18.

through human reason and by human speech. The Spirit of Truth is Christ Himself by His Spirit guiding and teaching still.[130]

Manning saw here the fulfilment of Isaiah's prophecy: 'All your children shall be taught by Yahweh' (Is. 54:13). And the words of the prophet became a constant theme in his writings on the subject of the rule of faith.

Manning had been looking, from his early days as a pastor in Lavington, for the faith of the day of Pentecost. Now he had come to see that Pentecost did not end at sunset, leaving the historical sciences to find out what the Holy Spirit had taught the apostles on that day. Pentecost was not an event of the past, but a permanent reality in the Church. This is the central idea running through the fourth volume of sermons: 'The day of Pentecost is a perpetual miracle. It stands in its fullness even until now, and we are partakers of its presence and its power.'[131] The original 'inspiration of the Apostles became illumination in the Church. The illumination of the Holy Ghost is as perpetual as His presence. His office is, as His presence, "for ever"; that is, unto the end of the world.'[132]

The infallibility of the Church is the result of this perpetual illumination by the Holy Spirit. He described infallibility as being made up of two elements: 'perfect certainty in the object revealed, and spiritual illumination in the subject which perceives it, that is, the Church itself'. The infallibility of God who reveals is mirrored by the infallibility of the Church, which receives without distortion the content of the revelation. He summarized his thought on the matter as follows: 'What has been said amounts to this: that the doctrines of the faith, fully and clearly revealed by inspiration in the beginning, were fully and clearly apprehended by the Church.'[133] 'Shake this foundation', Manning would add, 'and faith becomes uncertainty.'[134]

The uninterrupted work of the Holy Spirit in the Church is absolutely necessary for the perpetual preservation of truth. The 'presence of an *infallible* Teacher is as necessary to the infirmities of human reason, as the presence of an omnipotent Comforter is necessary to the infirmities of the human will'.

---

[130] *ASer* iv. 97.   [131] Ibid. 103.   [132] Ibid. 169; see also 172.
[133] Ibid. 172.   [134] Ibid. 171.

Without such a presence, omnipotent and infallible, the will and reason of man 'would be in bondage to evil and to falsehood'.[135] The truth revealed by God would soon have been deformed and corrupted, had it been left to unaided human reason to understand, preserve, and transmit it. 'Is it possible to believe', Manning asked, 'that the supernatural illumination of the Spirit was so given as to rest upon no higher base than reason, discovery, criticism, and analogies of nature?'[136]

Some, arguing from the analogy of nature, could perhaps say that 'as certainty is found nowhere in nature, it is not to be demanded in revelation; that a measure of uncertainty, that is, of probability, is involved in the idea of moral trial, and that the facts of nature shew us on what laws revealed truth is to be sought and held; and that therefore the whole analogy of our condition is opposed to the supposition of an unerring witness preserving and propounding truth by Divine appointment in the Church'.[137] Manning, in his response to that objection, acknowledged the analogy of nature as an instrument at the service of God's revelation. Its role is to clear away 'supposed objections [preliminary objections to revelation and faith in general, or to particular doctrines of faith] by fact; it [also] raises a probability that revelation is, like nature, the work of God; and that the analogy we trace in part, may extend beyond our range of observation. Thus far it invests nature with a divine character, and makes it the basis of faith.'[138]

In a letter to Robert Lowe, Manning tried to express more plainly what he had said in the sermon: the analogy of nature is good and useful when applied to revelation consequently, '(1) to clear away objections against Revelation which would equally smite nature. (2) To raise a presumption—as the spring of the Resurrection. (3) To raise a *probability* that what we cannot see will be like what we can see, because as far as we can see there is a proportion.'[139] It would be a serious

---

[135] *ASer* iv. 172.   [136] Ibid. 170.   [137] Ibid. 162.

[138] Ibid. 157.

[139] Manning MSS Bod., c. 662, fo. 178, letter dated 3 Apr. 1850. R. Lowe became leader writer of *The Times* in 1850. Later on, after a long political career, he was appointed 1st Viscount Sherbrooke in 1880.

mistake, though, to use the analogy antecedently, to determine either the limit of the Faith as to its content, or to prescribe the manner and kind of the divine procedure to be followed by God in revealing himself.[140]

Revelation stands on its own proper evidence. 'We must receive it [revelation] in its own light and upon its own proper proofs.' Manning continued the argument by asking: 'What, then, is this proper evidence on which revelation, or, as we shall better say henceforth, the Church and the Faith, repose?' The answer was obvious: the faith rests 'upon no presumptions or probabilities deduced before the fact, that is, upon no *a priori* reasoning. We are not able to say before the fact whether any revelation shall be given or not; or, if given, to what extent, to what end, on what evidence, or how secured, and the like. In this, nature is silent as death. Analogies have no existence. All our proofs are after the event. The fact attests itself, and reveals its own outline, character, and conditions.'[141]

The proofs of revelation are not found in the analogy of nature, but 'in a series of supernatural facts, in original revelations, in spiritual consciousness, in the words of inspired Scripture, in apostolical traditions, in the testimony of the Church, in the definitions of Councils, in the collective discernment of men sanctified by the Spirit of God'.[142] These supernatural facts—which have no counterpart or analogy in nature—are the only ones which reveal the manner of God's dealings with man and the truths of faith. 'The supernatural inspiration of the Church is a perpetual illumination above the laws of nature. Its conditions, limits, and modes of operation are all its own.'[143] Were man's belief to be limited by his natural experience, he would never be able to rise to the experience of the supernatural. Moreover, Manning considered as enemies of the Faith those who applied wrongly the analogy of nature. 'They not only use the analogy of nature antecedently to the proper proof, so as to prescribe *a priori* the manner in which the Divine revelation has been put and left, but ultimately even against it. In fact, they are but the fine end of nat-

---

[140] Cf. *ASer* iv. 158.   [141] Ibid. 164.   [142] Ibid. 168.
[143] Ibid. 165.

uralism.'[144] When the analogy of nature is pressed beyond its proper range, then the analogies existing between the counter-parts 'soon run into a supposed identity, and the faith sinks into a mere natural religion'.[145]

What is natural cannot determine what and how the super-natural should be, Manning kept on repeating. If that were to be the case, it could, for example, be concluded that there are three Gods, because in nature each person is one man and several persons several human natures. The revelation is super-natural, and the supernatural has its own laws—different from and above those of nature—and it can be reached only by faith. Having settled that point, he added rhetorically: 'because among men the father is before the son, cannot the ever-lasting Son be co-eternal with the Father? ... Because human traditions grow corrupt, may not divine traditions be kept pure? ... Because natural truth is an uncertain light, may not the light of Christ be sustained by Himself infallible and clear?'[146]

4. *The Nature of the Act of Faith*

Manning had already established two factors in the formula of the certainty of faith: the certainty of the original revelation, based on God's infallibility, and the certainty of the faith in its preservation and transmission, guaranteed by the presence of the Holy Spirit in the Church. There was, however, another element in need of satisfactory explanation: how does the indi-vidual believer reach the certainty of faith? As far as Manning was concerned, any knowledge worthy of the name should be certain in the two senses of the word: the truth itself should be objectively certain, and, on the other hand, the one who knows should be certain about its being true.

What, then, is the faculty by which the certainty of revealed truth is to be apprehended by the individual?, Manning asked. The response was not long in coming: 'The whole word of God answers at once, By faith.'[147] Unfortunately, men seemed to have lost sight of the true nature of faith. He consid-ered that the controversies of the last centuries had led to two

---

[144] Cf. *ASer* iv. 162.   [145] Ibid. 159.   [146] Ibid. 166.
[147] Ibid. 168.

evils: they had dethroned the Church from its role as formal object of faith, and they had degraded faith itself as a virtue.[148] The different definitions of the nature of faith being proposed were unsatisfactory: 'Some will have it to be a speculative assent to truths revealed; and some, to correct them, will have it to be a principle of moral action; and others, to set both sides right, join together these two definitions in one, and tell us that faith is a principle of moral action springing from speculative assent to truths revealed.'[149]

According to Manning, these were only partial answers, separating what is and acts in unison. Moreover, they turned faith into 'an effect without a cause, or with a simply human cause, and within the natural endowments of the human intelligence'.[150] The latter was their more serious error: human reason can never be the foundation of the knowledge of faith nor the basis of certain knowledge about the supernatural, nor the origin of the act of believing. This is why he rejected the attempts of those who looked to the analogy of nature or to probabilities for the foundation and source of the act of faith. For them, as Manning saw it, the act of faith consisted in man's decision to believe what God has revealed; man would draw that conclusion after weighing the probabilities about a particular truth or system being of divine origin, ascertaining in what direction the scales moved. Those who thought along these lines accepted that human reason cannot reach the supernatural truths which are the object of faith, but, once they were revealed, the act of faith was a human act. Theirs was a 'certainty' based on probabilities.[151] Manning could not be satisfied by that type of certainty; neither could he accept that the act of faith was in substance a human act: as in the case of Peter at Caesarea Philippi, it was not given to man by flesh

---

[148] Cf. ibid. 376.   [149] Ibid. 376–7.   [150] Ibid. 377.

[151] A certain amount of confusion may be generated by the different concepts about what constitutes 'certainty', whether it be seen merely as a subjective quality of the assent or as a quality both of the assent and of the truth to which the assent is given. It seems that in Butler the term 'probability' is opposed to 'demonstration', rather than to 'certainty', and that he left the door open for a certainty based on probabilities (moral certainty). Manning's 'certainty', on the other hand, is a knowledge which excludes doubt, and which can never be reached as a conclusion based on probabilities; the probable character of the premises would not allow the conclusion to rise above the level of a probable truth.

and blood, but by the Father who is in heaven. Then, what is faith? And how is it generated in man?

Manning had spoken of action and consent springing from faith. Now he added, 'but what is that cause or power which is before both the assent and action of faith?' And he answered: 'What but faith itself?'[152] A faith which has no human cause, but is only in God's power to grant. In the sermons Manning stressed the quality of faith as an infused grace of God: 'Faith is a spiritual consciousness of the world unseen, infused into us, in our regeneration, by the supernatural gift of God.'[153] The Holy Spirit is the foundation of the certainty of revelation in itself, and also of the certainty with which man accepts God's revelation. He inspires this certainty in man with the gift of faith. 'Faith means trust in divine authority.' A trust which is 'an infused grace of God, by which the soul casts its whole confidence upon the authority of God. The infallibility of God is the foundation of that trust.'[154] It generates in the believer a certainty founded on revelation. The concept of revelation contains the idea of a *clear and infallible knowledge* of the truth given direct from God to man.

Probability, Manning would say, is the best 'that nature can give in most things, but the least truth in the kingdom of God is greater than it'.[155] Manning saw divine faith as consisting in an infusion of supernatural grace, illuminating the intelligence to know and inclining the heart to believe. There was no other path to certainty, as he explained, a few years later, to Robert Wilberforce, then on the brink of conversion to Rome:

I fancy that you are looking for what God does not give. I mean a conviction which precludes the exercise of faith. Except in figures and numbers there is no [human] conviction which excludes the possibility of the contrary being true. ... A deist in becoming a Christian has no more than a conviction which excludes *reasonable* fear that Christianity may turn out not to be true. Reason can go no further, and until upon the motives of credibility supplied by reason he makes an act of faith, he can raise no higher. ... As a student of Aristotle and Butler you know all this better than I.[156]

---

[152] *A Ser* iv. 377.   [153] Ibid.   [154] Ibid. 171.
[155] Ibid.
[156] Quoted in *P* ii. 36–7, letter dated 20 Jan. 1854.

From now onwards, he will insist on the idea of faith as a gift, with the same structure in the Christians on the day of Pentecost as in the rest of believers down the centuries: 'this divine gift, as it was, at the first, not discovered but received, so it has been, not critically proved, from age to age, by intellect, not gathered by inductions or by the instruments of moral reasoning, but preserved and handed on by faith'. The office of reason, then and now, is 'not to discover and attain, but to illustrate, demonstrate [!], and expound'.[157]

The knowledge of faith is a means, the most perfect one granted by God, for man to gain access to reality; it 'is that power of spiritual perception analogous to sense, that is, to sight, hearing, and feeling; and also to affection, that is, to love, fear, and desire. It is as wide as the whole soul of man, uniting it in one continuous act'.[158] Its object is a world of spiritual realities which cannot be apprehended except through it. Faith does not contradict or oppose the natural powers; its role is rather to complement and to perfect them. The experience of the senses gives man a perception of the visible world, and the intellect adds its interpretation; sense and intellect are not in opposition, they complement each other. Such is the case with faith: the intellect 'corrects and exalts sense; faith corrects and exalts both'.[159]

The gift of faith perfects man as a whole: it 'has been defined as the perfection of the will and of the intellect—of the will as it sanctifies, of the intellect as it illuminates, of both at once as it issues in its congenial fruits'.[160] Faith helps the proper acts of both potencies; it is an active principle: 'Acting towards God, it issues in trust, love, prayer, contemplation, worship; towards man, in charity, gentleness, self-denial; upon ourselves, in abasement, discipline, and penance.'[161]

Manning hastened to add that the supernatural gift of faith was infused into us, as a virtue, by the Spirit of God, 'but in its acting depends upon our will'.[162] Like all other gifts from God, it 'is subject to the will of man'. Consequently, it 'may be used or abused, matured or neglected, made perfect or perverted'.[163] Faith could be defined as 'a moral habit, having

[157] *ASer* iv. 172. [158] Ibid. 378. [159] Ibid. 379.
[160] Ibid. 380. [161] Ibid. [162] Ibid. 378.
[163] Ibid. 381.

its root in the will'.[164] Man's moral character has, therefore, a determining influence in the act of faith. The effort to purify one's conscience, the habitual exercise of prayer, frequent communion, etc., help faith to mature; sin and worldliness, on the other hand, deaden and blur that spiritual perception, in the same way as human defects and vices affect the exercise of the intellect and the will.

The home and resting-place of the truth of faith revealed by God is the Church of Christ. In the Church truth is 'one, perfect, absolute, and binding; admitting no diminution or addition, election or choice. It is all contained in the baptismal creed, as is all the law of sanctity in the ten commandments, not expressly, but by deep implication; and the authority on which we receive both is one,—the Church teaching in the name of Christ.'[165] The entirety of revealed truth, as proposed by the Church, is binding on those who belong to it; the very nature of faith excludes a partial reception of the truths proposed by the Church.

In one of the sermons, Manning considered the case of those who, because of not having the truth proposed to them, do not come to know it, and that of those who, because of some deeply ingrained prejudice, cannot recognize the truth of revelation when confronted with it. He affirms that 'no ignorance of truth is a personal sin before God, except that ignorance which springs from personal sin'.[166] If that is the case, why should men need the teaching of a visible Church? Would it not be enough to leave man to discover and follow truth with his own, unaided reason? To Manning's mind, the question ignored how great a treasure the possession of the truth of revelation is: it brings life to those who possess it, in the measure of their knowledge and acceptance of that truth. Moreover, Manning added, those who asked that question did not understand the moral role of the Church as a means for the probation of man.

5. *The Analogy of Nature and Probabilities*

Manning's fourth volume of sermons, and particularly the sermon entitled 'The Analogy of Nature', marked an impor-

---

[164] *ASer* iv. 386.   [165] Ibid. 84.   [166] Ibid. 75.

tant departure from Butler's ideas in the *Analogy*, and from the standpoint of men like Keble, Pusey, and Gladstone. These felt that the shipwreck of the Oxford Movement was due, in good measure, to the neglect of Butler's principles. Keble had pointed this out in 1846, in a letter to Ryder: 'I am sure it is long since I dreamed of "maintaining the cause" of all truths I firmly believe, or of "finding sufficient answers" to all objections. In such matters I should have made shipwreck long ago, had I not accepted, and tried to act upon the theory of Bishop Butler—that theory which seems now to be so sadly despised and forsaken by so many of our friends.'[167]

In 1847, Keble tried to remedy that deficiency with the publication of his *Sermons Academical and Occasional*. The long preface was meant as a diagnosis of the illness affecting so many of the old Tractarians, and as a prescription to arrest the stream of conversions to Rome. Pusey had urged him repeatedly to reassure those who were anxious and discouraged by recent events, and Keble's *Sermons* tried to give direction to what was left of the Oxford Movement by steering it clear of the rock on which the allegiance to the Anglican Church of so many Tractarians had broken up. He charted the treacherous coast along which ran the course of the revival of Catholic principles, and clearly defined the danger to be avoided at all cost: the yearning for certainty—absolute certainty—in matters of faith. This wayward desire had led a certain number of the Tractarians to Rome. The long preface to the volume of sermons was Keble's effort at unmasking that unhealthy urge, for the benefit of those still in the Anglican Church. The yearning for certainty, he wrote, was 'a generous and devotional feeling; still it is a feeling, not reason, and proceeds on an inadequate view of the necessary imperfection of this our mortal state'.[168] Keble thought that this 'longing

---

[167] Letter dated 22 May 1846, quoted by Newsome, *Parting of Friends*, 311. Newman was one of those friends, and Keble had offered him before his secession to Rome the same advice (see Newman, *Correspondence*, 320). Gladstone also saw in Butler the antidote for the new ideas of development: 'I am persuaded', he wrote to Manning (28 Dec. 1845), 'that Bishop Butler if he were alive would in his quiet way tear the whole argument [Newman's] into shreds' (British Library, Gladstone Papers, Add. MS 44247, fo. 279).

[168] Keble, *Sermons*, p. x.

after assurance'—the craving for 'perfect rest of mind and heart'—'might perhaps not unaptly be called the "last infirmity" of saintly spirits. As the tender and anxious conscience is won by the expectation of some peculiar, untried repose, to be found in Roman Catholic confessionals only; forgetting that the same treasure of pardon is by God's mercy already within its reach; so the restless argumentative intellect thinks to take refuge in the doctrine of infallibility.'[169] The preface argued that conversion to Rome was not the safer path, on moral grounds, and that, on the other hand, the analogy of nature militated against the existence of certainty in the knowledge of the matters of faith.

Keble followed Butler's argument in *The Analogy of Religion*, where Butler had dealt with the objection which, arguing from the lack of clarity in revelation, denied its divine origin. The deist claimed that, if God had really given a revelation, he would have accompanied it with an unmistakable proof of its truthfulness, and its content would be plain to all. This argument, Butler said, was an a priori argument, deducing from what we think reasonable how God should have acted. We are not justified in assuming that this is the case with revelation. As a matter of fact, Butler added, the analogy of nature would have us think otherwise. The truths of Christian revelation, like those of nature, are, and can be, apprehended only imperfectly by us. Probable evidence is, in most cases, the highest achievable evidence; but moral certainty could be built on the foundation of cumulative probabilities. Probability is the guide of life, and man should not pretend to enjoy absolute certainty where God only intended probable knowledge for him. Gladstone would say that this was the reason why Butler, the mildest of men, would pronounce such a severe sentence on the claims of the Popes; it was born of his horror at the daring and presumption of their claim to infallible knowledge.[170]

Butler saw in this a disposition of Providence, a moral design: it was part of man's moral test. Faith would have no

---

[169] Keble, *Sermons*, pp. lxvi–lxvii.
[170] Cf. W. E. Gladstone, *Studies Subsidiary to the Works of Bishop Butler* (Oxford, 1896), 105–6.

merit if the knowledge of divine truth were to impose itself on our minds with an absolute certainty; that would be a worthless and compulsory assent. Evidence in matters of religion needs to be weighed carefully, and where the evidence falls short of being conclusive, the effort to determine its proper value is more of a probation for man than would be the case if the evidence were to be overwhelming. The examination of the evidence requires the exercise of a series of virtues: the fickle and worldly man would be inclined to excuse himself from accepting the revealed truth, and its demands, on the plea of its uncertainty, while the virtuous man would be more inclined to make it his own. God may deliberately hide himself from men, and his hiddenness is not just 'the divine response to the corruption of their minds. It is rather the theory that those disposed to seek the truth with full seriousness might have to be presented with obstacles to test their moral determination.'[171]

Manning had dismissed the analogy of nature, probabilities, and the natural light of the individual mind—aided in some general way by grace—as sources of the act of faith. If this were the case, the highest evidence achievable would be only a moral evidence or 'moral certainty', as Butler and Keble would call it: a mere probable evidence. This, Manning thought, would imply uncertainty 'both in the subject and in the object. Is it possible to believe', he asked, 'that this scheme of probabilities (that is, of uncertainty) in doctrine, and of imperfection (that is, of doubt) in evidence, is part of the probation of the regenerate within the revelation of the faith?'[172] He had a different idea about the nature of man's probation. Submission to the teaching Church was, in Manning's mind, the essential element of man's probation and regeneration. As he saw it, there is on man's part—as a consequence of sin—an unwillingness to submit to the Church. This ordinance of God seems to him unreasonable and arbitrary; his intellect and his will rebel against it. He finds it difficult to believe that pastors—whom he sees as human and defective—are commissioned to teach infallible truth; he also finds it difficult to

---

[171] T. Penelhum, 'Butler and Human Ignorance', in Cunliffe (ed.), *Butler's Moral and Religious Thought*, 137.

[172] *ASer* iv. 170.

submit to the discipline dictated by an order of men, and to preserve the unity of brotherhood. Man's rebellion, which destroys the image of God in him, is corrected by his submission to the discipline of the Church. In so doing, man conforms to the image of Christ, the obedient Son of the Father, and his inner unity is restored.[173]

Thus, the probation of man does not consist in his discovering or not discovering the truth of faith by himself, aided by grace and his moral rectitude. Manning considers that this avenue leads to spiritual pride and rationalism. The Church's mission is not to call man 'to weigh the value of truth in the balance of the individual reason, but to call upon the individual will to surrender itself to the sweet yoke of Christ'.[174] 'Latitudinarian errors and proud indifference' were the moral opposites of the humility required for the act of faith, and they were not without moral responsibility.

Manning's central idea in his fourth volume of sermons was the continuous presence and permanent teaching office of the Holy Spirit in the Church. As he put it in the ninth sermon, 'Is it possible to believe that the supernatural illumination of the Spirit was so given as to rest upon no higher base than reason, discovery, criticism, and analogies of nature?' And he would drive home the absurdity of that position with the words of St Paul to the Galatians: ' "Are ye so foolish? Having begun in the Spirit, are ye now made perfect by the flesh?" (Gal. 3:3)'.[175]

Keble, on the other hand, had stressed Butler's idea of the role of the moral element in the actual acceptance of revealed truth. More than as a help inclining the intellect to accept the truths which appear to the intellect as probable, he seems to have conceived man's moral disposition as a light guiding man to find the truth. The knowledge of God in faith and love assists man in discerning clearly the truth perceived confusedly through probability: 'He that is willing to do His will, he shall know of the doctrine, whether it be of God.'[176] Probability leaves ample room for the moral sense to correct the

---

[173] See above Ch. I, sec. 6.   [174] *ASer* iv. 84.   [175] Ibid. 170.

[176] Keble, *Sermons*, p. xvi. Newman also found Keble's theory incomplete. For Newman's philosophical departure from Butler and Keble see his *Apologia pro Vita Sua* (Oxford, 1913), 19–21.

errors and limitations of the intellect. Keble also contended that probable knowledge was more consistent with the proper understanding of the nature of faith and hope as described in Holy Scripture, 'since "hope which is seen is not hope": and "faith is the substance", the realizing, "of things hoped for", the "evidence, or making venture", of things not seen. When objects therefore, either earthly or heavenly, present themselves to the mind as distinctly as though they were seen, there is no room any longer for either hope or faith, properly so called.'[177]

Manning rejected this contention on the grounds that Keble had disregarded the nature of the act of faith; he had also failed to consider that, although a truth may lack intrinsic evidence, its truthfulness may be supported by extrinsic evidence: that is, the truthfulness and omniscience of the one propounding it. Curiously enough, Manning's departure from Butler's ideas had a Butlerian foundation. As far as he was concerned, to use the analogy of nature to determine the degree of certainty or uncertainty of God's revelation was as much an a priori procedure as the rationalist ideas that Butler was trying to refute. He felt that Butler's conception of the act of faith had degraded it to a natural act: the act of weighing and deciding on a series of probabilities presented to the intellect; a purely human act, in which both the intellect and the general rectitude of the will played the decisive part. Manning rejected this position: faith is based not on 'probability' but on a double certainty. First, the truth revealed presents itself to us as infallibly true; secondly, the subjective act of faith does not originate with a judgement of the believer about probabilities, but has its origin in God who grants it to man.

Manning had circulated the proofs of his *Sermons* among a few of his friends. Gladstone answered in detail Manning's contention as to the analogy of nature; he rejected infallibility outright. For him, as he wrote at this time, 'faith essentially

---

[177] Ibid., p. xi. Coleridge had put forward similar ideas: moral rectitude was a sure guide to religious truth; those who looked for certainty were ready to sacrifice the moral excellence of faith to a cold, mechanical, compulsory assent to an evident truth (see B. Reardon, *From Coleridge to Gore: A Century of Religious Thought in Britain* (London, 1971), 72, 114).

involves the idea of what we have called probable evidence; for it is "the substance of things hoped for, the evidence of things not seen"; and "what a man seeth, why doth he yet hope for"?'[178] Robert Wilberforce, on the other hand, could not fault Manning's logic, but found it difficult to accept his conclusions, and he would have preferred it if Manning had used the word 'indefectibility' rather than 'infallibility'. He also asked whether the sermon had been written against Keble's preface. No, it had not, Manning answered; he had written it in 1847, while he was ill, before the preface appeared.[179] Allies was enthusiastic about the *Sermons*, particularly sermon 9 on the analogy of nature. Had he read it before, the sermon could have saved him from years of uncertainty. His judgement upon the volume—half in jest, half seriously—was that Manning should be brought before the Court of Arches:

You have been not so much attacking a single point here and there in the Articles of our faith, as overthrowing the whole ground on which the Anglican Church originally went and now stands. When you speak of inhering in the infallibility of the Church Catholic, it is a language and a thought unknown to all her writers, and utterly alien to her action and life for three hundred years. How has she lived save on criticism of the text of Scripture, criticism of antiquity[?][180]

Manning's correspondence with Robert Wilberforce in the years following the publication of his last volume of Anglican sermons dwells repeatedly on the themes sketched in it. On 22 January 1851, he expressed his alarm at the 'strange and sad words I have heard from good men about "craving for certainty", and "uncertainty being the utmost sphere of moral probation"'. He could not understand how they could affirm such a thing. 'Is it the probation of Faith', he asked, 'to be uncertain whether there be a True and proper Trinity of Persons—whether there be a Real Presence—or any Holy

---

[178] Gladstone, 'Probability as the Guide of Life', in *Studies Subsidiary*, 362. He started writing these studies in 1845.

[179] Manning MSS Bod., c. 655, fos. 131–2, letters dated 14 and 16 Nov. 1849. In a letter to Gladstone (21 Nov. 1869) he seemed to suggest that he had written the sermon with Keble's preface in mind (British Library, Gladstone Papers, Add. MS 44249, fos. 125–30).

[180] Ibid., c. 657, fo. 196, letter dated 29 Jan. 1851.

Ghost? And if not in these, why in any truth whereby we must be saved?'[181] Pusey and Keble had a false view of moral probation, and this was perhaps more dangerous than their doctrinal errors; he was concerned for the faith of their followers. In 1854 he would still be playing the same themes in Robert's mind:

Do you mean that the ground of your faith is *probability*? What, then, is the office of the Holy Spirit? You know that it is a condemned proposition to say that "the supernatural assent of faith can consist with only a probable knowledge of revealed Truth". See Viva, *Prop.* XXI Innocent XI. Look at my old nonsense on the Analogy of Nature, and your own better sense in the Sermon before the University of Oxford at the end of your Erastianism. This is not consistent with the presence and office of the Holy Spirit, the Guide and Light of the Church.[182]

Manning's fourth volume of sermons built upon contemporary Tractarian ideas about the Church, an ecclesiology to which he himself had made important contributions. The Tractarians' understanding of the nature of the Church developed gradually. Härdelin has remarked how 'the idea of the Church as an organism, as the mystical body of Christ, which forms so prominent a feature of the thought of the Fathers, was not developed by the Tractarians until a later stage'.[183] The principle of apostolic succession, the prerogatives of the episcopate, the idea of the Church as a means of grace, the concept of the regeneration of Christians through their union with Christ and their life in him, were the steps that led the Tractarians to the vision of the Church as a living body: Christ's Mystical Body. It was a gradual, but, it might be added, almost inexorable progress. Asking the question about the nature of the Church opened the door to a hundred others; thereafter, the logical development of their tenets and the reading of the Fathers could hardly fail to bring the doctrine of the Mystical Body of Christ to the forefront of Tractarian thinking about the Church.

It would be no mean task to chart in detail the springs which fed Manning's thought. It has been pointed out that his

---

[181] Ibid., c. 656, fo. 111.
[182] Quoted in *P* ii. 40, letter dated 28 Feb. 1854.
[183] Härdelin, *Tractarian Understanding*, 72.

'sermons bear in many, though not all respects, a notable like-ness to Pusey's'.[184] Manning, and also Robert Wilberforce, seem indebted to Pusey's tract on scriptural views of baptism when they speak about the incorporation of the Christian into Christ and the Christian's life in him. It might be more diffi-cult, and it would require detailed study, to ascertain the extent of Newman's influence, if any, on Manning's eccle-siology; echoes may have grown too faint here, and ideas too widely spread and generally accepted, to identify direct influ-ences. It is easier, however, to detect the many obvious simila-rities between Manning's fourth volume of sermons and Robert Wilberforce's book on the Incarnation, although their regular intercourse and copious correspondence during the late 1840s and early 1850s would make it hard to determine the extent of their mutual influence, and what precisely they owed to each other. This may be particularly the case where the theology of the Church and of the Eucharist is concerned.

What is beyond doubt is that, on the basis of opinions com-monly held among the Tractarians, Manning developed the concept of the Church as the Mystical Body of Christ—its unity and infallibility—well beyond the ideas of men like Pusey or Robert Wilberforce. The latter, in his book on the In-carnation, still spoke of the theory of the three branches, and of the Church's loss of the gift of infallibility with their separa-tion. Again, Manning's doctrine about the nature of the virtue of faith, and of its genesis, can also be said to be a new development, beyond common Tractarian thinking.

---

[184] G. Rowell, 'Remember Lot's Wife—Manning's Anglican Sermons', *Recusant History*, xxi. 2 (Oct. 1992), 170. D. Forrester, e.g., has pointed out 'how closely bap-tismal regeneration was bound with a notion of Christian life as a mysterious incor-poration of the individual into the Humanity of God Incarnate' (*Young Dr. Pusey* (London, 1989), 192). O. Chadwick has, in his turn, remarked on Pusey's contribu-tion to the Tractarian concept of the Church as the Body of Christ: he 'almost *feels* the individual's incorporation into the Body. His language is more mystical ... than the language of any other Tractarian' (*Spirit of the Oxford Movement*, 39).

III
Conversion: 'To Add, to Develop, to Perfect'

A. LAST STEPS TO ROME

1. Deep Convictions Militant against the Heart

Newman's book on development had made Manning rethink his position with respect to the Anglican rule of faith. He thought that it was no longer tenable as an instrument to attain certainty in the knowledge of the truth of the Faith: it was incomplete and, in its present formulation, equivalent to private judgement. He had to find an answer to the fundamental question: *Quo judice?* He discovered it in 1847: the Church was the final judge in controversies about the Faith, and she was infallible in her judgements because of the perpetual presence of the Holy Spirit.

Having reached the conviction that infallibility was an essential property of the Church, and in spite of all his doubts, Manning remained in the Church of England for almost another four years. The Anglican Church did not lay claim to infallibility; was this another of those Catholic truths which, like the sacramental system, the Tractarians had been called to restore to their proper place in the Church of England? A true but forgotten doctrine might be restored in a true Church; was the Anglican Church a part of the true Church? It was a painful question, and the final answer was to be even more so.

His letters to Robert Wilberforce chart the meandering course of that lengthy process, and are the best means at our disposal for following it. On 5 February 1848, while the Hampden case was raging in England, Manning wrote from Rome: 'I cling to the Church of England, because, trusting that it is a portion of the visible Church, it partakes of this undoubted divine property', infallibility.[1] But this was not an absolute belief and, in the following line he added: 'If it does not partake

---

[1] Manning MSS. Bod., c. 655, fo. 63.

of this property it affords no foundation for my Faith. It is use-
less to offer me antiquity for my foundation. What do I know
of antiquity?'[2] The appeal to antiquity was a barely masked
exercise in private judgement. As he wrote to Pusey in May
1850: 'we appeal to Antiquity—to seven Councils—and the
undivided Church of the past, not claiming this guidance [of
the Holy Spirit]. And this seems to me to be *a corporate exercise
of private judgment*: judging by *reason*. ... Upon what do we
found our exposition of the Faith of the undivided Church,
but upon an intellectual criticism of the Fathers? This seems
to me to be only a *learned form of private judgment*.'[3] Around the
same time, he told Robert that Pusey and Keble seemed to
'have given up the Divine Tradition as the Supreme authority,
and to apply private judgment to antiquity, as Protestants do
to Holy Scripture'.[4] And in January 1851 he summed up
these thoughts by saying that the Anglican rule of faith was
'manifestly private reason, judging by way of historical
criticism'.[5]

External events contributed to Manning's unsettlement and
growing doubts about the Church of England. The appointment of Renn Dickson Hampden, Regius Professor of Divinity
at Oxford,[6] to the see of Hereford had shown, he wrote on 12
February 1848, the 'separation of the English Episcopate from
the whole episcopate under heaven, the denial of Catholic doctrine in *substance* by a large body of the English Priesthood ...
and the rejection of Catholic doctrine in *form*, by the rejection
of Catholic tradition as the rule of Faith, the historical fact
that the Church of England has made common cause with
Protestantism ... all these have for a long time deprived me of
the power of claiming for it the undoubted guidance of the
Holy Spirit along the path of Catholic Tradition'.[7] That was
not all. This 'event has brought out a miserable truth, namely

[2] Manning MSS. Bod., c. 655, fo. 63.
[3] Ibid., c. 654, fos. 382–3, letter dated 4 May 1850.
[4] Ibid., c. 655, fo. 217, letter dated 15 June 1850.
[5] Ibid., c. 656, fo. 99, letter dated 7 Jan. 1851.
[6] Hampden's appointment as Regius Professor (1836) was imposed by Melbourne
on the University against the wishes of the Archbishop of Canterbury and of the
majority of its members. The University, subsequently, censured Hampden for his
heterodox views.
[7] Ibid., c. 655, fo. 65.

that the Civil Power is the ultimate judge of doctrine in England, a principle which is not more heretical than atheistical'.[8]

The Hampden case, and, later on, the Gorham judgement, seemed to Manning to give the same answer to the *Quo judice?* question, one which denied Manning's fundamental belief about the Holy Spirit's perpetual presence and teaching in the Church. Those instances appeared to confirm the conviction which had been growing in his mind that the Church of England did not share in the endowment of infallibility, which she did not claim; or in that of unity, which she did claim. Hampden's consecration, he believed at the time, was the final nail in his coffin: 'the Court of Queen's Bench plus Hampden's consecration declares the Civil power to be *ultimate* and supreme even in spiritual obligations. This overthrows the only defence I have ever been able to make of our position. If it be true I am myself one of the foremost in believing it to be fatal to our claims as a member of the visible Church. I cannot evade this; and I cannot obey it. If it be finally confirmed I am at an end.'[9]

His correspondence with Gladstone did not mention the theme of infallibility, but there were in it some references to the unity of the Church. During his illness of 1847 Manning had reviewed his ideas on unity, and he had come to see—still somewhat vaguely—the role of the Pope in preserving it. That is why he did not follow Gladstone in his confessed 'insularity', writing to him from Rome on 3 April 1848:

I never had much of it and feel that every year has convinced me more deeply that Protestantism is heretical, and Nationalism is Judaic. I remember you saying that the English Monarchy is an idea which commands the veneration and affections of your mind in a way beyond what I am likely to feel. On the other hand '*Tu es Petrus*' and '*Credo in Unam Catholicam Ecclesiam*' reveal to me a divine Monarchy claiming a sentiment of loyalty to a Person in Heaven before which all other kingdoms melt away. I trust that your insularity does not limit the full living practical realization of this transcendent law of Faith and action.[10]

---

[8] Ibid., fo. 66; for Manning correspondence with S. Wilberforce see Newsome, *Parting of Friends*, 337 ff.

[9] Ibid., fos. 67–8, letter dated 11 Mar. 1848.

[10] Manning MSS Pitts, box 1, folder 8.

The final act, though, was not so close as Manning had led Robert Wilberforce to believe. His return to England stayed the ultimate decision. His 1848 *Charge* tried to present the best possible interpretation of the Hampden case, by pointing out that Hampden had not formally been declared heretical by an ecclesiastical court.[11] Manning was ready to err on the side of hope, but he was not fully satisfied by the argument. In the meantime, the whole doctrinal system remained as clear and obvious to him as before. And, a year later, on 28 December 1849, he wrote to Robert: 'My whole reason seems filled with one outline. The Faith of the Holy Trinity and of the Incarnation subdue me into a belief of the indivisible unity, and perpetual infallibility of the Body of Christ. ... I am forced to believe that the unity of His Person prescribes the unity of His visible kingdom as one, undivided, whole; and that numbers are an accident. It was once contained in an upper chamber; it may be again; but it must always be one, and indivisible.'[12] What was stopping him from leaving the Church of England? He felt himself divided, as he saw it, between truth and love. The emotional side of Manning clung to the Anglican Church, and he still hoped against hope that his conclusions with respect to it would be proved wrong, and that the exercise of the civil power as ultimate judge on doctrinal matters would be denounced by the Anglican Church as a usurpation and against the nature of the Church.

The Gorham appeal dispelled his last doubts. His correspondence during the months preceding the appeal evinced clear signs of how far removed Manning now was from the position held by some of his friends. Pusey, writing in December 1849, had spoken of the Council of Trent and its definitions, saying that he could not receive

on authority what does not come to me on the authority of the whole Church ... I could not subscribe the Council of Trent (as now interpreted), for for this it matters not whether the Articles are more or

---

[11] Hampden's views, when he was appointed Regius Professor by Lord Melbourne in 1836, had been censured only by Oxford University's Convocation, which deprived him of the right to appoint Select Preachers.

[12] Manning MSS Bod., c. 655, fos. 142 and 144; see also letter dated 27 May 1850, ibid., fo. 213.

fewer which I could not sign—except on the belief that the Roman Church alone were the Church of Christ. And I can see no ground to anathematize the Russian Greek Church as well as our own. The claim several times made parenthetically in the Council of Trent, to be 'mater omnium et magistra', is surely unhistoric...[13]

Manning could not accept the principle on which Pusey had worked out his response to Trent: that is, the branch theory. It was against his deep conviction about the presence and work of the Holy Spirit in the Church. In June he wrote to Pusey describing how he viewed the question in dispute:

I seem to see no choice but this—the voice of God speaking always by His Church, or the reason of man judging of Revelation. That the Divine Spirit guides the Church in Faith is to me a manifest doctrine of revelation. That this guidance has ceased to rule the Church seems to me repugnant to Faith. That it therefore guides it now is inevitably a matter of Faith. But how can it be said that the Greek, Latin, and English Church are under this guidance? The supremacy as between the East and the West, the Sacrifice as between us and both (to say nothing of Regeneration in Baptism as of a matter as yet only in peril) seems to overthrow the idea of one universal guidance. Also I observe that the Greek Church claims to be the True Church and to possess alone this guidance.

So does the Roman.

But we appeal to Antiquity—to seven Councils—and the undivided Church of the past, not claiming this guidance. ... The Greek Church will not accept our exposition of the Seven Councils. Much less the Roman.

... Has not our Lord invested the Church with the office of declaring by a lineal and perpetual tradition what was and is the Faith in all ages?[14]

He had been able to defend the acquiescence of the Church to Hampden's nomination on the basis that he had not been formally condemned as unorthodox by an ecclesiastical court. That was not the case with Gorham: his bishop and the archbishop's court had judged his doctrine on baptismal regeneration erroneous. The problem now was not whether the Crown would judge in favour or against the ecclesiastical court in a

---

[13] Letter quoted in H. P. Liddon, *Life of Edward Bouverie Pusey*, iii (London, 1894), 207–8.

[14] Manning MSS Bod., c. 654, fos. 381–3, letter dated 4 May 1850.

doctrinal matter, but whether the Church acknowledged the Crown's power to do so. The question was once again reformulated: 'Does the Royal Supremacy carry a claim to review by appeal the declarations and interpretations of the Courts of the Church in matter of doctrine?'[15] As a matter of fact, Manning feared more a decision in favour of the doctrine of Baptismal Regeneration than one against it. The wrong decision would probably galvanize the opposition to the present interference of the State in matters doctrinal, whereas the right one would mislead many into thinking that all was proper. As he told Gladstone, 'A judgment right in matter, cannot heal a wrong in the principle of the Appeal.'[16] Even if they were to decide rightly, he wrote to Robert Wilberforce, it would not be a decision of the Church, but 'an independent and absolute judgment of the Crown in matter of Faith'.[17] This would make the civil power the ultimate interpreter of the Church's formularies and the ultimate judge in controversies about the Faith, the final expositor of doctrine. 'No higher power is claimed by Pope or General Council,' Manning exclaimed.[18]

2. *Gorham and 'The Appellate Jurisdiction of the Crown'*

'[A]ll Divine authority in England is at stake, all Divine law for the intellect and for the will,' Manning wrote to R. Wilberforce.[19] The nature of the appeal implied putting forward the claim that the jurisdiction of the Crown was assumed to be in *eadem materia* with that of the spiritual courts, *coextensive* with all their jurisdiction, *superior* to them.[20] This would destroy the supernatural foundation of the Church. Manning maintained that the Church was infallible, and no other external body was such; thus, in matters of Faith the tribunal and the judge should be purely spiritual, and within the Church. The appeal took the final decision in matters of faith out of the Church's hands, and gave it to a civil court: 'the final interpretation of doctrinal formularies—which is equivalent to

---

[15] Letter to R. Wilberforce, 12 Jan. 1850, Manning MSS Bod., c. 655, fos. 150–1.
[16] Manning MSS Pitts, box 1, folder 9, letter dated 31 Dec. 1849.
[17] Manning MSS Bod., c. 655, fo. 157, letter dated 18 Jan. 1850.
[18] Letter to Pusey, 4 Jan. 1850, ibid., c. 654, fo. 379.
[19] Ibid., c. 655, fo. 202, letter dated 10 May 1850.
[20] Cf. letter to R. Wilberforce, 18 Feb. 1850, ibid., fo. 168.

definition—... is thus removed out of the Church to the Civil Powers'.[21] The civil court was just a human body, and its judgements could be based only on human reason. This procedure would inevitably lead to rationalism.

Everything conspired to urge Manning in the same direction. In June he could write to Robert: '*Logically* I am convinced that the One, Holy, Visible, Infallible Church is that which has its circuit in all the world, and its centre *accidentally* in Rome.'[22] Recent events, including the Hampden case, had not changed the position of the Church of England, only revealed it. It was the disclosure of a position untenable *ab initio*. Hope-Scott played an important role in helping Manning realize that the present exercise of Royal Supremacy was not a recent abuse, something accidental to it, but an essential element of the Anglican Church. As early as 29 January 1850, Hope-Scott had written to his friend:

You have a theory of allegiance based upon ecclesiastical principles, while I have not. But when you adopted that theory, had you fully considered the facts? If you had, it ought still to hold good, for I maintain that nothing, in principle new, has befallen us in the case of Hampden, or, as yet, of Gorham. But if you have not hitherto read Erastianism in the history of the Church of England since the Reformation, then I fear you and I have much to discuss before we can meet upon common ground.[23]

Discuss they did, and, after the failed protest against the Gorham judgement, Manning published, as a letter addressed to the Bishop of Chichester, *The Appellate Jurisdiction of the Crown in Matters Spiritual*; it was dated 2 July 1850. The Gorham judgement, and its acceptance by the Church of England, implied for Manning a dramatic departure from what until then he had considered the basic principles of the Church of England, as a branch of the universal Church. The letter pointed out what he believed those principles to be, and how the judgement had violated them.

The Church, Manning explained, had been entrusted by Christ with the custody of the Faith and the holy sacraments. For 'the perpetuity of the Church, and for the preservation of

[21] Letter to Pusey, 4 Jan. 1850, ibid., c. 654, fos. 378–9.
[22] Ibid., c. 655, fos. 224–5.
[23] Quoted in *P* i. 527.

the Truth, He has pledged His own perpetual presence and the guidance of the Holy Spirit'. She 'possesses a sole, supreme, and final power, under the guidance of its Divine Head, and responsible to Him only'. The Church of England, in its measure and sphere, enjoyed 'the same guidance as the whole Church at large'.[24] She had in her the fountain of doctrine and discipline, and it 'has no need to go beyond itself for succession, orders, mission, jurisdiction, and the office to declare to its own members, in matters of Faith, the intention of the Catholic Church'.[25] But Manning could not think of the faith of the Anglican Church in isolation from the universal Church: faith is the belief of the Church dispersed throughout the world. A particular or local Church had no life except in so far as it is part of the Church Universal. 'The Church in every land', he would say, 'is the Church throughout the world sojourning as in a place, and there teaching and ruling by the whole weight of the Divine Office committed to the Church Universal ... The only superior known to the local Church is the authority of the Church universal.'[26] The Church of England was for Manning the presence and action of the universal Church in a particular place, active with the virtuality of the Church Catholic and with her authority. The unhappy suspension of communion between East and West, between the Roman and the Anglican Church, was a fact to be deplored, not a normal state.

It was essential to stress that in the Reformation the Church of England had not accepted 'the supremacy of the Crown instead and in place of the supremacy of the Universal Church; but resumed the full, free, and final exercise of its own Spiritual office, legislative and judicial, within its own proper sphere'.[27] A particular Church cannot hand over to the Crown powers which are inconsistent with the divine sovereignty of the Church Universal. Thus, the Royal Supremacy was 'strictly and simply a civil or temporal power over all persons and causes in temporal things, and over Ecclesiastical persons and causes in the temporal and civil accidents attaching to them'.[28] These legitimate, and custom-sanctioned, principles

[24] Manning, *Appellate Jurisdiction*, 4.
[25] Ibid. 5.   [26] Ibid. 22–3.   [27] Ibid. 23.
[28] Ibid. 6.

of the ancient jurisdiction of the Royal Supremacy over the Church had been stretched beyond their proper limits by the statutes of Henry VIII; Charles I, however, would have corrected the abuse and restored the limits of the ancient jurisdiction. Manning refused to acknowledge the following claims of the Royal Supremacy:

1 That Princes have, or can have, any inherent spiritual authority, or become fountains of spiritual jurisdiction, so far as it is spiritual.

2 That they may exercise a directive or legislative power in matters purely spiritual.

3 That they may re-hear and review with a power of discretion and determination the judicial sentences of the Church in matters purely spiritual.[29]

The Crown did not possess the prerogative of receiving appeals in matters of doctrine. 'The Church is final and sole in its Divine office .... The Apostolic commission [to teach and rule] did not depend for its exercise upon the licence of Princes—it descends direct from Him who is over all supreme,'[30] and for centuries it was exercised in spite of the opposition of the civil power.

The above principles had been ignored by the appeal. The civil authority had claimed for itself a power 'to judge and to declare that the Faith and Formularies of the Church admit of this or of that interpretation, of this or of that latitude'; that was 'nothing less than a power which subjects the whole faith of the Church to the judgment of the Prince'.[31] This was a late case of the old *Ejus est religio cujus est regio*, and a most serious violation of the divine commission of the Church. She 'alone possesses the deposit of the Word of God, or Christian faith, contained in the Holy Scripture, with its true interpretation, as a trust committed to it by its Divine Head'.[32]

The power to judge in matters of faith had been committed to the Church by Christ. Manning added that, in a certain sense, the 'whole office of the Church, in respect to doctrine, may be called judicial'.[33] He used the term 'judicial' in this

---

[29] Ibid. 18–19.   [30] Ibid. 21.   [31] Ibid. 31.
[32] Ibid. 34.   [33] Ibid.

context analogically, as opposed to a legislative power to create and promulgate law; that is, the Church cannot create or change an article of faith. The Church's only role is to interpret and to declare the truth revealed by God. Thus, he inveighed against those who said that doctrine was untouched by the Gorham decision because the formularies remained the same. 'Doctrine', he stated, 'is not a written, but a living truth ... If books were doctrine, no sect could be in heresy so long as they retained the Bible. If creeds were doctrine, the Socinians, who recite the Apostle's Creed, must be acquitted. But books and forms without their true interpretation are nothing.'[34] And that interpretation, the doctrine of faith, is always to be found in the oral exposition of the Church as universal teacher.

The act of the Appellate Jurisdiction transferring the decision in matters of faith from the tribunal of the Church to an external and secular judge had momentous consequences. It not only isolated the faith of the Church of England from the faith of the universal Church; even more, it lowered faith to the level of human opinion by destroying authority. Faith believes because of the authority of God, who reveals, and because of the propositions of the Church, teaching with his authority. To question or to reject her teaching authority in a particular doctrine of faith amounted to rejecting it altogether. 'If I have authority to affirm,' Manning wrote, 'another has equal authority to deny the same doctrine. Henceforth, we speak in our own name; not by authority at all, but by opinion; and if one article of faith is thus without authority, what article is more than an opinion? for opinion, and not faith, will be the principle and basis of all our teaching.'[35] The final conclusion was clear: the Church of England was in danger of 'abdicating the Divine authority to teach as sent by God, and a body which teaches under the authority of human interpretation descends to the level of a human society'.[36]

He felt justified in saying to Robert Wilberforce that the pastors of the Church of England, in their passive acceptance of the Gorham judgement, had 'betrayed the Divine authority of faith—not an article alone, but the whole principle of Divine authority in Faith'.[37] It was a confession, he wrote years later,

[34] Manning, *Appellate Jurisdiction*, 35.   [35] Ibid. 44–5.   [36] Ibid. 44.
[37] Manning MSS Bod., c. 656, fo. 99, letter dated 7 Jan. 1851.

then a Catholic, of their being unconscious of a divine commission and assistance to teach the truth of faith. This responded to the fundamental truth of the case: the Church of England 'could not speak for God, because it was not the organ of His voice'. Men, 'slowly and painfully', 'yielded to the truth, that what they had believed to be divine was not a Church just then fallen from unity and faith, but a human society, sprung from private judgment, established by civil power'.[38]

Manning seemed to have decided to ignore Allies's conclusions in his pamphlet *The Royal Supremacy Viewed in Reference to the Two Spiritual Powers of Order and Jurisdiction*, published at the beginning of 1850. Allies had claimed that the Royal Supremacy was not a late usurpation, but the foundation-stone on which the Church of England had been built at the beginning of its separate existence. But when, in September 1850, Allies's *The See of Peter* appeared, Manning confessed that, although the author had deformed his book by a few things, it provided him with a mass of evidence 'which would be immoral to put aside'.[39]

Event followed closely upon event. Just before the summer of 1850, Gladstone was urging his friends to commit themselves not to take any steps towards Rome for a certain period of time. Manning would not do so: time, he wrote to Gladstone, 'is not measured by the dial but by events, that is not chronological but moral'.[40] God keeps the time of conscience. The restoration of the Catholic hierarchy in England by Pius IX, at the end of September 1850, was the third and final sign that Manning had been awaiting from God. He described its full significance in 1863: the 'supremacy of the Vicar of our Lord had reasserted itself in England, and claimed of all men submission to its direction. The royal supremacy paled before the splendour of the head of the Church of all nations upon earth.'[41] What the Church of England did not claim for

---

[38] *CSer* i. 105.

[39] Letter to R. Wilberforce, 19 Sept. 1850, quoted in *P* i. 560.

[40] Manning MSS Pitts, box 1, folder 9, letter dated 22 May 1850. See also Manning's letter to R. Wilberforce, 22 May 1850, Manning MSS Bod., c. 655, fo. 205.

[41] H. E. Manning, 'The Work and the Wants of the Catholic Church in England', *Dublin Review*, July 1863, repr. in *Miscellanies*, i. 40.

itself—or had abdicated—was being claimed by the Pope: a jurisdiction sovereign and independent of any civil power, an authority which did not submit its claims to any human authority, but based them on a divine commission.

In his capacity as Archdeacon of Chichester, he was asked to convoke the clergy to a meeting against papal aggression. He did so. The meeting took place on 22 November. Manning had formally resigned his archdeaconry the previous day, and made public in the meeting his disagreement with the proceedings. On 28 November he wrote to an unknown correspondent, explaining the reasons for his actions: 'I can take no part with any movement which is inconsistent as I believe this to be with the principles which tend to restore the Church of England to the unity and communion of the universal Church.'[42] As he confessed in another letter, he could 'lift no hand in so bad a quarrel either to defend a Royal Supremacy which has proved itself indefensible, or against a Supremacy which the Church for 600 years obeyed'.[43]

By now his foot was in the river, and it was cold. Some of his friends—like Bellasis, Dodsworth, and Laprimaudaye—had gone down into the water, and were over. His heart was sad at the thought of leaving home, church, and flock. They had been all to him for eighteen years. He felt lonely, and the high tide of human sorrow at times engulfed his mind and clouded his judgement.[44] The end, however, was nigh. Manning, on 6 December 1850, wrote to Gladstone in the following terms: 'I do not believe that the Church of England is more than a provisional institution.'[45] This, he continued, was not a rash

---

[42] Manning MSS Bod., c. 662, fo. 265.

[43] Manning to Lord Campden, 14 Jan. 1851, ibid., fos. 270–1.

[44] See his letters to R. Wilberforce, Oct. 1850–Mar. 1851. He carried the painful memory of that separation well into his Catholic life. In Advent 1851 he left a moving description of those feelings: 'What memories of Lavington, and Sunday night, and of Advent. But all is in God's hands. That was a time of peace, as the time before was a time of beauty and happiness. Now it is all three, but with reality, sharpness, loneliness with God, and a sense of certainty and of eternity. ... Certainly, if there were no such a thing in the world as the Catholic Church, it [Lavington] would have been a blessed life' (Diary, quoted in *P* ii. 11). The memory of his married life also kept coming back to him, but he would not go back to that happiness of nineteen years before, even if it were granted to him sevenfold. He looked forward to meeting Caroline in heaven, after a life of work here on earth (cf. Ushaw College Archive, Manning to Mary Wilberforce, letter 38, dated 7 Sept. 1852).

[45] British Library, Gladstone Papers, Add. MS 44248, fo. 113.

judgement provoked by recent events; 'it is the deep conviction of long years of patient silent thought. You thought me hasty. I may have seemed so, for events have precipitated conclusions which for long years have hung suspended, waiting only for some change in the law of proportion to give them form.'[46] Gladstone, who had not been party to Manning's confidential expansions to Robert Wilberforce, tried everything in his power to keep his friend within the Anglican Church. All to no avail: Hope-Scott and Manning, two of Gladstone's closest friends, were received together into the Catholic Church on 6 April 1851.

3. Rome: The Rule of Faith Revisited

Wiseman communicated to Talbot[47] the good news of Manning's conversion and the part that the hierarchy commotion had played in it: 'I am sure that [to know this] will console the Holy Father,' he wrote. He added how Manning, after his reception, 'had said to Allies that "it was wonderful how many doubts and difficulties had completely vanished, and [that] he was perfectly happy" '.[48] Had he come to see clearly the primacy of the Pope? Had he discovered the place of the infallibility of the Pope in the schema of the infallibility of the Church?

Soon after his conversion, on 25 June, Manning was ordained a Catholic priest. The following autumn he moved to Rome, to the Accademia Ecclesiastica. There he was to spend the years 1851–4, alternating his stay in Rome with extended periods in England, escaping from the hot Roman summers. He soon found that the public schools did not suit his needs, and he read at home, directed by some of the Roman professors; he came to know well the main Roman theologians of his time: the Jesuits Perrone, Passaglia, and Schrader. In his letters

---

[46] Ibid., fo. 114.

[47] Mgr. George Talbot, son of the 3rd Baron Talbot of Malahide, was ordained as an Anglican clergyman, and was later received into the Catholic Church (1842). After ordination as a Catholic priest, he served for some years in Southwark before moving to Rome. Wiseman introduced him to Pius IX, and Talbot soon became his confidant and adviser on English matters, in which he strongly supported Wiseman's and Manning's line.

[48] Venerable English College Archive, Talbot Papers, Rome, letter 1007, dated 14 Apr. 1851.

he speaks of how he was reading moral theology, an area in which he felt particularly deficient, Giovanni Perrone's *Compendium*, and other works. It seems that Carlo Passaglia acted as his main director of studies, guiding him, among other things, in his study of the *Summa Theologica*. Manning had long conversations with him, and told Robert Wilberforce that they discussed many of the points and elaborations which had filled his mind during his years as an Anglican. He felt that the answers he had found to the different questions he himself had raised were, on the whole, correct: 'It is to me a delight to have a living voice to answer the questions which past years have helped me to make. And I am truly thankful to find how, in the main, I have rightly kept to the end of the thread.'[49]

It would be difficult to define the precise influence that his acquaintance with the Roman school of theology had on his thinking about the question of infallibility. It is obvious, though, that he did not owe to it his doctrine of the Mystical Body of Christ. Passaglia was perhaps the first Catholic theologian to have developed a detailed conception of the Church as the Mystical Body of Christ; still, Passaglia's book *De Ecclesia Christi*, published together with Schrader, did not appear until the years 1853–4, three or four years after Manning's fourth volume of Anglican Sermons.[50] Möhler's *Symbolik*, which Manning was reading in the mid-1840s, could have been another Catholic influence on the evolution of his vision of the Church. There are reasons, however, to affirm that his main sources of inspiration—shaped by the original illumination received by his reading of Cano—were Scripture and the Fathers of the Church, in particular St Augustine—the sources which had fed Möhler's own theology.

The same could be said with respect to infallibility. The original discovery and its subsequent elaboration preceded his conversion by about four years; here he had been helped by his knowledge of the Catholic theologians of the past, Cano in particular. As a result, the main lines of his ideas on the matter

---

[49] Letter dated 25 Jan. 1852, quoted in *P* ii. 27. See also extracts from his journal, in *P* ii. 18–20.

[50] Cruz (*Spiritus in Ecclesia*, 248) thought that Manning's theology of the Mystical Body had its sources in Passaglia and Schrader.

of infallibility can be found in his Anglican writings and letters. As a Catholic, he may have completed them in some respects, particularly in what refers to the infallibility of the Pope, but the main arguments remained the same: the living presence of the Holy Spirit in the Church, the reality of the Mystical Body of Christ, and the infallibility of the Church consequent to that presence. These themes were part of his original vision, and were to remain with him for the rest of his life.

In 1852, during one of his sojourns in England, Manning gave four lectures at Southwark Cathedral which were later published under the title *The Grounds of Faith*. The lectures read like a Catholic rewriting of his Anglican sermon *The Rule of Faith* (1838), after a quarter of a century of intellectual development that had led him, through conversion, into the Catholic Church. In the lectures he carried on the dialogue with the questions which had occupied his mind for many a year, and also addressed the queries and objections which had been raised in his correspondence with Robert Wilberforce, Pusey, and Gladstone. The fourth lecture, in particular, answered Keble's arguments in the Preface to his *Sermons Academical and Occasional* (1847) against joining the Catholic Church. In it, he outlined the basic points of his Catholic approach to the Anglican Church, an approach which would find a more detailed expression in subsequent sermons, lectures, and pastoral letters.

The first lecture opened with words reminiscent of those he had used in 1838: 'My purpose is to speak of the grounds of Faith; I do not mean of the special doctrines of the Catholic theology, but of the grounds or foundation upon which all Faith rests.'[51] This was a vital task at all times, 'because as the end of man is life eternal, and as the means to that end is the knowledge of God, and of Jesus Christ whom He hath sent, our whole being, moral, intellectual, and spiritual, demands that we should rightly know, and by knowledge be united with, the mind and will of God'.[52]

Manning affirmed that the knowledge of the rule of faith is the only means to avoid religious confusion and scepticism. If scepticism had made such inroads in many minds, it 'is because

---

[51] *Grounds*, 1.   [52] Ibid. 2.

the Rule of Faith is lost, and the principle of certainty destroyed. ... The effect of this is that men have come to state, as scientifically certain, that there is no definite doctrine in revelation. ... The objective certainty of truth is gone.'[53] Consequently, as he had said as an Anglican, and would repeat in his sermon before the First Council of Westminster (1852), opinion becomes the ultimate rule of faith.[54]

For Manning, proper and true knowledge should be clear and definite; it should also be certain. 'If we have not a definite knowledge of what we believe, we may be sure we have no true knowledge of it.'[55] A blurred and contourless perception cannot properly be called knowledge, whether in the field of natural sciences or in that of faith. In such a case, we may have a guess, or conjecture, or probability, but not proper knowledge. Any kind of knowledge worthy of this name should be certain in two senses: it should include the objective certainty of the truth in itself, and also subjective certainty. In other words, 'that the proofs of that truth are either self-evident, or so clear as to exclude all doubt'; and 'that we are inwardly convinced, by the application of our reason to the matter before us, of the sufficiency of the evidence to prove the truth of it'.[56] The knowledge of faith should also enjoy that double certainty: 'He that has not certain faith has no faith.'[57] He rejected the contention of those who said 'that to crave for certainty implies a morbid disposition'. The prophets craved certainty; so did the apostles and the evangelists. Conversely, 'the contrary disposition is worthy of rebuke. How can we venture to content ourselves with uncertainty in matters where the truth and honour of God and the salvation of our own souls are at stake?'[58] Some would perhaps contend that uncertainty is the proper climate of faith, that 'probability is the atmosphere in which faith lives, and that if you extinguish probabilities, faith dies'.[59] These people, Manning thought, were promulgating a new virtue, the essence of which would be 'to be uncertain of the truth and of the will of God; to hold our faith on probabilities'.[60]

---

[53] *Grounds*, 4–5. [54] Cf. *CSer* i. 104. [55] *Grounds*, 8.
[56] Ibid. [57] Ibid. 10. [58] Ibid. 10–11.
[59] Ibid. 11. [60] Ibid.

In a later sermon, 'Truth before Peace' (1864), he tackled a different, though connected argument, which he summarized by saying that ' "England prides itself on its piety and its free-dom"; that "earnest men will always be inquiring"; that "the Apostles urged inquiry into natural religion, into the visible creation, into Scripture"; that they "appealed to the burning curiosity and yearning after something better, which was the chief feature of their age"; that "this is the age of inquiry; that inquiry is the rule"; and that "the source of inquiry is doubt" '.[61] Manning accepted the principle as valid as long as it applied to the natural world and to the world without faith. On the other hand, if that were to be said of 'the world illumi-nated by the faith and the Church of Jesus Christ, it is', he held, 'self-evidently false. They who have not the truth whole and perfect, must be always inquiring, always doubting. Not so they who are "taught of God".'[62] They had already found truth; nothing remained but to hold fast to it. As he had said in the fourth lecture of *The Grounds of Faith*: 'the very idea of re-velation involves the properties of definiteness and certainty, because the knowledge divinely revealed is presented to us as it exists in the mind of God'.[63] Therefore, 'where faith begins uncertainty ends'. Faith 'terminates upon the veracity of God; and what God has spoken and authenticated to us by Divine authority cannot be uncertain'.[64]

Manning was clear about what he had to say to his interlo-cutors: 'we are saved by truth; and truth which is not definite is no truth to us; and indefinite statements have no certainty; and without certainty there is no faith'.[65] Truth is not to be trifled with; borrowing a leaf from his Anglican writings, he said: 'Truth bears the stamp of God, and truth changes man to the likeness of God.'[66]

Men have God's revelation to gain access to salvific truth. But the revealed word of God, Manning said, poses a problem of interpretation: 'Scripture is not Scripture except in the right sense of Scripture,'[67] and that sense is what needs to be determined. Let us say, Manning added, that we reject private

[61] *CSer* ii. 239.   [62] Ibid. 240.   [63] *Grounds*, 60.
[64] Ibid. 11.   [65] Ibid. 24.   [66] Ibid. 19.
[67] Ibid. 24.

judgement and introduce, as Anglicans do, the test of the historical tradition of the Church. This does not solve the problem. Individual reason has shown itself unable to deal with a small book and to determine its true interpretation; how can it deal with the literature of six centuries of Christianity? Here, said Manning, 'we touch upon another difficulty even more pressing and more vital. We have now the test by which to discover the truth; but where is the mind by which that test shall be applied?'[68] This was where Manning had found himself after reading Newman's *Development of Christian Doctrine*: the nature of revelation demanded a test, and the test demanded a judge. He concluded: 'a perpetual doctrine tested by a perpetual rule needs a perpetual judge'.[69]

There were only two possible ways of access to the revelation of God: an infallible teacher or a mere human one. 'If there exists in the world no teacher invested with divine commission to guide all others, either every several local church is invested with a final and supreme authority to determine what is true and what is false; that is, possesses the infallibility denied by objectors to the Universal Church itself; or else, no authority under heaven respecting divine truth is more than human.'[70] To claim that the definition of what is divinely revealed is the privilege of a human authority would not lead, even remotely, to any sort of certainty, but rather to rationalism, subjectivism, and scepticism; not to faith, but to the destruction of it. And his own times, Manning thought, afforded ample evidence of this fact.

One could appeal to the promise made to the apostles of a permanent teacher, the Holy Spirit. But, he asked, if 'you believe that the Holy Spirit does still teach in the world, how does He teach?'[71] It is obvious that He does not teach each man by immediate inspiration. The one answer left was that the Holy Spirit teaches through the Church. 'But if through the Church, through what Church? How are we the better or the wiser by knowing that the Spirit of God teaches the world at this hour, and that He has an organ through which to speak, if we know not which, nor where that organ is?'[72] It

---

[68] *Grounds*, 43.   [69] Ibid. 44.   [70] Ibid. 71.
[71] Ibid. 14.   [72] Ibid. 15.

was a fundamental question, the answer to which defined the one true way of salvation.

In that respect, the branch theory was found wanting by Manning. 'If these three bodies, then, be indeed the one Church, the Church is divided. ... These three bodies, brought by theory into unwilling combination, refuse, in fact, to be combined. They can be united only upon paper.'[73] They disagree over the essentials of the faith, and even over which doctrines are essential to it. This could not be called unity, Manning said. There is one only Church, and this is not a result of combining different separate parts; to say otherwise is to deny the visible unity of the Church in its government and its doctrine. The differences between Anglicans and Catholics were obvious and deep. So were those between Catholics and Greek Orthodox, like the disputed question of the primacy of the Pope. 'In the baptismal faith we profess to believe in one Holy Catholic Church. Surely the question whether or no there be on earth a supreme head of the Church divinely instituted, is as much part of the substance and exposition of that article as any other point.'[74] This Church should be one, and visibly so. 'How shall an invisible church carry on the revelation of God manifest in the flesh, or be the representative of the unseen God: the successor of visible apostles, the minister of visible sacraments ...?'[75] It would contradict the whole mode of God's dispensations to man.

The office of the Holy Spirit as infallible guide of the Church, admitted by Anglicans for the first centuries of Christianity, was not ended with the appearance of divisions among Christians. If that were to be the case, if 'the office of the Church to teach the truth and to detect falsehood, to define the faith and condemn heresy, be suspended, we know not now with certainty what is the true sense even of the Articles of the Creed'.[76] There would be no judge on earth to decide the disputes about matters of faith. But if the universal Church is the judge of doctrine, then it 'must be infallible; for if it may err, who shall determine whether it errs or no? ... It comes, then, by the force of rigorous argument to this, that either the

[73] Ibid. 63–4.   [74] Ibid. 69.   [75] Ibid. 64.
[76] Ibid. 68.

universal Church cannot err, or that there is on earth no certainty for faith.'[77] Manning had made his own Wiseman's argument.

This infallible Church could only be, Manning concluded,
the Roman Catholic Church. 'No other Church but this one
interpenetrates in all nations, extends its jurisdiction wheresoever the name of Christ is known, has possessed, or, I will say,
has claimed from the beginning, a divine primacy over all
other Churches; has taught from the first with the claim to be
heard as the Divine Teacher ... Whatever may be said in
theory, no other, as a matter of fact, from the east to the west,
from the north to the south, claims to be heard as the voice of
God.'[78] Moreover, Manning added, the Church of Rome had
been acknowledged as the uncontaminated fountain of truth
by the undivided primitive Church of the first centuries, and
the primitive Church was recognized as infallible by the Anglicans. True, the Roman Church's claim had been disputed almost from the beginning, but this did not tell against it: all
articles of the Faith have been controverted. Manning turned
the argument around: the fact that its authority had been disputed from the very begining was just a corroboration of the
fact that it had been claimed *ab initio*.

Man, unaided, could not have attained the knowledge of revealed truth, and once this has been handed on to him by
God, he would not have been able to preserve it unadulterated
if the bases on which it rested were purely human. Truth
would turn into opinion, and this would also have serious consequences for moral life. When 'the objectivity of truth is lost,
the obligation of law is gone'.[79] It is not possible for a human
authority to bind fellow creatures under pain of sin unless it
possesses a divine authority so to do.

The message of the lectures can be summarized briefly: 'We
believe ... that we have no knowledge of the way of salvation
through grace, except from the revelation of God'; 'neither
have we any certainty what that revelation was, except
through the Church of God'.[80] 'The teaching of the One,
Holy, Universal, Roman Church ... is to us the voice of God

[77] *Grounds*, 46.   [78] Ibid. 61.   [79] Ibid. 82.
[80] Ibid. 25, 28.

now, and the foundation of our faith.'[81] These were words that Manning would repeat that same year in his sermon before the First Provincial Council of Westminster. He saw the whole doctrinal edifice and the moral life of the Church as resting on the keystone of its infallibility. 'The unity and the infallibility of the Church of Jesus Christ, these are our principles, and this shall be our safety,'[82] Manning told the assembled bishops. The following year, in a sermon entitled 'The Certainty of Faith', he returned to the same theme. The fullness of the kingdom of faith consists of three divine gifts: an infallible testimony, an inward witness in man's reason, and charity to kindle the heart and to inspire the will. The infallible testimony of the Church 'is the true and formal object of our faith, which is surer than all sense, higher than all reason, perfecting both. Faith has a certainty of its own above all other kinds; above the certainty of science, different in its nature, loftier in its reach, deeper in its convictions; for it unites the reason of man with God, the eternal changeless truth'.[83]

Those who rejected the witness of the Church, her infallibility, were the heirs of a long tradition of incredulity: 'there are those who profess to believe the divine power and commission of the Apostles, but refuse to believe the divine mission and power of the Church; and yet, in the days of the Apostles, they would have equally appealed from them to the authority of Moses'.[84] It was a human temper of rebelliousness before God's claims that had never ceased to produce new shoots.

B.   MANNING'S CATHOLIC ECCLESIOLOGY
(1851–1865)

Manning's residence in Rome ended in 1854, after repeated requests from Wiseman for his return. On 7 May he wrote to Robert Wilberforce with the news: 'So far as I know I am come home for good. And my purpose is to continue in London the life I was living in Rome, that is, to live in community with three or four, having a library, chapel, and refectory in com-

---

[81]   Ibid. 60.   [82]   *CSer* i. 194.   [83]   Ibid. 207.
[84]   Ibid. 201.

mon. I find this both intellectually and spiritually a great help. And I shall set apart a room for you.'[85] This was not a new idea with him, for about a year earlier he had already mentioned it to Robert, not yet a Catholic: 'My hope is to find some one or two priests who will give themselves to study, writing, and preaching—to live in community, as Merton and All Souls should have been. Why should not you be the Warden?'[86] Manning's hopes were, for a moment, very close to becoming a reality. Unfortunately, Robert's conversion and subsequent decision to become a priest were closely followed by his premature death in 1857. Neither was Manning to enjoy the peace and quiet for 'study, writing, and preaching' he was looking forward to. As he wrote in 1863, surveying the years since his conversion, 'the constant and increasing press of active work . . . for the last ten years, has rendered it difficult, if not impossible, for me to find the quiet or time necessary for writing'.[87]

The period from his return to England until 1865, when he was made Archbishop of Westminster, was one of intense activity, including, among other things, representing Wiseman in his numerous suits in Rome and the founding of the Oblates of St Charles. His name was mentioned several times when a vacancy on the episcopal bench occurred, or even as a possible coadjutor to Wiseman. There were few substantial publications during those years: only individual sermons, included later in the volumes of his *Sermons on Ecclesiastical Subjects*, and his lectures on the temporal power of the Pope. In 1865, shortly after his appointment as Archbishop, he published a treatise which had been in the making for some time: *The Temporal Mission of the Holy Ghost, or Reason and Revelation*. It was a sort of systematic exposition of themes and ideas that had been the constant subject of his sermons in previous years: the Church as the Mystical Body of Christ, inhabited by the Holy Spirit: one, imperishable, and infallible. It devoted particular attention to the teaching role of the Holy Spirit in the Church.

He felt very deeply the need to insist on those points in order to ensure the proper understanding of the nature of the

---

[85] Quoted in *P* ii. 41.   [86] Letter dated 13 June 1853, quoted in ibid. 33.
[87] *CSer* i. 1.

Church, and to rest faith on solid foundations. This was particularly necessary in those countries where, as in England, the
dominant culture was Protestant, with the consequent blurring
of the formal object of faith. In his concern to foster the proper
concept of the rule of faith, he even lectured the English
bishops, assembled for the Second Synod of Westminster
(1855), on the infallibility of the Church.

1. *The Holy Spirit in the Church: The Mystical Body of Christ*

Manning's last volume of Anglican sermons already contained
most of the elements that intervened in the structuring of his
thought on this matter as a Catholic. There is, however, a
clear development in his views, more by the way of completeness than of change. The vision of the Church as the Mystical
Body of Christ, and the perpetual presence of the Holy Spirit
in it, is always before his eyes, the constant point of reference
for the whole of his ecclesiology. And he would fall back on it,
when confronting the different problems that presented themselves to him or to the Church.

The permanent and active presence of the Holy Spirit is the
keystone of Manning's vision of the Church. 'It is not by accident, or by mere order of enumeration', he said, 'that in the
Baptismal Creed we say, "I believe in the Holy Ghost, the
Holy Catholic Church". These two articles are united because
the Holy Spirit is united with the Mystical Body.'[88] He repeated time and again that the Church 'is not the name of a
multitude, but of a supernatural unity, the Head and the
Body, Christ mystical'.[89] It is not a collection of individuals
brought together by a common ideal or way of life, it is rather
a living and organically unified reality.

The Wisdom of God had inhabited the tabernacle of Christ's
humanity. There was 'another house still to arise, built upon
His own Incarnation—that is, His mystical body'.[90] It was
the work of the Holy Spirit to 'create' the Mystical Body of
Christ on the day of Pentecost, and since then he had preserved
its life and helped its operations.

Until the day of Pentecost the mystical body was not complete.
There could be no body till there was a Head. There was no Head

---

[88] *TM* 36.   [89] *CSer* i. 118.   [90] Ibid. 150.

until the Son was incarnate; and, even when incarnate, the completion of the body was deferred until the Head was glorified; that is, until the Incarnate Son had fulfilled His whole redeeming office in life, death, resurrection, and ascension, returning to enthrone the Humanity with which His eternal Person was invested, at the right hand of the Father. Then, when the Head was exalted in His supreme majesty over angels and men, the creation and organisation of the body was completed.[91]

The Ascension was the 'condition ordained of God for the advent and perpetual presence of the Third [Person]. And the coming of the Holy Ghost is likewise declared to be the condition of the creation, quickening, and organisation of the Mystical Body.'[92] The whole body was knit together by the Holy Spirit. Till Pentecost 'the members were not united to the Head, nor to each other, nor as a body to the Holy Ghost. ... And these three unions were constituted by the mission of the Holy Ghost from the Incarnate Son.'[93]

The Holy Spirit is to the Mystical Body what the soul is to the body of man. The Spirit of God—in an analogy taken from the creation of man in Genesis—is the breath of supernatural life breathed by God into the Church: he 'entered into the mystical body, and breathed into it the breath of life',[94] 'inhabiting that body, and diffusing His created grace throughout it, animates it as the soul quickens the body of a man'.[95] Manning saw the Holy Spirit as the Mystical Body's 'life, soul, and mind'.[96] The Church contains, therefore, in the Holy Spirit, the power of self-edification.[97]

The Head and the members constitute one Mystical Person. Quoting St Augustine, Manning would say that the Church is "una quaedam persona", "unus perfectus vir"; or, as the Apostle says, "the Spiritual man, who judgeth all things, and himself is judged of no man"'.[98] This body has a lineal identity, and is a moral person.[99] She is 'a new creation of omnipotence',[100] something which the world had not seen before. In her is found 'the fullness of the mystery of the Incarna-

[91] *TM* 58–9. [92] Ibid. 41. [93] Ibid. 68–9.
[94] *CSer* i. 418. [95] *TM* 66. [96] *CSer* i. 118.
[97] Cf. H. E. Manning, *The Office of the Holy Ghost under the Gospel* (London, 1857), 9.
[98] *CSer* i. 118; see also *Four Evils*, 106.
[99] Cf. *CSer* ii 243.
[100] *CSer* i. 15.

tion—the prolongation of its presence upon earth, the extension of its powers'.[101] Therefore, the Church is 'Jesus teaching and reigning upon earth: by His Spirit and His Word, He is present still, and will be, to the consummation of the world'.[102] The work which Christ had begun in his physical body is 'continued by His Mystical Body, through which He went and preached to all the nations of the world'.[103]

The union of the Holy Spirit with the Church is an indissoluble one: the Church would not be able to live without the Spirit, and it is part of Christ's promise that the Church will remain for ever. To reinforce this idea, Manning added that the union of the Holy Spirit with the Church on Pentecost Day is 'after the analogy of the Incarnation'. Through the Incarnation, the divinity and humanity of Christ are united in one person, 'never to be divided, by the indissoluble link of the hypostatic union, so the Holy Spirit united Himself to the mystical body on that day, never to depart from it; to be its life, guide, and voice to the end of time'.[104] A union which can never be dissolved because it results from 'a Divine act, analogous to the hypostatic union, whereby the two natures of God and man are eternally united in one Person. So the mystical body, the head and the members, constitute one mystical person.'[105] Manning devoted many a page to insisting on the indissoluble character of this union between the Holy Spirit and the Church. He had an eye on the need to refute the Anglican theory which, while maintaining the infallibility of the Church in the first six hundred years of her existence, affirmed that the infallible guidance of the Holy Spirit had ceased when the process of separation of what it called the three branches of the Church started. For Manning, this theory implied a clear denial of the true office of the Holy Spirit in the Church; it affirmed that the Church is on probation, and that the power and prerogatives of the Holy Spirit 'depend upon the conditions of the will of man'.[106]

[101] *CSer* ii. 8.   [102] Ibid. 13.   [103] *CSer* i. 419.

[104] *CSer* ii. 10; see also *CSer* i. 19.

[105] *TM* 66. Manning seems to have taken this analogy from Petavius. He made it clear that the union of the Holy Spirit and the Church was not hypostatic, given that the 'human personality of the members of Christ still subsist in this substantial union' (ibid. 63).

[106] *CSer* i. 245.

The union of the Holy Spirit with the Church is wholly different from the union between the Holy Spirit and the individual soul. The Holy Spirit, God's grace, granted to the individual may be refused entrance into the soul by the man's will or rejected after having once been accepted. The union of the Holy Ghost with the Church, on the other hand, is 'not conditional, but absolute, depending upon no finite will but upon the Divine will alone, and therefore indissoluble to all eternity';[107] 'though individuals may fall from the Body, the Body can never be parted from the Spirit of God, who dwells in it'.[108] The Church 'is not like an individual upon probation, as if the endowments and prerogatives of the Holy Spirit depend upon the will of man. It is itself the instrument of probation to individuals. It is through the Church that God confers His grace and truth upon mankind; and by the bestowal of grace and truth that He tries us one by one.'[109]

If the union of the Holy Spirit with the Church does not depend on any finite will, neither do his operations within it. The Spirit is in the Church to perform a work which is to last until the end of the world, until the whole number of God's elect is full. 'A perpetual work', Manning argued, 'demands a perpetual office and a perpetual operation.' It also demands 'a perpetuity in the means of its accomplishment. ... What are the means whereby the Elect of God are made perfect but grace and truth? and the work of sanctifying and illuminating is as perpetual as the chain of the Elect ... The whole office, therefore, of the Holy Spirit is as perpetual and indispensable as His presence.'[110] Doctrines and sacraments, the means and instruments to carry out that work, shall therefore be perpetually and divinely preserved, until the work is finally accomplished.[111] Although each individual can deprive himself of the Holy Spirit's illumination and sanctifying grace, the sin of man cannot suspend any of the operations of the Holy Spirit in the Church. Human misery cannot prevent the sacraments granting grace, even when administered by an unworthy minister; neither can it corrupt the voice of the Holy Spirit in the Church.[112]

[107]   *TM* 65; see also *CSer* i. 239–40.
[108]   *CSer* i. 19.   [109]   Ibid. 242.
[110]   Ibid. 235–6.   [111]   Cf. ibid. 13.   [112]   Cf. *TM* 67.

Manning had brought side by side the sanctifying and the teaching operations of the Holy Spirit, as complementary and inseparable. The two offices of the Holy Spirit, as teacher and sanctifier, were intimately related, and depended on each other. He had pointed this out in the fourth volume of his Anglican sermons, and, before that, in *The Unity of the Church*. He reiterated this idea once again: 'How is it that any one can fail to perceive that the condition of our sanctification is Truth, and that the perpetuity of the office of the Sanctifier presupposes the perpetuity of the office of the Illuminator?'[113] The presence and the operations of the Holy Spirit are always necessary if the life of grace and the knowledge of truth are to be preserved in the Church. Only he can grant the gift of grace, a share in God's life in Jesus Christ; only he can preserve from corruption the truth that God has revealed, a share in the mind of God. The Holy Spirit 'both teaches and sanctifies, without intermission, with a perpetual divine voice and a perpetual sanctifying power; or, in other words, the divine action of the day of Pentecost is permanent, and pervades the world as far as the Church is diffused, and pervades all ages, the present as fully as the past, to-day as fully as in the beginning'.[114]

2. *The Endowments of the Church: Infallibility*

The union of the Holy Spirit with the Church is the source of her supernatural endowments, 'which can never be absent from it, or suspended in their operation'.[115] They are 'derived from the Divine Person of its Head, and the Divine Person who is its life. As in the Incarnation there is a communication of the Divine perfections to the humanity, so in the Church the perfections of the Holy Spirit become the endowments of the body.'[116] The Church, as a result, 'became one with a twofold unity, essential and intrinsic, visible and external, because Jesus, its Head, is one and indivisible. It became indefectible, because Jesus is life eternal. It became infallible, because Jesus is eternal truth, and its intelligence is perpetually illuminated by His intelligence, and its voice governed by His voice.'[117]

---

[113] Ibid. 82.   [114] Ibid. 75–6.   [115] Ibid. 36.
[116] Ibid. 67; see also *Fourfold*, 117.
[117] *CSer* i. 419; see also *TM* 73–4 and *Fourfold*, 117 ff.

As far as the Faith is concerned, the Church enjoys an immutable *'knowledge, discernment,* and *enunciation* of truth; and
that in virtue of its indissoluble union with the Holy Ghost,
and of His perpetual teaching by its living voice'.[118] It could
not be otherwise. The perpetuity and indefectibility of the
Church were clearly revealed in Christ's promise that the
gates of hell should not prevail against it. 'This includes the
perpetuity and indefectibility of the Faith on which the Church
is built. If the superstructure be indefectible, much more the
foundation: and the union of the Faith with the Church is
therefore perpetual and indefectible. They are divinely united,
never to be divided.'[119]

The Holy Spirit speaks in the Church, and through the
Church, in a continuous office of teaching: 'the body of Christ
is the organ of His voice'.[120] Manning dwelt repeatedly on the
words of the apostles in the first of the Church's Councils:

'It hath seemed good to the Holy Ghost, and to us, to lay no further
burden upon you than these necessary things' (Acts 15: 28). What
words are these for men to speak! 'Who hath known the mind of
the Lord? or who hath been His counsellor?' (Rom. 11: 34) Who
can declare the mind of the Holy Ghost? This was their prerogative,
this was the endowment bestowed on the Church of God. It could
speak in the name of the Holy Ghost, because it could discern by
His light, and decree by His assistance.[121]

Manning saw in this the fulfilment of Isaiah's prophecy (Is. 59:
21), announcing God's new covenant with his people: ' "My
spirit that is in thee, and My word that I have put in thy
mouth, shall not depart out of thy mouth, nor out of the
mouth of thy seed, nor out of the mouth of thy seed's seed,
saith the Lord, from henceforth and for ever". That is, there
shall come a day when thou shalt have a teacher in the midst
of thee who shall not err, who cannot mislead, whom thou
shalt follow in safety.'[122]

Manning proceeded to add a point that for him was fundamental: the Holy Spirit exercises His teaching office in the

---

[118] *TM* 36.   [119] *CSer* i. 20.
[120] *TM* 73; see also ibid. 205, and *CSer* i. 18.
[121] *CSer* ii. 12. In 1871 he would say: 'The Church of Christ possesses the truth; it
possesses His mind, it knows it always' (*Fourfold*, 122).
[122] Ibid. 4.

Church not just on rare isolated occasions but uninterruptedly. He is actively present in its teaching, 'not only from council to council ... with an intermittent and broken utterance, but always, and at all times, by its continuous enunciation of the faith, as well as by its authoritative dogmatic decrees'.[123] The infallibility of the Church is not confined in its exercise to the dogmatic definitions of Popes and Councils, with long intermediate periods in which it remains dormant. In 1869, in his encyclical about the coming Council, he would return to this theme: 'through all those eighteen centuries its [the Church's] active infallibility has been, not intermittent but continuous, both in its Episcopate with its Head, and in its Head as Universal Pastor and Teacher, both of pastors and flock'.[124] God's providence reached both the natural and the supernatural world: 'as the preservation of the world is the work of creation by the same omnipotence perpetually produced, so the illumination of the Church is the perpetual fullness of His inspiration, which descended on it on the day of Pentecost'.[125] Pentecost, as he kept on repeating, is not an event of the past but the permanent state of the Church. The Holy Spirit is in the Church, and, through her, 'enunciates to this day the original [pentecostal] revelation with an articulate voice, which never varies or falters'.[126]

The office of the Holy Spirit as illuminator includes, according to Manning, several operations, the first of them being 'the original illumination of the Apostles, and through them of the whole Church throughout the ages'. Since then, he has preserved that which was revealed, assisting the Church at the same time 'to conceive, with greater fullness, explicitness, and clearness, the original truth in all its relations'.[127] Manning would also describe this process as the 'progressive unfolding of the inward sense and consciousness of the Church',[128] which was for her what the awakening consciousness of self and the world is for the individual human being. The Holy Spirit unfolds the mind of God in the Church.

This he does by 'freely and gently acting upon the intelligence of the mystical Body: not overbearing its operations,

---

[123] *TM* 36–37. [124] *Privilegium*, ii. 149. [125] *CSer* i. 237.
[126] *TM* 84. [127] Ibid. 83. [128] *CSer* i. 131.

but perfecting its perceptions and its powers ... until it had adequately apprehended and, with unerring precision, expressed [a particular truth]'. The Holy Spirit assists the mind of the Church—one continuous and universal intelligence embracing the whole Body of Christ in every age and land—'to penetrate, to analyze, to apprehend, to harmonize, and to define the doctrines of the original revelation.'[129]

The adequate enunciation of the truth perceived is of the utmost importance for the preservation and transmission of revealed truth. Therefore, the help of the Holy Spirit could not fail the Church in her effort to give verbal expression to divine truth; he assisted her 'in the choice, selection and consideration of the very words in which to express the doctrines of Faith'.[130] The Church would find it virtually impossible to teach the Faith or to judge on doctrinal matters if she were not able to express in suitable words her apprehension of revealed truth.

Manning could then speak of defined dogma as 'the true intellectual apprehension, and the true verbal expression of the truths and facts of the Divine Revelation'.[131] It is something precious to the Church: 'a new and profounder insight into the intelligence of God, an enlarged knowledge of "the things of God" '. To her, every dogma is 'a heavenly treasure, dear and priceless, living and giving life. ... Dogma has a sacramental power of its own.'[132] Manning, with this unusual expression, wanted to convey his old idea of truth's permanent power to conform man to the image of God, communicating to him God's life.

Manning defended the immutability of dogma as he defended the immutability of natural truth. He felt that both were under attack. In the *Temporal Mission* (1865), he described the main lines of what in later years would be known as Modernism, at the time making incursions into Protestant theology. It pretended to reform the old dogmatic teaching, alleging 'that the old dogmatic formulas were a true expression

---

[129] *CSer* i. 131–2.   [130] Ibid. 132; see also *TM* 230.

[131] *APUC* 20; see also *Fourfold*, 121–2.

[132] *CSer* i. 135–6. In a typical overstatement he added that '[e]ven the syllables of its sacred language shed abroad the illumination of truth, the motives of obedience, the fervour of devotion'.

of the rude and uncultured religious thought of the early Middle Ages: that the progress of the human intelligence in the matter of Christian thought demands a new expression; that this expression will not be dogmatic but "moral and spiritual"; that the nineteenth century has a theology of its own, which, if not already formed, is forming under intellectual and spiritual impulses, the momentum of which is irresistible'.[133] The old Catholic dogma, according to these people, would be a dead trunk hampering progress.

Manning did not understand those who saw dogma as an enemy of freedom, a constraint on the expansion of intellectual life. They thought that 'the human reason, by submitting itself to faith, becomes dwarfed; that faith interferes with the rights of reason; that it is a violation of its prerogatives, and a diminution of its perfection'.[134] He called that pure superstition. The opposite happens to be the case: 'The truth will make you free,' he liked to repeat. 'God sent His Son into the world, divided and distracted as it was by contentious teachers, that He might abolish all human usurpation over the reason of mankind, and redeemed it into a divine liberty of truth.'[135] Dogma does not set a limit to the expansion of the intellect; it is, rather, a barrier separating truth from the regions of error. Those who reject faith, the voice of the Holy Spirit, 'inevitably forfeit the divine freedom which our Lord has purchased for the human intellect through His most precious Blood: and forfeiting this divine freedom, they fall under the authority and into a bondage of human teachers'.[136]

It is also the Holy Spirit, he had written in 1855, 'who chooses the times and the seasons when such definitions [of faith] shall be made'.[137] With his assistance the Church is able to discern 'not only of the truth, but [also] of the opportunity of declaring it ... . We are sure that the "homoousion" is true, and that the fourth century was the opportunity divinely chosen for its declaration. We know with the certainty of faith that the Immaculate Conception is true, and we are certain that this time was the opportunity divinely chosen for its

---

[133] *TM* 242.   [134] *Four Evils*, 3.   [135] *CSer* ii. 246.
[136] *CSer* i. 232; see also *Fourfold*, 53.
[137] *CSer* i. 132.

definition. The event is proof.'[138] This principle would be at the forefront of Manning's mind during the First Vatican Council, when the opportuneness of the definition of papal infallibility was being discussed. At that time, even inopportunists like Moriarty could write: 'If it is the secret counsel of God that the infallibility should be defined, there must be not only truth in the definition, but also some great need of it which we do not foresee.'[139] Were papal infallibility to be defined, he wrote on another occasion, 'the opportuneness will then have ceased to be a question'.[140]

3. *The Church as the Interpreter of Holy Scripture*

Manning also dealt with a theme dear to him from the time of *The Rule of Faith* (1838) and *The Unity of the Church* (1842). Christianity was not dependent upon the Scriptures of the New Testament to be born; the Faith *was* before the Scriptures were written. It was derived from, and it still depends upon, 'the order of divine facts introduced into the world by the Incarnation; among which facts, one is the perpetual presence of a Divine Teacher among men'.[141] The Holy Spirit had taught the primitive Church the divine truth, and, when the writings of the New Testament were spread throughout the Church, Christians interpreted them in the light of the faith they had previously received. To affirm that Christianity is to be derived from the Bible, and that the dogma of faith is to be limited to what is written in it, is the same as saying 'that the Spirit is bound by the letter; and that in the place of a living and Divine Teacher, the Church has for its guide a written Book'.[142] Those who upheld this opinion impoverished the Church and reduced it to the condition of the Jewish people in the old dispensation: the Jews had a Book, but they were unable to discover in Christ the Messiah announced by the prophets; their present counterparts were unable to discover in the Church the active presence of the Holy Spirit. While Christ was among the Jews, he 'interpreted to them the sense, and con-

---

[138] *APUC* 51–2.

[139] Letter to Newman, 28 Apr. 1870, quoted by C. Butler, *The Vatican Council, 1869–1870* (London, 1962), 300.

[140] Letter to Newman, 14 May 1870, ibid. 320.

[141] *TM* 183.   [142] Ibid. 188.

firmed the authenticity of the Books of Moses and of the Prophets with a Divine witness'.[143] But the Jews appealed from
the living voice of a divine teacher to the letter. The same
error was still repeated in Manning's day. The Holy Spirit is
to the Scriptures of the New Testament what Jesus was to
those of the Old. Manning was fond of repeating: 'the letter
kills, the spirit vivifies'. The letter, without the Spirit to give it
its true interpretation, might be a hindrance rather than a
help to gaining access to truth.

Those who were left with only the 'letter' ignored a fundamental fact: revelation was originally recorded 'upon the
mind of the pastors, or the *Ecclesia docens*, the Church teaching
the world; and upon the mind of the flock or the *Ecclesia discens*,
the Church learning throughout the world'.[144] It was written
by the Holy Spirit, first and foremost, 'upon the intelligence
and heart of the living Church, and sustained in it by His presence'. Manning affirmed that the New Testament 'is a living
Scripture, namely, the Church itself'.[145] There inhabits the
Holy Spirit, the author and writer of all revealed truth, the
perpetual teacher of the world. And the New Testament 'in
spirit and in truth', is the revelation of the day of Pentecost.
'This is the original, of which the written Scripture is but a partial and subsequent transcript, ... pointing to the living and
Divine Teacher as the only guide into all truth'.[146]

The Scriptures, chronologically, were written after Christians had believed and lived the Faith for at least a generation:
'It was not till the faith had been everywhere preached, believed, defined in creeds, recorded in the mind of the universal
Church, embodied in sacraments, and manifested in its perpetual worship, that the New Testament was formed.'[147] 'We
neither derive our religion from the Scriptures, nor does it depend upon them. Our faith was in the world before the New
Testament was written.' Even more, 'Scripture itself depends
for its attestation upon the Witness who teaches us our faith,
and that Witness is Divine.'[148] Without the testimony of the
Church 'we should not have known that a revelation had ever
been given'. Thus, it does not make sense to believe in the

[143] Ibid. 185.   [144] Ibid. 191.   [145] Ibid. 190.
[146] Ibid. 195–6.   [147] Ibid. 193.   [148] Ibid. 181.

Scriptures while, at the same time, disbelieving the Church which delivers the Scriptures to us: 'it is the Church alone that testified to us the existence of Holy Scripture. We should not have known with divine certainty that sacred books had ever been written, much less their inspiration; or what inspiration is; or the number and names of the books ... or the reading and sense of the text—but for the supernatural witness and discernment of the Church.'[149]

The Church judges of the books, being divinely assisted to distinguish God's Word from human words. It follows that she is also the only one able to understand its message and judge of the right interpretation of the sacred books. She is 'the sole fountain of all judgments as to the faith ... It alone in the world knows the revelation of God, its contents and its limits; and therefore it alone can judge what truths are contained in it, what is accordant, what is discordant with it.'[150] The Church is the only one empowered to decide in the controversies about the faith, and its judgements 'are infallible and therefore final'.[151] Time did not erase from Manning's memory the lessons of the Gorham case.

In short, 'this science of God, incorporated in the Church [on the day of Pentecost], is the true key to the interpretation of Scripture'. And that science of God 'bore witness to the whole revelation of the day of Pentecost; it fixed the meaning of the Scriptures by the evidence of divine facts'.[152]

Among those divine facts determining the meaning of Scripture should be included the living Church. This introduces us to another important theme in Manning's thought. He maintained that the Church is 'not only the interpreter, but [also] the interpretation'[153] of the Scriptures. The Church's life declares and fixes the true interpretation of the sacred books. In 'its unity, universality, and authority, in its faith, sacraments, and action upon the world'[154] the Church proclaims the true meaning of Holy Scripture. The New Testament recognized and presupposed this order of divine truths and facts; they are 'the actual and the scientific key to their [the sacred books]

---

[149] *CSer* ii. 250.   [150] Ibid. 249.   [151] Ibid. 252.

[152] *TM* 196.

[153] *CSer* ii. 250; see also *TM* 200.

[154] *CSer* ii. 250.

true interpretation'.[155] Therefore, it makes no sense to proclaim, for example, that there are only two sacraments, no sacrifice, no real presence in the Eucharist, because there are not 'explicit' references to them in Holy Scripture. This might be argued from a purely scriptural point of view; but, leaving aside the argument, the life of the Church has expressed in words and in life its faith in the seven sacraments, the sacrificial character of the Mass, etc. The faith of the Church and her living reality were the true keys to the interpretation of the sacred books, and they are still the only ones able to unlock the meaning of Scripture.[156]

The Holy Spirit, Manning said, summarizing the argument, is 'the author and teacher of the whole revelation of Christianity, the guardian of the Sacred Books, and the interpreter of their sense: and the Church in all ages, one and undivided, is the perpetual organ of His voice'.[157] The Church diffused throughout the world, both pastors and people, were filled by a consciousness of this faith. 'And in the light of this consciousness the whole sense of Scripture, I do not say in all its contents, but in all that bears upon the faith and law of God, is instinctively clear to it.'[158]

What, then, of antiquity? Manning did not forget his Anglican background and experience; he wrote with his old co-religionists in mind, and with a clear apologetical end. As he saw it, the facts of antiquity were also 'transparent in the light of its [the Church's] perpetual consciousness of the original revelation'.[159] As a matter of fact, Manning affirmed, the Church 'has no antiquity. ... [It] is always primitive and always modern at one and the same time; and alone can expound its own mind, as an individual can declare his own thoughts.'[160] Manning's conclusion was a straightforward one: 'The enunciation of the faith by the living Church of this hour, is the maximum of evidence, both natural and supernatural, as to the *fact* and the *contents* of the original revelation.'[161] Thus, the Church's doctrine is incorrupt, as pure as on the day of Pentecost; incorruptible, because of the perpetual

---

[155] *TM* 198. [156] Cf. ibid. [157] Ibid. 205.
[158] Ibid. 201–2. [159] Ibid. 218. [160] Ibid. 239.
[161] Ibid. 214.

presence of the Holy Spirit; immutable, because it is incorruptible; and, therefore, primitive.

In *The Grounds of Faith*, Manning summarized his whole argument in two conclusions, which he repeated in his sermons
and in *The Temporal Mission of the Holy Ghost*: first, man has no
knowledge of the way of salvation except through the revelation of God; secondly, man can have no certainty about the
content of the revelation except through the Church. She is
'the organ by which the Holy Spirit speaks on Earth, and the
vessel in which the Heavenly light always burns in undimin-
ished splendour'.[162]

4. *Faith's Formal Object*

Manning affirmed that faith's first step is to believe God, who
reveals himself to us; a belief based on God's omniscience and
truthfulness. The 'formal object of faith [is] the veracity of
God revealing His Truth to us, and not only by an act of revelation eighteen hundred years ago, but also by sustaining His
revelation, whole and inviolate, in all its fullness and integrity,
through all times, and by proposing it to us by His Divine
voice in every age'.[163] God speaks now in the voice of the
Church. 'The ultimate authority, then, on which we believe,
is the voice of God speaking to us through the Church. We believe, not in the Church, but through it: and through the
Church, in God.'[164] He could therefore say: the 'voice of the
living Church of this hour, when it declares what God has revealed is no other than the voice of the Holy Ghost, and therefore generates divine faith in those who believe';[165] this is 'the
basis of divine certainty and the rule of divine faith'.[166] Faith
is not just belief in God and in a certain number of connected
truths, but rather believing God and believing the Church,
through which he speaks. Believing in the Church is a fundamental act of the virtue of faith; remove that foundation, and
there is faith no longer: 'When the Divine authority of the
Church manifests itself to our intellect, it lays its jurisdiction

---

[162] *CSer* i. 241.   [163] Ibid. 24.
[164] *Grounds*, 50; see also H. E. Manning, *The Internal Mission of the Holy Ghost* (9th
edn., London, n.d.), 74.
[165] *TM* 86–7; see also *Fourfold*, 52.
[166] *TM* 86.

upon our conscience to submit to it. To refuse is an act of infidelity, and the least act of infidelity in its measure expels faith; one mortal act of it will expel the habit of faith altogether.'[167]

He insisted time and time again on these ideas, which he considered of vital importance: our only access to God's revelation is in the Church and through the Church. The 'proposition of the Church is the test of the Revelation of God. ... We have no contact with the Revelation of God, except through the proposition of the Church. We are in contact with the Scriptures, because the Church proposes them to us as the written word of God; we are in contact with tradition, because the Church proposes tradition to us as the unwritten word of God. We are in contact with antiquity, because the Church proposes antiquity as its own past experience. Antiquity is no more than a period in the mind of the Church: for the mind of the Church is continuous'.[168] Without 'the perpetual and supernatural witness of the Church, how should we know, with divine certainty, the revelation given to man eighteen hundred years ago?'[169]

A denial of the infallibility of the Church implied denying the presence and action of the Holy Spirit in it: 'they who deny the infallibility of the Church, deny also the guidance of the Holy Spirit'. But that was not all. Manning considered that those who rejected the Church's infallibility did also 'either in part or in whole deny the office of the Third Person of the ever blessed Trinity'.[170] This amounted to a Trinitarian error. For Manning, the 'perpetuity of the dispensation of the Holy Spirit is shadowed forth in the mystery of the Holy Trinity'. And he thought that there were 'reasons in the analogy of faith, which, if express proof in words were wanting, would suffice' to define his role in the Church.[171] St Gregory Nazianzen had spoken of the Holy Spirit as 'the Perfecter'. Manning, quoting him, would write: the 'mystery of the Divine Trinity has its perfection in itself in the third and last Person of the ever blessed Three. So also in the outward operations of God.'[172] He saw that perfecting role of the Holy Spirit in the

[167] *Workings*, 16–17.   [168] *APUC* 46–7.   [169] *CSer* ii. 244–5.
[170] *CSer* i. 243; see also *TM* 23 and *Internal Mission*, 472.
[171] *CSer* i. 233.
[172] Ibid.; see also *Internal Mission*, 466–9.

work of creation; it was apparent in the Incarnation; and the same could be said of the work of redemption. 'What the Second Person began, the Third Person continued. ... He is come to take up and to carry on to the end of the world the dispensation of grace. The Perfecter is now in the world to finish the work of the kingdom of God.'[173] Faith in the Blessed Trinity, according to Manning, demands the right faith in the office of the Holy Spirit; and 'one direct and inseparable consequence [of that faith] is faith in the infallibility of the Church'.[174]

The Church claims authority to judge and to define matters of doctrine, and to impose those definitions on the faithful. She demands their assent to them as one having the power to bind men to believe. During the Vatican Council Manning prepared many notes, in his neat handwriting, on theological issues; these were intended either for his use or for the use of those who shared his outlook. In one of those notes, speaking of interior assent, he said that he did not want 'to dwell upon the obvious truth that interior assent can be required by no authority but that which is infallible'. This demand, he added, 'would be tyrannous and intolerable, slavish and corrupting, if the Church were not infallible'.[175] Only an authority which cannot err is entitled to demand interior assent: the obedience of reason and will. The Church's authority has its foundation in truth. It is truth 'that generates authority', Manning said, 'not authority that generates truth';[176] he 'that has the truth has power, and none other but he'.[177] Truth comes first, authority follows from it; 'for authority is truth convincing the intelligence with its light, and binding the will by those convictions, and by the authority of God which pervades them'.[178] And truth's power to command acceptance springs from man's calling to pursue it and make it his own. This is particularly so in the case of the highest truth about God and man, as contained in God's revelation. The Church

---

[173] *CSer* i. 234–5.   [174] Ibid. 231.

[175] Manning MSS Pitts, box 7, folder 7 (Vatican Council Documents, vol. 3). The State acts as if it were infallible. The analogy of the civil power, used by De Maistre, would justify the Church acting likewise; but Manning pointed out in the same paper that the analogy falls short of the reality of the Church when it comes to matters of doctrine. He thought that De Maistre had been misunderstood on this point.

[176] *CSer* ii. 249.   [177] Ibid. 248.   [178] Ibid. 249.

is in possession of the truth because it has the mind, the truth, of God, and having 'the truth of God [it] has also the power and authority of God'. Manning concluded by saying that the 'Church binds men to believe, because it is divinely guided to teach them what they are bound to believe'.[179] It is an imperative command, and, of its nature, lays a serious obligation on man. 'If indeed, God the Holy Ghost be in the midst of us, and if it be God the Holy Ghost Who speaks to us through the one Holy Catholic and Roman Church, then it imposes its doctrines on the consciences of men under pain of eternal death.'[180]

Already in 1854, in a letter written to Robert Wilberforce, Manning had made a confession of his faith in 'One God, one Spirit of Truth, one Church, one Theology, one Living Judge. *Authoritative* only because *divinely guided*.'[181] The infallibility of the Church was, for Manning, a matter of faith, but it was one for which he found abundant support in reason; it also bore the hallmark of experience.

5. *Infallibility in the Church and in its Various Members.*

The Mystical Body of Christ, Manning said, was anointed with the unction of the Holy Spirit, and the endowments of the Head became the endowments of the body. He added, however, that this outpouring of the Holy Spirit had descended upon the members of the Church 'in his own order and measure—upon the Pontiffs with a perpetual divine assistance; upon the Episcopate diffused throughout the world, sustaining it in the light of truth; upon the Church in its Councils, preserving it from all error; upon the faithful of every tongue, who cannot err in believing, because the Church cannot err in teaching'.[182] This meant that the Church possessed a twofold infallibility: 'the passive, whereby the whole body was pervaded by a luminous consciousness of the Revelation of God ... the active, whereby the Church, with unfaltering voice and the precision of a supernatural intelligence, propounds the dogma of faith and the law of morals in every land and in every age'.[183]

---

[179] Ibid. 248.   [180] Ibid. 23.
[181] Letter dated Holy Thursday, 1854, quoted in *P* ii. 41.
[182] *CSer* ii. 310.   [183] *CSer* i. 292.

Manning described in a terse sentence the source of the passive infallibility: the Church 'cannot err in believing; for God is its teacher'. The first act of faith is to believe God, an infallible teacher; the believer, searching for divine truth, cannot lose his way with that guide. The illumination of the day of Pentecost had pervaded the whole Church: the 'Bishop on his throne, the Doctor in the schools, the peasant in the fields, the little child at his mother's knee, all alike are illuminated and sustained by the passive infallibility which replenishes the whole mystical Body'.[184] This universal consciousness—passive infallibility—manifests itself in different ways: it is 'expressed in every form of word and witness, by liturgies and offices, by homilies and by feasts'.[185] The whole life of the Church—how the faithful express their faith in life and prayer, in celebration and worship—is a witness to her faith.

The Church also has a divine assistance when teaching the faith: that is, 'the gift of active infallibility which sustains the whole body of its pastors, whether spread throughout the world, or congregated in council; and also in an eminent way the person of the Vicar of Jesus Christ'.[186] The collective body of the pastors 'is the organ of the Holy Spirit of truth, and their voice is the active infallibility of the Church'.[187] Individuals—lay people and pastors—may err, but their error leaves no stain upon the mind of the Church, upon its belief or its teaching; the seeds of corruption cannot lodge and germinate in its faith. It could be said, paraphrasing Manning, that the Church cannot err in teaching because God is the teacher.

Manning made clear that the distinction between an active and a passive infallibility did not distribute the members of the Church into two groups: teachers and taught. All members of the Church are believers and are taught by the Church. The authoritative teachers of the faith are, in their turn, disciples: 'Jesus made His Apostles to be disciples before He sent them forth as Doctors. ... What He did for them, the Church does for us. *Doctores fidelium, Ecclesiae discipuli*. The doctors of the faithful are the disciples of the Church, because the unction which is upon it teaches them all things. ... They learn to be-

---

[184] *CSer* ii. 246.   [185] *CSer* i. 130.   [186] *CSer* ii. 247.
[187] *TM* 234.

lieve as the Church believes, and to teach as the Church teaches.'[188] 'The Church is the teacher of the pastors, as the pastors are the teachers of the flock.'[189] The pastors have to be taught by a divine teacher before they can teach others: 'The dogma of faith is infused into them by the light of the Church before they speak in its name; and the faithful, by their mouths, hear not the voice of an individual, but of the universal Church of all ages and of all lands.'[190] Manning seems to have had in mind Newman's *On Consulting the Faithful in Matters of Doctrine* when he added that individual pastors are not infallible, one by one, but that 'the Church which guides them is. They must be unfaithful to it before they can err; and even then "the ears of the faithful" would be, as of old, purer than the "lips of the priest". The instincts of a Catholic child would detect the novelties of human error.'[191]

In *The Temporal Mission of the Holy Ghost*, Manning described the organs through which the Holy Spirit speaks in the Church, 'the organs through which that infallibility is exercised'. He also 'noted the degrees of authority possessed by them, and the kind and degrees of assent required by the acts and words of the Church or of its members'.[192] The voice of the Holy Spirit can be heard, he wrote, in the Baptismal Creed, which 'represents at this day, in all the world, the preaching of the Apostles and the faith of Pentecost'; Holy Scripture—known to be such, and rightly understood—is also the voice of the Holy Spirit. We also hear him speak in the tradition found all over the world 'running up beyond Scripture and the General Councils'; in the decrees of the General Councils; in the definitions and decrees of the Roman pontiffs speaking *ex cathedra*; in the unanimous voice of the saints who 'in any matter of the Divine truth or law can hardly be believed to be other than the voice of the Spirit of God'.[193]

---

[188] *CSer* ii. 327–8. Manning frequently used the words of St Gregory quoted here; among other occasions, in his speech to the Council on 25 May 1870 (cf. *M* lii, col. 250A).
[189] *TM* 233–4.   [190] *CSer* ii. 247.   [191] Ibid.
[192] *TM* 93. Manning's enumeration of the organs of infallibility is little more than a summary of Cano's scheme of the theological sources, and their authority, as described in *De Locis Theologicis*.
[193] Ibid. 86–90.

'Consensus Sanctorum sensus Spiritus Sancti est.' In 1847, these words of Melchor Cano had set Manning on the path to becoming a Catholic. Now, in 1865, he qualified this principle by saying: 'though there is no revealed pledge of infallibility to the Saints as such, yet the consent of the Saints is a high test of what is the mind and illumination of the Spirit of Truth'.[194] The voice of the theologians or doctors also has a certain amount of weight and should be taken into consideration, although it does not generate or demand an act of divine faith. Something similar can be said of the Fathers of the Church, whom Manning mentioned surprisingly after the saints and doctors of the Church: 'The voice of the Fathers has weight as that of the saints and doctors, and also as witnesses to the faith in the ages in which they lived, and yet they cannot generate divine faith nor afford a divine certainty.'[195]

He rounded off the argument by saying that, if the relation between the Church and the Holy Spirit 'be absolute and indissoluble, then all its enunciations by Pontiffs, Councils, Traditions, Scriptures, and universal consent of the Church, are divine, and its voice also is divine, and identified with the voice of its Divine Head in heaven'.[196]

6. The Infallibility of the Pope

In 1847, Manning had confided to Laprimaudaye his belief in the Pope's role as focal point for the unity of the Church; he was the centre around which the episcopate found its unity: *Episcopatus unus est*. The concept had started then to take shape in his mind, although there were still many grey areas in and around it. The following years brought with them a strengthening of this conviction, leading him eventually to accept the supremacy of the Pope and his infallibility. We do not know when this actually happened. Although Manning maintained that infallibility was one of the endowments of the Church, he did not yet, in early 1851, have a definite concept of the primacy and infallibility of the Pope. His opinions, as described in his letter to Gladstone of 17 March of that year, seem to have had a certain 'Anglo-Gallican' flavour. He wrote: 'the highest *active* form [of evidence and decision] is the Church in council, countersigned by the reception of the Church diffused'.[197]

It may have been that his doubts on this matter were among those which baptismal grace clarified for him. In any case, either then or during his sojourn in Rome, for the purpose of study, he soon came to espouse the doctrine of papal infallibility. It found its way into his Southwark Cathedral lectures in 1852, barely a year after his conversion. If Manning's fourth volume of Anglican sermons had been a manifesto of his belief in the infallibility of the Church, *The Grounds of Faith* (1852) was a confession of his belief in the infallibility of the Roman Church: 'The teaching of the One, Holy, Universal Roman Church ... is to us the voice of God now, and the foundation of our faith.'[198] Manning acknowledged that the primacy of Rome had been denied from the beginning, but he felt that this fact, rather than telling against it, reinforced the argument in favour of its claim. 'Tell me', he said, 'that the waves have beaten upon the shore, and I tell you that the shore was there for the waves to beat upon.'[199] St Leo's words to the Council of Chalcedon—which he had already read in 1847—were a clear expression of awareness in Peter's successors of their role in the Church, one expressly acknowledged by the Fathers of the Council. No other Church, he would say, 'has claimed from the beginning, a divine primacy over all other Churches; has taught from the first with the claim to be heard as the Divine Teacher'.[200]

Manning was even clearer in his sermon to the First Synod of Westminster (1852). There he spoke to the assembled bishops of the heresies which had afflicted the Church in all times, and of how at certain moments they had penetrated 'into every place except that one to which denial of faith has never come'; and then, when the time was ripe, 'by Peter spoke the Divine Head, who gave to His Vicar upon earth the authority and power to speak'.[201] Christ had announced the storms which would be unleashed against the Church; he had promised that they would break upon the rock of Peter, which would withstand them all.

[197] Manning MSS Pitts, box 1, folder 9.
[198] *Grounds*, 60.   [199] Ibid. 53.   [200] Ibid. 61.
[201] *CSer* i. 99.

The sermons preached in the years following his return from Rome developed further the theme of the infallibility of the Pope and its relationship to the infallibility of the Church. The Supreme Pontiff, he told the Second Synod of Westminster (1855), is 'the pillar of supernatural illumination; the immovable centre of universal tradition; the Heir of the promise, "I have prayed for thee that thy faith fail not" '.[202] The recent definition of the dogma of the Immaculate Conception was a clear manifestation of this: 'The Church, through its Visible Head has spoken, but the utterance', he said, 'is the voice of the Spirit of God';[203] the Holy Spirit had promulgated the definition. Peter had been the organ of the Holy Spirit on Pentecost Day, and he had never ceased to be such. The voice of the Church was the voice of the Holy Spirit, and Peter's voice was the voice of the Church. The whole Church 'spoke through the lips of the Vicar of Jesus Christ, when but the other day he defined to the world by his infallible voice the Immaculate Conception of the Mother of God'.[204] Years later, he would be even more specific: the whole Church acts when the Pope acts, 'for it is all contained in him, and where the Head acts, all act with him'.[205]

Manning defined more clearly the relationship between the infallibility of the Roman Pontiff and the infallibility of the rest of the Church in his sermons around 1860. He thought that the 'endowments of the body are [also] the prerogatives of the Head', and they are in it in a pre-eminent way: 'the illumination which is diffused throughout the whole body of the Church resides eminently in the Episcopate, but resides preeminently and above all in the chief of Bishops, the Pastor of pastors, the Vicar of the Incarnate Word Himself'.[206] These

---

[202] *CSer* i. 131. Manning, at this time, seems to have made a clear distinction between what he considered as part of revealed truth and what was to be demanded as part of Catholic faith. In a letter to Miss Stanley, 27 Nov. 1854, answering some of the objections suggested to her by Gladstone, Manning asserted that it was 'no point of Faith that the Popes even speaking *ex cathedra* are infallible' (Manning MSS Bod., c. 661, fo. 85). Mary Stanley was considering the possibility of becoming a Catholic, and maintained a correspondence with Gladstone and Manning. Manning tried to answer the objections raised by Gladstone, who argued the case against conversion. She became a Catholic in 1856.

[203] *CSer* i. 133.   [204] *CSer* ii. 18–19.   [205] *CSer* iii. 85–86.
[206] *CSer* ii. 19.

prerogatives are not only pre-eminently in the head, they flow from it to the whole Church. Peter is the Rock, 'from whose foot these living sources of the manifold perfections of the Church pour forth their streams'.[207] In 1861, in a letter to Talbot, he spoke of the infallibility of the Pope 'as the only true and perfect form of the Infallibility of the Church'.[208] The infallibility of the Pope is the only perfect infallibility on earth, because it depends only on that of the divine Head of the Church in heaven. The infallibility of the Bishops, on the other hand, teaching or not in Council, and that of the rest of the believers, depends on the infallibility of the Pope.

Only in 1867, in his pastoral about the forthcoming Council, did Manning explain at greater length these expressions. He wrote:

The formation of the Church is traced in the order of the Baptismal Creed. God sent His Son into the world to be made man. The Incarnate Word, in Whom were hid all the treasures of wisdom and knowledge, became the fountain of grace and truth, of doctrine, and of jurisdiction, to the world. To the chief of His Apostles He conveyed by the Holy Ghost all His communicable prerogatives, and thereby constituted him His vicar upon earth. Peter became the head and guide, the fountain of doctrine and jurisdiction, to the Apostles. The Church sprang from him, and was formed, as St Cyprian says, like the seamless robe of our Lord, from the top throughout ... The organisation of the Church was unfolded from the plenitude of its head. The prerogatives of stability, perpetuity, and indefectibility in the head became endowments of the body united to him. But they existed in Peter before they were communicated to the Church, and before the Church was organised to which they were to be communicated.[209]

Thus, the supernatural gift of infallibility 'resides first in its [the Church's] head, next in the whole episcopate united with him ... [The] fountain of infallible teaching is the Divine Head in

---

[207] *CSer* i. 305–6.

[208] Letter dated 5 Aug. 1861, quoted in *P* ii. 160. The letter was written at a time when Manning's book on the temporal power of the Pope was being criticized in Rome; he was not unduly worried by the criticism, he wrote: 'The one truth which has saved me is the infallibility of the Vicar of Jesus Christ, as the only true and perfect form of the infallibility of the Church, and therefore of all divine faith, unity, and obedience.'

[209] *Privilegium*, i. 22–3.

heaven, through the organ of the visible head of the Church on
earth ... the prayer of the Divine Head of the Church sustains
the faith of Peter. ... The Faith of Peter is, by a Divine assistance, perpetual in the Church; and is therefore, by its intrinsic
stability, indefectible and infallible.'[210]

Among contemporary theologians, the Jesuit Clement
Schrader, professor at the Roman College and at Vienna, is
perhaps the one who makes this point most clearly.[211] Manning was familiar with his work, and they worked together
very closely during the First Vatican Council. It is difficult to
say with any degree of certainty, however, whether Manning
borrowed the idea from him. Whatever the case may be, it fits
well with his conception, as developed in the fourth volume of
Anglican sermons, of the Church as the Mystical Body of
Christ, where all its prerogatives flow down from the Head,
Christ, to the body. Analogically, the Pope, as the visible head
of the visible Church, has a somewhat similar relation to it.

He expressed these ideas in *The Temporal Mission*. The
Roman Pontiffs, as vicars of Christ, Manning wrote there,
have a 'twofold relation, the one to the Divine Head of the
Church of whom they are representatives on earth, the other
to the whole body. And these two relations impart a special
prerogative of grace to him that bears them.'[212] Manning considered the infallibility of the Pope from that double standpoint: 'The Vicar of Jesus Christ', he wrote, 'would bear no
proportion to the body if, while it is infallible, he were not. He
would also bear no representative character if he were the fallible witness of an infallible Head.'[213]

The infallibility of the Roman Pontiff is the foundation of
the unique prerogatives of the Church of Rome. She is the
only particular Church which cannot err, and her faith has always been considered as the standard to which all other par-

---

[210]   Privilegium, i. 23–5.
[211]   See e.g. his *De Unitate Romana* (Friburgi Brisgovia, 1862), 337 ff. Other authors
who propounded similar ideas were Capellare, Perrone, and Liberatore, the German
canonist Philips, etc. The Preparatory Theological Commission of the Council put
forward similar ideas (cf. *M* xlix, col 673BC). It included among its members theologians like Perrone, Franzelin, Hettinger, Schrader and Guidi. Manning's library contained a large number of treatises on the Pope's primacy and infallibility, among
them, most of the authors he quotes in his pastorals.
[212]   *TM* 88–9.   [213]   Ibid. 89.

ticular Churches should conform, the test of orthodoxy. 'What is the sense of all this', Manning asked, 'but that the indefectibility and infallibility of the Pontiff, by a singular privilege, pervades the Church of which he is pastor?'[214] But it is important not to forget that 'the prerogative of Peter is the cause, the fidelity of the Roman Church the effect'.[215]

Manning's insistence on the need for the definition of papal infallibility was based on this fundamental conviction that the Church receives its infallibility through the Pope. A denial of his infallibility would leave the infallibility of the Church under a cloud, and, deprived of its foundation, it would soon be called into doubt. This he defended in his speech to the Council on 25 May 1870. Mgr. Gasser, in his speech to the Council on behalf of the deputation *De Fide*, criticized this theory in rather strong terms: it had saddened him, he said, to hear some Council Fathers speak in those terms.[216] Manning, however, did not seem to be moved by Gasser's arguments, and, in his Pastoral explaining the Council decrees, he said that the definition did 'not decide the question whether the infallibility of the Church is derived from him or through him. But it does decide that his infallibility is not derived from the Church, nor through the Church. The former question is left untouched.'[217] There seems to be little doubt that Manning, after the Council, continued to hold his previous ideas on the relationship of the Pope's infallibility to that of the Church, although he acknowledged that this was an open question.

The Pope's *ex cathedra* definitions were infallible. As for the object of his infallibility, Manning thought that it extended 'to the whole matter of revelation, that is, to the Divine truth and the Divine law, and to all those facts or truths which are in contact with faith and morals';[218] that would include truths of the natural order in spheres like ethics, philosophy, and politics. The definition of the object area covered by the Church's infallibility was one of the main subjects under discussion before, during, and after the Council.

[214] *Privilegium*, i. 26; see also *Privilegium*, ii. 148.
[215] *Privilegium*, i. 28. Manning's words addressed the contemporary controversy about whether infallibility resides in the *Sede* or in the *Sedente*.
[216] Cf. *M* lii, col. 1214CD.
[217] *Privilegium*, iii. 90.   [218] *TM* 89.

IV
Rationalism, Protestantism, and the Church of England

A. Rationalism and Protestantism

1. *Faith or Rationalism*

Manning's idea of the Church included, as an integral part of it, a clear conception of the access of man to revealed truth. He had already described it in *The Grounds of Faith* (1852). Now, in the introduction to *The Temporal Mission of the Holy Ghost* (1865), he plainly described how he viewed the alternative before man when confronted with God's revelation. As he put it: 'my object in the following pages is to show that the reason of man has no choice but to be either the disciple or the critic of the revelation of God'.[1] He also wanted to demonstrate that faith does not detract from the perfection of human reason; on the contrary, faith perfects and elevates reason. He numbered the theses he wanted to prove:

1 That to believe in revelation is the highest act of the human reason.

2 That to believe in revelation, whole and perfect, is the perfection of the reason.

3 That to submit to the voice of the Holy Spirit in the Church is the absolute condition to attain a perfect knowledge of revelation.

4 That the Divine witness of the Holy Spirit in the Church anticipates the criticism of the human reason, and refuses to be subject to it.[2]

He considered that to denounce the doctrinal authority of the Church as tyranny would be 'as unreasonable [as] to talk of the tyranny of science and the bondage of numbers'.[3] It is 'no bondage', he would say, 'to know the truth, and no freedom

---

[1] *TM* 3; see also *Fourfold*, 5.   [2] *TM* 9.   [3] *CSer* ii. 249

to be in doubt'.[4] The very nature of revelation presupposes the submission of the intellect to a teaching authority. 'The revelation of faith is no discovery which the reason of man has made for himself by induction, or by deduction, or by analysis, or by synthesis, or by logical process, or by experimental chemistry. The revelation of faith is a discovery of itself by the Divine Reason, the unveiling of the Divine Intelligence, and the illumination flowing from it cast upon the intelligence of man.' If that is the case, how 'can the illumination of the faith diminish the stature of the human reason? How can its rights be interfered with? How can its prerogatives be violated? Is not the truth the very reverse of all this? Is it not the fact that the human reason is perfected and elevated above itself by the illumination of faith?'[5] Reason is raised to the most pure and perfect knowledge of God, the most perfect knowledge of the nature of man, and of the most elevated morality.

Man's intellect cannot be the judge but only the disciple of revelation. Reason's role, as a judge, is confined to 'estimating the motives of credibility', judging of the evidence in support of Christianity as a divine revelation. 'This process of reason is the preamble of faith. Once illuminated, the reason of man becomes the disciple of a Divine Teacher.'[6] Moreover, when taught by the Holy Spirit, the 'highest discursive powers of the reason are developed by revelation, which elevates it from the contemplation of the first principles and axioms of truth in the natural order to a higher and wider sphere, unattainable by the reason without faith'.[7] Man's only access to supernatural truth is through God's revelation. After the event, Manning would say, he still needs a divine teacher to understand the revelation properly and to avoid corrupting it.

As far as the interpretation of revealed truth was concerned, there were only two possible answers to the *Quo judice?* question: 'the individual proceeding by critical reason, or the Church proceeding by a perpetual Divine assistance'.[8] Man may receive the knowledge of God either from an infallible divine teacher or from a fallible human one. The first leads to

---

[4] *APUC* 22.
[5] *Four Evils*, 4; see also *Fourfold*, 13–16.
[6] *TM* 94.   [7] Ibid. 122.
[8] Ibid. 30; see also *Fourfold*, 12.

the true knowledge of God, the second—as he had pointed out many a time in the past—to rationalism, subjectivism, and indifferentism.

Manning's discovery of the indissoluble union of the Holy Spirit with the Church had made him see 'at once that the interpretations or doctrines of the living Church are true because Divine, and that the voice of the living Church in all ages is the sole rule of faith, and infallible, because it is the voice of a Divine Person. I then saw that all appeals to Scripture alone, or to Scripture and antiquity, whether by individuals or by local Churches, are no more than appeals from the Divine voice of the living Church, and therefore essentially rationalistic.'[9] Human reason becomes then the one and supreme judge; the 'Private Judgment of individuals exercised critically upon history, philosophy, theology, Scripture, and revelation ... is ultimately all that remains to those who reject the infallibility of the living Church.'[10]

2. *The Reformation: Development and Forms of Rationalism*

The history of the Christian faith has been punctuated by a long series of heresies. There is no doctrine or article of the Creed which has not been controverted in the nineteen centuries of Christianity. The denial of the divinity of our Lord was followed by the rejection of the divinity of the Holy Spirit; then came errors about the sacraments, and many others. Manning saw the progress of heresy moving gradually through the doctrines confessed in the Creed. In his time, heresy had come in turn to assail one of the Creed's last articles: the visible Church's existence, and its divine authority. This error had its roots in the Reformation. Its substance was to be found not in the denial of particular doctrines—like transubstantiation, purgatory, indulgences, and the like—but in a much more fundamental principle: the denial of the true rule of faith, the formal rejection of the divine voice speaking perpetually in the Church. What 'is the chief and master heresy of the last three hundred years, but a denial of the perpetual office of the Holy Ghost[?]'[11] That was also true of the Anglican Reformation. It had as its confessed aim to impugn certain doctrines,

---

[9] *TM* 29.   [10] Ibid. 91–2.   [11] *CSer* i. 137.

or corruptions, introduced into the purity of the primitive faith by the Church of Rome. In fact, Manning wrote, it 'consists formally in the rejection of the Divine voice of the Church—in effacing from the minds of the English people the whole idea of a visible and divinely endowed Church, with supernatural offices'.[12]

Private judgement gave birth to the Reformation; since then, it has gone on to generate schism after schism. Manning described the causes of that process succinctly: 'Each Protestant church, as it was established, contained within itself the principle both of its creation and dissolution, namely, private judgement.'[13] Private judgement had set in motion the ongoing process of division and subdivision among the Reformers, adding continually to the ever-increasing number of Protestant sects.

The rejection of the rule of faith was also the root from which rationalism grew: the 'first cause of Rationalism ... was the rejection of the Divine authority of the Church of Jesus Christ three hundred years ago'.[14] The perpetual teaching office of the Holy Spirit in and through the Church is for Manning the foundation of truth and certainty, the guarantee of the preservation of the original revelation and of its transmission in all its integrity. He expressed it in a clear formula: 'The one fountain of truth is God; the only sure channel of truth is His Church, through which God speaks still.'[15] Thus, the rejection of the infallibility of the Church by the Protestant Reformation had set its followers on an inclined plane towards rationalism; a plane 'on which, if individuals may stand, generations cannot'.[16] Protestantism resolved itself in time into rationalism 'by a law of production so legitimate, by an intellectual law so certain, that, I think, any one who would give himself sufficient time and apply sufficient industry to follow the history of unbelief in the last three hundred years would see it to demonstration'.[17]

Manning described, in general lines, the steps of the progress from private judgement to rationalism. As he saw it, the conclusion followed necessarily from the premises set by the

---

[12] Ibid. 34. [13] *Grounds*, 2–3. [14] *Four Evils*, 14.
[15] *Grounds*, 79. [16] *Workings*, 27. [17] *Four Evils*, 14.

Reformation. Once the presence of a divine teacher upon earth was denied, this led at once to a rejection of the supernatural character and office of the Church, and subjected all doctrines to the examination and criticism of man. There were few alternatives open to the Reformers: either to admit that the Holy Spirit taught individuals one by one or to accept that human reason is left to its own devices in pursuing the truth of revelation. The first proposition was soon found theoretically untenable, and practice made its unsoundness even more apparent. It was obvious that revelation had not been made to men individually, and that it did not spring up by inspiration in the inward consciousness. Unaided human reason was the only access to revealed truth still open: 'The rejection of the Divine authority', wrote Manning, 'necessarily throws men upon the only alternative—human criticism applied to Scripture, to antiquity, to Fathers, to history, to Councils, and to the acts of the Holy See.'[18] It could not be otherwise, for they 'who do not rest upon the divine office of the Church rest on history alone'.[19] And the historical sources of Christianity were to be found in Holy Scripture, inspired by God, and in the works of the early Christian writers, witnesses of the primitive faith.

Men went on to examine the human evidence upon which the doctrines of Christianity reposed. Thus, Manning wrote, they 'began to apply human reason to criticise, to test, to measure the credibility, both extrinsic and intrinsic, of every article of the Faith. I say, first, the extrinsic credibility; that is, whether it could be historically proved that this or that doctrine was believed in the beginning and has been believed ever since: secondly, the intrinsic credibility; that is to say, whether this or that doctrine was in itself reconcilable with the human reason.'[20] Human reason, working out by itself what was credible and probable, could not fail to downgrade revelation to a mere human level, and to produce a variety of interpretations, constantly eroding the common ground held by 'believers', and, therefore, ever enlarging the constituency of doubt and uncertainty in matters of faith. To reject the living voice of the Spirit in the Church meant that 'all things would be in a

[18] *Four Evils*, 18; see also *TM* 91–2.
[19] *Grounds*, 23.   [20] *Four Evils*, 15.

perpetual flux of mutation and uncertainty; so that for three hundred years the amount of Christianity that has been believed on this human and critical basis has been perpetually diminishing, and the residuum which is left upon that foundation now is incalculably less than that with which men started three hundred years ago'.[21]

The Reformation, according to Manning, had originally broken the union between the Spirit and God's word, that which God had joined by an inseparable bond. Once the Reformers had rejected the guidance of the Spirit, it followed next that 'the word departed from their lips. They clutched at it with jealousy, and they found in their hands the written word alone: *Litera occidit, spiritus autem vivificat* (2 Cor. 3: 6). The letter that killeth was left behind, the spirit that giveth life departed. The word was interpreted no more by the light of the Holy Ghost, no more by an infallible Guide, but by the interpretations of man and the light of the human intellect.'[22]

The Anglican Reformation offered a clear example of what was to follow. 'The reformers of the Church of England took for the basis of their religion, not the perpetual and infallible teaching of the Spirit of Jesus in His Church, but the Bible. A written book was erected in the place of the living Teacher, so as to exclude His supreme living voice. Anglican Christianity was to be based upon the Bible.'[23] Unfortunately, that foundation, Manning contended, 'Anglicans have ruined under their own feet'.[24] The Scriptures, separated from the Church, which is their custodian and interpreter, became lost in a maze of contradictory interpretations. And he quoted St Jerome's words in support of the principle that the Gospel consists not in the words of Scripture but in the sense; when the sense is misinterpreted, then the words of the Sacred Books become mere human words: 'When the right sense is lost, the Scripture is lost.'[25] As history had shown, 'when the interpretation goes, faith in the inspiration of Scripture speedily follows. The course

---

[21] Ibid. 16.

[22] *CSer* ii. 27. Manning contended that the 'transmission of truth in the world is not by books, but by men; not by parchments and rolls, but by living intelligences and wills formed by the Spirit of God. Written records and formularies of faith are of little avail when the living teachers are in error, or contradict each other' (ibid. 131).

[23] Ibid. 191–2.   [24] Ibid. 192.   [25] *TM* 205.

of Biblical criticism, both in Germany and in England, shows that men do not long believe in the divine inspiration of books which are rendered incredible by misinterpretation.'[26] The paradox of Anglicanism, and of Protestantism of every shade, was that those who had claimed to be most scriptural ended up being the most unscriptural: 'the system which founded itself upon the claim to be essentially and above all Scriptural, is ending in denying the inspiration and authenticity of Holy Scripture'.[27] And Manning would quote the authors of *Essays and Reviews*, and Dr Colenso's works, as samples of those who, encouraged by German criticism, were already moving in that direction. This was still far from being the general spirit of the Anglican Church, but the seeds had been planted in the Reformation, and they could not but grow in time to full stature.

In time, those false premises led necessarily to the destruction of Christianity altogether. The divine authority of the Church, according to Manning, keeps the human mind from converting faith into the subjective imaginations of the individual reason. Remove the check of the Church, and religious belief becomes

a kind of waking dream. For what is dreaming but the perpetuity of human thought running on unchecked by waking consciousness, which pins us down to order and rule by fact and by reality? ... In like manner, the visible Church, with its rule of faith, its authoritative teaching, its order, its discipline, its worship, is that outer world in which we move. It keeps the spiritual mind in limit and in measure. Dissolve it, and the mind weaves on in its own fancies, throwing off heresies, eccentricities, and falsehood.[28]

This is what the *Syllabus of Errors* had tried to correct by condemning, in propositions 3 and 4, the opinions of those who saw human reason as the sole and sufficient judge of truth and falsehood, and as the source of all the truths of religion.

Manning acknowledged that rationalism was not a single uniform phenomenon. Under its name were gathered a variety of intellectual approaches to reality, closely related, yet distinct. For the sake of clarity he would distribute them into two main groups: 'those who reject all revelation and those

[26] *TM* 206–7.   [27] Ibid. 207.   [28] *Grounds*, 80–1.

who profess to receive it'.[29] He called the first 'fully-developed'
or 'absolute' rationalism; he referred to the second as 'imperfect', 'moderate' or 'incipient' rationalism. The perfect, or
fully developed, rationalist accepts the existence of God, that
being forced upon him by nature. 'But, while these men believe
in a God of nature, nevertheless they reject the revelation
which He has given them of Himself.'[30] Their thought 'is
founded upon the assumption that the reason is the sole *fountain*
of all knowledge relating to God and to the soul, and to the relations of God and of the soul'.[31] The system was provided
with a safety-valve: the collective reason of the human race
would serve as a corrective to the excesses of the individual
reason. In summary, 'reason is therefore the *source* and the *measure* or the *limit* of what is credible in the theology of rational religion. This, necessarily, excludes all supernatural
revelation.'[32]

Moderate rationalism, on the other hand, while retaining a
belief in God's revelation to man, rests 'upon the assumption
that the reason is the supreme *test* or *judge* of the intrinsic credibility of revelation admitted in the main to be supernatural'.[33]
It admits its existence, 'but it constitutes the reason as the
judge by critical inquiry of the contents of that revelation, of
the interpretation of Scripture, and of the witness of antiquity'.[34] Moderate rationalism professes belief in revelation,
but 'only so much as, upon private criticism and its own judgment, the individual mind is disposed to retain'.[35] Moderate
and absolute rationalism shared a common origin, the rejection
of the divine voice of the Church; they also tended to a common end, a purely natural religion or vague deism. Manning
maintained, as we have already seen, that 'the human reason
can only stand related to the revelation of God, either as a
critic, or as a disciple in the presence of a Divine Teacher'.[36]
There is no middle ground between those two points where
man's reason can take its stand. 'In both [absolute and moderate rationalism] the reason is the critic of revelation. In the latter, it rejects portions of revealed truth as intrinsically

---

[29] *TM* 6.   [30] *Four Evils*, 13–14.   [31] *TM* 7.
[32] Ibid.   [33] Ibid. 8.   [34] Ibid. 9.
[35] *Four Evils*, 20–1.   [36] Ibid. 21.

incredible; in the former, it rejects revelation as a whole for the same reason.'[37] Reason, here, is no longer a disciple; it has become a judge.

Manning considered that only 'the inconsequence of those who hold this system [moderate rationalism] arrests it from resolving itself into its ultimate form of perfect Rationalism'.[38] These people no longer have faith, because they reject the divine authority teaching in the Church, the source and foundation of faith. And Manning added, he who 'shall believe all the articles of faith, and yet reject one of them, in that rejection rejects the whole Divine authority upon which all the articles of the faith alike depend'.[39] He might accept a divine text, but the interpretation was human, reason being the test and measure of what was to be believed.

How long could moderate rationalism hold its ground before reaching the stage of fully-developed rationalism? Manning thought that it was just a matter of time. 'Protestantism is running its natural career. ... Its incoherences, contradictions, internal repulsions, endless contentions, are doing their work with an unrelenting certainty. The Reformation is devouring itself, and all its many forms of contradiction are resolving themselves into Rationalism and simple unbelief.'[40]

The 'real ultimate question between the Catholic Church and all [the] Christian bodies separated from it', Manning thought, 'is not one of detail but of principle. It is not a controversy about indulgences, or purgatory, or invocations and the like, but of the divine tradition of dogma, its certainty and its purity'.[41] The Catholic Church confesses the perpetual presence of the Holy Spirit teaching the Faith, in and through the Church, and preserving revelation from corruption. The rejection of the Church as the channel of the Holy Spirit's teaching action in the world was for him the fountain and source of all heresy and, ultimately, of indifferentism: 'men have come first to deny, and then to disbelieve the existence in the world of a foundation, divinely laid, upon which revealed truth can certainly rest'.[42] The denial of the office of the Holy Spirit in the Church led to the loss of the rule of faith, and

---

[37] *TM* 8.   [38] Ibid.   [39] *Four Evils*, 22.
[40] *CSer* i. 380.   [41] *TM* 226.   [42] *Grounds*, 22.

this, in its turn, opened the door to 'the denial of the foundation of certainty in faith'. Once the principle of certainty had been removed, 'certainty was broken up, and the principle of uncertainty introduced'.[43] Protestantism had torn itself from the source of certainty, and this was followed in due course, as the logical conclusion of its generative principle, by the loss of belief in the objectivity of truth: 'To deny that there exists for the faith any higher than human authority, is to destroy the objectivity of truth.'[44] And the rejection of the divine voice speaking in the Church had 'let in the flood of opinion, and opinion has generated scepticism, and scepticism has brought on contentions without an end'.[45] It could not be otherwise: if the 'office of the Church to decide questions of faith has been suspended, then the world at this hour has no teacher'. There is no longer a divine teacher upon earth, and 'there exists no judge on earth to say who has the truth in this dispute'.[46] Or, rather, each individual is constituted supreme judge, from whom there can be no appeal. Man had been left at the mercy of rival human teachers, and with them came contradiction, with contradiction uncertainty, and with uncertainty doubt.

B. MANNING'S CATHOLIC VIEW OF THE CHURCH OF ENGLAND

Manning was rather reluctant, after his conversion, to launch into an open attack on the Anglican Church; he did not want to be involved in controversy. He conceived the role of the Catholic Church in England as one of building up the whole edifice of revealed truth, restoring and completing the structure of partial truth still standing in the Anglican Church. It should not be a work of demolition. He was loath to contribute to the internal divisions already existing and multiplying within the Church of England. For him, it was a matter of personal feeling and also of charity

The Anglicanism of the Reformation is upon the rocks, like some tall ship stranded upon the shore, and going to pieces by its own

---

[43] Ibid.   [44] Ibid. 79.   [45] *TM* 225.
[46] *Grounds*, 68.

weight and the steady action of the sea. We have no need of playing the wreckers. It would be inhumanity to do so. God knows that the desires and prayers of Catholics are ever ascending that all which remains of Christianity in England may be preserved, unfolded, and perfected into the whole circle of revealed truths and the unmutilated revelation of the faith.[47]

Still, the circumstances of the times, and the whole bent of his thought, forced him to speak frequently, sometimes even harshly, about the Anglican Church.

1. *Anglicanism's Progress*

Manning did not draw a distinguishing line between Protestantism and Anglicanism: they had been generated by a common principle, and had developed along common lines. The vast majority of Anglicans, while disagreeing in almost every other aspect, found common ground in opposing the idea of an infallible teaching Church as 'a human superstition or a spiritual tyranny'.[48] To his mind, the 'master heresy of the English race is to deny the presence of any infallible authority upon earth'.[49]

It had taken many generations to unfold the full consequences of the original error. The process had gone further and faster in Germany. Manning thought that only a divine intervention had prevented the Anglican Church from going that far: 'That which in Germany produced pure Rationalism, in England, but for the interposition of God, would have produced the same general disbelief of Christianity.'[50] However, the course of the Anglican Church was a downward one; error grew larger all the time, while truth disappeared. 'Every error which has sprung up in it adheres to it still. Its doctrines vanish, its heresies abide. All its morbid humours are absorbed into its blood. The Lutheranism of Edward the Sixth; the Hierarchical Calvinism of Elizabeth; the Ceremonial Arminianism of James; the Episcopalian Antiquarianism of the two Charleses; the Latitudinarianism of William the Third ... all coexist ... together, in open contradiction, and almost perpetual controversy.'[51] This was the inevitable consequence of the Angli-

---

[47] *TM* 225–6; see also *Grounds*, 13.
[48] *CSer* i. 41.   [49] Ibid. 56.   [50] *Grounds*, 88.
[51] *CSer* i. 57.

can schism, 'because separation from the Holy See is separation from the Universal Church, and to be separated from the Church is to be deprived of its divine guidance and support';[52] that is, the presence and assistance of the Holy Spirit. Truth, like a body deserted by the soul or like a branch detached from the vine, then began its long process of decomposition within the Anglican Church. There was no provision in it to arrest that process. The Church of England did not pronounce judgement among its factions, and there was not within it any infallible authority or test of certainty to be applied in order to discern truth from error. All the different and contradictory schools which made up the Church of England were in it by right. 'It would be untrue', Manning maintained, 'to represent any one of these schools of error as the legitimate voice or exponent of the Anglican Church. They are all equally so, and all equally not so. They each claim so to be, and deny the legitimacy of all the rest.'[53]

There had been, though, a reaction against that downward trend of faith within the Anglican Church, and that effort to recover the foundations of faith had begun with the rejection of the principle of private judgement. Manning traced the origins of that theological school to the Elizabethan period. It had 'sprung up within the Established Church, basing itself upon Catholic tradition, and claiming to found its faith not upon private judgement, but upon the rule of Vincent of Lerins, namely, on that which was believed "at all times, every where, and by all men".'[54] Its adherents had conducted a courageous campaign to recover the lost inheritance of Catholic truth, and to defend that under attack. A measure of their success was that they had created the illusion that the Anglican Church was still part of the great Catholic family. Unfortunately, they were only a school, and a small one at that, within the Anglican Church. However, Manning acknowledged that they had performed a providential service in slowing down the decline towards rationalism within the Church of England.

There is, in Manning's thought and writings during the 1860s, a progressive recognition of the providential character of this movement towards Catholic faith and worship. He saw

---

[52] Ibid. 25–6.   [53] Ibid. 57.   [54] *Grounds*, 41–2.

it as the work of the Holy Spirit, 'drawing men, step by step, out of the illusions and falsehoods of the Anglican separation into the unity of the only Church'.[55] Manning, like Newman, considered that the internal logic of the Tractarian Movement, as intended by the Holy Spirit, led to Rome. However, Manning was quick to add, it was a movement of men, not of the Anglican Church. The Holy Spirit was 'preparing the hearts of men beforehand for the advance of His Church',[56] by restoring 'the line of continuity between the intelligence of the English people and the intelligence of the universal Church'.[57] This had been broken at the Reformation, and it was now providentially re-established by the introduction of Catholic doctrines and practices within the Anglican Church. Truths and practices, long before forgotten or neglected, were now preached and defended, though not yet fully expressed and believed, by a numerous body within the Church of England.

Unfortunately, that return towards the fullness of truth was not general within Anglicanism. The hold of faith over the people of England had grown continually weaker: the 'masses are moving away'. To this negative diagnosis, Manning added a note of cautious optimism: 'individuals in great numbers are returning towards the light'.[58] He did not think that this signalled a recovery for the Church of England; it worked in a different direction. The heirs of the Oxford Movement were trying to cure the wounds that the Anglican Church itself was opening in its own body, but they were unable to identify and tackle the cause of the illness. They laboured under the same fundamental error as their opponents: they could not see that to enthrone man as judge of Scripture and Tradition was as much private judgement as making private judgement the interpreter of the Scriptures. Manning considered them 'entangled in a circle which is never discovered until the divine

[55] Inaugural Address to the Academia, Session 1866–7, in *Miscellanies*, i. 178. See also 182 and 183.

[56] Ibid. 187.

[57] 'On the Subjects Proper to the Academia', Session 1863–4, in *Miscellanies*, i. 83.

[58] Inaugural Address, Session 1866–7, in *Miscellanies*, i. 178. Manning considered that the two schools which were tearing Anglicanism apart, the Anglo-Catholic and the Critical, were moving away from each other so fast 'that nothing can restrain them from reaching their natural points of rest', Rome or rationalism (Inaugural Address, Session 1868–9, in ibid. 262).

fact of the presence and office of the Holy Ghost in the mystical body becomes intelligible to them'.[59] That was a Catholic truth which those who belonged to this school had still to recover. As he had written to Miss Stanley in 1851: 'The difference between the Church of England and the Church of Rome is not so much in *what* they respectively believe (though it is there also) but in *why* they believe it.'[60] That difference 'is not one of doctrine and details. It is a question of the Presence and Office of the Holy Ghost.'[61]

There were, in Manning's analysis, two great tendencies at work within the Anglican Church: 'the one a tendency to exaggerate the importance of the external forms of worship and discipline; the other, to concentrate itself in an internal Pietism'.[62] One bore 'the appearance of Catholic doctrine and of Catholic tradition'; the other, 'earlier in date, [sprang] from the very substance of the Reformation itself, preoccupying the Anglican communion, a school of pure Protestant theology'.[63] In the conflict between these two schools, the 'Pietistic or Puritan school, under the name of Evangelical, gradually prevailed more and more in imparting its character to the popular religion of the Anglican Church'.[64] They still lived together, side by side—Anglicanism and Puritanism, he calls them this time—'the ruins of the outer and the inner life of the Catholic Church, from which they separated at the Reformation and then split asunder. This accounts', he added, 'for the dryness of Anglicanism, and the disembodied vagueness of evangelical pietism.'[65]

Manning said that there had been a time when it was thought that the Catholic school was 'the substance of the Anglican Church, and the Protestant a parasite: a malady which, though clinging closely to it, might yet be expelled and cast off'.[66] Then a crisis arose: the Gorham case. The civil appeal showed that the secular power had a jurisdiction on spiritual

---

[59] *TM* 78
[60] Manning MSS Bod., c. 660, fo. 59, letter dated 4 July 1851.
[61] Ibid., fo. 184, letter dated 29 Dec. 1853.
[62] *CSer* i. 45.   [63] *Grounds*, 74.   [64] *CSer* i. 46.
[65] 'Notes and Reminiscences', quoted in *P* i. 68.
[66] *Grounds*, 74.

questions coextensive and superior to that of the bishops. Before that moment, there had been men who

once trusted that those who claim to be the pastors of this people could teach them truly; but in the midst of contradiction they have asked for guidance, and waited in vain for a response. When the faith, by confession of their very teachers, was openly denied, they looked up with inquiring gaze to the authority which they had believed to be divine. They asked in vain. ... The authority in which they trusted failed, because it had no consciousness of divine commission. It could not speak for God, because it was not the organ of His voice.[67]

The Gorham case had shown that the Anglican Church was a human society, as human as the will which had set it up at the Reformation. Manning was reliving his own personal experience when he wrote: 'Slowly and painfully they yielded to the truth, that what they had believed to be divine was not a Church just then fallen from unity and faith, but a human society, sprung from private judgment, established by civil power; human in its origin, human in its authority, and because human without divine office or power from the first. The land once fair in their eyes became a wilderness.'[68]

He saw signs of future decline in the Anglican Church: the growth of ignorance of the supernatural among the multitudes living in towns and cities, the contradictions, confusion, and uncertainty among her teachers and guides. In 1855 he had written about the Church of England's proved and manifest impotence to rule and incapacity to teach:

It cannot judge, it cannot decide: it may not legislate: it dares not to solve its own perplexities: it has not mind or courage to define its own doctrine. There is no voice to be heard: no divine certainty, no divine guide in the seat of its councils. And lastly, never was there a time when the public opinion, the supreme infallibility which guides and teaches in England, was so absolute in its will. It is bearing all before it down the stream to a deeper indifference to all positive revelation.[69]

In the introduction to the volume *England and Christendom* (1867), which collected some of his previous writings on the

---

[67] *CSer* i. 105.   [68] Ibid.; see also *Grounds*, 78.   [69] *CSer* i. 141–2.

subject, he added that this was the natural consequence of the national character of the Church of England. In a national Church comprehensiveness takes the place of truth, and it has to do so if it is to preserve its character as a national Church. Thus, 'the tendency of the Church of England to conform itself to the state of opinion among the English people, so as to reflect their subjective contradictions instead of witnessing to objective truths, has been elevated to a test of its perfection'.[70] Articles of the Creed were removed to make room for people. It had even been said that Christianity was not essential to a national Church but only a blessed accident, a providential bonus.[71] As an Anglican, Manning had already noted with disquiet the theories being put forward in Germany claiming that the Christian Church in each country should be the spirit of the nation expressing itself through an organization of its own. He felt now that what in Germany was a philosophical doctrine had been long ago introduced into England on grounds of political expediency.

The process of dissolution was relentless, and the Anglo-Catholic party within the Church of England was powerless to arrest it; the general body was moving in a different direction, leaving those who held Catholic views more and more isolated. As Manning saw it: 'Whatsoever be the partial reaction of opinion in individuals or fragments of the Anglican body towards a more positive faith, I cannot note in the body as such, any tendency but one of further departure from unity, and of a lower descent in unbelief.'[72] Each period of its history brought with it a further erosion in the belief of Anglicans as a whole, and Manning saw each of these descending steps as the nemesis after a collision with the Church of God.

In the final analysis, the controversies of the last 300 years had resolved themselves into a simple alternative: a choice between 'Rome and rationalism, between the divine certainty of faith, and the instability of human opinion: between the presence of a Divine Teacher and the solitude and darkness of the human soul';[73] the human reason testing the doctrines of revelation or the human reason submitting as a disciple to the teaching of a divine Person. It was no longer a matter of choice between 'Anglo-Catholicism or Roman Catholicism, but between Rationalism and Christianity; that is, Rationalism or Rome'.[74]

Pusey was later to misquote those words, as he had misquoted Newman's reference to the Church of England. Newman had described it as a 'barrier against errors more fundamental than its own'; at the touch of Pusey's pen those words metamorphosed into 'a bulwark in God's hands against infidelity'. When it came to Manning, his alternative between Catholicism and rationalism became in Pusey's hands an alternative between Catholicism and atheism. Manning refuted that false accusation in his pamphlet *The Workings of the Holy Spirit in the Church of England* (1864), writing:

I do not believe that the alternative before us is Catholicism or Atheism. . . . If a man, through any intellectual or moral aberration, should reject Christianity, that is Catholicism, the belief of God and of His perfections stands immutably upon the foundations of nature. Catholicism, or Deism, is the only ultimately logical and consistent alternative, though, happily, few men in rejecting Catholicism are logically consistent enough to reject Christianity. Atheism is an aberration which implies not only intellectual blindness, but a moral insensibility.[75]

The alternative between Catholicism and rationalism, Manning felt, had become a public and practical question in England. Some, in their effort to recover Catholic truth, had moved forward to embrace the fullness of the Faith; others, because of intellectual and social reasons, had retreated from that step in the only direction possible: namely, towards rationalism. They had thrown themselves back 'in the direction of German criticism, as the only assignable reason for not submitting to the Catholic Church'. The inevitable decline which followed had led them to go a long way in a very short time: 'Many who are now prominent in the anti-catholic movement in England, specially in public life, were once on its frontier, and, parted from their former colleagues and convictions,

<hr />

[74] *E&C* iii. 79.   [75] *Workings*, 24–5.

actually on the threshold of its unity, I may say ad limini [sic] apostolorum.'[76] It was an unavoidable decline.

2. *Schism and Heresy*

Manning claimed that 'the relation of any body or people to the Church or to the Faith may be measured by their relations to its head. Their attitude towards Rome will give the exact appreciation of their attitude towards the Revelation of Jesus Christ.'[77] Henry VIII had removed England from their allegiance to Rome; a human authority had dismissed a divine one, and had enthroned itself in its chair. That set in motion a process which, once initiated, could not be arrested. Because of its break with Rome, 'the mind and spirit of the Universal Church has no influx into the Anglican communion'.[78] England had rent itself from the source of certainty of faith, and the rejection of this divine authority of the Church had shattered the unity of faith in England.[79] Then, '[w]ith schism came contradiction; with contradiction uncertainty, debate, and doubt. ... And private judgment, working out its result in individual minds, caused schism after schism.'[80]

He did not, however, utterly condemn his fellow Englishmen. 'The English people are indeed in heresy, but I do not call them heretics. God forbid!', Manning would say.[81] The Anglican Reformation had been

the sin of the Rulers, not of the people; of the Pastors, not of the flock. It was not until after long years of force, and fraud, and unrelenting cruelty, of persecution unto death, with frequent but fruitless armed risings in defence of their faith, that the poor of England fell under the power of their masters. They were robbed of their faith, and separated from the Church of God by conquest; and their children have been born into the ruin of their inheritance, and are in schism by no conscious, much less by any perverse election of their will.[82]

'They have never known their rightful inheritance. They have

---

[76] *CSer* i. 61. Manning did not mention names here. He may have had in mind people like James Anthony Froude or Mark Pattison. In a letter of 1854 he mentioned R. Isaac Williams as one who, he felt, had been untrue to himself and to truth (cf. *P* ii. 36).

[77] Ibid. 34. [78] *Grounds*, 77. [79] Cf. *Four Evils*, 22.

[80] *Grounds*, 2–3. [81] *Four Evils*, 23. [82] *CSer* i. 72.

grown up believing what has been set before them by parents
and by teachers ... They have never made a perverse election
against the truth.'[83] Generations had gone by. Manning had
already pointed out, when speaking as an Anglican about the
Dissenters, that those who had been born into schism were,
naturally, less responsible than those who had caused it, and
the moral guilt grew less as the schism or heresy became ingrained in the common mind and social culture.[84]

The condition of those outside the Church was a question
which had exercised Manning's mind even before becoming a
Catholic, and he had studied it as far as Dissenters and non-
Christians were concerned. He had addressed it in *The Unity
of the Church* (1842), and in his fourth volume of Anglican sermons (1850) he devoted the sermon entitled 'Christ Preached
in Any Way a Cause of Joy' to this subject. Manning defined
in it his approach, which he was to maintain and develop
after becoming a Catholic, to the difficulty presented by the
multiplication of Christian sects and the moral status of those
who belonged to them. He felt that any knowledge of God,
even partial and perhaps contaminated by a certain degree of
error, was better than no knowledge at all. The knowledge of
God, he thought, brings about mighty changes in the soul; it
is a living and life-giving truth. Through it, man becomes
aware of God's love for him and of his sinfulness, and he is
brought under the law of responsibility.

In 1850 Gladstone, in his effort to detain his friend in the
Church of England, had pointed out how, years back, Manning himself had confessed he could not doubt the workings of
grace in the Anglican Church. Manning answered that he
had not changed his mind: he still believed that 'God's mercy
is upon all who are faithful to their light be it what it may'.[85]
He saw his conversion as the work of grace, leading him in his
effort to be faithful to the light. God's mercy had made him
see what he had not seen before. In 1890 he would describe
how the Holy Spirit was in action among those looking for
truth with a sincere heart, although separated from the
Church, and particularly among those who had received the

[83] *Four Evils*, 23.   [84] Cf. *Unity*, 315.
[85] Manning MSS Pitts, box 1, folder 9, letter dated 17 Nov. 1850.

sacrament of baptism. True Catholic principles upheld that God wishes all men to be saved and that grace is given to all, even infidels; those who co-operate with it receive an increase of grace in their souls, while the virtue of penance restores grace to those who have lost it through sin and cannot receive the sacrament of penance; all those who seek truth belong, at least, to the soul of the Church. His personal experience confirmed the doctrine. He also had 'intimately known souls living by faith, hope and charity'; that is, living holy lives. He thought this 'as undoubtedly the work of the Holy Ghost as I have ever seen'. And, he added, 'I have received into the Church I do not know how many souls in whom I could find no mortal sin.'[86]

Divisions were to be deplored, but Manning maintained that the right approach to other bodies was to rejoice in the good that they had and to work so as to build upon it. 'All that can be done to foster and ripen the elements of truth ... is the duty and work of charity.' He was against an aggressive policy towards those communities: 'To overthrow, on the plea of re-construction, is to do the office of one whose name is the De-stroyer. God's temple is to be built up by a labour of construction which preserves with jealous and loving tenderness all that has life and truth.' He thought that, by following this approach, in the effort 'to add to and raise upward to perfection whatsoever of truth and faith exists in the most imperfect, we [the Anglican Church, at that stage] should win many a soul. Men are not won by contradictions, nor persuaded by refutations, but by the expansion, enlargement, and perfect exhibition of the truths they hold in germ. This is the divine rule of controversy, the only evangelical principle of conversion.'[87] After becoming a Catholic, he would tell his co-religionists that they should be familiar with those truths of faith solidly rooted in the minds of the people of England in order to build upon them.

---

[86] 'Autobiographical Note', quoted in *P* ii. 780–1. The same note described how different was the general perception of Catholics at the time.

[87] *ASer* iv. 73–4. In 1890 he contrasted the two methods: 'There are two ways of solving a problem. The one to show that every other conception is impossible; this is polemical and destructive. The other to show that the true conception is evident. This is positive and expository' ('Autobiographical Note', quoted in *P* ii. 789).

Still, in 1850, he had acknowledged that some could object
to the above concepts and *modus operandi*: 'It may be said that
this is equivalent to denying the visibleness and divine institution of the Church, the necessity and grace of the holy Sacraments; that it substitutes personal sincerity for the true faith,
and goes all length with the latitudinarian theory, which either
makes truth indifferent, or God all mercy.' Manning answered
by saying that 'truth has life in it to those whose heart is right
with God'.[88] The measure of truth possessed or presented to individuals is determined by circumstances over which they
have little control: truth may have not been proposed to
them, or the education they have received has created such a
strong prejudice that it prevents them from recognizing truth
when confronted with it. Invincible ignorance is no personal
sin, and 'no ignorance of truth is a personal sin before God, except that ignorance which springs from personal sin'.[89] What
really mattered was whether man was faithful to the light of
truth he had received; '[if] the heart be right with God, He
will weigh the rest in a balance of compassion'.[90] As he would
say: 'Truth is given for the probation of man; the probation of
man is not ordained for the sake of truth.'[91] Moreover, the acceptance of the truth seen as such implicitly contained many
other truths, even the whole of revealed truth: 'No eye but
God's can read the mysteries which are received by implicit
faith.'[92] These principles, he added, applied 'to every Christian
sect according to its measure, and to every individual born
into it'.[93] He summarized his thought in a phrase which
seemed to require some further clarification: 'God has bound
us to seek His grace through His Church; but He has not
bound Himself to give grace and salvation in no other way.'[94]
Upon those who were faithful to their light, whatever it might
be, would rest the mercy of God, and they would be partakers
of his grace.

---

[88] *ASer* iv. 74.   [89] Ibid. 75.
[90] Ibid 78; see also *Fourfold*, 33 ff.
[91] *ASer* iv. 78.   [92] Ibid. 80.
[93] Ibid. 77. In 1842 he had said how a body which had broken away from the
Church had forfeited the character of a Church, but that it would be false to conclude
that its members had forfeited their hope of salvation (cf. *Unity*, 349).
[94] *ASer* iv. 82.

This was not latitudinarianism. The 'duty of believing the whole and perfect truth is still absolutely binding on pain of sin to all who know it'.[95] That was a great responsibility. After his conversion, looking back at those who had been with him for most of the journey, Manning felt that among them were those who, having reached the threshold of truth, had recoiled from crossing into its fullness. God alone could judge their reasons for doing so, but Manning thought that some were motivated by human considerations, and he had serious misgivings as to their standing in God's eyes. In 1854 he wrote to Robert Wilberforce: 'I see men who once believed with even clearer light than I did, now professing not to believe this or that particular; and what is worst of all, I believe they say so truly; for what ought to be obeyed when believed, passes away. ... If I trust the men who speak, I the more fear for them, for the truth has been lost.'[96]

In the early 1850s, Manning's main fears in this respect were for his friend Robert Wilberforce. He was afraid that he might be untrue to himself and to truth. Robert, to Manning's mind, was looking 'for what God does not give': 'a conviction which precludes the exercise of faith. Except in figures and numbers there is no conviction which excludes the possibility of the contrary being true. It is not impossible even that Jesus Christ is not come in the flesh. I mean it does not involve a contradiction in its terms to suppose that the Christian History is a myth.' The proper use of reason and private judgement was to examine the evidence as to whether God had instituted an infallible authority in the Church. 'Reason can go no further, and until upon the motives of credibility supplied by reason he makes an act of faith, he can rise no higher.'[97] Private judgement stopped short of the final step; it provided a reasonable probability that Christianity was true, and could do no more. Only faith could add certainty to the confession of Christian faith. 'We go by our own taper to the altar of light, and then put our taper out for ever.'[98]

---

[95] Ibid. 80.
[96] Letter dated 20 Jan. 1854, quoted in *P* ii. 36.
[97] Ibid. 36–7.
[98] Manning MSS Bod., c. 656, fo. 200, letter to R. Wilberforce, dated 16 June 1851.

During the First Vatican Council, Manning would welcome the first schema *De Ecclesia,* among other reasons, for its treatment, in chapter 7, of the principle *extra ecclesia nulla salus.* He felt that there was great ignorance on the subject, among both Catholics and non-Catholics. 'Catholics despaired of the salvation of non-Catholics and non-Catholics rejected the Catholic doctrine as incompatible with divine mercy and justice. This misunderstanding was a great obstacle to conversions, Manning complained, and his efforts to clarify the Church's position were met with the charge that he was mitigating the Church's doctrine without proper authority.'[99]

Englishmen were in a state of invincible ignorance, and their prejudices were so strongly rooted in their minds and hearts that, in good measure, they were unable to detect the light of the true Faith. 'They were born into an atmosphere in which all lights are distorted and all colours change their hue. Truth and falsehood have shifted places, and the history of the English reformation is a traditionary fable.'[100] Prejudice was a powerful force. The hatred of the Catholic Church—'into which we English are born, as into the fall of Adam'[101]—was the fruit of centuries of anti-Catholic propaganda. And this deep-seated prejudice was married to the conviction that there is no divine voice now teaching on earth: 'the Anglican Reformation has entirely cancelled from the intelligence of the English people the whole idea of the Church divinely founded, endowed with supernatural attributes, and teaching with divine, and, therefore, infallible certainty'. This meant, that, as shown by the universal experience of those who had exercised the evangelical ministry in England, 'the last article of the Creed, which enters, and that slowly, and for a long time painfully, into the English intelligence, is the nature and office of the Church: or to speak theologically, the formal object of Faith, and the divinely ordained conditions of its manifestations to the world'.[102]

[99] Cwiekowski, *English Bishops,* 220. Manning considered that English Catholics, because of 'an antagonistic attitude of mind, bitter and hardly charitable' towards Anglicans, 'held with all rigour the axiom *extra ecclesiam nulla salus*' ('Autobiographical Note', quoted in *P* ii. 778)—an attitude born of centuries of persecution and discrimination.

[100] *CSer* i. 192–3; see also *Workings,* 15.
[101] *Privilegium,* i. 102.   [102] *CSer* i. 58.

Manning, however, did not despair of the eventual conversion of England to the Catholic Faith. He was confident that the conjunction of the virtues of the English race and the grace of God might open their eyes to see the illusion, and enable them to break the spell under which they had lived for so long. Ezekiel's vision of the 'Valley of the Dry Bones' was before his eyes. He felt that Providence might again draw good from evil, and make the global empire of the British people a vehicle for the expansion of the Catholic Faith.[103]

3. *The Establishment: The Shirt of Nessus?*

After the court decision on some of the authors of *Essays and Reviews*,[104] the old cry for disestablishment of the Anglican Church was raised anew. The ills of the Church of England, it was said, were consequent upon its condition as a Church established by law; remove the cause, and the patient would soon recover its former strength. Not many voices echoed this call. Still, Manning would have to answer the charge of not having distinguished, in his commentary on the court's decisions, between the Church and establishment. That was a theme congenial to him, one on which he had tried his hand before, while still an Anglican.

As far as he was concerned, the court decisions on the authors of *Essays and Reviews* had once more revealed the internal contradiction that lay at the very heart of Anglicanism. In the Reformation the Anglican Church had declared herself independent of external jurisdiction, and self-sufficient for the preservation and declaration of doctrine, and for the determination of all controversies over matters of faith. While claiming this power, the Church of England had almost in the same breath denied being endowed with infallibility, confessing that particular Churches were liable to error, and that they had in fact erred. It followed that, even if the bishops or Convocation were to give a unanimous decision on a controverted point of

---

[103] Cf. ibid. 112–14 and 378 ff.; see also *CSer* ii. 251 ff.

[104] *Essays and Reviews* was published in 1860. The authors applied to the Bible the modern methods of textual criticism, suggested testing biblical miracles by scientific criteria, argued against the doctrine of eternal damnation, etc. They were denounced by the Archbishop of Canterbury, and some of them were brought before the Court of Arches under a charge of heresy.

doctrine, this could not be the basis for human certainty, even less for divine certainty. Convocation can only 'give a human judgment, even on matters of revealed faith; and therefore it can generate in the minds of men only a fallible opinion'.[105] Lord Brougham's speech against Bishop Blomfield's proposed law to amend the appellate jurisdiction of the Crown in matters of doctrine had made it abundantly clear that, in the eyes of the country as a whole, the decisions of the bishops would have no weight and would carry no power of convincing. The position, Manning thought, was an untenable one, 'for the common sense of Englishmen would refuse to submit in appeal, on matters of faith, to the judgment of a bench of bishops, who disclaim infallibility, and are openly divided against themselves'.[106]

The parliamentary statutes of the Tudors made it clear that the power to judge on appeal all causes of controverted doctrine belonged to the Crown: a judge which, like the bishops, disclaimed infallibility. Even more, the Crown did not even claim to 'judge of the truth of the matter brought before it'.[107] The Crown was 'invested with a power to admit or to exclude doctrines upon the exercise of its own *discernment*, all the while disclaiming the power to pronounce them to be *true*, and claiming only to pronounce them to be legal'.[108] The judgement of the Crown confined itself to declaring whether a particular doctrine was in open contradiction to the Anglican formularies. But, Manning would say, the cause of the evils which afflicted Anglicanism was the Anglican Church itself, not the Crown or its Privy Council: 'If the Church of England were the Church of God, the tribunals could do it no harm. It is Anglicanism which *generates* the errors. The tribunals only *legalise* them. The Anglican system is the source of all its own confusions, which the law contemptuously tolerates.'[109]

Those who looked at establishment as the cause of the Anglican Church's evils, and thought of disestablishment as the solution for its ills, were prey to a misconception. Establishment was not a shirt of Nessus for the Anglican Church; 'my belief', Manning wrote in 1864,' is that when the Church of England

---

[105] *E&C* iii. 49.   [106] *E&C* ii. 12.   [107] *E&C* iii. 56.
[108] Ibid. 44.   [109] *E&C* ii. 28–9.

lost its inheritance in the universal Church, the principle of all spiritual and intellectual disease was developed in its blood, and ate into its bone. I do not believe that it is a poisoned vestment which is put upon it from without, but a morbid and manifold disease which is ever reproducing itself from within.'[110] Disestablishment could do little or nothing to remedy the evil.

By the late 1860s, however, Manning conceived a more positive view of disestablishment. He acknowledged that some good had followed from the 'moral disestablishment' of the Church of England by the Test and Corporation Acts and by Catholic Emancipation. They had thrown the Church of England upon its inner spiritual and intellectual resources, and that had resulted in a revival, which further disestablishment would only accelerate. Manning considered this a highly desirable development, which would increase the religious zeal and activity of the country as a whole. 'If this be so ... then the course of public legislation would assuredly not be less Christian. The public opinion of the country would be more so; and the legislature must ultimately be governed by public opinion.'[111] The preservation of Christianity, and the improvement of moral and social conditions in England was a task which required the co-operation of all the Christian denominations. Manning considered that Catholics were bound to co-operate with Anglicans and Dissenters 'in everything which is not contrary to faith or morals';[112] and he was always ready to share a platform with Anglicans or Dissenters to defend a good cause—a practical ecumenism which did not imply a change in Manning's theological conception of the Church of England: Anglicanism was Protestantism.

Anglicans readily acknowledged that 'Protestantism is essentially rationalistic, but deny that Anglicanism is Protestant'.[113] Manning, on the other hand, maintained that they were intimately related, if not identical, to each other: both appealed from the voice of the living Church; both alike rejected its

---

[110] Ibid. 24.

[111] Inaugural Address, Session 1868–9, in *Miscellanies*, i. 291. Von Arx has studied some of these points in his article 'Manning's Ultramontanism'.

[112] 'Autobiographical Note' (1890), quoted in *P* ii. 782.

[113] *E&C* iii. 50.

divine infallible authority. It did not matter what they appealed to; the basis for that appeal was the same: 'the refusal
of the living voice of the Church as the rule of faith'.[114] If
there was no infallible authority, the only criterion by which
to interpret Holy Scripture—or Scripture and Tradition—was
human reason, and the position was, therefore, essentially rationalistic: there is 'nothing intermediate between divine faith
and human opinion'.[115] Human reason was to determine
which books have been inspired and their interpretation: the
'ultimate certainty upon which it rests, even the Scripture, its
authenticity, interpretation, inspiration, is a human, and therefore a fallible, tradition'.[116] This was rationalism. This procedure could generate neither a human nor a divine certainty; it
could not generate faith. A human authority 'can bind no
man to believe in its decisions; for no man can be under obligation to make an act of faith in a teacher who may err'.[117] The
individual was left to the devices of his private judgement; he
was 'free to revise all judgments of a teacher who disclaims
infallibility'.[118]

This, naturally, had momentous consequences as far as the
act of faith was concerned. Following the above principles, the
'distinction between reason and faith is thus obscured; and the
generic difference between the last act of reason and the first
act of faith . . . is effaced from the minds of most Anglicans'.[119]
Manning had ample personal experience in this respect. What
they called faith was a personal opinion based on reason or sentiment, or both. This erroneous concept of the act of faith
made it very difficult for Anglicans to find the true Faith, and
it was a serious obstacle in their dialogue or controversy with
Catholics. The terms they used were equivocal. The Catholic
position, Manning summed up, was that reason 'leads us to
the feet of a Divine Teacher; but thenceforward His voice,
and not our balancing of probabilities, will be the formal motive of our faith. . . . My faith terminates no longer in a cumulus
of probabilities gathered from the past, but upon the veracity
of a Divine Person guiding me with His presence.'[120]

[114] *E&C* iii. 51.   [115] Ibid. 53.   [116] Ibid. 57.
[117] Ibid. 59.   [118] Ibid.   [119] Ibid. 75.   [120] Ibid. 75–6.

Rationalism was not an external agent, working on the Church of England from the outside. The civil courts had not opened the door for it to steal into the Anglican Church. It was a habit of thought which had conceived Anglicanism and all the dissenting bodies which had separated from it. 'The Churchman differed from the Socinian, and the Socinian from the Deist as to the number of articles in his creed; but all alike consented to test their belief by the rational evidence for it.'[121]

4. *A Bulwark against Infidelity?*

The publication of *Essays and Reviews* (1860) had signalled the beginning of a new crisis in Anglicanism, and the subsequent court decisions on the contributions of Rowland Williams and H. B. Wilson increased the atmosphere of gloom among those of the Catholic party in the Church of England. The highest ecclesiastical tribunal, excepting only the Queen in council, had pronounced in the cases of Williams and Wilson. Manning saw in the decision of the Court of Arches an official recognition of the legitimacy of rationalism within the Anglican Church. His analysis concluded that the decision, 'though in some degree adverse to the liberty claimed by the Rationalists, nevertheless gives to that school a substantive existence, and incorporates its principles by public law in the system and rights of the Church of England'.[122] In Manning's summary, the Court of Arches upheld the following principles: that the Church of England held as inspired and canonical the books of the Old and New Testaments, but it did not define what inspiration was; that the inspiration of parts of a particular book could be denied; that those parts which were considered inspired could be interpreted freely, provided the interpretation did not contradict the articles and formularies of the Church of England, which were vague and ambiguous enough 'to permit liberty and largeness of interpretation, of which everyone may avail himself as his conscience and critical faculty may require'.[123] This, for Manning, was pure rationalism: whatever was retained or rejected, was retained or rejected 'upon the

---

[121] *E&C* i, p. xxiii, quoting from *Essays and Reviews*, 257.
[122] *CSer* i. 52.
[123] Ibid. 53.

principle of Rationalism, that is, of human testimony tried by the same criterion'.[124]

The judgement of the Court of Arches was raised in appeal to the Privy Council. The judgement was delivered on 8 February 1864. It went beyond the decision of the Court of Arches, opening 'a large[r] area of biblical criticism and theological enquiry to free discussion among the clergy', and rendering 'a large part of the conventional teaching of the Church unenforceable at law'.[125] The Anglo-Catholic party was not idle in the face of those events. Pusey's pamphlet on the legal force of the judgement of the Privy Council in Wilson's case (1864) was part of the reaction against the threat posed by the *Essays and Reviews*. In his pamphlet, Pusey made some remarks which were to stir Manning into action. He described the reaction of English Catholics before the recent events as follows: 'A class of believers joined in the triumph. And while I know that a very earnest body of Roman Catholics rejoice in all the workings of God the Holy Spirit in the Church of England, (whatever they think of her,) and are saddened in what weakens *her* who is, in God's Hands the great bulwark against infidelity in this land, others seemed to be in ecstasy of triumph at this victory of Satan.'[126] It was generally believed that Manning was included among those who rejoice at Satan's victory. He had recently been accused of having changed from being slow, cautious, and moderate before his conversion to being violent and unreasonable; from being over-English before to being now Ultramontane. Pusey was to disclaim later on, in his *Eirenicon* (1865), that he had included Manning and Wiseman in that group; by then, after Manning's broadside in his *The Workings of the Holy Spirit in the Church of England* (1864), they were already engaged in open polemic, and more of the capital ships of both sides were about to join the action.

Manning felt that he could not leave unanswered Pusey's claim that the Church of England was a bulwark against infidelity. On the contrary, Manning thought that the Anglican

---

[124] *CSer* i. 54.

[125] J. L. Altholz, *Anatomy of a Controversy: The Debate over Essays and Reviews, 1860–1864* (Aldershot, 1994), 109.

[126] E. B. Pusey, *Case as to the Legal Force of the Judgment of the Privy Council in re Fendall v Wilson* (London, 1864), 3–4.

Reformation and the Anglican Church were the 'true and original source of the present spiritual anarchy of England. ... [The Church of England], so far from being a barrier against infidelity, must be recognised as the mother of all the intellectual and spiritual aberrations which now cover the face of England.'[127] He tried to substantiate this charge by applying those principles that were so dear to him. The Church of England, he would admit, could be called a 'barrier against infidelity' by grace of the truth that she still retained; but she was, at the same time, a source of unbelief in the measure in which she denied other truths, and here he included not just particular doctrines but the very foundations of the faith. The Church of England propagated unbelief

by principle, and in the essence of its whole system. What is the ultimate guarantee of the Divine revelation but the Divine authority of the Church? Deny this, and we descend at once to human teachers. But it is this that the Church of England formally and expressly denies. The perpetual and ever-present assistance of the Holy Spirit, whereby the Church in every age is not only preserved from error, but enabled at all times to declare the truth, that is the infallibility of the living Church at this hour—this it is that the Anglican Church in terms denies.[128]

The true barrier against infidelity is the faith in the divine voice perpetually speaking in the Church, keeping the deposit of faith incorruptible, interpreting and propounding the revelation infallibly, resolving the controversies about the Faith. Thus, it was becoming more and more evident 'that in the flood of unbelief pouring at this time upon England, the sole barrier to the inundation, the sole guardian and keeper of Holy Writ in all the integrity of its text and meaning, ... the sole, immutable, and unerring interpreter of its meaning is the Catholic and Roman Church'.[129]

Manning did not regard the Church of England as a *teacher of truth*, 'for that would imply that it teaches the truth in all its circumference, and in all its divine certainty. Now this is precisely what the Church of England does not.' It had, besides, 'destroyed in itself the power of [so] doing',[130] by rejecting the

---

[127] *Workings*, 29–30.   [128] Ibid. 34.   [129] *TM*, 221.
[130] *Workings*, 21.

infallible authority of the Church. Manning was willing to call
it 'a teacher of Christian truths', but not a teacher of Christian
truth, 'because it rejects much of that truth, and also the divine
principle of its perpetuity in the world'.[131] It had to be admitted that the Anglican Church had preserved and taught
more truths than the German Protestants, but it undermined
the evidence of the truths it still retained in a double way, because (a) 'It has detached them from other truths which by
contact gave solidity to all by rendering them coherent and intelligible'. (b) 'It has detached them from the Divine voice of
the Church, which guarantees to us the truth incorruptible
and changeless.'[132] He concluded: 'How can this be regarded
as "the great bulwark in God's hand against infidelity"?'[133]

These were hard words, and harder things were to follow.
Manning had borne witness 'to the presence and voice of a
divine, and therefore infallible, teacher, guiding the Church
with His perpetual assistance, and speaking through it as His
organ'. He had also 'borne witness that the Church through
which He teaches is that which S. Augustine describes by the
two incommunicable notes—that is "spread throughout the
world" and "united to the Chair of Peter"'.[134] Manning was
fully aware of the corollaries which followed from these pre-
misses: 'If the Catholic faith be the perfect revelation of Christianity, the Anglican Reformation is a cloud of heresies; if the
Catholic Church be the organ of the Holy Ghost, the Anglican
Church is not only no part of the Church, but no church of
divine foundation. It is a human institution sustained as it was
founded by a human authority, without priesthood, without
sacraments, without absolution, without the real presence of
Jesus upon its altars.'[135]

The fact that Manning recognized the workings of the Holy
Spirit in the Church of England could not be of great consola-
tion to men like Pusey. The Holy Spirit, Manning had added,
was active in the whole world and among every nation even
before the Church came into existence. He continued his operations in individuals outside the Church, but his presence
and action would necessarily be more abundant among those

---

[131] *Workings*, 22.   [132] Ibid. 30.   [133] Ibid. 35.
[134] Ibid. 41–2.   [135] Ibid. 42.

who have been regenerated by baptism. Manning qualified this statement. What he had just said did 'not recognise the grace *of* the Church of England as such'. Grace 'works not *by* it, nor *through* it, but *in* it and among those who, without faults of their own, are detained by it from the true Church of their baptism'.[136] As a matter of fact, the grace they received was not granted to detain them in the Church of England, but to call them out of it.[137]

He added that he did not rejoice, but lament, over any further loss of truth in the Anglican Church. In his introduction to *England and Christendom* he quoted an old sermon of his published in the fourth volume of Anglican sermons: 'Christ Preached Every Way a Cause for Joy'. There he had affirmed that any light is better than darkness, and that in the least measure of truth there is cause for rejoicing. Now he expressed his conviction that anything which undermined the truths still taught by the Church of England drove the people further and further away from the Catholic Church. Manning did not look forward to the Anglican Church being swept away by a flood of infidelity. He desired to see the Church of England pass away 'under the action of a higher and more perfect truth' that would make the lingering embers in it rise into a burning flame. Then, all the Christianity 'which survives in Anglicanism would be perfected by the restoration of the truths which have been lost, and the whole would be fixed and perpetuated by the evidence of a Divine certainty and the voice of a Divine Teacher'.[138] The mission of the Church in the world is not to destroy but 'to fill up the truth'.[139]

Manning foresaw that his words would seem 'heartless, cruel, unfilial, unbrotherly, ungrateful' to Pusey. He had never spoken so strongly about the Church of England. It seems that, when doing so, he had in mind more than just Pusey's phrase, and that he was also addressing certain developments then taking place within the Catholic Church. Was he also making use of the opportunity to correct, without making explicit reference to them, some of Newman's expressions? Many people thought so, and Newman himself seems to have

---

[136] Ibid. 18 and 20.   [137] Cf. ibid.   [138] Ibid. 28–9.
[139] Ibid. 24.

been of that opinion, although he expressed it rather cau-
tiously—at least, in public. Manning later disclaimed all intention of attacking Newman;[140] Newman, for his part, declared
that he had never made his own what the rumour said. Neither
seems to have truly believed the other's disclaimer. What is a
fact, however, is that several times in his text Manning used
the word 'barrier', Newman's word, instead of 'bulwark', the
word used by Pusey.[141]

5. *An* Eirenicon *and the APUC*[142]

Manning's judgement of the Church of England could not but
draw a response from Pusey; Manning had denied to the Anglican Church everything that Pusey felt it stood for. Pusey
wrote to Newman expressing how hurt he was by Manning's
letter: he has 'denied us every thing, except what in a greater
degree Dissenters had too'.[143] He seemed to have forgotten,
though, that Newman had said as much in his *Difficulties of Anglicans* (1850): 'If I let you plead the sensible effects of supernatural grace, as exemplified in yourselves, in proof that your
religion is true, I must allow the plea to others [Wesleyans] to
whom by your theory you are bound to deny it. ... [H]ave
they not more remarkable phenomena in their history, sympto-
matic of the presence of grace among them, than you can
show in yours?'[144] The comparison with the Dissenters was
not a new one, and the High Church party in the Church of
England had contrived to answer it many a time. In his *Eirenicon*, Pusey was to move along well-trodden paths.

Manning's charges against the Anglican Church, Pusey
thought, could be grouped together under two headings:
(a) the errors of the Anglican Church; (b) the rejection of the
infallibility of the Church. He counter-attacked by saying that
the Catholic Church itself was not free from error—devotion
to Our Lady being a conspicuous example; indeed, the Angli-

---

[140] Cf. letter to Ullathorne, 5 Aug. 1867, Manning MSS West., Manning–
Ullathorne Correspondence, *U* 78.

[141] Cf. *Workings*, 30, 33, 34–5.

[142] Association for the Promotion of the Unity of Christendom.

[143] *LD* xxii. 99.

[144] J. H. Newman, *Certain Difficulties felt by Anglicans in Catholic Teaching* (new edn.,
2 vols., London, 1897), i. 88.

can Reformation had been a protest against such abuses. Manning's fundamental charge, though, was that the Church of England had rejected the doctrine of the infallibility of the Church. Pusey addressed this in detail, and made use of Ward's articles in the *Dublin Review* to rebut the charge and turn it against the Catholic Church. 'The last charge which Dr. Manning brings against the Church of England', Pusey wrote, 'is, that "it formally denies" the "perpetual Divine voice" of the Church.'[145] He rightly pointed out that the main stress in Manning's words was on the term 'perpetual'. Pusey claimed that the Anglican Church did not deny the infallibility of the Church, in the past or at the present time. Manning's mistake, according to him, originated in a false assumption: 'that, in denying the infallibility of the Roman Church by itself, we are "denying the infallibility of the living Church at this hour"; because, on his hypothesis, the Roman Church is, alone, the living Church, to the exclusion of the Eastern Church and of ourselves'.[146]

The Church of England, Pusey claimed, was in possession of infallible truth and accepted the infallibility of the Church of all times. She had infallible truth resting on an infallible authority, that of the primitive Church, and, he added, we 'do not need the present agency of an infallible Church to assure us of the truth of what has been ruled infallibly'.[147] Besides, the Church of England not only accepted that the Church had been infallible in the past, but also that it would be infallible now if it were to be united and act in unison. The Holy Spirit still speaks in the Church when its three branches 'teach the same faith which was from the beginning ...; and, if need required, they could at this day declare concurrently any truth, if it should appear that it had not, as yet, been sufficiently defined, against some fresh heresy which should emerge'.[148] The 'whole' Catholic Church had not collectively sanctioned error, and what it had or might collectively sanction in the future would be certain truth: a truly General Council would now be as infallible as those the primitive

---

[145] E. B. Pusey, *An Eirenicon: In a Letter to the Author of 'The Christian Year'* (London, 1865), 82.
[146] Ibid. 83–4.   [147] Ibid. 96.   [148] Ibid. 84.

Church. This, Pusey felt, was the theory of the Gallican divines, who set the test of infallibility in the reception of a particular doctrine by the whole Church. To Pusey's mind, the main difference between him and Manning was that the latter identified the Church with the Roman Church, while Pusey saw it in the union or concurrent action of its three constitutive branches: the Anglican, the Roman, and the Orthodox.

On the other hand, Pusey added, the infallibility of the Pope—the corner-stone of Manning's argument—was not accepted by the whole Church, not even by all Roman Catholics: the Orthodox and the Anglicans rejected it, and so did the Gallicans within the Church of Rome. What was more, it had never been declared a dogma of faith. Were the Roman Church to declare it so in future, it would find itself enmeshed in a web of inextricable difficulties. The *Dublin Review* was claiming for the Pope an infallibility which covered the *Syllabus* and *Quanta Cura*, and 'consequently, for every like expression of the Pope's mind, to be *the very word of God*'.[149] Thus, it would have 'to be shown how any statement of any Pope which has since been abandoned, is consistent with such infallibility'.[150]

There were fundamental issues involved in the controversy. The main argument concerned the concept of the unity of the Church, and what constituted it. Ironically, Pusey, in his *Eirenicon*, had repeated, almost verbatim, the ideas about unity and infallibility which Manning had published in *The Unity of the Church* (1842), and which he would formally retract in *The Temporal Mission of the Holy Ghost* (1865).

Manning, who in the meantime had been made Archbishop of Westminster, did not answer Pusey's *Eirenicon* directly. He thought that it had been written at Keble's behest, and in order to prevent people from entering the Catholic Church. To Manning's mind, Pusey had confirmed the contention put forward in *The Workings of the Holy Spirit in the Church of England*: 'that the Anglican Church appeals from the living voice of the Church at this hour, thereby denying its Divine authority'. Dr Pusey's *Eirenicon* had done precisely that, 'thereby confirming the argument of my Letter'.[151] Still, the points raised by

---

[149] E. B. Pusey, *An Eirenicon*, 304.   [150] Ibid. 305.   [151] *E&C* i, p. xiv.

Pusey would be taken into consideration in his subsequent works. *The Temporal Mission of the Holy Ghost*, published that same year, addressed some of the issues; others were to be tackled in his pastoral letter on the APUC.

In *The Temporal Mission* he dismissed Pusey's appeal to antiquity, to the infallible primitive Church. Anglicans maintained, Manning said,

that the only certain rule of faith is to believe that which the Church held and taught while yet it was united and therefore infallible. Such reasoners fail to observe, that since the supposed division, and cessation of the infallible voice, there remains no divine certainty as to what was then infallibly taught. To affirm that this or that doctrine was taught then where it is now disputed, is to beg the question. The infallible Church of the first six centuries—that is, before the division—was infallible to those who lived in those ages, but is not infallible to us. ... Its infallibility does not reach to us, for the Church of the last twelve hundred years is by the hypothesis fallible, and may therefore err in delivering to us what was taught before the division.[152]

For Manning, once the existence of a permanent divine doctrinal authority had been denied, the points of faith decided by the General Councils while the Church was still united were no longer safe. 'There needs only an individual of sufficient intelligence and sufficient influence', he had written in *The Grounds of Faith*, 'to rise up and call them in question. If the interpretation of the decrees of the Councils of Nice or Ephesus be disputed, an authoritative exposition of these ancient definitions is required. But this cannot be obtained unless there still sit on earth a judge to decide the law.'[153]

That, however, was accidental. The main point of contention was the concept of the Church's unity. Pusey acknowledged the infallibility of the present-day Church almost as much as Manning did. The all-important difference consisted in their divergent concepts of what the Church is and, therefore, of what constitutes its unity. Manning's concept of the Church, as we have seen, rested on the perpetual and inseparable union of the Holy Spirit to it, and the consequent perpetual endowments of unity (intrinsic and visible at the same

---

[152] *TM* 78–9.   [153] *Grounds*, 70.

time), of holiness and of infallibility. Pusey's idea of the *Ecclesia Anglicana* rested on the acceptance of an externally divided Church which, at the same time, had preserved its essential unity. The universal Church was still infallible, although its infallibility was suspended in so far as the Church was prevented from acting in unison by the divisions which had broken its visible unity.

Manning was to dwell on the concept of unity in his pastoral *The Reunion of Christendom* (6 January 1866), and in doing so was to address together the issues raised by Pusey and by the APUC. He saw them sharing the same basic error on a fundamental point of faith, and he felt the need to act on the matter promptly and clearly. Manning considered that vital principles for the Church were at stake. As he had written in 1852, 'The unity and the infallibility of the Church of Jesus Christ, these are our principles and these shall be our safety.'[154] These principles were now openly attacked by Pusey, and, at the same time, they seemed to be obscured in the minds of many of those Catholics who had given their names to the APUC.

The Association for the Promotion of the Unity of Christendom, heir to previous initiatives for corporate reunion, had grown out of the enthusiasm and sanguine hopes of Ambrose Phillipps De Lisle, a pre-Tractarian convert to Catholicism with a bent for romantic and grandiose schemes. In his letters to Propaganda he gave the impression that the number of Anglicans committed to the scheme of reunion was much larger, and their determination to seek reunion with Rome stronger, than they actually were. Those who had set up the association declared that they looked forward to a corporate reunion of those three great bodies which claimed for themselves the inheritance of the priesthood and the name 'Catholic'. They professed that they did not want, at that stage, to compromise any principles that those separate bodies might uphold; their only aim was to pray for unity.

The Catholic hierarchy, from very early on, looked with suspicion on the initiative. In 1857, within a year of the setting up of the association, Cardinal Wiseman wrote a strong memorandum to Propaganda about the APUC. In it he referred at

[154] *CSer* i. 194.

length to the unfounded hopes or 'dreams' of Mr Ambrose
Phillipps De Lisle. The Cardinal also mentioned that the tone
of Phillipps De Lisle's expressions 'tend to strengthen the Anglicans in their intrenchments, and to make them more confident of the validity of their orders, and to encourage them to
look for the conversion of the whole body, rather than for that
of individuals'.[155] Wiseman had carefully read Phillipps De Lisle's *On the Future Unity of Christendom*, and he objected to the
way in which he spoke of ' "the three great denominations"
(the term itself is Protestant) "of Christians", i.e. "Catholics,
Greek, and Anglicans," as though they were all equal, and
could treat of religious union upon a footing of equality'.[156]
The unionists, he added, had tried to obtain his support, and
had pretended that he held views similar to those of the association; he, for his part, had made every effort to dissociate
himself from their principles in the strongest possible terms,
telling Phillipps De Lisle—as he reported to Propaganda—
that he 'had always been far from allowing the slightest prerogative to the "Church" (as it professes to be) of England,
whether in the matter of orders, of missions, of sacraments, or
of instruction in doctrine; that, on the contrary, he had im-
pugned all right, on the part of Anglicanism, to the name of
church; and that he had warmly, and not ineffectually, invited
each one singly to save his own soul by leaving a system of
falsehood and error'.[157]

However, no action was taken to discourage Catholics from
joining the association, and a year after its formation, it
counted 1,000 Catholics among its membership of 7,000. The
majority of members of the association, though, belonged to
the Anglo-Catholic party, and they became the dominant influence within it. Wiseman had promised Propaganda to keep
an attentive eye on its doings, and to act if that were required.
The need for action presented itself to the bishops after the
foundation of the *Union Review* by Lee, to succeed the *Union*

[155] Quoted in W. Ward, *Life and Times of Wiseman*, ii. 483.
[156] Ibid. 485. Phillipps De Lisle was aware of Wiseman's opposition to the APUC
and to his pamphlet; see letter to Lee, 4 Sept. 1857, quoted in M. Pawley, *Faith and
Family: The Life and Circle of Ambrose Phillipps De Lisle* (Norwich, 1993), 299. The *Rambler* and the *Dublin Review* were also highly critical of De Lisle's pamphlet.
[157] W. Ward, *Life and Times of Wiseman*, 483–4.

Newspaper. The latter, until then the organ of the association, had, by its advocacy of 'Romish' practices, alienated many moderate High Churchmen. The newly born *Union Review*, as a reaction, 'was anxious to adopt a measured and cautious tone, but in developing this approach to assuage Anglican susceptibilities it succeeded in offending Roman Catholics by a sustained antagonism to individual conversions and bitter attacks upon well-known converts'.[158] The *Review*, intentionally or unintentionally, was 'encouraging disharmony among the body of Roman Catholics, setting "old Catholic" against convert'. What galvanized the bishops into action, though, was its advocacy of the branch theory: 'ample evidence could be culled from it [the *Review*] of the views of leading members of the Association to give weight to the papal rescript when it declared that the Association "has resulted from a view, put forward by it in express terms, that the three christian Communions, the Roman Catholic, the schismatic Greek and the Anglican, though separated and divided one from another, yet with an equal right claim the title Catholic" '.[159] Not all members of the association held those views, but most of them did, and there was a danger of scandal, as it could be presumed that the Catholic members shared those ideas.

Manning shared the misgivings of the Cardinal. In his address to the Academia in 1863 he referred to some Catholics who thought that 'the duty of Anglicans is to remain where they are with a view to spreading their opinions in the Established Church: in other words, that individuals may postpone, or even refuse, to submit to the Church in the hope of bringing about what I may call a corporate union of the Churches'. He considered that this opinion involved a fundamental misunderstanding; it could only 'rest upon the erroneous assumption that the Anglican Establishment is as truly a Church as the schismatical Greek Church'.[160] That was not the case, given that the Church of England lacked the essential elements which made up a particular Church: apostolic succession, valid orders, valid sacraments, and orthodox doctrine.

---

[158] V. A. McClelland, 'Corporate Reunion: A Nineteenth-Century Dilemma', *Theological Studies*, xliii/1 (Mar. 1982), 25.
[159] Ibid. 27.   [160] *Miscellanies*, i. 82.

The Catholic bishops commissioned Bishop Ullathorne to write to Propaganda to denounce the association and its principles, which he duly did on 26 April 1864; he also sent some issues of the *Union Review*, to illustrate the case. The Holy Office's answer, dated 16 September 1864, came as a cold shower to the members of the Association: it condemned the branch theory, implicit in the declaration of the APUC, as 'a heresy overthrowing the nature of unity, and the Divine Constitution of the Church'; consequently, it added, it would be unlawful for a Catholic to join the association, 'in as much as it is an implicit adhesion to heresy, and to an intention stained with heresy'.[161]

The blame for the APUC's condemnation was laid by general opinion at Manning's door. This was to be a lasting tradition. Wiseman tried to set the record straight, and he wrote to a correspondent: 'it is not true that the recent letter of the Holy See has been obtained by representations made by Mgr. Manning'.[162] Ullathorne himself tried to dispel this false opinion in his pastoral on the APUC question, but the charge against Manning lingered on. Dr Littledale affirmed that the rescript against the APUC had been issued in consequence of a petition in which Manning was the main mover; that, to his mind, disqualified it, 'since the name of so accomplished a master of the art of suppression and misstatement is almost enough of itself to demolish any rescript based upon his presentation'. He acknowledged that Ullathorne had denied this to be the case. That went to show Manning's astuteness, Littledale said: he had misled Cardinal Patrizi, and had also been 'effectual in concealing its own workings from Bishop Ullathorne'.[163] That Manning was not sympathetic to the association is beyond doubt, but although there are some references in his letters to Propaganda about the APUC, they are for the most

---

[161] Manning's translation in *APUC* 6.

[162] Letter dated 26 Nov. 1864, quoted in W. Ward, *Life and Times of Wiseman*, ii. 491.

[163] Quoted in W. B. Ullathorne, *The Anglican Theory of Union as Maintained in the Appeal to Rome and Dr. Pusey's 'Eirenicon': A Second Letter* (London, 1866), 5. Recent studies have shown the unfounded nature of Littledale's allegations; see e.g. E. B. Stuart, 'Roman Catholic Reactions to the Oxford Movement and Anglican Schemes for Reunion, from 1833 to the Condemnation of Anglican Orders in 1896' (D.Phil. thesis, Oxford, 1987); see also Pawley, *Faith and Family*, 298, esp. 311.

part of a passing nature and could have had little influence on Propaganda's response.

The disappointment of members of the association was great, and they felt themselves gravely misunderstood. An Address, signed by 198 Anglican clergymen, was sent in the summer of 1865 to Cardinal Patrizi, trying to clarify those points which they considered the Holy Office had misinterpreted. Its principal aim was to explain the matter of the three branches, or communions. They maintained now that, when the APUC spoke of Anglicans, Orthodox, and Roman Catholics as having an equal claim to call themselves 'Catholic', they were treating of the question of *fact*, not of *right*.

The new Archbishop-elect was asked by Rome for his comments on the address, and he was not slow in sending them. The association had been '*in no sense misunderstood*'. Their answer clearly manifested their mind:

> They say that they do not believe that there are three Churches *de jure*, but only *de facto*. But this denies (1) the exclusive unity of the Catholic and Roman Church, and (2) its exclusive infallibility, and (3) the universal duty and necessity of submission to it. These three points they do not hold. They hold that the three are all alike *de facto* Churches. ... Under the disguise of this theory lies hid the old assumption of the *divisibility* [mere breach of the visible unity] of the Church, and its consequent loss of *perfection* only. And this assumes also the suspension of infallibility, and, therefore, of the perpetual Divine assistance of the Holy Spirit.[164]

Manning's letter, and subsequent visit to Rome, had considerable influence in shaping the response of the Congregation of the Holy Office to the letter of the 198 Anglican clergyman. He felt the urgent need for an authoritative declaration. The 'unionists', he wrote to Ullathorne, claimed the support of the bishops, and many Catholics were being deceived. He considered that the way to clarify those misunderstandings would be for each bishop to publish individually the forthcoming document from Rome, and to show their personal sentiments. 'For my part', he added, 'I am ready to come out more strongly than ever.'[165]

---

[164] Letter to Talbot, 18 July 1865, quoted in *P* ii.281.

[165] Manning MSS West., Manning–Ullathorne Correspondence, *U* 34, letter dated 25 Aug. 1865.

The letter of the Congregation, dated 8 December 1865, was handed first to the representatives of the Anglican clergymen who had written to Cardinal Patrizi. Talbot sent a copy to Manning as soon as he possibly could. In the accompanying letter Talbot wrote: 'I think that you will admire it. It contains all your ideas on the subject, as they made your instructions their rule.'[166] Manning, however, was not entirely satisfied with the Congregation's reply. He felt that the letter was 'very solid and dignified, as far as it goes'. Still, he had hoped for more, 'but it will do'.[167] To make it really do, Manning published the letters from Rome with a long commentary, in which he developed at great length the points made in them. He prefaced his remarks with a brief narrative of the events which had led to the exchange of letters, and then, for the benefit of his flock, presented a clear synopsis of the principles contained in the answers of the Holy Office:

1 That the unity of the Church is absolute and indivisible, and that the Church had never lost its unity, not for so much as a moment of time ever can. ... There is, therefore, both *de jure* and *de facto*, only one Church, one by a numerical and exclusive unity.

2 That the Church of Christ is indefectible, not only in duration, but in doctrine, or in other words, that it is infallible, which is a Divine endowment bestowed upon it by its Head; and that the infallibility of the Church is a dogma of faith. ...

3 That the Primacy of the Visible Head is of Divine institution, and was ordained to generate and to preserve the unity both of faith and of communion, that is, both internal and external, of which the See of Peter is the centre and the bond.

4 That therefore the Catholic and Roman Church alone has received the name of Catholic. ...

5 That no one can give to any other body the name of Catholic without incurring manifest heresy ...

6 That whosoever is separated from the one and only Catholic Church, howsoever well he may believe himself to live, by this one sin of separation from the unity of Christ, is in the state of wrath.

---

[166] Talbot to Manning, 1 Dec. 1865, quoted in *P* ii. 284.
[167] Manning to Talbot, 11 Dec. 1865, quoted in *P* ii. 284.

7 That every several soul under pain of losing eternal life, is
  bound to enter the only Church of Christ, out of which is
  neither absolution nor entrance into the kingdom of heaven.[168]

It is difficult to see what else Manning could have expected
from the Congregation: the letter dwelt clearly with those topics—unity and infallibility—which he felt were threatened.
He prepared his pastoral, and sent the draft to some people
asking for their opinion. Ullathorne thought that some things
in it were sharp, but Grant did not think them so. Manning
did not want to sound sharp, and, following Ullathorne's advice, corrected some points in it. His efforts were not totally
successful; many thought that it marked a change of tone,
harsher now, from previous utterances on the subject.

The fundamental difference involved in the exchange of letters between the association and Propaganda or the Holy Office, as with the controversy between Pusey and Manning,
concerned the concept of unity of the Church. Manning's pastoral on the APUC was considered generally as aimed at
Pusey's *Eirenicon*. Bringing the two together, under one theological umbrella, has been controversial ever since. The association felt itself misrepresented by Rome, claiming that it did
not have a proper doctrine on unity, and that it did not identify itself with the articles published in its organ, which represented the opinions of the individual writers. In the same way,
it has been recently said, Pusey 'had no links with the APUC
and the APUC had no theology of the Church'.[169] How did
they come to be associated? For some, the cause would be
purely accidental. The publication of the *Eirenicon* so soon
after the condemnation of the APUC would explain why the
two were seen as closely related: '[t]hey both suffered from
being linked with one another. The APUC was seen as essentially Anglican and only conceiving of a reunion based on the
Branch Theory; the *Eirenicon* was mentally fixed under "unionist" and therefore trying to prevent individual conversions.'[170]

---

[168] *APUC* 8–10. The last two points need to be read in the light of Manning's
ideas, described already in this chapter, on the position of those who are outside the
Church.
[169] Stuart, 'Roman Catholic Reactions', 186.
[170] Ibid.

It was more than a mere circumstantial coincidence, however. That Pusey, and almost the totality of the Anglican members of APUC, supported the branch theory is beyond
dispute. On the other hand, the profession by the APUC that
it had no theology of the Church clashed with the public perception of the association, based on the uniform character of
the utterances of the *Union Review*. Besides, its official language
in dealing with Rome has been charged with 'incompetence
(or deliberate ambiguity)', even by those who accuse Rome of
harshness in its dealings with the APUC.[171] This ambiguity,
which people like Phillipps De Lisle did little to clarify, more
than justified the way in which Rome and the English Catholic
bishops acted. Pusey and the association were banded together
by Manning, not because he considered Pusey a 'unionist' in
the strict sense of the word—although he wrote with ideas of
reunion in mind—but because he saw them as sharing the
same fundamental error about the nature of the Church. It
should also be added that Manning's main concern, and also
Propaganda's, was not what Pusey and the Anglican members
of APUC might think about the unity of the Church, but how
far the existing ambiguity might go in confusing the issue in
Catholic minds.

For Manning, unity could only take place in truth. 'We are
ready', he wrote in his pastoral, 'to purchase the reunion of
our separated brethren at any cost less than the sacrifice of a
jot or a tittle of the supernatural order of unity and faith.'[172]
Agreement in truth should always precede unity, and the sig-
natories of the letter to Cardinal Patrizi could probably have
underwritten that statement. 'Truth alone generates unity. It
was the dogma of faith which united the intellects of men as
one intelligence. ... From this unity of intellects has sprung
the unity of wills.'[173] Truth is the cause, unity the effect. But
truth, Manning added, could not be found 'till we have submitted ourselves to a teacher who cannot err'. The only infallible teacher is God himself, and unity was to be achieved 'by
surrendering reason and will to His divine voice, teaching
through His only Church'. As he liked to repeat: 'We must be

---

[171] Cf. ibid. 170.   [172] *APUC* 16–17.
[173] Ibid. 23–4; see also *Fourfold*, 124 ff.

taught by God before we can be at peace one with another.'[174]
The unity of the Church is created 'by the submission of all
wills to one Divine Teacher through the pastors of the Church,
specially the one who is supreme on earth'.[175] Thus, there
could be no unity which did not accept this fundamental truth
of faith: 'We can offer unity only on the condition on which
we hold it—unconditional submission to the living and perpetual voice of the Church of God. If this be refused, it is not
we who hinder unity. For it is not we who impose this condition, but the Spirit of Truth who abides in the Church for
ever.'[176] The visible unity of the Church, the outward expression of its internal unity, was the 'landmark which God has
set up to bound the Fold of Salvation ... They who teach that
the Anglican separation and the Greek schism are parts of the
Catholic Church violate a dogma of faith.'[177] This was a truth
that Christians are as bound to believe as that of baptismal
regeneration.

Pusey had looked to Gallicanism for support on the question
of infallibility. According to Gallican principles, the reception
by the whole Church was the guarantee of the infallibility of a
doctrine. Gallicanism in fact, Manning argued, offered little
support for Pusey's contention. Bossuet, and Gallicans as a
whole, maintained the idea of the visible unity of the Church.
Manning quoted Bossuet's words about the Catholicity of the
Council of Trent: it was a true Council, 'as it is certain that it
is received and approved in that respect by the whole body of
the Churches which are united in communion with that of
Rome'.[178] Bossuet might have thought that the infallibility of
the Pope could be denied, but he accepted the unity and infallibility of the Catholic Church in communion with the Roman
Pontiff. Thus, Manning concluded, Anglicanism stood condemned not only by Ultramontane principles, but also by Gallican ones.

Manning admitted that some Anglicans were ready to accept the decrees of the Council of Trent, but that was not
enough for reunion, because they would accept them according
to their own interpretation. 'To profess a readiness to accept

[174] *CSer* ii. 238-9.   [175] *APUC* 24.   [176] Ibid. 17.
[177] Ibid. 26.   [178] Ibid. 32

the Council of Trent, if it be interpreted according to our opinion, is not to subject ourselves to the authority of the Council, but to subject it to our own judgement.'[179] That was equivalent to receiving the Council upon the principle of private judgement. This procedure 'would make no man a Catholic. To receive the Council of Trent only because we critically believe its decrees to be true, and not because its decrees are infallible, is private judgement'. But in that case, Manning added, we 'should not be submitting to them, but approving them. The formal motive of our approval would be not the divine authority of the Council, but the judgment of our private spirit.'[180] The APUC and Pusey occupied the same ground. In Manning's view,'[i]f a man were to hold the whole Catholic Theology and the decrees of the eighteen General Councils on the principle of the *Eirenicon*, he would not be a Catholic. He would be as true a Protestant as Luther or Calvin. It is not the believing of isolated doctrines, but the act of Divine Faith, terminating in its formal motive, the veracity of God through the living voice of the Church, that makes us Catholic Christians.'[181] 'The Anglican system,—including its most advanced developments of Anglo-Catholicism, Unionism, Ritualism,—rests upon one and the same basis; and the period which commenced with 1830 and the *Tracts for the Times*, diverse as its phenomena may be, is nevertheless in principle, in procedure, and in result, as purely and simply rationalistic as the period from 1688 down to that date.'[182] Ritualism, to single one out, was just 'private judgment in gorgeous raiment'.[183] Pusey, Manning claimed, had not answered his argument, he had merely confirmed it; and he added: 'every *Eirenicon* against the Catholic Church is a fresh reinforcement to the Rationalism of England'.[184]

Pusey also charged Manning with wanting to impose on Anglicans, as a truth of necessary belief, the infallibility of the Pope, when it had never been defined as a dogma of faith, and when even some Catholics, like the Gallicans, denied it.

---

[179] Ibid. 39.   [180] Ibid. 41.
[181] *E&C* i, pp. lxxxii–lxxxiii. In his speech to the First Vatican Council (25 May 1870), Manning affirmed that belief in the infallibility of the Church is the only adequate motive for conversion to the Catholic faith (cf. *M* lii, col. 258A).
[182] *E&C* i, pp. li–lii.   [183] Ibid., p. lxxxiii.   [184] Ibid., p. lii.

This was a charge constantly repeated by Anglican controversialists, and Manning felt it very deeply. He acknowledged the fact, but he countered the argument by telling the faithful of his diocese: 'it must be always borne in mind, and explicitly declared to our flocks, that the infallibility of the Pope, speaking *ex cathedra*, is an opinion protected by the highest authority',[185] and it would be temerity—as Alexander VIII had declared— to oppose it. It was an opinion which had been considered *proxima fide* by the most renowned theologians.

Manning maintained that reunion was not just a question of believing a little more or a little less of dogma. It implied a fundamental choice between a divine faith and rationalism. 'Unionism is outwardly a reaction against latitudinarianism; inwardly it promotes it. There can be but two principles and two tendencies: the one, divine faith ... the other, of human criticism, disguise it as you may in texts of Scripture, or in patristic learning, or in sceptical history, or rationalistic interpretation, the tendency of which is always to wider formulas and diminished truth, to comprehension of communion, and loss of faith.'[186]

There was no point in talking about the 'essentials' of the Faith. What are essentials? Who has the power to determine what is essential and what is not? By whose judgement are we to ascertain it? 'I had thought', Manning would say in answer, 'that the word "essentials" had long ago departed with "fundamentals", into the Limbus of infantine theology.'[187] For those who accepted the principle of infallibility, there was no question of a little more or a little less of dogma; implicit in their faith in the infallibility of the Church was belief in everything that the Church had defined as revealed or might define in the future as belonging to the deposit of revelation: 'The Church knows only one essential truth, and that is, the whole revelation of God.'[188] For those who did not accept the principle of infallibility, there was no question of more or less. They did not have faith, only an opinion based on private judgement. In any case, Manning would add, the 'circle of essentials [in the Anglican Church] has so short a radius, that it is diffi-

[185] *APUC* 44.　　[186] Ibid. 68.　　[187] *E&C* i, p. lxiv.
[188] *Grounds*, 25.

cult to enclose in it any perfect Christian truth'.[189] Manning
put it very simply in a letter to Ullathorne:

I am very glad you have written about Dr. Pusey's Book. What you
say is most true. It shows a simple unbelief in the two articles of
the Creed,—the Holy Ghost and the Church. I am surprised and
sorry that men should fail to appreciate this. ... I see Dr. Pusey is
again writing in answer to me about '*explanations*' [of terms and concepts used]. What can explanations do for a man who does not believe the Voice of the Explainer to be divine? He may agree with
the explanations, but that is not faith. Can Dr Pusey be really so
blind?[190]

Pusey wrote two more *Eirenicons;* they went unanswered. The
argument, as far as Manning was concerned, had already
been exhausted. Pusey and the unionists were men of great
zeal. They had struggled hard to preserve and recover Catholic
principles; it was a gallant effort, but they were building on
sand.

The rule of faith and the nature of the Church's unity were,
for Manning, the two points on which all ecumenical dialogue
resolved itself. He thought that the convocation of the First
Vatican Council offered a new ecumenical opportunity. In
the event, the terms, for different reasons, were unacceptable
to both Greeks and Anglicans. The Archbishop of Westminster, when announcing it to his flock, clearly defined the conditions for communion: 'The General Council ... will be
convened by the Roman Pontiff; and will be composed of
those who believe, as an article of Divine faith, the visible
unity and infallibility of the Catholic and Roman Church.'[191]

[189] *E&C* i, p. lxv.
[190] Manning MSS West., Manning–Ullathorne Correspondence, *U* 40, letter
dated 15 Mar. 1866.
[191] *Privilegium*, i. 88.

V

Conflicts at Home

1. *The Spirit of the* Rambler *and the* Home and Foreign Review

Manning, while dealing with Pusey's remarks and the APUC question, had an eye on developments within the Catholic Church which deeply worried him. He had, for some time, been concerned about the growth among Catholics of a school of thought which, if successful, would introduce into the Church the evils he saw afflicting Anglicanism. His fears were openly expressed in a letter to Ullathorne dated New Year's Day, 1863:

I am very glad you are following up the *Rambler*. The whole system of opinion both Philosophical and Theological seem to me false and highly dangerous. You are of course aware that the independence of revelation claimed for society and science is a new reproduction of a Tübingen theory. In these last months I have had constant evidence of the progress of rationalism and absolute unbelief not only out of the Church but among Catholics: and I believe we have a storm coming which will try the faith of many. What has ravaged Germany will pass over England, with modified results perhaps, but with extensive loss of faith.[1]

Manning felt that the storm-clouds, which had been gathering in Germany for some time, had already started to appear over the intellectual horizon of English Catholicism.

Manning had in mind the theories of the Tübingen Protestant school of theology, and the influence it had on Catholic thinking. He was fully aware of the importance of the debate which had been raging in Germany among those who had at heart the renewal of Catholic theology. The question of theological method had divided German theologians into two opposing camps. Mainz and Würzburg had become the main

---

[1] Manning MSS West., Manning–Ullathorne Correspondence, *U* 8. Manning had previously encouraged Wiseman to act against the *Rambler* (cf. J. L. Altholz, *The Liberal Catholic Movement in England* (London, 1962), 39).

centres of those who looked for the revival of theology in a renewal of the scholastic tradition. Meanwhile the 'New German Theology', conceived in the Catholic Faculty of Theology in Tübingen, paid more attention to the historical dimension of the truths of faith: revealed truths, ecclesiastical institutions, etc., would be better understood when placed in historical context and taking into consideration their development in time. The new problems arising from scientific discoveries, and the progress and rigour of historical studies, had prompted these German Catholic scholars to search for a theological method capable of meeting the new challenges. The old speculative theology was deemed wholly inadequate for that purpose. The new method, they argued, should be modelled on that of the positive sciences, while not losing sight of the supernatural character of revealed truth. They would confront Protestant and rationalistic scholarship with their own weapons, and in the process rescue Catholic intellectuals from the inferiority complex which afflicted them. In the course of the century some theologians connected with the Tübingen school, in response to questioning by Protestant historians of traditional conceptions of the origins of Christianity and of medieval developments, became more and more concerned with the historical dimension of faith, stressing the role of historical studies in theology to the detriment of other methodological elements. Döllinger, at Munich, was the most representative figure of this school. For him, in the final analysis, it was history's role to determine the content of revelation, which it was to glean from the records which contained it. Progressively he came to reject the idea of a development of doctrine, an integral element of the Tübingen method. The scholars of Döllinger's circle also claimed complete intellectual freedom, limited only by a few dogmatic definitions, in contrast to the greater respect shown by the new scholasticism for the pronouncements of the Church's magisterium, as guided by the Holy Spirit.[2]

---

[2] As background to the debate about the theological method see G. A. McCool, *Catholic Theology in the Nineteenth Century: The Quest for a Unitary Method* (New York, 1977); also E. Hocedez, *Histoire de la Théologie au XIXe siècle* (3 vols., Brussels and Paris, 1947–52).

Döllinger was being translated into English in the pages of the *Rambler* and, subsequently, in those of the *Home and Foreign Review*, with Acton as moderator and main mouthpiece of this school of thought. The principles were explicitly described, not without personal touches by Acton, in the pages of those periodicals. Their sympathizers were men inspired with a reverential respect for the new scientific methods, which, in their view, preserved science from contamination by prejudice or party spirit. Thus, 'learning ceased to be hostile to Christianity when it ceased to be pursued merely as an instrument of controversy—when facts came to be acknowledged, no longer because they were useful, but simply because they were true'.[3] Religion had nothing to fear from science: the scientific method guaranteed the certainty of the truths reached by it, and truth could not be an enemy of faith. Acton had very much at heart the desire to disarm two widespread prejudices, which he described in a letter to Newman in July 1861:

I cannot bear that Protestants should say the Church cannot be reconciled with the truths or precepts of science, or that Catholics should fear the legitimate and natural progress of the scientific spirit. These two errors seem to be almost identical, and if one is more dangerous than the other, I think it is the last. So that it comes more naturally to me to be zealous against the Catholic mistake than against the Protestant. But the weapon against both is the same, the encouragement of the true scientific spirit, and disinterested love of truth.[4]

According to Acton, an incompatibility between science and faith could arise only in the minds of those 'who have not learned to distinguish what is divine from what is human—defined dogma from the atmosphere of opinion which surrounds it,—and who honour both with the same awful reverence'.[5] The men of the *Rambler* or the *Home and Foreign Review* were not afflicted by that particular complaint. One of the essential principles of both reviews was the clear recognition

---

[3] J. E. Acton, 'Cardinal Wiseman and the Home and Foreign Review', *Home and Foreign Review*, 1862, repr. in *The History of Freedom and Other Essays*, eds. J. N. Figgis and R. V. Laurence (London, 1909), 453.

[4] *LD* xx. 6.

[5] Acton, 'Cardinal Wiseman', 458.

first, of the infinite gulf which in theology separates what is of faith from what is not of faith,—revealed dogmas from opinions unconnected with them by logical necessity, and therefore incapable of anything higher than a natural certainty—and next of the practical difference which exists in ecclesiastical discipline between the acts of infallible authority and those which possess no higher sanction than that of canonical legality. That which is not decided with dogmatic infallibility is for the time susceptible only of a scientific determination, which advances with the progress of science, and becomes absolute only where science has attained its final results.[6]

Acton clearly affirmed that God's revelation is made up of truths and facts which although 'absolute and objective in themselves, are not and cannot be known to us except through revelation, of which the Church is the organ'.[7] The philosopher could not contradict them without going outside the sphere of his competence. History, though, had a different relationship to revelation. The latter was a historical fact which could be gathered from historical sources. 'God's handwriting', Acton would say, 'exists in history independently of the Church, and no ecclesiastical exigence can alter a fact. The divine lesson has been read, and it is the historian's duty to copy it faithfully without bias and without ulterior views.'[8] Only the historian, who has deeply studied and practised the historical method, is in a position to sift truth from error, gathering it by historical research.

Some felt, not without foundation, that the new school aimed at substituting history for theology, and that in it there was little room for the magisterium of the Church. Nothing below an infallible pronouncement had more weight or authority than the acquirements of the individual or individuals putting it forward, were they the Congregation of the Index or the Pope himself. It went without saying how little regard the school of Döllinger and Acton had for scholastic theology, on which most of the utterances of the Roman Pontiffs and the Roman Congregations were founded. The Germans, in Acton's own words, had 'ceased to regard them [the scholastic theologians] as equals, or as scientific divines at all. Without

[6] J. E. Acton, 'Conflicts with Rome', *Home and Foreign Review*, Apr. 1864, repr. in *History of Freedom*, 484.
[7] Ibid. 473. [8] Ibid.

impeaching their orthodoxy, they learned to look on them as men incapable of understanding and mastering the ideas of a literature so very remote from their own, and to attach no more value to the unreasoned decrees of their organ [the Congregation of the Index] than to the undefended *ipse dixit* of a theologian of secondary rank.'[9]

While particular questions—such as education and the temporal power of the Pope—may have been the occasion of the frequent clashes of the *Rambler* and the *Home and Foreign Review* with ecclesiastical authority, Manning's opposition was directed, rather, against the principles that inspired them. He saw in them a semi-rationalistic approach to faith, which could, in due course, lead only to absolute rationalism. It was on this basis that he denounced the *Rambler* to Propaganda in 1862, asking for the review to be included on the Index.[10]

2. *History and Faith*

Acton's words about history ascertaining the content of revelation had a particularly familiar ring for Manning. They resembled voices returning from his Anglican past. In 1838, as we have seen, he had made his own Palmer's words about how to determine the truths belonging to universal tradition: their existence was a historical fact, to be established 'on the same sort of evidence as proves any other historical fact'. It had taken him many years to discover the presence of a divine teacher in the Church, and to break away from what he now saw as the ever-deepening downward spiral of rationalism. The ghost that he had thought buried in the past was raising its head again, and it had to be laid to rest anew.

Manning referred on several occasions to the relationship between history and faith, sometimes while addressing Protestant critics, on others when referring to Catholics of the school of historical criticism. Naturally, his most explicit denunciations coincided with the controversies over the infallibility of the Pope, specially in his pastoral after the First Vatican Council. However, the ideas he expressed at this juncture had been conceived, and in good measure brought out into the open, in

---

[9] J. E. Acton, 'Conflicts with Rome', 476.
[10] Cf. SCPF, *Scritture Riferite nei Congressi, Anglia 1861–1863*, fos. 341–2 and 515–16.

his Anglican years. To Manning's mind, the school of scientific historians laid down 'as a principle that history is tradition, and tradition history: that they are one and the same thing under two names'; this implied 'a tacit elimination of the supernatural, and of the Divine authority of the Church'.[11] His fundamental question was: 'Are we to understand ... that the words and acts of the Fathers, and the documents of human history, constitute the Rule of Faith, or that the Rule of Faith depends upon them, and is either more or less certain as it agrees or disagrees with them? or, in other words, that the rule of faith is to be tested by history, not history by the rule of faith?'[12] According to Manning, the supporters of these ideas seemed to accept two principles: one explicitly, that a doctrine cannot be defined until the historical difficulties are solved;[13] the second, implicit in the first, was more insidious, undermining the very foundations of the faith of the Church. It considered that the doctrinal authority of the Church and the certainty of dogma depended, 'if not altogether, at least in part, on human history. From this it would follow that when critical or scientific historians find, or suppose themselves to find, a difficulty in the writings of the Fathers or other human histories, the doctrines proposed by the Church as of Divine revelation are to be called into doubt, unless such difficulties can be solved.'[14]

[11] *Privilegium*, iii. 123–4. It is interesting to compare Manning's and Newman's ideas on the subject. Newman dealt with the relation of history to dogma in his 'Letter to the Duke of Norfolk' (1874), in *Difficulties of Anglicans*, ii. 309–13. His notes to the 3rd edn. of *The Prophetical Office of the Church*, in *VM* i (lecture I, n. 2; lecture II, nn. 1 and 3; lecture XI, n. 3) are also illustrative of their concurrence in the main arguments on the subject.

[12] *Privilegium*, iii. 121.

[13] J. Fessler, Secretary of the First Vatican Council and himself a historian, had this sort of proposition in mind when he wrote: 'If before doctrinal matters were decided in the Catholic Church, we had always had to wait until all the difficulties were cleared away, General Councils would have had a long time to wait' (*The True and False Infallibility of the Popes* (London, 1875), 17). Manning was perhaps more sceptical about the possibility of reaching generally agreed, definitive, firm conclusions on many historical problems.

[14] *Privilegium*, iii. 121. This idea had not been clearly stated before the First Vatican Council. Manning seems to have taken it, at least in its formulation, from the Constitution *Dei Filius*, ch. 3, sect. 6. He himself had suggested its insertion there, probably borrowing it from ch. 9 of the first schema *De Ecclesia*.

Manning's answer to the question was clear and uncompromising: 'Human history is neither the source nor the channel of revelation.'[15] A Catholic does not deduce his faith from history, fact, or antiquity; the reason being that 'faith was revealed and taught before history, fact, or antiquity existed. ... The Church, which teaches him now by its perpetual living voice, taught the same faith before as yet the Church had a history or an antiquity. The rule and basis of faith to those who lived before either the history or antiquity ... existed, is the rule and basis of our faith now.'[16] 'The Church itself is the Divine witness, teacher, and judge, of the revelation entrusted to it.'[17] The pastors of the Church, or *ecclesia docens*, 'divinely sustained and guided to guard and to declare the faith', were 'antecedent to history, and are independent of it'.[18]

He acknowledged that it would be legitimate to ask the question, 'If you reject history and antiquity, how can you know what was revealed before ... history and antiquity existed?' His answer was: 'The enunciation of the faith by the living Church of this hour, is the maximum of evidence, both natural and supernatural, as to the *fact* and the *contents* of the original revelation.'[19] The Third Person of the Blessed Trinity is now teaching in the Church, as he was then, with a divine and infallible voice; 'history, and antiquity, and facts ... of the past vanish before the presence of an order of facts which are divine—namely, the unity, perpetuity, infallibility of the Church of God'.[20] The followers of the school of historical criticism were more or less explicitly rejecting the perpetual office of the Holy Spirit in the Church. They appealed 'from the traditional doctrine of the Catholic Church, delivered by its common and constant teaching, to history interpreted by themselves'.[21] This would be an 'inverted and rationalistic method of extracting dogmas from the facts of history'.[22] History is not the source of faith, neither is it the method of theolo-

---

[15] *Privilegium*, iii. 125.   [16] *TM* 214.   [17] *Privilegium*, iii. 123.

[18] Ibid. During the Vatican Council, while Hefele was claiming in his speech, 17 May 1870, that historical difficulties militated against the definition of papal infallibility, Manning wrote in his notes: 'Non sumus in scholis sed in oecumenico Concilio congregati. Interrogandi sunt non historici, et critici, sed vivum Eccl[esi]ae oraculum', quoted in Cwiekowski, *English Bishops*, 324.

[19] *TM* 214.   [20] Ibid. 216.   [21] *Privilegium*, iii. 128.

[22] *TM* 216. Newman, in his 'Letter to the Duke of Norfolk', wrote: 'He who

gical proof. Manning quoted Cano's rules about the authority
of history and its role in theology. Cano's main principle was
that history 'can afford no adequate motive of divine
certainty'.[23] History could provide some probable arguments,
sometimes even a certain one, but based only on a human
and, therefore, fallible authority.

History was not an exact science. Not even the new rigorous
historical method could turn it into a proper science, made up
of certain principles and conclusions. Manning examined
what the sources were from which history was built up. It was
fashioned from documents 'written by uninspired human
authors, transmitted by documents open to corruption,
change, and mutilation, without custody or security, except
the casual tradition of human testimony and human criticism,
open to perversion by infirmity and passion of every kind'.[24]
If such was the raw material for the work of history, 'who and
what are the workmen? Has any of them, or have they altogether, the promise of Divine assistance to interpret history
against the living witness of the Church of God? They appeal
to the past, which is dead and speechless, save as it echoes
their own voices.'[25] The school of historical criticism, however,
had obviated these objections and rendered them ineffective

by the simple introduction of one additional compound, their own
personal infallibility. The universal Church assembled in Council
under the guidance of its Head [the Vatican Council had just
taken place] does not, cannot, and what is worse, will not, know its
own history, or the true interpretation of its own records and acts.
But, by a benign though tardy provision, the science of history has
arisen, like the art of extracting sunbeams from cucumbers, to recall

believes the dogmas of the Church only because he has reasoned them out of History,
is scarcely a Catholic' (*Difficulties of Anglicans*, ii. 312).

[23] *TM* 91.

[24] *Privilegium*, iii. 133; see also *Grounds*, 37. Fessler also pointed out the difference
between a divine source and a human one. He considered history of value for theology as a corroboration of doctrinal statements or as offering an opportunity for
clarifying them further because of the historical objections put forward in apparent
contradiction to particular truths (cf. *True and False Infallibility*, 22–3).

[25] H. E. Manning, *Religio Viatoris* (5th ed., London, n.d.), 84. Döllinger's blunder
in denying the ecumenical character of the Council of Florence (*Allgemeine Zeitung*,
21 Jan. 1870) would offer a glaring example of a historian falling victim to both scientific fraud and his own anti-infallibilist passion (cf. V. Conzemius, 'Lord Acton and
the First Vatican Council', *Journal of Ecclesiastical History*, xx (Oct. 1969), 279).

the Church from its deviations to the recognition of its own true mis-
deeds. Such higher intelligences may be called and revered as the
Pontiffs of the Realm of Criticism. We are warned, however, not to
profane this awful Hierarchy of superior persons by further
analysis.[26]

Manning's sense of humour did not lead him to underesti-
mate the dangers inherent in the principles of that school, for
he considered that 'under this pretext of scientific history lurks
an assumption which is purely heretical'[27]: the appeal from
the divine authority of the Church to another authority.
Lutheran and Calvinistic Protestantism had appealed to Holy
Scripture, interpreted by private judgement; Anglicanism to
the faith of the undivided Church, with some adding the consent of the Fathers. The new German and English school, according to Manning, 'places itself in constant antagonism to
the authority of the Church, and, to justify its attitude of antagonism, appeals to "scientific history" '.[28] The 'appeal from
the light of faith to the light of history' implied an appeal
'from the supernatural to the natural order; a process, as I
have said again and again, consistent in Protestants and Rationalists: in Catholics, simply heretical'.[29] These ideas would
weaken the hold of many Catholics on the rule of faith by exalting history and deprecating the teaching authority of the
Church. God's will is different, Manning would say. He wants
man to learn the doctrines of revelation not 'by criticism on
past history, but by acts of faith in the living voice of the
Church at this hour'.[30] Those theories posed a serious threat.
They had already perverted the faith of some, and, according
to Manning, others would follow: many people had been partly
deceived, and partly intimidated, by the tone and by the apparent or real scholarship of the leaders of the party.

Manning did not reject history. The Church had indeed a
history recorded in documents, and the 'tradition of the
Church may be historically treated; but between history and
the tradition of the Church there is a clear distinction'.[31]
Tradition, for Manning, is made up of two divine elements:

[26] H. E. Manning, *Pastime Papers*, ed. W. Meynell (London, n.d.), 72.
[27] *Privilegium*, iii. 126.   [28] Ibid. 127.   [29] Ibid. 135.
[30] *Privilegium*, ii. 126.   [31] *Privilegium*, iii. 123.

the word of God, written and unwritten, and the teaching authority of the Church. Just as the Church alone 'can judge of the true sense and interpretation of Holy Scripture, it alone can judge of the true sense and interpretation of the acts of its own Pontiffs and Councils'.[32] To appeal from the judgement of the Church to history would be equivalent to 'Lutheranism in history'.

Manning, following Schlegel, considered the witness of the Church to be the greatest historical authority for the events of her own history. 'The Church is a living history of the past. It is the page of history still existing, open before his eyes. Antiquity to the Catholic is not a thing gone by; it is here, still present.'[33] Manning saw the Church as a living witness, whose consciousness stretched from Pentecost morning to the present day. Consequently, she is 'a sufficient motive to convince a prudent man that Christianity is a divine revelation', and a motive of credibility 'sufficient for the act of faith in the Church as a divine witness'.[34]

The conclusive crisis for the school of historical criticism was unleashed by Döllinger's manifesto at the Munich Catholic Congress of September 1863, called as an attempt to foster unity among German Catholic scholars. His opening address about the past and the present of theology compared the Roman and German theological methods. The latter, he claimed, were defending the Faith with all the weapons of modern scholarship, while the former were still using the rusty tools of scholasticism. He demanded complete freedom for the theologian whenever dogmatic definitions were not at issue, and gave the impression of claiming for the new German theology a role almost equivalent to that of the Church's magisterium.[35]

This time, the voice which spoke out against the principles he espoused was not the voice of Mainz or Würzburg, or of an English bishop, but that of the supreme authority in the Church. On 21 December 1863, Pius IX addressed a letter to the Archbishop of Munich in which he clearly stated, among other things, that the assent of faith should be given not only

---

[32] Ibid. 129–30.   [33] *Grounds*, 37.   [34] *Privilegium*, ii. 125.
[35] Cf. 'The Munich Congress', *Home and Foreign Review* (Jan. 1864), 209–44.

to the dogmatic definitions of Ecumenical Councils or of Roman Pontiffs', 'it must also be extended to those things, which through the ordinary teaching of the whole Church throughout the world, are proposed as divinely revealed and, as a result, by universal and constant consent of Catholic theologians are held to be matters of faith'.[36]

The letter to the Archbishop of Munich was published on 5 March 1864. Acton, in the April 1864 issue of the *Home and Foreign Review*, summarized in clear sentences the substance of the Munich brief:

In the present condition of society the supreme authority of the Church is more than ever necessary, and must not surrender in the smallest degree the exclusive direction of ecclesiastical knowledge. An entire obedience to the decrees of the Holy See and the Roman congregations cannot be inconsistent with the freedom and progress of science. The disposition to find fault with the scholastic theology, and to dispute the conclusions and the method of its teachers, threatens the authority of the Church, because the Church has not only allowed theology to remain for centuries faithful to their system, but has urgently recommended it as the safest bulwark of the faith, and an efficient weapon against her enemies. Catholic writers are not bound only by those decisions of the infallible Church which regard articles of faith. They must also submit to the theological decisions of the Roman congregations, and to the opinions which are commonly received in the schools. And it is wrong, though not heretical, to reject those decisions or opinions.[37]

On 8 March, Acton had written a letter to Simpson which clearly defined the position of the *Review* and the way forward. He felt, though, that 'the open aggressive declaration, and the will to enforce obedience', were 'in reality new'. This placed the *Review*, he added, 'in flagrant contradiction with the government of the Church'.[38] He did not want to hide or disguise in public how far the principles contained in the Munich brief were in opposition to those upheld by the *Home and Foreign Review*. The *Review* had not only expressed opinions contrary to

[36] Letter *Tuas libenter* (Dz-Sch 2879), transl. taken from G. Van Ackeren (ed.), *The Church Teaches* (Rockford, Ill., 1973), 84.

[37] Acton, 'Conflicts with Rome', 482.

[38] Acton to Simpson, 8 Mar. 1864, in J. E. Acton, *The Correspondence of Lord Acton and Richard Simpson*, eds. J. L. Altholz, D. McElrath, and J. C. Holland, iii (Cambridge, 1975), 185.

those of the brief; it existed for the very purpose of so doing. Acton publicly acknowledged the position in which the editors found themselves. 'It is the design of the Holy See not, of course, to deny the distinction between dogma and opinion ... but to reduce the practical recognition of it among Catholics to the smallest possible limits. A grave question therefore arises as to the position of a *Review* founded in great part for the purpose of exemplifying this distinction.'[39] Part of that distinction was to declare that the Pope was not infallible, and that 'there is no institution from which this [infallible] knowledge can be obtained with immediate certainty. A Council is not *a priori* œcumenical; the Holy See is not separately infallible. The one has to await a sanction, the other has repeatedly erred.'[40]

The awkward position in which the *Home and Foreign Review* had been placed by the brief was to be resolved by its closure in 1864. The *Review*, according to Acton, was to be sacrificed on the double altar of truth and of obedience to authority: it would be as wrong to abandon principles which had not ceased to be true as to defy the legitimate authority of the Church, which had condemned them.[41] The withdrawal of the *Home and Foreign Review* from the arena did not imply that the principles it had maintained were by any means dead. Acton spoke of the need to wait for better times.

3. *Ward on Infallibility*

Acton's parting shot could not fail to draw fire from the *Dublin Review*. In July of the same year Ward published his essay 'Rome and the Munich Congress', wherein he clearly defined the error which was to be his target: that the assent of faith is due to no doctrines other than those which the Church has expressly defined. His contention was that to maintain 'that the

---

[39] Acton, 'Conflicts with Rome' 484.

[40] Ibid. 477.

[41] Simpson would agree with the course proposed by Acton: 'It is clearly impossible', he wrote, 'to carry on a professedly Catholic Review on our principles, as it is for us to change our principles at every wind of pastoral that may blow across the Alps ... Of course you will let it be clearly understood that we in no sense accept the views of Pius IX' (in *Correspondence of Acton and Simpson*, iii. 186).

Church taught no doctrines as of faith before she defined them, is to say that before heresies arose she had no faith at all'.[42] Manning could have made that sentence his own, and it is quite likely that he was the source of it. It was reminiscent of what he had said in answer to those who affirmed that faith was based on Holy Scripture alone: had there been no faith in the Church till the canon of Holy Scripture was formed? The volume in which Ward collected his essays in the *Dublin Review* was dedicated to the Archbishop, in recognition of Ward's debt to Manning's constant teaching that 'there is no security for religious truth, except in the most humble and unreserved submission to the Church, on all matters which are related ever so remotely to faith and morals'.[43] Thus, he felt as imperative the need to clarify the degree of assent due to the different declarations of authority, and, in particular, to those of the Roman Pontiffs and of the Roman Congregations. Ward considered that this all-important methodical ground had not been cultivated with the attention that it deserved, and he decided to study it thoroughly. As far as he could see, men of the *Home and Foreign Review* stamp regarded the rulers of the Church much as they 'might regard Balaam's ass: they are made the organs of a divine utterance ... at certain very wide intervals, but are otherwise below the ordinary level of humanity, in their apprehension of God's works and ways'.[44]

The fundamental principles Ward was fighting for were: the Church is infallible; the 'infallibility which the Catholic Episcopate possesses collectively, the Holy Father possesses individually, as the Church's teacher';[45] the 'Pope's infallibility is precisely co-extensive with that of the Ecclesia Docens'.[46]

Ward developed his ideas starting from a proposition which he considered 'indubitable on Catholic principles ... that the

---

[42] W. G. Ward, 'Rome and the Munich Congress', *Dublin Review*, July 1864, repr. in *The Authority of Doctrinal Decisions which are not Definitions of Faith, Considered in a Short Series of Essays Reprinted from the 'Dublin Review'* (London, 1866), 2.

[43] W. G. Ward, *Authority of Doctrinal Decisions*, p. v.

[44] W. G. Ward, 'Rome and the Munich Congress', 25.

[45] Ibid. 9.

[46] W. G. Ward, 'Rome, Unionism, and Indifferentism', *Dublin Review*, July 1865, repr. in *Authority of Doctrinal Decisions*, 84.

Church *possesses* whatever infallibility she *claims*.[47] The *Ecclesia docens* cannot claim an infallibility that she does not possess: 'If she is mistaken in considering herself infallible on one class of questions, how can we take her word for her infallibility on another?'[48] The same could be said of the Pope and his infallibility. He had to be infallible in all those pronouncements in which he claimed to speak infallibly. It could not be otherwise. If he were to be mistaken once in considering himself infallible when he was not, there would be no guarantee that he would be infallible on any other occasion. Thus, he felt that all the arguments could be resolved into one of fact: '*Does* the Pope claim to teach doctrine ex cathedra in Allocutions, Encyclicals, and the like?'[49]

The Pope taught *ex cathedra*, according to Ward, when he spoke as universal teacher and demanded the assent of the faithful to a particular doctrine. Ward seemed to imply that the mere fact of demanding interior assent was a sufficient sign of an *ex cathedra* infallible pronouncement, and he would express his surprise in a letter to Manning when the latter put forward a different view: 'Are there 10 people in the world who think themselves bound to accept his [the Pope's declarations] with *interior assent* while not thinking them *infallible*? I did not know there was any such person, till you expressed your opinion. A man like Monsell would be fully as disgusted with your opinion as with mine.'[50] Where Monsell would have been disgusted, others might have been confused, as Manning did not clearly explain this point in his writings. As we have seen, he affirmed that only an infallible authority could demand interior assent. His thesis that some of its pronouncements, although not infallible, still called for interior assent

[47] W. G. Ward, *Authority of Doctrinal Decisions*, p. xi. This was a basic principle which Ward repeated innumerable times during the controversy with Ryder (see *A Letter [to] the Revd. Fr. Ryder on his Recent Pamphlet* (London, 1867), 18; etc.).[48] W. G. Ward, 'Extent of the Church's Infallibility—the Encyclical "Mirari Vos"', *Dublin Review*, Jan. 1865, repr. in *Authority of Doctrinal Decisions*, 43.

[49] W. G. Ward, *Authority of Doctrinal Decisions*, p. xii.

[50] Ward to Manning, n.d., quoted in D. McElrath, *The Syllabus of Pius IX: Some Reactions in England* (Louvain, 1964), 150. Did Manning come to agree with Ward in later years? In 1875 he would write: 'It is an axiom in morals *Lex dubia non obligat*. But if it be doubtful whether the Syllabus is *ex cathedra*, I am not bound to receive it with interior assent' (*The Vatican Decrees in their Bearing on Civil Allegiance* (London, 1875), 16).

seems to rest on the high degree of probability that, being made under the guidance of the Holy Spirit, they would be exempt from error.[51]

Ward considered that Gregory XVI had claimed to speak infallibly in his encyclical *Mirari Vos*. That was for him more than enough to prove the infallibility of all encyclicals: 'no human being ... will admit the doctrinal infallibility of this Encyclical, while he hesitates in attributing the same quality to that whole class of Papal decrees which it represents'.[52] The acceptance by the episcopate of the Pope's doctrinal pronouncements would also identify them as infallible, on Gallican principles.

Again, the fact of the Pope designing a doctrinal document for the general guidance of the faithful identified it, to Ward's mind, as an *ex cathedra* pronouncement. It was clear that this had been the Pope's intention in some letters or briefs addressed to individuals, as in the case of Günther's condemnation or in that of the Munich Brief. From this he concluded that '[a]ll the doctrinal instructions contained in these addresses [allocutions, encyclicals, letters to a bishop, etc.] are ex cathedra'.[53] It was rather more difficult to qualify the character of those doctrinal decrees of Roman Congregations which the Pope had made his own by confirming them and ordering their publication. Ward, on this particular, declared: 'Such decrees, if promulgated by the Pope's express command, are probably ex cathedra.'[54]

Infallibility, though, did not cover all the doctrinal statements introduced in a particular papal document, but only that doctrine which the Pope intended to teach. Thus, '[i]f the

---

[51] Ward also accepted the possibility of an internal assent to a non-infallible decree based on probability, although he confined it to the level of decrees of the Sacred Congregations not confirmed by the Pope. Their familiarity with the doctrine of the Church, the Pope's supervision and direction of their work, and the general providence of God over the purity of the Faith would guarantee the soundness of those decrees (cf. 'Doctrinal Decrees of a Pontifical Congregation', in *Authority of Doctrinal Decisions*, 133 ff.).

[52] W. G. Ward, 'Extent of the Church's Infallibility', 45.

[53] W. G. Ward, *Authority of Doctrinal Decisions*, p. x.

[54] Ibid., p. xvi. The decrees of the Pontifical Congregations which had not been directly approved by the Pope did not demand intellectual interior assent, although—Ward thought—they, on the grounds of probabilities, deserved a certain interior assent (cf. 'Doctrinal Decrees', 133 ff.).

doctrinal reasons even for a doctrinal declaration are not infallible, much less can infallibility be claimed for the doctrinal reasons of a disciplinary enactment'.[55]

Quanta Cura and the *Syllabus* were also infallible on the above principles. However, Ward acknowledged that neither of them were definitions of faith, as the Bull *Ineffabilis Deus* had been. They also covered many areas not directly connected with faith and morals. This went to prove, he argued, that (a) the Church is also infallible when she condemns a proposition with a censure less severe than that of heresy, as approaching heresy, being scandalous, etc.; (b) that there is an 'enormous number of *philosophical* truths, on which she may infallibly pronounce; and this because of their intimate connection with the Apostolic Deposit'.[56]

He acknowledged that his ideas were not accepted by all Catholics, and that there were 'two propositions'—contrary to the theory he was propounding—'which may be held by a Catholic, at all events, without forfeiting his title to Catholicism. He may hold (1), that the Holy See is not infallible, even in those definitions of *faith* which it may put forth, unless the Catholic Episcopate expressly or tacitly adhere to them; and he may hold (2), that the Pope and bishops united are fallible, when they condemn a thesis, not precisely as heretical, but as deserving some lesser censure';[57] others would not accept the infallibility of the Pope's instructions which were not definitions of the Faith. Such were not excluded from the body of the Church, but they were 'unsound Catholics'; their error was a fundamental one and violently anti-Catholic; 'they commit, moreover, as we must maintain, (materially at least) mortal sin'.[58]

Theirs was, therefore, a rather precarious condition, and it would be difficult for anybody holding those ideas to avoid a downward progression towards more fundamental errors. Ward then described the successive steps that led a Catholic towards apostasy:

First, he refuses to believe any Catholic doctrine which is not strictly defined. Next, as to the defined doctrines themselves, he more and

---

[55] W. G. Ward, 'Extent of the Church's Infallibility', 50. [56] Ibid. 38.
[57] Ibid. 36. [58] W. G. Ward, 'Rome, Unionism, and Indifferentism', 107.

more chooses to confine his acceptance of them to the lowest sense
which their words will grammatically bear, instead of studying the
Church's full intention. Then a current of thought finds outward
vent, which has long been silently proceeding; and he both thinks
and speaks of the Church's rulers with compassionate contempt.
... [The] time could not be far distant, when he would find himself
in a direct opposition to the Church's teaching.[59]

There was little doubt that he was referring to Döllinger and
Acton, and those associated with them.

Wilfrid Ward was to point out later that although his
father's 'logic was more moderate than his rhetoric, it was his
rhetoric which gave the tone to his works and decided their
effect'.[60] This is true only up to a certain point. The inner
logic of his ideas was probably missed by most of his contemporaries; Ward's conclusions, on the other hand, were clear
enough, and not a few people found some of them rather extreme. People like Newman and Ryder particularly resented
his branding of those who did not go along with him to his
final conclusions as unsound and disloyal Catholics, and as
committing mortal sin, at least materially. Ward exonerated
them from that charge only on the plea of invincible ignorance.
They thought this a source of scandal for both Protestants and
Catholics. The former might come to consider Ward's view as
the only legitimate one for Catholics to maintain, and would
then feel further alienated from the Church; Catholics, for
their part, could be unnecessarily upset in their faith by the implications of Ward's theories. He was free to maintain them,
Newman thought, but he should not impose them on others.
'Let me observe then', Newman wrote to him, 'that, in former
years *and now*, I have considered the theological differences between us as unimportant in themselves; that is, such as to be
simply compatible with a reception, both by you and by me,
of the whole theological teaching of the Church in the widest
sense of the word "teaching".' But now, he added, 'by exalting
your opinions into dogmas', Ward was dividing the Church.
'I protest then again, not against your tenets, but against
what I must call your schismatical spirit. ... I pray God that

[59] W. G. Ward, 'Rome and the Munich Congress', 25.
[60] W. Ward, *William George Ward and the Catholic Revival* (London, 1893), 183.

I may never denounce, as you do, what the Church has not denounced.'[61] He confessed that he preferred to act in the spirit of the old maxim: '*In necessariis unitas, in dubiis libertas, in omnibus charitas.*' Ward subscribed to the principle, but he drew differently the circle encompassing truths of necessary belief.

4. The Ward–Ryder Controversy: A Duel by Proxy?

Ryder was the man to attempt to rid Newman, and those who thought like him, of that quarrelsome layman. He claimed, in 1867, that Ward's ideas on the subject had their origin in his 'craving for ideal completeness'. This led him to an a priori argument which took the leap 'from our notion of what should be, to what it *is*'.[62] Ward, he continued, in search of the most effective system to 'beat this wretched wild world into subjection', had built up a system which recommended itself to him 'as the best moral discipline, and as most satisfactorily supplying a moral want'.[63] Ward's ways, then, could not be but God's ways! The strategy had been suggested by Newman: before dealing with Ward's opinions, Ryder should show 'from Ward's character of mind how untrustworthy he was'.[64] It is doubtful whether this was the correct approach in the circumstances. What seems to be beyond doubt is that Ryder misunderstood Ward's fundamental reason for the theory that he had put forward on the subject.

Among other things, as would be pointed out to Ryder, it was not a new theory. In its general outline, the Pope's infallibility and the subjects it covered were common opinion among theologians. During the Ward–Ryder controversy, a good number of those consulted or who volunteered their views agreed in principle with Ward's main conclusions. Earlier on, in 1865, Cardella, when asked his opinion of the ideas put forward in the *Dublin Review*, answered by saying that

[61] Letter dated 9 May 1867, *LD* xxiii. 216–17. Ward admitted in one of his pamphlets that even some of those who tended to agree with him had cautioned him against his *peremptoriness*, as injuring the very cause he wanted to promote (cf. *A Second Letter to the Revd. Father Ryder* (London, 1868), 12). He acknowledged the fact, but seems to have found it difficult to check his language.

[62] H. I. D. Ryder, *Idealism in Theology: A Review of Dr Ward's Scheme of Dogmatic Authority* (London 1867), 9–10.

[63] Ibid. 8.

[64] Newman to Canon Walker, 11 May 1867, *LD* xxiii. 227.

Ward's and Dr Murray's views were without doubt Roman Catholic doctrine.[65] A representative sample of current theological opinion can also be found in the study by the Preparatory Theological Commission of the First Vatican Council, in February 1869, of Cardoni's Vote on the infallibility of the Roman Pontiff. The Commission counted among its twenty-four members such eminent theologians as Perrone, Franzelin, Schrader, and Hettinger. In their answers to eight questions on the subject, taken from Cardoni's Vote, they unanimously affirmed that the Pope was infallible as a public person, with an infallibility coextensive in its object with that of the Church—that is, even in his minor censures and in non-revealed matters connected with the deposit. Opinions were divided, however, on whether the decrees of the Roman Congregations were infallible once they had obtained the approval of the Roman Pontiff. The majority seem to have thought that they were, or could be, infallible; others were of the opinion that to be so they required a special act of the Pope, equivalent to an act *ex cathedra*, not just a simple approval.[66] It is also worth mentioning that, during the Council, the Theological-Dogmatic Commission would point out that the fact that a doctrinal decree was directed to a particular person did not necessarily exclude its being addressed to the universal Church.[67] On the other hand, Ward's identification of the demand of internal assent as one of the hallmarks of an infallible decree had led him to conclusions far beyond the limits of common theological opinion. Here he found himself open to criticism on purely theological grounds, and that from a quarter he did not expect: that of the Roman theologians.[68]

Ryder maintained that their main difference consisted in Ward's insistence on the infallibility of *all* encyclicals, allocutions, etc. Ryder did not accept the infallibility of encyclicals *per se*; nor did he acknowledge the infallibility of all minor cen-

---

[65] Cardella to unknown correspondent, letter dated 29 Dec. 1865, Birmingham Oratory Archive, Ryder Papers.

[66] Cf. *M* xlix, cols. 668–73.

[67] Cf. *M* lii, col. 940A, also col. 1225BC.

[68] At first, the agreement of the Roman theologians on the interior assent due to encyclicals, allocutions, etc. made Ward think that these theologians maintained the infallibility of all those documents. He soon discovered that this was not always the case.

sures, if this were to imply that the propositions so condemned
were all certainly false. Ryder's *Idealism in Theology* showed, on
the other hand, how far Ryder and Newman, from whom
Ryder had imbibed most of his ideas,[69] would go along with
Ward. 'I have ever conceived myself to be an Ultramontane,'
Ryder would say.[70] He confessed that he accepted the infallibility of the Pope in his definitions of faith. That covered
those truths which are contained in the *depositum* or which
might certainly be deduced from truths contained in it.
Furthermore, he acknowledged that encyclicals were written
under the special guidance of the Holy Spirit, and that the general course of these instructions could not be other than holy
and true.[71] The presumption is in favour of the truth of such
pronouncements: 'the mere fact that one is speaking, whose
every word has so important a share in the Divinely-guided
policy of the Church, must generate "a violent presumption",
as Amort calls it, in favour of the truth of what he is saying'.[72]
They go so far to tie the Church to the particular line they
take that, were they to foster error, this fact would militate
against Christ's promise that the gates of hell would not prevail
against his Church. They should be received with respect and
obeyed by all Catholics. All the doctrinal instructions contained in the encyclicals, Ryder said, 'at least after they have
been received without protest by the Church, must be presumed to have a sort of infallibility, to use the term improperly,
viz: an *ex post facto* immunity from all substantial error of faith
or morals'.[73] This was far from a statement of Gallican principles, but rather an echo of Newman's view of the '*securus iudicat
orbis terrarum*'.

In Ryder's eyes, Ward had lost sight of the difference between certain and probable religious truths. There is, he said,
'a wide sphere of probable religious truth, approximating
more or less closely to certainty, but never reaching it, within

---

[69] Many of Newman's ideas on this subject in the *Apologia* and, in particular, in his
letters to Pusey in 1867 (letters dated 22 and 23 Mar. 1867, *LD* xxiii. 98–100, 104–
7) found their way into Ryder's answer to Ward.

[70] Ryder, *Idealism in Theology*, 13.

[71] Cf. ibid. 16.

[72] H. I. Ryder, *A Letter to William George Ward, Esq., D.Ph., on his Theory of Infallible
Instruction* (London, 1868), 15.

[73] Ryder, *Idealism in Theology*, 17.

which we are bound to yield not merely the practical assent of obedience, but also a certain degree of internal intellectual adherence, varying according to the nature of the case'.[74] He argued 'that any one, who should mentally reject as untrue, even whilst punctiliously obeying, any official utterance of the Holy Father, on the ground that it was not infallible, would not only be acting unreasonably, but even sinfully against the *pietas fidei*'.[75]

Pietas fidei was a concept, rich in content, which Ryder had borrowed from Newman, and which he made explicit as the controversy with Ward unfolded. Because of the assistance of the Holy Spirit, the antecedent probability of the truth of the doctrinal instructions in encyclicals, etc., weighed heavily in their favour. They required interior assent. Here, however, Ryder parted ways with Ward. The interior assent demanded by these pronouncements of the Pope was not an absolute interior assent. Only infallible utterances demanded an absolute interior assent. The *pietas fidei* imposes on the faithful the duty of presuming the Church right until 'proved wrong, or, at least, until there be a rational ground of doubt'.[76] The *onus probandi* was on the other side. Ryder considered the existence of those grounds for doubt highly unlikely; he even went as far as saying that he believed that such foundations for dissent, 'even supposing their existence, from the nature of the case, cannot be discovered'.[77] Therefore, it would not only be sinful but also unreasonable to reject those doctrinal instructions.

He complained that Ward, in trying to buttress the infallibility of the Pope, was damaging the cause he wanted to defend. To make the Pope unable to speak except infallibly—which was more than Ward had ever claimed—would amount to a 'most inconvenient gift, which, like the golden touch of King

---

[74] Ryder, *Idealism in Theology*, 24.

[75] Ibid. 25. This was a concept which Newman used repeatedly. See his letters to Pusey quoted in n. 68 above; also his letter to Flanagan, 15 Feb. 1868, in J. D. Holmes (ed.), *The Theological Papers of John Henry Newman on Biblical Inspiration and on Infallibility* (Oxford, 1979), 155). The same ideas appeared later on in Newman's 'Letter to the Duke of Norfolk', 257–8, 339, 345.

[76] Ryder, *Letter to Ward*, 37.

[77] Ibid. He seems to imply that this would be the case at least at the time of the pronouncement, and quite probably afterwards.

Midas, is calculated to check the free action of its possessor'.[78] Ward, like Saul when arming David to meet Goliath, was forcing upon Catholics 'an equipment, in which, however it may become himself, the majority of them cannot even walk, still less fight'.[79]

Ryder's argument was partly deformed by its tone, in the attempt to ridicule Ward, and by suggesting that adulation and flattery of authority were among the principal aims of those who, like his courtiers with Canute, exaggerated the power of the Pope. His sense of humour, sometimes sharp and pointed, was on other occasions a poor imitation of Newman's irony and, in general, rather unsuited to the theme in hand, taking 'from the dignity of so momentous a controversy'.[80] Ullathorne judged Ryder's pamphlet inopportune, and Manning concurred with this opinion. 'I fear', Manning wrote to Ullathorne on 11 May 1867, 'that it will gravely complicate matters which were tangled enough already.'[81] To Talbot he wrote: 'Fr. Ryder of the Edgbaston Oratory has published an attack on Ward's book on Encyclicals. Dr. Newman sent it to Ward with a letter *adopting* it, and saying that he was glad to leave behind him young men to maintain those principles'.[82]

Flanagan, writing to Ryder at the time of the publication of *Idealism*, described the possible sources of opposition to his ideas in England:

My opinion is that by 3 schools (if they are distinct) you are looked upon as a semi-heretic, if not worse. *First* that Manning and his school entirely agree with Ward is not to be doubted. The quotation at p. 14 of W[ard]'s letter from Manning's work (neither of which I have seen) are, I think conclusive, both as to condemned propositions, and encyclicals, etc. *Next* we have the Ushaw school as represented by Dr. Gillow. He is furious, and if he had his will would commit you and your essay to the flames. *Lastly*, I fancy, the London Or[atory] are against you. This is only my own inference.

---

[78] Ryder, *Idealism in Theology*, 17–18.

[79] Ibid. 62.

[80] Russell to Ryder, letter dated 27 May 1867, Birmingham Oratory Archive, Ryder Papers. Others among Ryder's supporters also took exception at the tone of his response to Ward.

[81] Manning MSS West., Manning–Ullathorne Correspondence, *U* 75.

[82] Quoted in *P* ii. 320. See Newman to Ward, letter dated 30 Apr. 1867 (*LD* xxiii. 197).

They will stick up for anything Faber has written. Now he has committed himself distinctly to the 'Ecclesiastical Faith' view.[83]

It was an accurate prediction. On the other hand, the Jesuits Garside and Coleridge were in favour of Ryder, and so were Edmund Knight of Oscott and Russell of Maynooth, the latter with some qualifications; Moriarty, Bishop of Kerry, found himself somewhere between Ward and Ryder.

The ensuing war of pamphlets between Ward and Ryder did little to help them understand each other or to clarify the issues. It did help, however, to clarify the meaning they attached to some of their words. In the course of the controversy, both of them had to acknowledge the lack of accuracy of their language at certain points, and had to explain or correct some of their expressions. The public soon lost interest in the dispute: Ryder confessed, in his private correspondence with Ward, that his *Idealism* had sold well and almost paid the printer's bill; his *Letter to Ward* had not sold at all.[84]

Ward's logician's mind militated against the idea of demanding interior assent to a non-infallible proposition; his common sense could perceive, on the other hand, how easy it would be for men to find a rational ground for doubting whatever they disliked.[85] Ward felt that Ryder's opinions led to conclusions which, although removed from Ryder's mind, others would draw. Ryder, to Ward's mind, denied that the Pope had spoken infallibly when the Roman Pontiff had said that this was the case. Thus, he totally undermined the infallibility of the Pope in any other pronouncement. Ryder, on the other hand, could not visualize Ward's fundamental principle, and how it forced him to the conclusions he reached.

[83] Quoted in McElrath, *Syllabus*, 162.

[84] Ryder to Ward, dated 24 Apr. 1868, St Andrews University Library, Ward Papers, box vii, no. 258. We do not have information about the sales of Ward's pamphlets, but they probably suffered a similar fate. The Ward–Ryder correspondence, begun as a means of clarifying the theological issues dividing them, while not altering their respective points of view on the subject, became more personal and friendly as time went by. Ward would later welcome Ryder's response to Dr Littledale's *Plain Reasons against Joining the Church of Rome* (1880) (see H. I. D. Ryder, *Catholic Controversy. A Reply to Dr Littledale's 'Plain Reasons'* (London, 1881)). At that time W. G. Ward told his son Wilfrid that Fr. Ryder was 'by far the best theologian in England' (W. Ward, 'Fr. Ignatius Ryder. A Reminiscence', in *Ten Personal Studies*, 117–18).

[85] Cf. W. G. Ward, *Second Letter*, 18.

Perhaps the only real point of interest in the war of pamphlets was that Ryder made an explicit declaration of the infallibility of minor censures, and clarified his description of the subject-matter covered by the gift of infallibility. In *Idealism*, he had—unknowingly, it seems—narrowed it to encompass only those truths which were part of the deposit or could be deduced from it. Russell and Moriarty had pointed out to him how this was far less than what was generally admitted by theologians.[86] Consequently, in his *Letter to Ward*, he quoted Newman's reference in the *Apologia* to the infallibility of the Church in the *pomeria*, those subject-matters which bear upon religion, and where a mistake would be equivalent to the gates of hell prevailing against it and a failure in her mission as pillar and bulwark of truth. That would include the canonization of saints, attributing error in faith and morals to a book, etc.[87]

Ward changed his stance little, but was forced to admit the theoretical possibility that some *obiter dicta* in the pontifical acts might be infallible, given that one of the propositions of the *Syllabus* had been an *obiter dictum* in the original document. On the question of the infallibility of encyclicals *per se*, Ryder and Ward maintained their initial positions. Only later, when confronted with the objections of the Roman theologians, would Ward modify some of the conclusions that he had defended during the controversy with Ryder.

In contention was another important point, which became more prominent as the controversy went on: to whom does the definition of what is an *ex cathedra* pronouncement and what is not belong? What authority is entrusted with the authentic interpretation of infallible pronouncements? Ryder had raised these points, in passing, in his *Idealism*. He, with Newman, considered that the Pope's words were always in need of interpretation, and that this was the task of theologians. 'None but the *Schola Theologorum*', Newman would write years later, 'is competent to determine the force of Papal and Synodal utterances, and the exact interpretation of them is a

---

[86] Cf. Russell to Ryder, letter quoted in n. 80; also Moriarty to Ryder, letter dated 20 May 1867, Birmingham Oratory Archive, Ryder Papers.

[87] Cf. Ryder, *Letter to Ward*, 7–9.

work of time.'[88] It required a slow and careful process of theological discernment, which, Ryder thought, would hardly suit
the hot haste of the *Dublin Review*. Ward, on the other hand,
maintained that it is 'for the Ecclesia Docens ... and not for
private theologians, to decide the extent of her own infallibility'.[89] Manning agreed with him on this point: the interpretation of an infallible pronouncement could not be the
province of a fallible authority. The Council of Trent was for
him a clear example of this principle, since its interpretation
had been reserved to the Holy See.

5. *Manning and Ward*

Newman considered that Manning shared the ideas expressed
in Ward's articles: Ward was according to Manning, who was
according to the Pope. When deliberating whether to respond
to Pusey's *Eirenicon*, he felt that he could do it well, 'but not, except at the expense of theories and doctrines, which the Archbishop thinks of vital importance, and which I cannot
receive'.[90]

Manning and Ward had collaborated closely since the beginning of Ward's editorship of the *Dublin Review*. They both
viewed with growing alarm the spirit of the *Home and Foreign
Review* spreading in England, and were united in their effort
to eradicate that mentality from English Catholicism, substituting for it a more loyal adherence to the magisterium. Manning, when writing to Ward in early 1865, could speak of 'our
position'. Both felt that they had to speak out: 'If we are silent
these men will mislead public opinion.' The only course open
to them was 'equal explicitness; and the enunciation of the
highest truths'. Boldness was prudence, half-truths the real
danger. Manning agreed with Ward's strategy: 'It seems to
me that we can do nothing surer nor more practical than to
pursue the line you have begun and to keep to it almost exclu-
sively; I mean, the exposition of the Pontifical Acts.' He also indicated how this exposition was to be carried out: 'we must

---

[88] Newman, 'Letter to the Duke of Norfolk', 176. He would ask, on another occasion, 'Who could ever guess *what* is condemned, what not, in a *Theses Damnata*, without such a work as Viva? (letter to Canon Walker, 17 June 1867, *LD* xxiii. 254).

[89] W. G. Ward, *Letter to Ryder on his Recent Pamphlet*, 20.

[90] Letter to Allies, 11 Oct. 1865, *LD* xxii. 72.

disclaim [though] to be the interpreters and derive our interpretation, as far as we can from Rome, or interpret them avow-
edly as private writers, and with submission'.[91] This call for
restraint went mostly unheeded. The end result was that
Ward's excesses were also generally attributed to the Archbishop, as Ullathorne was to deplore in his letter to Manning
of 9 May 1866: 'I am deeply convinced that the *Dublin's* extreme line tends to conjure up reaction. I know it does, and I
should care less for that if people did not persist in making
you the sponsor of Mr. W.'[92]

Ward had acknowledged his debt to the Archbishop on the
subject of infallibility. They were to reach somewhat similar
conclusions, but this did not always mean that they had followed the same path or that they shared all their ideas. Ward
had more of a mind of his own with respect to Manning than
Ryder with respect to Newman. Ward claimed that encyclicals
were infallible on the logical ground that no interior assent
could be demanded to a non-self-evident proposition unless it
were infallibly proposed. Manning's starting-point was a different one: the Holy Spirit speaks through Peter whenever he
speaks as teacher of the Universal Church, and his voice is infallible. Manning, while agreeing on the whole with Ward's
conclusions, did not hide his doubts about many points in his
writings. His letter to Talbot of 25 February 1866 gives clear
insight into his mind on the subject: 'Ward and Faber may exaggerate, but they are a thousand times nearer to the mind
and spirit of the Holy See than those who oppose them. Between us and them there is a far greater distance than between
them and Dr. Pusey's book.'[93] Later on, though, when sending
Ward's book to Talbot, he manifested his general agreement
with its content: 'I send you a book of Ward's on the authority

---

[91] Manning to Ward, letter dated 12 Jan. 1865, St Andrews University Library,
Ward Papers, box 7, no. 196.

[92] Quoted in Leslie, *Henry Edward Manning*, 276.

[93] Quoted in *P* ii. 323. This was an opinion which the *Union Review*, in its desire to
discover divisions among Catholics, would share with Manning. While Ryder, 'by
accepting Papal infallibility seems to place himself technically on common ground
with his antagonist, there is really a great gulf between them, but little more than
an ideal barrier between him and ourselves' ('Father Ryder and Dr Ward on Infallibility', *Union Review*, v vol. (Jan.–Dec. 1867), 349). Manning might exaggerate; in
the *Review*, it looked like wishful thinking.

of Encyclicals. It is ably done and is the sole and only book we have on the subject. This it is that has brought on him the charge of extravagance. But I am confident that in Rome it will not be thought so.'[94] Talbot himself had noticed Ward's exaggerations, but he had looked benignly upon them, writing to the author: 'it is a book most useful and opportune at the present moment. Perhaps here and there you have erred a little on the right side, but that is of no importance. It is much better and safer to believe too much than too little and no one can make a mistake by being guided in all he does by what comes from the Holy See.'[95]

Manning's doubts about Ward's 'exaggerations' were fully expressed after the publication of Ryder's pamphlet: 'Would you oblige me', he wrote to Talbot, 'by asking F. Brunengo to read over Ward's book on Encyclicals, and mark any doubtful passages. I will do so too, and compare in Rome. *I must know with certainty what to state*.'[96] The Roman theologians did indeed express some reservations about Ward's book. They agreed with him on the general principles of the infallibility of the Pope, but there were a number of points in Ward's writings which were arguable. Consequently, Ward was later to make an explicit acknowledgement to the effect that, in his book and in his controversy with Ryder, he had extended infallibility beyond what was generally held by theologians. He left a record, in his *De Infallibilitatis extensione* (1869), of those statements which had been censured in Rome. Against what he had originally said, he accepted that not all encyclicals, allocutions, or apostolic letters contained *ex cathedra* pronouncements, and that not all documents quoted by the *Syllabus* were infallible. He also acknowledged that many theologians were of the opinion that the fact of demanding internal assent to a doctrinal declaration did not identify it *per se* as an infallible pronouncement (although he was still inclined to think that it was so). Again, he added, some theologians of repute maintained that a doctrinal declaration by one of the Roman Con-

[94] Letter dated 4 Mar. 1866, quoted in *P* ii. 389.
[95] Quoted in McElrath, *Syllabus*, 135.
[96] Letter dated 3 May 1867, quoted in *P* ii. 320.

gregations did not become infallible by the mere fact of being confirmed by the Pope.[97]

Manning generally agreed with Ward about the infallibility of encyclicals and other Papal pronouncements. In *The Temporal Mission of the Holy Ghost* (1865) he maintained that the 'Definitions and Decrees of Pontiffs, speaking *ex cathedra*, or as the Head of the Church and to the whole Church, whether by Bull, or Apostolic letters, or Encyclical, or Brief, to many or to one person, undoubtedly emanate from a divine assistance, and are infallible'.[98] Ward used similar words in the preface to his book. In regard to the object, or subject-matter, covered by infallibility, Manning declared: this 'extends to the whole matter of revelation, that is, to the Divine truth and the Divine law, and to all those facts or truths which are in contact with faith and morals'; and revealed truth 'is in contact with natural ethics, politics, and philosophy'. These truths of philosophy, 'being in contact with the faith, they fall within the infallibility of the Church'.[99] He was also explicit in considering infallible the censures of propositions below those declared heretical. In them 'the assistance of the Holy Spirit certainly preserves the Pontiffs from error; and such judgments are infallible, and demand interior assent from all'.[100] There was a fundamental difference, however, in the reasons behind their agreement. Ward, as we have seen, differed from Manning about the connection between interior assent and infallibility. Logical considerations made Ward think that internal assent could not be demanded to a non-infallible proposition; Manning did not agree with him here. He was motivated by a theological principle: the fact that the Holy Spirit speaks in the Church when it teaches. The exercise of the active infallibility of the Church, in its teaching, had not been intermittent, in isolated and rare occasions, like Councils and dogmatic definitions. The Holy Spirit has been continuously assisting the Church in the understanding of revelation, and in the infallible enunciation and proposition of the Faith generation after generation.[101] Man-

---

[97] Cf. W. G. Ward, *De Infallibilitatis extensione: Theses quasdam et quaestiones theologorum judicio subjicit Gulielmus Georgius Ward* (London, 1869), 33, 39, 41.

[98] *TM* 87–8.   [99] Ibid. 89–90.   [100] Ibid. 90.

[101] Cf. ibid. 36–7 and 84.

ning and Ward were in harmony in the general outline of their ideas, but it may safely be said that the Archbishop did not necessarily follow where the layman went, stretching the logic of his principles to breaking-point.

In the field of political thought their disagreements were even more fundamental. Manning—against Ward's explicit statements on the subject—maintained that the principles of the revolution of 1789 were not incompatible with Catholic doctrine: 'In a moment of haste and precipitation, some French writers and politicians have interpreted the condemnations in the Syllabus as a condemnation of the principles of 1789. . . . We would desire to believe, if we can, that those principles . . . are . . . reconcilable with the great laws of political morality which lie at the foundations of human society, and are consecrated by the sanction of the Christian world.'[102] He was fully in agreement with the efforts of Catholics like de Broglie and the Abbé Godard to remove the supposed contradiction between the principles of 1789 and the doctrines of the Church.

It has been suggested, on the other hand, that Newman, 'who . . . condemned emphatically the Liberalism of the Munich school, felt strongly the intellectual enlargement which, with all its shortcomings, it promised for Catholic education and speculation. He shrank from an abrupt logical challenge, which might simply irritate its members, and might lose their services for the Catholic revival.'[103] As he repeatedly declared in his letters, he did not want to impose as matters of necessary belief those propositions which he did not consider part of the Faith to be professed by all Catholics, even though he might have accepted them himself. It was his avowed aim to avoid in-

---

[102] *Privilegium*, ii. 17.

[103] W. Ward, *Ward and the Catholic Revival*, 167. Acton was fully aware of their differences: 'Newman has great sympathy with our cause, in as much as he is enlightened and liberal and highly cultivated, but I do not believe he really understands our theory, and certainly would no more admit it than De Buck' (letter from Acton to Simpson, 7 Feb. 1864, in *Correspondence of Acton and Simpson*, iii. 172). Contrast Acton's words (quoted on p. 203) with Newman's ideas on the subject in his lecture 'Christianity and Physical Science' (1855) (cf. *The Idea of a University* (new edn., London, 1907), 452). Acton also believed that Newman's theory of development was likely to lead people astray as it offered a means to circumvent the historical difficulties on the path of the definition of the Pope's infallibility. This is eventually what happened (see *LD* xxv. 57–8).

troducing theological opinions while declaring the doctrine of the Church. The *Apologia*, he wrote to Flanagan on 15 February 1868, 'was addressed to Protestants *in order to show* them what it was that a Catholic fairly undertook in the way of theological profession, when he became a Catholic. I myself, for instance, have ever held as a matter of theological opinion the Infallibility of the Pope.'[104] His letters to Pusey, written around March 1867, are also very important in showing the full import of his thought. Against Pusey's talk of a 'minimum' to be demanded of those who seek reunion, Newman clearly defined faith's formal object. Faith, he affirmed, is not a code made up of certain definite articles or a written creed. The act of faith 'must ever be partly explicit, partly implicit; viz. "I believe *whatever* God has revealed, whether I know it or not"; or "I believe whatever has been and whatever shall be defined as revelation by the Church who is the organ of the revelation" '.[105] The Faith rests on the Church, and she 'is the teacher of the whole faith'. Applying this principle to the Pope's infallibility he said: 'I think that the Church *may* define it ... but that she *will* not *ever* define it.'[106]

If Newman had hopes of the philosophical and historical movement represented by the Munich school, Manning felt sympathy for the movement of Lacordaire and Montalambert, which he hoped might contribute to the Catholic Revival. And both, Newman and Manning, 'shrunk from pressing logical conclusions which might kill this prospect. Each was a movement full of heterogeneous life; and they hoped that dangerous elements might be discarded, and the life utilised for the Church. In these hopes Ward had no share whatever.'[107] Manning did not want to set Church and society in opposition to each other, or to exclude Catholics from playing an active part in the political life of the systems born from the principles of the French Revolution. Newman was similarly anxious to avoid a divorce between the intellectual life of his time and Catholic thought, and wanted to stop Catholics forming an intellectual ghetto, isolated from contemporary science and

---

[104] Newman, *Theological Papers*, 155.
[105] Letter dated 22 Mar. 1867, *LD* xxiii. 100.
[106] Letter dated 23 Mar. 1867, *LD* xxiii. 105.
[107] W. Ward, *Ward and the Catholic Revival*, 167.

culture. Manning, who likewise felt that danger, saw a different remedy for it: only a clear concept of the infallibility of the Church and the Pope offered the key to unlocking the problem of the relationship between faith and reason; without it, the problem would remain for ever an insoluble one.

6. *The 'Catholic Spirit'*

According to Manning, Catholics, in order to confront the world successfully and to make a really positive contribution to the solution of its ills, should be fully imbued with what he called 'Catholic spirit'. He conceived it as a 'habit of mind' with distinctive 'signs or rules'; a habit that should be found in every 'true Catholic student'. The Feast of St Edmund of Canterbury in 1865 offered him the opportunity to describe it in detail to his students and future priests at St Edmund's, Ware. The echoes of the last broadside of the *Home and Foreign Review* had not completely died away, and Manning wanted to show how the true Catholic spirit was in clear opposition to the temper of mind displayed by the supporters of that school.

Five characteristics, or signs, came together to define the 'Catholic spirit'. The first sign of a Catholic spirit, he said, is 'a loving submission to the Church ... a joyful and thankful obedience to the Church as a divine guide; and a generous and unreserved conformity of our whole nature and mind, intellectual and spiritual, to its guidance and direction'.[108] This is the natural disposition of those who know the Church to be the Body of Christ. To the voice of the Holy Spirit, speaking in it, they render not only 'a bare submission of outward obedience, or of silence', but 'an inward assent and affiance of heart'. They obey 'not only the dogma of faith delivered by Councils, but the whole spirit and mind which pervades the discipline, worship, and devotions of the Church'.[109] This was a principle worlds apart from those advocated by the *Home and Foreign Review*.

The second sign is 'devotion to the Saints', under which heading he included the Fathers and Doctors of the Church. 'Next to the infallible voice of the Church, there is no guidance so certain as the doctrine of the Saints.' He then went on to

---

[108] *CSer* ii. 328. [109] Ibid. 329.

quote Cano: 'Theologians boldly say, that what the Saints unite in teaching is undoubtedly true. "The consent of the Saints is the sense of the Holy Spirit".'[110] This is not their only contribution to building up the Catholic spirit; in the saints, Catholics find 'not only the dogma of faith, but instincts, discernments, intuitions in matters both near to the faith and remote from it, which are most salutary for our guidance'.[111]

Scholastic theology, which had been summarily dismissed by Döllinger in his Munich speech, was given a prominent place by Manning in the make-up of the Catholic spirit. Its third sign is 'deference to theologians'. When 'the theologians of the Church agree, no individual without temerity can oppose them. ... They have a claim ... to our deference, not only on the ground of intellectual superiority, confirmed by an unanimity in some things and a wide consent in others, but also as doctors of the faithful, in whom a higher intellectual cultivation was elevated by a larger illumination [being some of them also great saints]. Their judgments and decisions cannot indeed make matter of faith, but they certainly make matter of moral certainty.'[112]

In 1860, in one of his sermons, Manning made large claims for theologians. Peter, he said, had received from our Lord the two keys of jurisdiction and knowledge. But, he added, 'the key of knowledge has been entrusted by St Peter himself to the Orders of Religion ... so now it is to the Orders of Religion that we come for the toils and fruits of theology matured in rest and silence'.[113] He saw the constitution of the Church as finely balanced, however,

God has so tempered all things together in His Church, that to the apostolic authority, to the episcopate sitting in its consistories and its councils, all, even the doctors and teachers of the religious life, must come, as to the fountain of jurisdiction and of light, of discernment and of judgment. On the heads of the Apostles and their successors rests the *gratia veritatis*, the special gift and unction of the Faith. And they sit as judges on the illuminated labours of all; for they rule the Church, and are the guardians of the Faith, and with them in its fullness is the grace of Pentecost ... All the theology of

110 Ibid.   111 Ibid. 330.   112 Ibid. 330–1.
113 *CSer* i. 301.

the Church, dogmatic and mystical, passes at last under the judgment of the Church in its Hierarchy, and of its Supreme Pontiffs,
and is corrected by its discernment, and stamped with its
authority.[114]

Manning, in this context, would often quote St Irenaeus's
words about the bishops possessing the 'unction of truth'.

A 'fear and suspicion of novelty' was, for Manning, the
fourth sign of the Catholic spirit. Truth, he said, is immutable,
although it may always be defined with greater precision. The
terminology may be new, but the truth is always as old as the
revelation of faith. The true Catholic student is suspicious of
new doctrines, new interpretations of Holy Scripture, and new
principles in philosophy. 'He will take his stand upon the
sacred terminology and scientific tradition of the Church in its
schools; and will not be tempted to depart from them for any
novelties, howsoever alluring.'[115] Manning then fired a direct
shot at the Munich school: the above principle was particularly
relevant in the present circumstances, when 'we hear, not
from Protestants only, but even from some Catholics, that the
scholastic philosophy and theology are antiquated, unfit for
modern thought, and must be replaced by new methods and a
new criticism of history and of antiquity, in order to lay the
basis of science and to generate faith'.[116]

The fifth and last sign is 'mistrust of self'. 'A Catholic student', Manning wrote, 'will be confident wheresoever the
Church has spoken, or the consent of Saints or of theologians
goes before him; but when he is left to himself he will have a
wholesome mistrust of his own opinions ... Confidence in our
own light is a virtue out of the Catholic unity, but a vice within
it. It is the maximum of certainty to those who have no divine
and infallible teacher; it is the minimum to those who are
guided by the Church of God.'[117]

It seems clear that, to Manning's mind, Newman was not
possessed of this 'Catholic spirit' which he had just described.
He agreed with Talbot on the danger posed by those imbued
with the spirit of the *Home and Foreign Review* and the school of
old Catholics, rallying round Newman:

<hr>

[114] *CSer* i. 301–2.   [115] *CSer* ii. 332–3.   [116] Ibid. 333.
[117] Ibid. 333–4.

Whether he knows it or not he has become the centre of those who hold low views about the Holy See, are anti-Roman, cold and silent, to say no more, about the Temporal Power, national, English, critical of Catholic devotions, and always on the lower side. I see no danger of a Cisalpine Club rising again, but I see much danger of an English Catholicism, of which Newman is the highest type. It is the old Anglican, patristic, literary, Oxford tone transplanted into the Church. It takes the line of deprecating exaggerations, foreign devotions, Ultramontanism, anti-national sympathies. In one word, it is worldly Catholicism, and it will have the worldly on its side, and will deceive many.[118]

Talbot was even harsher in his judgement of Newman. In his opinion, Newman lacked the true Catholic spirit because, 'by living almost ever since he has been a Catholic surrounded by a set of inferior men who idolise him, I do not think he has ever acquired the Catholic instincts'.[119]

Bodley also witnessed to Manning's mistrust of Newman's thought, saying that he 'sincerely believed that Newman was not an orthodox Catholic'.[120] And he quoted the following incident in support of this assertion. One evening, his conversation with Manning touched upon Newman, and after a time they moved on to theological ground. The Archbishop remarked: ' "From an observation you made" … "I gather that you are under the impression that Doctor Newman is a good Catholic". I replied that such was my vague belief. He retorted: "Either you are ignorant of the Catholic doctrine, or of the works of Doctor Newman" … After asking me which of Newman's books I had read, he proceeded to tick off on his tapering fingers, in his usual way, ten distinct heresies to be found in the most widely-read works of Dr. Newman.' Bodley's reaction was one of surprise: 'This seemed to me, at the time, on a par with Voltaire's discovery of a series of heresies in the Lord's Prayer.'[121] Years later, however, the Modernists' claim

---

[118] Letter dated 25 Feb. 1866, quoted in *P* ii. 322–3. It should be mentioned that Newman, in his 'Letter to the Duke of Norfolk', described what he considered a 'more scriptural, Christian, dutiful, happy frame of mind'; its traits closely resemble those mentioned above by Manning, with subtle differences with respect to concepts like *pietas fidei*, etc. (in *Difficulties of Anglicans*, ii. 339).

[119] Talbot to Manning, n.d., quoted in *P* ii. 323.

[120] Bodley, *Cardinal Manning*, 15.

[121] Ibid. 16–17.

of Newman as a precursor made him think that perhaps Manning was not so far off the mark as he had at first thought.

Admittedly, an after-dinner remark cannot be accorded too much credit as representing Manning's true perception of Newman's orthodoxy; besides, Bodley's use of words may not be entirely accurate. It is unfortunate that we cannot conjure up the tapering fingers ticking off Newman's heresies, and we are left to surmise what they were. A reasonable assumption would point in the direction of the rule of faith and of the permanent action of the Holy Spirit in the Church. Manning seems to have seen in Newman the spirit of the Oxford Movement, covered with a cloak of Tridentine definitions, which he would have reached by way of the Fathers and his doctrine of Development. Could he have read that in Newman's words in his 'Letter to Pusey'? There Newman had written: 'I am not ashamed still to take my stand upon the Fathers, and do not mean to budge.' That, however, was qualified by the words: 'Of course I maintain the value and authority of the "Schola", as one of the *loci theologici*; nevertheless I sympathize with Petavius in preferring to the "contentious and subtle theology" of the middle age, that "more elegant and fruitful teaching which is moulded after the image of erudite Antiquity". The Fathers made me a Catholic, and I am not going to kick down the ladder by which I ascended into the Church.'[122]

What is clear is that Manning thought that Newman's views about the infallibility of the Pope were minimalist, and that they obscured the permanent action of the Holy Spirit in the Church. It may be assumed that Manning would have pointed out to Bodley some of Newman's expressions which, because of their imprecision of language, left the door open to an unorthodox interpretation of his thought. The essay *On Consulting the Faithful* had got Newman into trouble for this reason, and his 'Letter to the Duke of Norfolk' ran a similar risk. In this latter case, Manning intervened to prevent any official or unofficial sign of disapproval from Rome. On 9 February 1875 he wrote to answer Cardinal Franchi's remarks about passages in the 'Letter to the Duke of Norfolk' which, in the opinion of some theologians in Rome, could mislead the faithful:

---

[122] J. H. Newman, 'Letter to Pusey', in *Difficulties of Anglicans*, ii. 24.

I warmly implore your Eminence to take no public steps as regard Father Newman's pamphlet, for the following reasons: The heart of Father Newman is as straight and Catholic as it ever was. His pamphlet has a most powerful influence over non-Catholics of this country. It makes a wholesome impression, specially on various Catholics of a difficult nature and of unsatisfied ideas. The aforesaid Father has never, up to the present, so openly defended the prerogatives and infallible authority of the Roman Pontiff, though he has always believed and preached this truth. The substance of the recent pamphlet is wholesome, but it is impossible not to notice certain propositions and a certain method of reasoning which is not in accord with the accepted mode of expression.[123]

Manning felt that no harm would follow from this; on the other hand, a rebuke would be a source of untold evil for the Church in England. There is little doubt that Manning might have held a higher opinion of Newman's orthodoxy had he been aware of the content of his correspondence, particularly that of his letters to Pusey and Flanagan.

Newman, for his part, was rather critical of the writings of the Archbishop. He wondered how the 'science necessary for a theologian and the *responsibility* weighing upon an ecclesiastical ruler'[124] had not inhibited Manning from indulging in the extraordinary 'rhetoric' which he had used concerning the infallibility issue. That was fair criticism, since Manning's rhetoric did disfigure at times the expression of his thought. Still, it has to be said that Newman was rather unfamiliar with Manning's writings and with the general framework of his thought. As he confessed in one of his letters,[125] he had not read Manning's *The Temporal Mission of the Holy Ghost*, *The Grounds of Faith*, or *England and Christendom*. It is also highly probable that he had not read the fourth volume of Anglican sermons. As for Manning's pastorals, Newman's letters give the impression of talking about them from what others had told him of their content, rather than from direct knowledge. Was this merely a literary device, to avoid direct criticism of the Archbishop? It seems unlikely.

---

[123] Quoted by Leslie, *Henry Edward Manning*, 281. Manning, though, did not further define in his letter just how 'straight and Catholic' Newman's heart had ever been.

[124] Letter to C. Jenkins, 2 Dec. 1875, *LD* xxvii. 383.

[125] Cf. letter to Mrs Helbert, 30 Aug. 1869, *LD* xxiv. 323–5.

7. 'The Catholic Spirit' and University Education

During the nineteenth century, Catholics in a position to benefit from a university education and wishing to attend the English universities numbered but a few hundred. On the other
hand, the amount of attention, time, and energy which the
English hierarchy devoted in the last third of the century to
university education was to be inversely proportional to the
portion of their flock concerned with the issue. The interests involved, and the personalities ranged in the opposing camps,
made sure that, for the best part of thirty years, the bishops
were to have this matter almost constantly before their eyes.

The removal of the religious tests from among the require-
ments for attending and taking degrees at the two ancient universities had opened the doors to those who, until then, had
been prevented from studying on religious grounds. Catholics,
as well as Dissenters, were now bound to examine very carefully the implications and the advisability of the new freedom
enjoyed by their members. In 1864, the Catholic Bishops were
directed by Propaganda to address the issue. Two questions
were then formulated: whether it was expedient for Catholics
to avail themselves of the opportunity now offered them of
studying at Oxford and Cambridge; and if so, should they join
the existing colleges, or should a Catholic college be founded
to receive them? The fruits of the bishops' deliberations, published on 13 December 1864, disappointed many expectations:
the bishops forbade Catholics to attend Oxford and Cambridge, either by joining the existing colleges or by entering a
new Catholic college set up to receive them.

The pastoral letters in which they announced to their respective dioceses this policy made plain the reason: Catholics
could not, without endangering their faith, attend the universities. The general moral doctrine about avoidance of occasions
of sin was used to buttress this decision: to expose youths at a
very impressionable age, when the most lasting intellectual influences are received, to the Protestant and rationalistic teaching then dominant in the universities would give occasion for
them to be shaken in the soundness of their religious convictions. No Catholic should expose himself to an occasion of
grave sin or loss of faith without a very serious reason, and the

bishops could not think of any such reason which would justify English Catholics attending Oxford and Cambridge. Some bishops cited the experience of Catholics who attended Trinity College, Dublin, to show that the danger was a proximate and real one.

Manning was generally seen as the inspiration and driving force behind the policy. That, however, seems to have more to do with popular demonology than with the facts of the case. He had made abundantly clear his opposition to allowing Catholics to attend Oxford and Cambridge, but to make him responsible for the policy exaggerates his influence with Wiseman and with the rest of the bishops. Wiseman, knowing what was being said about Manning's influence in the affair, wanted to keep his provost clear of the charge;[126] besides, Manning had no part in the bishops' deliberations in 1864. Did Wiseman impose on the bishops a policy which had been previously distilled in his ear by Provost Manning? This is hardly likely. The English bishops, who had more than once shown their independence of spirit in opposing Wiseman's policies at home and in Rome, would probably have done so again had they really disagreed with him on this issue. Manning was, on the whole, accurate when, years later, he described the reasons behind the Cardinal's actions:

If ever, therefore, there was anyone who, if it had been possible to sanction it, would have rejoiced over an association of prayer for the reunion of Christendom, and the return of Catholic youth to the Universities which Catholic England had created, it would have been our late Cardinal. But two things forbade him in any way to accept these invitations: his unerring Catholic instinct, and his keen intuition of the impossibility of combining fidelity to the divine tradition of the faith with the intellectual deviations and contradictions of modern England. His decision, therefore, on both these questions was prompt and final.[127]

---

[126] Wiseman rejected a suggestion from Manning about the form of his letter on the subject to avoid giving the impression that he was receiving—as was being said—all his inspirations from Manning, that he was under moral pressure, and that the text did not represent his own sentiments: 'Whatever, therefore, I write must be recognizable as mine' (Wiseman to Manning, 30 Nov. 1864, 'Unpublished Letters of Cardinal Wiseman to Dr. Manning', *Dublin Review*, clxix 339, p. 191).

[127] H. E. Manning, *The Office of the Church in Higher Catholic Education: A Pastoral Letter* (London, 1885), 5.

Manning was fully in agreement with the decisions of the hierarchy, and with the reasons they adduced. More than a year before their meeting, he had balanced the arguments in favour and against attendance of Catholics at Oxford and Cambridge in an article in the July issue of the *Dublin Review*.[128] The reasons in favour were clearly, though briefly, stated, but they were outweighed by the arguments against. Those who favoured the attendance of Catholics at the universities supported their contention with the need for a Catholic presence in public life. They saw the two traditional universities as the means by which Catholics could break out of their social isolation, and be incorporated into the mainstream of English society. Attendance at Oxford and Cambridge, they thought, would arm Catholics with the necessary intellectual tools to compete on equal terms with Protestants in the fields of literature and science, social and political life; their present inadequacies in those areas placed them at an obvious disadvantage. Besides, the personal relationships forged during those years would grant them easy access to future men of influence and power.

Manning was not indifferent to these arguments. He felt them as strongly as any, perhaps even more so. He could never reconcile himself to the idea of a fortress Church, hidden behind high walls, securing her intellectual and moral purity from contamination by avoiding all contact with the world. The Church had a mission to the world. It 'has a twofold work to do for mankind. Its first and primary, indeed, is to save souls, to lead men to eternal life. Its second, but no less true, is to ripen and to elevate the social and political life of men by its influences of morality and of law.'[129] He considered that the Church has a divine commission 'to enter into the most intimate relations with the natural society or commonwealth of men, or, in other words, with peoples, states, and civil powers'.[130] For this reason, he would deeply regret, in later years, the abstention of Catholics from exercising their duties as citizens in countries like France and Italy. He avoided

---

[128]   Cf. Manning, 'Work and Wants' (1863).
[129]   Ibid. 29.
[130]   H. E. Manning, 'The Catholic Church and Modern Society', *North American Review*, n.d., repr. in *Miscellanies*, iii. 310.

direct reference to Italy, however, so as not to clash with the official policy of the Vatican. He felt that abstention on the part of Catholics from social and, in particular, from political life had left social influence and political power in the hands of the enemies of the Church, and opened the door to a string of anti-Catholic laws. This was an abdication of natural duty and an indirect sanctioning of the separation of Church and State, Church and society, which had been condemned by the *Syllabus of Errors*. It was God's will, Manning thought, that the Church should always be in dialogue with society: 'the Church never withdraws from the State as such, which would be to abandon the natural society of man to its own maladies and mortality'.[131] And he added that the 'withdrawal of Catholics from the active service of the commonwealth, and the non-fulfilment of the duties of citizens and patriots, is a dereliction of duty, and unlawful in itself'.[132] In every situation, even a revolutionary one, the 'duty of using all civil powers and privileges still within reach for the welfare of the people, for the restoration of authority, and the maintenance of order, is a Christian and a Catholic duty'.[133] He thought that the Church had duties towards those political systems born of the French Revolution, even when they were anti-Catholic in many of their principles and pronouncements. In those situations, her aims should be: '(1) first, to guard and to conserve all the Christian faith and morals that still remain in them; (2) secondly, to minimise all the evils of their legislation or government; and (3) thirdly, to recall them by all influences to a better condition'.[134]

He particularly regretted the absence of a Catholic lay presence in English public life. It was true, he had written in 1863, that the 'social exile in which they had lived, and their exclusion ... from public and even private employments, have seriously diminished our capacity for usefulness'.[135] But that was an explanation which could easily be turned into an excuse. The situation was very much the same twenty years later; Catholics had still not made any appreciable progress in

---

[131] Ibid. 312.   [132] Ibid. 317.   [133] Ibid. 313.
[134] Ibid. 315.
[135] Manning, 'Work and Wants' (1863), 60.

the public life of England. Some blamed this on Catholics' lack of access to higher education. Could Manning not see that it was precisely the ban on Catholics frequenting Oxford and Cambridge that had prevented further Catholic advance and influence in the life of the country? That Manning could not draw this conclusion was due less to a lack of logical powers than to the very logic of his ideas on education.

The mission and duty of the Church, he would say, is to provide education: 'by its divine commission it is bound to form its own members. Their education in childhood and in youth is the inalienable duty of the Church.'[136] That included university education. Some might perhaps argue that, sooner or later in their lives, Catholics in England had to enter into the atmosphere and dangers of public life, that they had to enter into contact with anti-Catholic prejudices, a dominant Protestant culture, and rationalism. Was it prudent to cocoon them and to try to isolate them from the society of the world? Manning thought that not only was this impossible, but that their involvement in society was absolutely necessary; they should be fully immersed in it. It had to be thus, Manning would say,

but not until their Catholic formation is complete. The Church would abdicate its pastoral office if it were to suffer the formation of its youth to pass from its own hands into the hands of teachers external to its own intellectual and Catholic unity. And no Catholic parent, without dereliction of duty, can withdraw a son from the education of a Catholic College, and place him at the most critical period of his life, when youth is passing into manhood, under the influence of non-Catholic Universities, where the last Catholic formation of his youth cannot be given, and where the first Catholic formation of his boyhood may be destroyed.[137]

The dangers attached to attendance at Protestant universities were not the only reasons, in Manning's mind, for the banning of Catholics from Oxford and Cambridge. He felt even more keenly that, if Catholics were to attend them, Catholic education would remain an unfinished fabric, a machinery unable to turn out a finished product. It would also render impossible the building up of a Catholic culture. Manning felt that the

---

[136] Manning, *Office of the Church in Higher Education*, 18.
[137] Ibid. 19.

foundation of a Catholic university was an imperative need; without it the Church would not be able to perform fully its commission. Giving permission for Catholics to frequent Oxford and Cambridge would postpone *sine die* provision for that need. He was sorely disappointed, therefore, when, in 1864, the bishops, while banning Catholics from attending the two traditional universities, decided against setting up a Catholic university. As he wrote to Talbot: 'The bishops decided against the Protestant Universities in all ways; but that a Catholic University is not possible. To this I cannot agree. And I trust that they will be encouraged to attempt, or to let others attempt something to meet the needs of our laity. It would not do to prohibit, and to provide nothing. Many will go to Oxford and Cambridge; and the precedent will be set, and all hope of anything higher will be lost.'[138]

Thus, it can be said that Manning's 'concept of higher education was in no sense a negative one. The prohibition against the ancient universities has to be seen as but one facet of the much greater constructive project, the preparation of English Catholics for the formation of a Catholic University. Neither was the formation of such an institution an indication of a ghetto mentality'.[139] Catholics had a contribution to make to contemporary English thought, and a Catholic university was the appropriate means to enable them so to do. The prevalent intellectual atmosphere of the time was dominated by rationalism, in either its absolute or moderate varieties. It was Catholics to whom fell the task of rescuing human culture and society from what Manning did not hesitate to call a superstition: one, which, 'strange to say, pervades those who are willing to believe but little else'. The credal articles of this superstition were that 'faith and reason are at variance; that human reason, by submitting itself to faith, becomes dwarfed; that faith interferes with the rights of reason; that it is a violation of its prerogatives, and a diminution of its perfection'.[140]

Manning felt that two ideas should be safely anchored in every Christian heart at the end of the educational process:

[138] Quoted in McClelland, *Cardinal Manning*, 92–3.
[139] V. A. McClelland, *English Roman Catholics and Higher Education (1830–1903)* (Oxford, 1973), 353.
[140] *Four Evils*, 3.

first, the existence of a divine revelation, elevating and perfecting human knowledge; second, the divine institution of an infallible teaching authority. It was the task of Christian
education to leave deeply engraved in the Christian mind that
the

revelation of faith is no discovery which the reason of man has made
for himself by induction, or by deduction, or by analysis, or by
synthesis, or by logical process, or by experimental chemistry. The
revelation of faith is a discovery of itself by the Divine Reason, the
unveiling of the Divine Intelligence, and the illumination flowing
from it cast upon the intelligence of man; and if so, I would ask,
how can there be variance or discord? How can the illumination of
faith diminish the stature of the human reason? How can its prerogatives be violated? Is not the truth the very reverse of all this? Is
it not the fact that human reason is perfected and elevated above itself by the illumination of faith?[141]

Once Catholics had these fundamental principles well rooted
in their minds and had made of them a test for the acquisition
of human knowledge, they would be ready to enter into dialogue with the world and with the dominant ideas and principles
of the day. The purpose of a Catholic university education
was to help Catholics acquire human knowledge, and to learn
how to approach the culture of the day and scientific discoveries from a clear intellectual position. This was something
which could hardly be given them during the years of their
school education.

Manning felt that if Catholics were to serve their generation
in a truly Christian way, 'it must be by the boldest and clearest
enunciation of the great principles of Divine certainty in matters of Faith, and by pointing out the relations of Faith to
human knowledge, scientific and moral'.[142] This was an
approach, he thought, which recommended itself to English
people.

There is something downright, manly, and decided in it [the English character]; and it respects the same—that is, its own—qualities
in others as much as it despises and ridicules all servile or petty ea-
gerness to court its favour. Downright, masculine, and decided
Catholics—more Roman than Rome, and more ultramontane than

----

[141] *Four Evils*, 4.   [142] *TM*, p. vii.

the Pope himself[!]—may enter English society and be treated with good will and respect everywhere, if only they hold their own with self-respect and a delicate consideration of what is due to others ... No greater blunder could be committed than to try to propitiate Englishmen or English society by a tame, diluted, timid, or worldly Catholicism.[143]

Some might be tempted by the thought that English people could be won by compromise. Manning quickly dismissed that view: 'All the experience that I possess tells me that there is no greater illusion than this. The people of England expect us to be inflexible in all that makes us Catholic: and they confide readily in those who never compromise.'[144]

What made a man thoroughly Catholic, and thus distinct from his Protestant neighbours, was a firm belief in a divine authority still teaching the Faith in the world: that is, in the permanent presence of the Holy Spirit in the Church, and his constant and infallible magisterium. '*Sentire cum Ecclesia*—that is, to think and to feel with the Catholic Church—[would] be the test and note of a faithful Catholic.'[145] That meant to think and to feel with Rome. This was the sure principle and the firm foundation for Catholics moving across the stormy seas of present-day conflicting ideologies and rampant rationalism. Manning's article on 'The Work and Wants of the Catholic Church in England' (1863) finished with the following words: 'There is but one safety for us: "*Sentire cum Ecclesia*", in the whole extent of faith, discipline, worship, custom, and instincts—the most intimate and filial fidelity of intellect, heart, and will to the living voice of the Church of God.'[146] Only then, once the foundation was solidly established, could the Catholic make a positive contribution to the intellectual, social, and political life of his country. Manning's own presence in so many, diverse areas of public life—from social concerns to the Metaphysical Society—rested on those convictions.

Protestant England, on the other hand, was also in need of being confronted with those Catholic principles. The root of her errors and divisions was the denial of the presence of an

[143] Manning, 'Work and Wants' (1863), 65–6.
[144] Manning, *Office of the Church in Higher Education*, 20.
[145] Ibid. 14.
[146] Manning, 'Work and Wants' (1863), 71.

infallible teaching authority on earth; the remedy, its enthron-
ing in the mind of the people of the country. Here public opinion was overwhelmingly Protestant and opposed to a Church
divinely constituted and endowed with an infallible teaching
authority. 'The first principles and maxims of Catholic education—such as submission to a teaching authority, fear of error,
mistrust of our own judgments—are extinct. This spirit begins
in our schools, pervades our Universities, and animates the
whole of English society.'[147] Manning was also afraid of the influence that the general atmosphere of the country could have
on the habits of mind of English Catholics. In his report to Propaganda in 1867 about the state of his diocese, he pointed out
how it was not surprising that daily intercourse with non-
Catholics, reading their newspapers and books, would imbue
Catholics with some of their errors, 'more through ignorance
than through malice'.[148] Still, that was a worrying fact. The
atmosphere was there, he would write on another occasion:
'We cannot draw breath without inhaling it; and the effect of
it is visible upon men who do not suspect themselves of any
want of Catholic instincts. It has become unconscious; and
what strikes and offends foreign Catholics is hardly, or not at
all, perceived by those who are born into this atmosphere.'[149]
That subtle and imperceptible influence of the intellectual en-
vironment on Catholics made it even more necessary to insist
on those fundamental Catholic principles, until they were
deeply and safely engraved in Catholic minds.

Manning's opposition to allowing Catholics to study at Oxford or Cambridge had the above principles at heart. His opposition to Newman's going to Oxford, on the other hand,
had a twofold basis. It is true that he was afraid that the presence of Newman at Oxford would encourage other Catholics
to go there. But there was also another reason: Manning felt
that Newman was not in full possession of the elements that
made up the 'Catholic spirit', as he had described them, and
he could not accept with equanimity the idea of putting the
formation of Catholic university students in his hands. As has

---

[147] Manning, 'Work and Wants' (1863), 62–3.
[148] SCPF, *Scritture Riferite nei Congressi*, fo. 345.
[149] Manning, 'Work and Wants' (1863), 63.

been pointed out, 'there was his own personal unease at the influence that Newman, being Newman, would actually exercise in Oxford. He would tend to create Catholics after his own image; and it was not an image that Manning much liked.'[150]

A Catholic university would obviate these problems. It would also offer an additional advantage. Its contact with similar institutions, then growing in different countries of Europe and America, would help break down the intellectual insularity and national prejudices of English Catholics. Unfortunately, Manning's Catholic University College at Kensington was a failure. As usual, he consoled himself with the thought of the mysterious ways of Providence: good always comes out, in the end, from what men consider failure and defeat, if one is working for God's glory. Perhaps the time was not yet ripe for a Catholic university. In 1882, Manning, in light of the present set-back, looked into the future: 'That a college of higher studies for Catholic young men will one day be demanded is certain.' On that day, 'the timid and narrow counsels ... of those who desired to see our Catholic youth at Oxford and Cambridge, will be heard no more'.[151]

He had dreams of true and deep Catholic influence on every aspect of the life of the country, born from the pure spring of Catholic principles. He died with those dreams intact.

[150] Newsome, *Convert Cardinals*, 265–6.
[151] Manning, 'Work and Wants' (1882), 351.

VI
The Preparation of the Council

1. *The Agenda for the Council*

Pius IX's decision to convoke an Ecumenical Council had a long period of gestation. It seems that Cardinal Lambruschini had mentioned this possibility as early as 1849, as a response to the extraordinary needs of the times. Still, it was not until December 1864 that Pius IX informed the Curial cardinals of his intention of calling a General Council, an idea, he said, which had been in his mind for a long time. The cardinals expressed their favourable opinion, and the wheels of the machinery to prepare the Council were soon set in motion. In March 1865 the newly set up 'Congregation for the Future Council' started acting on its own suggestion of preparing, in draft form, the schemata to be discussed. The first step was to consult bishops all over the world about the matters that they considered should be addressed by the forthcoming Council, and in the following months, letters were sent to the bishops selected for the purpose. The original list did not include any English-speaking bishop among those to be consulted.

Henry Edward Manning was appointed Archbishop of Westminster by Pius IX in May 1865. In October of the same year, after his consecration in England and his journey to Rome for the pallium, he received a letter from Cardinal Caterini asking him to send his suggestions. His answer was prompt and clear. It followed the lines along which his thought had been running for many a year, expressing the intellectual convictions which had shaped his life.

To His Eminence Cardinal Caterini,
Prefect of the Sacred Congregation for the Council,
Rome.

Your Eminence,
It would not be difficult to give some vague answer to your letter of

26th of last month; to give an exact answer to a question so serious as the present one is very difficult.

The multiple perversions of error have grown forth so much in our days, particularly in England, that it is easier to compile them than to analyze them.

As in past centuries, so it is in our present time, that among the revealed truths there is always some particular truth which seems to become prominent or conspicuous as a sign of contradiction. In the first centuries, the first articles of the creed were under attack by the heretics; in later centuries those which came next; in these present days, the last articles of the creed are called into question. It may be said that the heresies of our time concern mainly the last paragraph of the creed, that is, the Holy Spirit and His temporal mission. All the heresies of the Pseudo-Reformation can be included under this heading: once the infallibility of the Church—the necessary corollary of the Holy Spirit's presence in the Church—has been rejected, then, all those divine things that hung on it perish; once the tree is cut the fruits and the leaves fall down. This is what has happened in England, that the notion of the Church as a body perpetually endowed and supported with supernatural gifts by the action of the Holy Spirit has almost completely disappeared from the minds of the English people.

Thus, taking into consideration the circumstances of my country, it seems most opportune to me that the supreme authority [of the Council] should make some pronouncement about the temporal mission of the Holy Spirit and about his perpetual and infallible assistance. This would serve to show more clearly the following truths:

1 That the Holy Spirit, after the Incarnation of the Word, had come into the world in a more eminent way, in order to undertake more powerful works.

2 That between the Holy Spirit and the Church there exists an indissoluble union—in the analogy of the Incarnation, but excluding an hypostatic union—from which flow the endowments and properties which inhere intrinsically and perpetually in the Church.

3 That the living and perpetual teaching is consequently infallible.

4 That, therefore, to appeal from the teaching Church is essentially heretical.

5 That the appeals to the testimony of the ancient Fathers, or to

the testimony of antiquity as some say, are clear manifestations of rationalism.

6 That the *vivae vocis* teaching given by the Supreme Pontiff on matters concerning faith, morals, or dogmatic facts is infallible.

Today, as your Eminence well knows, three centuries after the Reformation, this heresy, like Arianism in the time of St Gregory, is passing away. In those parts where the pestilence of Protestantism rages, the dispute is about the most fundamental principle of religion; that is, about the nature of divine faith. Today it is not just a particular doctrine of faith which is controverted, Christian revelation and the divine authority of the Church are being questioned. The possibility and the fact of revelation should be maintained against perfect rationalists; the presence and perpetual assistance of the Holy Spirit, and his perpetual and infallible voice in the Church, should be upheld against the imperfect rationalists, among whom should be counted the Anglicans. Thus, in the same way as the dogma of the Immaculate Conception of the Blessed Virgin Mary has been defined, it is to be expected that the dogma of the infallibility of the Church will be equally defined. In these present days we have reached the first foundation of the faith; the present time, the exposition of the faith and the ripeness of the matter itself, seem to demand urgently the promulgation by the supreme authority of the infallibility of the Church and of the Supreme Pontiff speaking *ex cathedra Petri*.

Thereupon, I, with my whole heart, humbly embrace the counsel of our Lord to extirpate the errors of this time, the only and always looked for remedy for the evils of the Church.

I remain the obedient and humble servant of your Eminence,

Henry Edward, Archbishop of Westminster.
Westminster, 15th November 1865.[1]

His controversy with Pusey and the APUC, the pamphlet war between Ward and Ryder, and the growth of what he called the spirit of the *Home and Foreign Review* reinforced in his mind the need for the definition. He trusted that the Council would find, under the guidance of the Holy Spirit, the solution to present-day problems; he also held that the Holy Spirit counts on man's effort and industry to obtain the desired result. Manning, therefore, acted decidedly on his own convictions about

[1] *M* xlix, cols. 170D–171D.

what the Church, and the world, needed most at that particular juncture.

2. The Jubilee of 1867 and Fr. Liberatore's Vow

His first passage of arms on the world's stage championing the doctrine of the infallibility of the Pope was to take place in 1867, during the celebrations in honour of the martyrdom of St Peter and St Paul. Some 500 bishops had gathered in Rome for the occasion. Making use of the opportunity presented by the Jubilee, the Pope announced publicly, in his allocution of 26 June, his intention of holding a General Council. The bishops present decided to respond to the Pope's announcement with an address; its drafting was entrusted to a commission of seven, Manning and Dupanloup,[2] Bishop of Orléans, among them. Ullathorne would later report as a certain fact that, on this occasion, Manning had 'got a hint from the Pope to check Orléans in the commission for drawing up the Address'.[3] Whether this is true to fact, or just a rumour, is difficult to determine. One thing is clear, however: Manning did not require any hint to spur him into action.

Haynald, archbishop of Kalocsa, was asked by the committee to produce a first draft to be submitted to the other members for study and approval. Haynald's text used the word 'infallible' several times when speaking about the Pope and his teaching. No objections were raised at the meeting of the committee, but Dupanloup suggested that Franchi, Archbishop of Thessalonica, should revise the text. After Franchi's revision the word 'infallible' was no longer included in the address, and it was supposed that the omission was due to Dupanloup's influence.

Manning's sanitized version of the proceedings in *The True Story of the Vatican Council* described the sequence of events at length. Haynald's draft, in outline,

was nearly as it was adopted at last; but in one point, bearing intimately on the history of the Council, it underwent an important re-

---

[2] During the Council Félix Dupanloup was to become the chief whip of the minority opposed to the definition of papal infallibility. In 1865 his pamphlet on the encyclical *Quanta Cura* and the *Syllabus* had helped render comprehensible for the general public the content of those documents.

[3] Letter to Brown, 26 Oct. 1869, quoted in C. Butler, *Vatican Council*, 123.

vision. As it originally stood, the word *infallible* was, in more places than one, ascribed to the office and authority of the Pontiff. To this word, as expressing a doctrine of Catholic truth, no member of the commission objected. It was however said that the word *infallible* had as yet been used only in provincial councils, or pastoral letters, or theological schools, but that it had not been inserted in the formal acts of any general Council of the Church, and that, inasmuch as the 500 bishops then in Rome were not assembled in council, it might be advisable not to seem to assume the action or office of a Council. These considerations were assented to by all. It was then proposed to insert the words of the Council of Florence, which was the last authoritative decree on the primacy of the Roman Pontiff. To this no objection as to the subject-matter was made; but it was urged that the draft address already contained expressions stronger than the decree of the Council of Florence, which only implicitly contains the infallibility of the head of the Church as the teacher of all Christians, for the address explicitly declares that 'Peter has spoken by the mouth of Pius'. To this it was answered that though beyond all doubt these words explicitly declare the voice of the Pontiff to be infallible as Peter's was, yet this acclamation of the fathers of Chalcedon and that of the third Council of Constantinople were always, and not unreasonably, set aside as of little weight in controversy, as little more than rhetorical amplifications of the authority of Leo and of Agatho. They were not doctrinal formulas, much less definitions, but only acclamations; and acclamations define nothing, and can form neither objects of faith nor terminations of controversy. It was therefore by the vote of almost all the seven members of the commission, if not indeed by the united vote of all, decided that the words of the decree of the Florentine Council should be inserted.[4]

The exchange of arguments seems to have been rather more heated than Manning gave to understand at first. In 1879, Manning wrote a note to answer Ollivier's contention[5] that the recollections in *The True Story of the Vatican Council* were not accurate, and that it had been Manning himself who had insisted on the insertion of the word 'infallible'. 'I did not press', he wrote, 'for the insertion of the doctrine [in the original draft], but I resisted the exclusion of the word unless the Florentine Decree were inserted in the Address.' Dupanloup

[4] *True*, 53–5.
[5] Cf. É. Ollivier, *L'Église et l'État au Concile du Vatican* (2 vols., Paris, 1879), i. 318.

opposed this, but the insertion of the decree of the Council of Florence was agreed. The episode did not quite end there. Manning takes up the narrative again: 'At our fourth session the Address was read again, but the Decree had not been inserted. I had foreseen that this might happen, and I had brought with me a transcript of the Decree which I gave to Mgr. Franchi. At our fifth session I found that still the Decree had not been inserted. And as I had again a prevision that this might happen, I had brought with me a second copy of the Decree, which was then incorporated into the Address.'[6] The tensions within the committee reached the bishops: 'you know', Ullathorne wrote to Bishop Brown on 26 October 1869, 'what a fight there was between them [Dupanloup and Manning], and what a different edition Orléans subsequently gave to the story from that we received on the spot'.[7]

In *The True Story of the Vatican Council* Manning would say 'that the impression made by the Centenary upon the minds of the bishops determined many to promote, by all means in their power, the closing of a controversy which had for centuries periodically disturbed the Church'.[8] Manning was among them. A small but significant event had taken place during the celebrations of the centenary, while the preparation of the address was going on. Manning told the story in a memorial written in 1881: 'On the eve of St. Peter's Day I and the Bishop of Ratisbon [Senestréy] were assisting at the throne of the Pope at the first Vespers of St. Peter; we then made the vow drawn up by P. Liberatore, an Italian Jesuit, to do all in our power to obtain the Definition of Papal Infallibility. We undertook to recite every day certain prayers in Latin contained in a little book still in my possession. The formula of the vow with my signature is bound up in my copy of *Petri Privilegium*.'[9]

---

[6] Quoted in Leslie, *Henry Edward Manning*, 214–15. Manning's volumes of Vatican Council documents contain the text without the Council of Florence's decree. In the margin are written, in Manning's handwriting, the words of the Council of Florence later inserted in the address (Manning MSS Pitts, box 7, folder 7, vol. viii).

[7] Quoted in Butler, *Vatican Council*, 123; see also Cwiekowsky, *English Bishops*, 67–9.

[8] *True*, 55.

[9] Quoted in *P* ii. 420. This volume is now at Pitts Theological Library (Emory University). The text had been previously published in the *Civiltà Cattolica* (fas. 414). The actual vow (pp. 19–20) contained a definition of papal infallibility. The text of the vow is in Italian.

The formula published by the *Civiltà Cattolica*, was to be used widely, particularly in France.

The jubilee of 1867 had a momentous significance for Manning. It had been, as far as he was concerned, a proof of how 'the primacy of the Roman Pontiff, with its full prerogatives and endowments, was vividly before the minds of the bishops'.[10] The words of the address were a confession—by the largest number of bishops ever gathered together—of their faith in the infallibility of the Pope. 'Without doubt', Manning said, 'the words did not explicitly declare the Roman Pontiff to be infallible, but half the episcopate of the Church would be not unreasonably accused of great temerity in their language if they had not believed the head of the Church to be in some special way guarded from error in his teaching.'[11]

3. *A Pastoral on the Pope's Infallibility*

The news of the forthcoming Council was now in the public domain, and Manning lost no time in fulfilling his vow: his pastoral *The Centenary of Saint Peter and the General Council* was dated 8 September 1867. As he had done before with the pastoral on the APUC, Manning sent the draft pastoral to Ullathorne on 5 September. Ullathorne answered at length on the 8th: 'My time has only let me run once over the Pastoral, and I have not been able to verify the quotations, but that you probably did not expect. I certainly should not put it out, were its responsibility on me, without modifications. And, in so formal a document as a Pastoral I should carefully mark the distinction between what is defined truth and what is theological exposition. What I would recommend would be to submit it to some very sound theologian', and he suggested either Perrone or Murray of Maynooth. Ullathorne felt that if it were published as it stood, 'there are things in it which will tend to embarrass rather than to help Rome'.[12] Manning incorporated Ullathorne's suggestions, and told him on the 9th that the draft had been sent to Murray. His answer was forwarded to the Bishop of Birmingham, who, on the 15th of the same month, wrote: 'Thank you for the sight of Dr. Murray's

---

[10] *True*, 55.   [11] Ibid. 52.
[12] Manning MSS West., Manning–Ullathorne Correspondence, *U* 84.

letter, I congratulate you in obtaining his suffrage to your theological accuracy.' He was, at the same time, somewhat suspicious: 'You do not however say whether the copy sent to him was the same that was sent to me or the one in which you informed me that you had made certain modifications.'[13] Yes, Manning would confirm, the 'proofs were the same: without the change of a letter'. The Bishop of Birmingham, in spite of Murray's judgement, was still doubtful about the appropriateness of publishing the pastoral: 'Theological accuracy is one thing, the *tempus omnia loquendi* is another.'[14] Manning hoped that he had not misjudged *de tempore loquendi*. In his mind, as he had already said on 9 September, the 'matter is no more than we were taught in Rome; and I feel that one of the causes of misunderstanding is that we have not sufficiently expressed it'.[15] Had the doctrine been put forward boldly and clearly, many of the difficulties which then afflicted the Church would have been prevented.

In his pastoral, Manning pointed out how the gathering of bishops in Rome in 1862 and 1867 had been a manifestation of the unity and universality of the Church, a reaffirmation of faith in the supremacy and the prerogatives of the prince of the apostles, in the person of his successor, a manifestation of the absolute adherence of the bishops to his authority and teaching. That was the great lesson from the jubilee which Manning wanted to expand upon for the benefit of his people: 'the perpetual office and action of Peter as the source of unity and infallibility to the Church'.[16]

Manning repeated what he had already said many a time.

The Incarnate Word, in Whom were hid all the treasures of wisdom and knowledge, became the fountain of grace and truth, of doctrine, and of jurisdiction to the world. To the chief of His Apostles He conveyed by the Holy Ghost all His communicable prerogatives, and

[13] Ibid., *U* 86.

[14] Ibid. Newman, after the publication of the pastoral, would agree with his bishop. He thought the Archbishop 'obviously wrong in introducing into his Pastorals the Pope's infallibility'. For his part, when writing the *Apologia*, he had borne in mind Ullathorne's advice that there should be no mixing up 'dogma with theological opinion, and that in a popular work theological opinions ought to be kept under' (*Theological Papers*, 155).

[15] Manning–Ullathorne Correspondence, *U* 85.

[16] *Privilegium*, i.16.

thereby constituted him His vicar upon earth. ... The indefectibility of truth, therefore, both in its conception and enunciation ... resides first in its head, next in the whole episcopate united with him;
so that the declarations and condemnations of the head of the
Church apart from the episcopate are infallible; and likewise those
of the episcopate, being united with him. ... [The] fountain of infallible teaching is the Divine Head in heaven, through the organ
of the visible head of the Church on earth.[17]

The centenary had been the celebration of the Chair of Peter,
and this 'is the power of Peter, and the place where it has
been divinely fixed'.[18] Peter's faith, sustained by Christ's
prayer, is 'transmitted and impersonated in his successors',
and it is, therefore, 'by its intrinsic stability, indefectible and
infallible'.[19] From this special prerogative of the Roman Pontiffs it follows that the particular Church of Rome cannot err.
The 'Chair of Peter has been held to be the test of orthodoxy,
the confirmer of Councils, the supreme tribunal of faith, the de-
stroyer of heresies, the end of controversies, an authority
which is subject to no appeal, to no reversal, to no revision, to
no superior upon earth'.[20] In confirmation of his words, he
could quote some expressions from Pius IX's Allocution on 26
June, together with the response of the bishops.

Manning felt that this clear doctrine had been obscured by
those who alleged that it was a novel opinion which, under
the name of 'Ultramontanism', had made its appearance but
recently, its main principle being 'put in act' by the Council
of Constance. There were those who thought that its rise at
that time owed much to ambition and to bureaucratic despot-
ism; then, after the Reformation, the breaking away from
Rome of the freedom-loving Teutonic nations allowed that
despotic theory to grow unchecked. Manning saw it differently. He considered the infallibility of the Pope to be the foundation of the life of the Church and of its mission, the
keystone holding the whole structure together. It was a doc-

---

[17] *Privilegium*, i. 22–4.   [18] Ibid. 24.

[19] Ibid. 25. Manning did not equate stability, indefectibility, and infallibility; he
saw them as 'three modes of expressing the same Divine fact' (*Privilegium*, ii. 149)—
that fact being the active presence of the Holy Spirit in the Church, from which the
stability, indefectibility, and infallibility of the Church follow.

[20] *Privilegium*, i. 26.

trine which had always been maintained by the Church: 'The Divine order has united the supremacy of truth and of jurisdiction in the same person; and from the Tradition of the Fathers and Councils, it is evident that the whole Church has believed the successor and the See of Peter to be not only supreme in power, but infallible in faith.'[21] As was his custom, he added a long list of quotations and authorities in confirmation of what he had just said. Ultramontanism was under attack not because it was a new doctrine; the real reason was that the 'greatest blunder in the world's eyes is Catholicism: the next greatest is Christianity. Ultramontanism is Catholic Christianity.'[22]

Manning made use of a practical example to illustrate the Pope's infallibility from a different angle: the relationship of the Pope to a General Council, which all accept as infallible. The prerogative of Peter, he would say, 'as the confirmer of his brethren is never so explicitly manifest as in the direction and confirmation of Councils. Every Council of the Church, from Nice to Trent, has reflected more visibly and vividly the supremacy and infallibility of the Chair of Peter.'[23] It belonged to the Pope, and to him alone, to convoke, direct, prorogue, translate, or dissolve a Council. The bishops in Council are judges of the faith, but it is important to understand in what sense they are such. 'If, at any time, in an Oecumenical Council, any dogma be defined which has already been defined by the Pope, or by other General Councils, the bishops act as judges, but are already bound to judge in conformity to what is already defined. But if the defining of anything not yet defined is in question, they are the judges in such sense that their judgments have no force to bind the conscience until the assent and confirmation of the Supreme Pontiff has been given.'[24] The need for confirmation by the Pope shows clearly the Church's awareness 'that from the head the influx [of infallible truth] descends into the members'.[25]

In *The True Story of the Vatican Council*, Manning, against conciliarist ideas, went on to say that the holding of Councils is

---

[21] Ibid. 58–9.   [22] Ibid. 39.   [23] Ibid. 70.
[24] Ibid. 78.
[25] Ibid. 72, quoting Brancatus de Laurea.

not essential for the Church to carry out her mission, although they are useful and sometimes necessary for particular times and errors; but the 'Church does not depend on General Councils for the knowledge of truth'.[26] He would point out how there is 'no divine commandment, no divine obligation, requiring that the bishops of the Universal Church should meet in one place'.[27] She 'is not infallible in virtue of General Councils, but General Councils are infallible in virtue of the infallibility of the Church. The whole Church, both the *Ecclesia Docens* and the *Ecclesia Discens*, diffused throughout the world, is infallible at all times. The Church discharges its office as witness, judge, and teacher always, and in all places.' The See of Peter and the episcopate diffused throughout the world—and united to the Roman Pontiff—'are so assisted by the perpetual presence of the Spirit of truth that they can never err as witness, judge, or teacher'.[28]

4. *The Opportuneness of the Definition of Papal Infallibility*

Having presented the case against the need for General Councils, as of absolute necessity for the life of the Church, Manning was then confronted by the task of showing the opportuneness of General Councils in general, and of the forthcoming one in particular. His main priority, however, was to defend the opportuneness of the definition of papal infallibility against the voices which started to be raised against it.

Councils, he said, are very effective against heresy and schism, and for the discipline of the Church. They 'confirm both truth and unity', as the faith of the Church is witnessed by the confession of the universal Church gathered in Council. They also 'set a mark upon their opposites which wither their growth and ensure their fall'. From a disciplinary point of view, Councils provide a means of gathering information about the needs of the Church which help to readjust its practice and laws; besides, the laws established in General Councils 'are far more acceptably carried through when the Supreme Pontiff makes such laws with the assent of General Council'.[29]

---

26 *True*, 14.   27 Ibid.
28 *Privilegium*, i. 77; see also *True*, 14 ff.
29 *Privilegium*, i. 80.

There was an obvious need, in Manning's mind, for the convocation of a Council at that juncture in the history of the Church. Times had changed since the Council of Trent, and the Church's discipline needed to be readjusted to the new circumstances. Again, the Church had to redefine its relationship to the new political order born after the French Revolution, so as to achieve peaceful co-operation between Church and State.

One great benefit arising from the coming Council would be the consciousness of the unity of the Church, and, with it, of its power: the 'conscious unity, universality, and power of the Church must be indefinitely elicited and strengthened by meeting in Council ... All who have been assembled at the centre of authority will carry back with them a consciousness of power which will spread through the whole Catholic unity; and this consciousness of unity is strength.'[30] The confidence born of this knowledge should mark the relationships of the Church with society, and with the State. Manning also thought that the unity of the Church would be reinforced if the Council were to put forward a clear statement on the nature and prerogatives of its Head: the Church's unity is based on truth, and truth rests on the infallibility of the Pope. He is the keystone on which the whole edifice rests, the source of its unity and infallibility.

The lull which followed the announcement of the Council was suddenly broken by the articles in the *Civiltà Cattolica* of February 1869, published as correspondence from France. They were based on two reports sent to Rome by the nuncio in Paris about the climate of opinion in the country with respect to the forthcoming Council. These reports seem to have originated within the circle of Veuillot, and they affirmed that the majority of French people were for the definition of papal infallibility. They hoped, the report continued, that the Council would be a short one, and that the unanimity of the Council would make long deliberations unnecessary; the definition of papal infallibility could, consequently, be carried by acclamation.

---

[30] Ibid. 92–4.

The ideas expressed in the *Civiltà Cattolica* could not but excite powerful feelings in more than one heart. Döllinger vented his anti-Romanist anger in a series of articles, signed by 'Janus', which started appearing in the *Allgemeine Zeitung* early in March. They were soon collected and published in book form, with translations into English and several other languages appearing during the summer of that year. The confessed aim of the articles was to assail that party which tried to carry out its plans 'either in ignorance of Church history or by deliberately falsifying it'.[31] The decadence of the Church, Janus said, had its ultimate root in the present form of the primacy. It had been meant, in God's plan, to be a source of strength for the Church; but the primacy had been transformed into the papacy in the Middle Ages, and in its present form was 'hindering and decomposing the action of its vital powers, and bringing manifold diseases in its train'.[32] Janus went on to state in clear terms that to 'prove the dogma of Papal Infallibility from Church history nothing less is required than a complete falsification of it'.[33] Only public opinion could prevent this happening, and it was Janus's responsibility to awaken public opinion to the danger, and to do so he was forced to bring forth the dark side in the history of the papacy. The book did not bear the names and titles of its author or authors. That was an intentional omission: the authors considered 'that a work so entirely made up of facts, and supporting all its statements by reference to the original authorities, must and can speak for itself, without needing any names attached to it'.[34]

Janus's spirit was a curious sort of revived Donatism, pointing to the human errors of Popes and bishops as clear disclaimers of their assumed prerogatives, such abuses being the clear signs of the erroneous character of the principle. Manning's attention may have been attracted by Janus's reference to Melchor Cano:

The third of the theological fathers of Papal Infallibility was Tap-

---

[31] 'Janus', *The Pope and the Council* (2nd edn., London, 1869), p. xviii. The articles seem to have been a collaborative effort, with Döllinger as the main author and the moving force behind them.
[32] Ibid., p. xix.   [33] Ibid. 49.   [34] Ibid., p. xxix.

per's contemporary, the Spanish Melchior Canus, who, like him, was at the Council of Trent. His work on theological principles and evidences was, up to Bellarmine's time, the great authority used by all infallibilists. But his experience of the effects of that system on the Popes and the *Curia* themselves is thus summed up in a later judgment, composed by command of the King of Spain, 'He who thinks Rome can be healed, knows little of her; the whole administration of the Church is there converted into a great trading business, a traffic forbidden by all laws human, natural, and divine'.[35]

The conclusion the reader was expected to draw was an obvious one, though far removed from the actual mind of Melchor Cano. That was, Manning thought, history at its worst: biased, and claiming for itself the certainty of an exact science. He judged it 'an elaborate attempt of many hands to destroy, by profuse misrepresentations of history, the authority of the Pope, and to create animosity against the future Council'.[36]

The Council stood condemned in the eyes of Janus even before its opening session. In the last paragraph of the book, he wrote: 'whatever course the Synod may take, one quality can never be predicated of it, namely, that it has been a really free Council. Theologians and canonists declare that without complete freedom the decisions of a Council are not binding, and the assembly is only a pseudo-Synod. Its decrees may have to be corrected.'[37] As an exercise in poisoning the wells, the book was a success, and it had a considerable influence in shaping the vision of future events. It unsettled many a mind.

Manning was directly affected by one of Janus's assertions. The book claimed that 'the whole plan of the campaign for fixing the infallibility dogma is already mapped out. An English Prelate—we could name him—has undertaken at the commencement of the proceedings to direct a humble prayer to the Holy Father to raise the opinion of his infallibility to the dignity of a dogma'.[38] Then, the plan hoped, it would be carried by acclamation. All the eyes turned towards Manning. Ullathorne seemed to have believed the report: 'I have it on second-hand authority', he wrote to Bishop Brown on 26

[35] Ibid., 379.   [36] *True*, 67.
[37] Janus, *Pope and Council*, 425.
[38] Ibid. 6.

October 1869, 'that the Archbishop was to have put the proposition about infallibility to the Council, and the priest is
named to whom he told it. I do not doubt myself but that
there was an understanding between him and Rome about
it.'[39] The official denials in the *Tablet* do not seem to have affected Ullathorne's belief in the accuracy of the report.

Numerous publications, mostly pamphlets, appeared around
this time, the greater part of them trying to stir up opinion
against the Council, and attacking the infallibility of the Pope
from historical precedents like that of Honorius. Germany,
though, was the country where the ferment created by Janus
was at its highest. The *Coblenz Memorial*, drawn up by lay people, expressed their concerns about the Council, and suggested
some of the areas which they considered should be the object
of study and reform by it. Montalembert, and the school of *Le
Correspondent* welcomed the *Memorial*, afraid of the possibility
of the Ultramontanists pushing even further the condemnation
of modern civilization and of the principles of the State forms
born of the principles of 1789. Meanwhile, those in favour of
the definition of papal infallibility were not idle. Dechamps,
Archbishop of Malines, published in June his pamphlet about
the infallibility of the Pope; it achieved a great success with
his moderate but unequivocal Ultramontanism, and it went
through numerous editions in a few months. August saw the
publication in several languages of *Observations on the Question,
whether it be Opportune to Define the Infallibility of the Sovereign Pontiff*, the work of Brentano, Döllinger's disciple. The pamphlet
was sent to most of the bishops, and it was to provide Dupanloup with much of the material for his own *Observations*.
The German bishops, assembled at Fulda in September for
their annual meeting, issued a joint Pastoral trying to reassure
their flocks about the forthcoming Council. In a significant
move, sixteen out of the twenty German bishops signed a separate letter to the Holy Father expressing their conviction that
the definition would be inopportune. The Hungarian and Bo-
hemian bishops expressed similar feelings. The French episcopate was too divided for common action. The other European
episcopates did not express a common opinion, although it

---

[39] Quoted in Butler, *Vatican Council*, 123.

was well known that Italian and Spanish bishops were solidly behind the definition. Newman looked on apprehensively. He welcomed Dechamps's pamphlet on the Pope's infallibility, and, on 3 September wrote to Monsell: 'There is an Essay of the Archbishop of Malines, a Redemptorist, on the Pope's Infallibility—very moderate, as I thought, and good—and agreeing with Fr. Ryder's pamphlet—and the view I should take myself, though I don't want it *defined*.'[40]

Manning's pastoral letter—*The Oecumenical Council and the Infallibility of the Pope* (Rosary Sunday, 1869)—was written against that background, and it was mainly concerned with the 'opportunity' of defining the infallibility of the Pope. He also intended to allay the fears of those who were afraid of an all-out attack by the Council on the principles of 1789. Manning started by confessing the obvious: he did not know what would be defined at the Council; he added that he had no anxiety as to its result, the Council being in the hands of the Holy Spirit. He was ready to accept its decrees, whatever the outcome, even if they were to go against his previous judgment. It goes without saying that he considered this eventuality highly unlikely. In his estimation, there were many and weighty reasons for the definition, while those which had been put forward against it were easily answerable.

The doctrine of the infallibility of the Pope, Manning said in the pastoral, is true and belongs to the deposit of faith. It is therefore redundant to ask whether it is or is not opportune to define it. 'Is not this question already closed by the fact that God has thought it opportune to reveal it? Can it be permitted to us to think that what He has thought it opportune to reveal, it is not opportune for us to declare?'[41] The *disciplina arcani* had no room in the present condition of the Church! It could be argued, Manning acknowledged, that not all doctrines need to be defined. But the doctrine of the Pope's infallibility had been denied, and the denials had given rise to doubts in many minds. It was not simply a latent and unobtrusive error; it was 'patent, notorious, importunate, and organised'.[42]

---

[40] *LD* xxiv. 326. Newman wrote in a contemporary note: 'Why is it, if I believe the Pope's infallibility I do not wish it defined? Is not *truth* a gain? I answer, because it can't be so defined as not to raise more questions than it solves' (ibid. 334).

[41] *Privilegium*, ii. 39.　　[42] Ibid. 43.

It had already produced ill effects, and more would follow: 'doubt generates secret antipathies, contentions, and mistrusts', and it keeps alive 'a theological and practical disunion in mind and feeling among the faithful'.[43] Manning painted a dark landscape of doubt, scandal to the weak, hindrances to the expression and expansion of truth, party spirit, mistrust of brethren and of pastors, as following from the obscuring of this doctrine.

The effects of this state of affairs were no less serious outside the Catholic Church. It had been argued that the definition would be an obstacle in the way of reunion with the Greeks, who recoiled from new words, and that it would also retard the return of Protestants to the unity of the Church, by increasing their prejudices against Catholic teaching. These arguments cut no ice with Manning: reunion had to be achieved by the acceptance of revealed truth, not by blurring its content. Even more, he thought that the conversion of Protestants was being delayed by the apparent contradictions among Catholics on the subject of infallibility. The unchecked disparity of opinions on this matter offered Protestants an opportunity for controversy. The definition of infallibility was, to Manning's mind, essential to the mission of the Church, especially in England. He had already expressed this same conviction in his 1867 pastoral: 'It is certain that the action of Catholic truth upon England has been weakened by the Gallican opinions.' Gallicans maintained the infallibility of the Church, but the inconsistency of their theories had given some foundation to the Protestant retort ' "What is the use of infallibility if you do not know where it resides?" ' And this has enabled them for two centuries 'to evade the force of the argument in which both Ultramontanes and Gallicans are agreed'.[44] The action and influence of truth were enfeebled, because the controversy obscured the infallible authority of the Church. This also had momentous consequences for the foundation of the Faith, given that the 'infallibility of the Church is the ordinary medium through which the material object, that is, the doctrine, of Divine faith becomes known to us';[45] or, to put it more precisely, the 'virtue of divine faith has for its formal motive the

---

[43] *Privilegium*, ii. 45.   [44] *Privilegium*, i. 55–6.   [45] Ibid. 57.

veracity of God, and for its ordinary means of knowing the revelations of God, the proposition of the Church'.[46] The Ultramontanism versus Gallicanism controversy, by obscuring the
authority of the Church, cast doubt on the principle of divine
certainty. That is why it was so important to clarify once and
for all the question of the infallibility of the Pope. The Church,
Manning said, teaches mainly 'by its Head alone'; he is 'the
teacher of the Church'.

> If there be any truth of the faith in which ambiguity is perilous, it is
> the Divine and infallible authority on which all faith reposes. The
> infallibility of the Vicar of Jesus Christ is the infallibility of the
> Church in its Head, and is the chief condition through which its
> own infallibility is manifested to the world. To convert this, which
> is the principle of Divine certainty, into a doubtful question, and
> one of the highest endowments of the Mystical Body, into a subject
> of domestic strife and fraternal alienation, is a master-stroke of the
> Enemy of Truth and souls.[47]

A doubtful infallible teaching, like a dubious law, would impose no obligation to believe; 'it cannot exclude doubt, and
for that reason cannot generate faith. Where faith is, doubt
cannot be; and where doubt is, faith ceases to be.'[48]

'Let it not, then, be imagined', he had claimed in 1867, 'that
this subject is remote from our pastoral work; or that we can
declare the truth, or guide souls as we ought, unless we clearly
and firmly comprehend the Divine procedure in revealing and
perpetuating the faith of Jesus Christ.'[49] The dissensions and
confusion generated by the controversies about infallibility pre-
judiced the whole mission of the Church; they 'tend to paralyse
the action of truth *ad intra*; and consequently, by giving a false
appearance of division and doubt among Catholics, upon the
minds of Protestants and others *ad extra*'.[50]

5. *Gallicanism*

Manning considered Gallicanism a royal theology, imposed by
royal pressure and opposed to the great theological tradition
of the French Church. The French monarchy had patronized
it in an attempt to revive the conciliarist ideas of the Old

---

[46] *Privilegium*, ii. 50. [47] Ibid. 47. [48] Ibid. 50.
[49] *Privilegium*, i. 58. [50] *Privilegium*, ii. 120

Sorbonne and, in the process, provide a doctrinal justification for its regalist ambitions. As a matter of fact, the Gallican Articles were but a feeble imitation of the Statutes of Henry VIII. Despots borrowed ideas from each other; they always sought to divide the unity of the Church. A universal united Church is a power that they are not able to control; a national Church, on the other hand, can be oppressed easily. 'So long as the Church is kept apart by the jealousies of governments and nations, it remains unconscious of the vast strength which arises from the unity of co-operation. Despots hate popes, and love patriarchs; for popes are sovereigns, and inflexible; patriarchs may become courtiers, and dependents.'[51] Theologically, Gallicanism was full of inconsistencies. It admitted the infallibility of the Church while rejecting the infallibility of the Roman Pontiff. It confessed the infallibility of the See of Peter while denying the infallibility of Peter's successors, because instinct told them 'that to deny the infallibility of the Roman See was to deny the infallibility of the Church, and to depart from the whole *praxis* of the Church for the first sixteen centuries'.[52] But the Gallican Articles affirmed 'that the judgments of the Roman Pontiff in matters of faith are not irreformable, unless the assent of the Church—that is, either congregated [in Council] or dispersed, either previously or subsequently— shall adhere to them'.[53]

It would be difficult for Gallicans, Manning thought, 'to show that such an opinion is to be found in the tradition of the Church'. Their theory was, rather, an inversion of the immemorial belief and practice of the Church, and it would be easy to show 'that the tradition of the Church is not to test the teaching of the Pontiffs by the assent of the Church, but to take the doctrine of the Pontiffs as the test of the doctrine of the Church. The Head spoke for the whole Body, and the utterances of the Head were the evidence of what the Body believed and taught.'[54] And Manning supported this assertion with a long list of quotations from Councils and Synods of the past, from Constance to Chalcedon. Even Gerson was called as a witness: he had said clearly that the infallibility of the

---

[51] *Privilegium*, i. 94.   [52] *Privilegium*, ii. 65.   [53] Ibid. 61.
[54] Ibid. 62.

Pope was the doctrine generally admitted in his time, and that any one who ventured to deny it would have been condemned for heresy. Manning summed up by saying: 'if for heresy, in what light did the consent of the faithful, and the tradition of the Church, regard the truth denied? The correlative of heresy is faith.'[55]

Manning felt that the spirit of Gallicanism, condemned innumerable times and almost defunct in France, had to be finally eradicated from the Church. The fact that no theological censure had been attached to the condemnation of the Articles of 1682 meant that they were put forward as an opinion which Catholics could hold without blame. In 1867 Manning had claimed—somewhat optimistically, perhaps—that England was free of Gallicanism: Gallicanism, he said, 'has no place among us. It has no existence in any of our colleges; it is not to be found in our clergy, secular or regular. It has no part in our laity.'[56] Even so, in 1869, he maintained that it posed a more serious danger to English Catholics than Anglicanism. The Anglican Reformation, he said, is external to the Catholic Church, 'in open heresy and schism. Gallicanism is within its unity, and is neither schism nor heresy. It is a very seductive form of national Catholicism, which, without breaking unity, or positively violating faith, soothes the pride to which all great nations are tempted, and encourages the civil power to patronise the local Church by a tutelage fatal to its liberty. It is therefore certain that Gallicanism is more dangerous to Catholics than Anglicanism.'[57]

Nationalism was for Manning one of the most serious dangers to the Church, and he had been inveighing against it since his Anglican days. If that cancer was not removed on time, it would weaken and finally destroy the unity of the Church. 'Gallicanism is nationalism: that which the Gospel casts out; that which grew up again in mediaeval Christendom.'[58] He called it 'Christian Judaism', and he conceived of it as national in spirit, against the universality of the Church; inward-looking and refractory to external influences, rebellious and reticent with regard to any authority which is

---

[55] Ibid. 93.   [56] *Privilegium*, i. 56.   [57] *Privilegium*, ii. 53.
[58] *Privilegium*, i. 40.

not its own. In a national Christianity, to be national would come before being Christian. This had been the root from which had grown the factional spirit that had divided the Sacred College and set up uncanonical Popes; it had provided the excuse for worldly avarice to get hold of the temporalities of the Church and for the civil power to impose its rule on it. Nationalism, he added, tends to exert a subtle and stealthy influence 'by which the national spirit invades and assimilates the Church to itself; and [produces] the bitter fruits of heresy and schism which that assimilation legitimately bears'.[59] Heresy built on the foundation of a schismatical Church is its legitimate issue. The history of England bore witness to this fact: English nationalism became the Anglican schism by the steady and constant encroachment of the civil power upon the liberty of the Church. 'The schism once complete, the work of heresy was inevitable, and was pursued at leisure.'[60]

Gallicanism, as contained in the 1682 Articles, was a mild form of the same illness. It caused great harm to the Church, and, if unchecked, would lead to a more serious condition. 'Anything that fosters this idea of National Churches,' wrote Manning, 'independent, except in a few vital relations, of the Holy See, powerfully excites a spirit which is not filial [opposed to the "Catholic spirit"]. An Episcopate which depends as little as it can upon the Pope, rears a laity which depends as little as possible upon the Episcopate.'[61] These were the tendencies unleashed by Gallicanism, and the definition of the infallibility of the Roman Pontiff, speaking *ex cathedra*, was needed 'to exclude from the minds of Catholics the exaggerated spirit of national independence and pride which has, in these last centuries, so profoundly afflicted the Church'.[62] The definition of the dogma of papal infallibility by the Council would clear up the atmosphere of confusion. The fact of being defined by an ecumenical council would help its reception by all, 'both by those who believe the infallibility of the Pontiff and by those who believe the infallibility of the Church'.[63]

England was not the only country endangered by unchecked Gallicanism. France had been the cradle of Gallican ideas,

<hr>

[59] *Privilegium*, ii. 52.   [60] Ibid.   [61] Ibid. 54.
[62] Ibid. 52.   [63] Ibid. 121.

and Manning felt that they could still strike root in it: 'the unity of the French nation renders it yet possible that influences and claims inconsistent with the liberty of the Church may still exist'.[64] Manning was aware of the fact that, although the majority of French bishops could not be accused of Gallicanism, some of Napoleon III's nominees had clear Gallican tendencies, and he expressed the desire that 'the Bishops of France should, in this first Council of the Vatican, stand forth to lead the voices of the Episcopate in asking that the infallibility of the Vicar of Jesus Christ may be declared by a decree of the universal Church'.[65] The invitation was not altogether flattering, as Manning used the parallel of the Dominicans and the Immaculate Conception of the Virgin Mary to illustrate what he meant. The Dominicans, having for a long time opposed the doctrine, had recently removed this blot from their history by asking for its definition.

6. *A Controversy on the Way to the Council*

Ullathorne thought Manning's 1869 pastoral moderate, 'until it reaches the Appendix on Maret's injudicious book',[66] but he considered that the Archbishop had 'committed a blunder by inviting the French bishops to bring the infallibility forward, angry as many of them are against him, and divided as they are into three parties'.[67] He was right. France may have not been 'put into a fury', but there was a good deal of hurt Gallican pride in the subsequent controversy between Manning and Dupanloup.

Maret's book appeared in September 1869, while Manning's pastoral was being given the finishing touches before publication. Maret identified the Church in Council as the supreme authority in matters of faith. On the other hand, his disavowal of the Pope's infallibility was couched in mitigated terms. He claimed that his book did not deny it, but brought it back to its true nature. As a matter of fact, he added, we 'acknowledge and prove that the Pope, by his right to *consult* or to *convoke*

---

[64] Ibid. 54.   [65] Ibid. 122.

[66] H. Maret, *Du Concile général et de la paix religieuse* (2 vols., Paris, 1869). Henri-Louis-Charles Maret, dean of the Theology Faculty at the Sorbonne, had been appointed titular bishop in 1861.

[67] Letter to Brown, 26 Oct. 1869, quoted in Butler, *Vatican Council*, 123.

the episcopal body, by the possibility in which he is of acting always in concert with it, possesses in virtue of the Divine order the assured means to *give* infallibility to his dogmatic judgments'.[68] The book had been sent to every bishop, and Manning had received his copy after the pastoral was ready for publication. He still managed to add an appendix to it, in which he tried to answer Maret's assertion that, 'apart from the episcopal body, the Pontiff is not infallible'.[69] This, to Manning's mind, denied the infallibility of the Pope altogether, and amounted to an inversion of our Lord's words. It was equivalent to saying: 'It is the brethren who confirm him, not he who confirms his brethren. The endowment of infallibility residing in the body flows to the Head when in consultation with the Episcopate. It is *influxus corporis in Caput*, not *Capitis in corpus*.'[70] Manning added: 'The doctrine maintained by me, under the guidance of every great master of theology of all Schools ... excepting only theologians of the Gallican school, is, that judgments *ex cathedra* are, in their essence, judgments of the Pontiff, *apart* from the episcopal body, whether congregated or dispersed.'[71] The concurrence of the episcopate with the Head of the Church is not necessary for an infallible judgement of the Roman Pontiff. Were it so, it would be the occasion of multiple practical difficulties. What would happen if the episcopate had not examined the matter or pronounced on it? 'How long were they [the Pope's acts] in this tentative state of suspended or conditional infallibility? Who has ever discerned and declared the epoch and the crisis after which they became judgments *ex cathedra*?'[72] Manning thought that, 'except in a few cases, we cannot be certain, by explicit proof, whether the episcopal body has concurred in those judgments or no'.[73]

Maret claimed that his ideas were reconcilable with the doctrines of moderate Ultramontanism, a claim Manning rejected outright. Maret's opinions, he said, 'seem to place the infallibility of the Church in the whole body as its proper residence,

[68] Quoted by Manning in *Privilegium*, ii. 139–40.
[69] Ibid. 140.
[70] Ibid. Ullathorne used a similar expression in his pastoral of October 1870 (see Butler, *Vatican Council*, 458).
[71] Ibid. 142.   [72] Ibid. 143.   [73] Ibid. 145.

and by result in its Head'. Ultramontanism, on the other hand, maintained 'that infallibility was communicated by the Divine Head of the Church to Peter as His visible representative and Vicar upon earth, and through him to his Successors and to the Church for ever.'[74]

Maret's book, as was to be expected, attracted the thunder of *L'Univers*. And, in the ensuing controversy, Manning's pastoral was part of the ammunition used by Veuillot. Dupanloup came to know of Manning's pastoral through the pages of *L'Univers*, and his attention focused in particular on Manning's reference to the Pope acting *apart* from the bishops in definitions *ex cathedra*. It was not the first time that Manning had used this expression,[75] but until now it had not attracted criticism.

Dupanloup, in his letter to the clergy of his diocese of 11 November, launched an all-out attack against the opportuneness of defining the dogma of the infallibility of the Roman pontiff in the forthcoming Council. He made clear that he did not want to refute the doctrine, which he himself had propounded, but the opportuneness of its definition. In so doing he misrepresented the motives of those who, like Manning, were promoting the definition for theological reasons. Dupanloup attributed it to the natural 'piété filiale du vouloir orner un père de tous les dons, de toutes les prérogatives'.[76] However, he added, in determining such delicate questions, one should not allow oneself to be guided purely by sentiment. The Church, Dupanloup continued, had not felt the need for a definition of the Pope's infallibility in eighteen centuries of existence; the belief in the Church's infallibility had sufficed until now. Why speak, then, of the need for a new definition, 'et de constituer dogmatiquement une nouvelle règle de foi?'[77] Dupanloup, like Newman, appealed to St Irenaeus: *Quod semper, quod ubique, quod ab omnibus* ... He also used another expression dear to Newman: *In dubiis libertas ... in omnibus charitas, in*

---

[74] Ibid. 148.
[75] It can be found, among other places, in his pastoral of 1867 (*Privilegium*, i. 18, 23, etc.).
[76] F. Dupanloup, *Lettre de Mgr. l'Évêque d'Orléans au clergé de son diocèse relativement à la définition de l'infaillibilité au prochain concile* (2nd edn., Paris, 1869), 3.
[77] Ibid. 1.

necessariis unitas. His main aim was to show the extravagances of the Ultramontanes, and both Ward and Manning came in for a fair deal of criticism. Manning's expression 'apart from the bishops' was quoted several times, and Dupanloup developed what he considered its corollaries. The Vatican Council would be the Council to make redundant all future Councils: 'Le Pape, "EN DEHORS DES ÉVÊQUES" pourra tout décider infailliblement, même les questions de foi, à quoi bon réunir les évêques?'[78] The bishops would no longer be needed as judges of the faith.

Dupanloup thought that Manning's mistake sprang from separating the Pope from the Church: the Pope, he would claim, cannot be separated from the Church; neither can the Church be separated from the Pope! It is doubtful whether Dupanloup had read Manning's pastoral, apart from the paragraphs quoted by *L'Univers*; it is beyond doubt, though, that he was unfamiliar with the context of Manning's ideas. It would have been difficult, otherwise, to suggest the possibility of Manning entertaining any thought of the Pope being separated from the Church. Manning felt that his thought had been misrepresented, and asked Dupanloup in a letter of 25 November to rectify the wrong impression given by his interpretation of Manning's words. The Bishop of Orléans had attributed to him the following expressions: the Pope is infallible when 'il pronounce seul "en dehors du corps épiscopal réuni ou dispersé"; et qu'il peut définir les dogmes seul, "séparément, indépendamment de l'épiscopat"; sans aucun concours exprès ou tacite, antécédent ou subséquent, des évêques'.[79] This was more than Manning had said. He acknowledged that the word 'indepéndamment' was to be found in his writings, but not '*séparément*'. The two words together did not appear in the Postscriptum: 'cette proposition n'est jamais sortie da ma plume'.[80] Maret's contention had been that the Pope was not infallible 'sinon avec le concours ou consultation de l'épiscopat'. Manning, in response, had tried to formulate the contrary thesis: the Pope is infallible 'apart from', 'c'est-à-dire, sans le

---

[78] F. Dupanloup, *Lettre de Mgr. l'Évêque d'Orléans*, 45.
[79] Ibid. 7.
[80] Manning to Dupanloup, 25 Nov. 1869, quoted in F. Dupanloup, *Réponse de Mgr. l'Évêque d'Orléans à Mgr. Manning* (Paris, 1869), 6.

concours ou consultation de l'épiscopat'. Dupanloup's conclusion that the sentences quoted implied the possibility of schism
or opposition ('emportent l'idée de scission ou d'opposition'[81])
was false, and misrepresented Manning's words.

Dupanloup, in his response to Manning's letter, gladly
granted that the Archbishop of Westminster did not maintain
the possibility of an opposition or breach between Pope and
bishops: 'Non, vous n'enseignez point une telle doctrine; vous
l'attribuer serait vous calomnier'.[82] He then went on to disclaim responsibility for the translation of Manning's words:
the translation used in his letter was that printed by *L'Univers*!
This was true up to a certain point: Manning had accepted
that 'indépendamment' was a proper translation of his
thought; *L'Univers* had rendered 'apart from' as 'séparément',
and had also used the words 'en dehors' in the translation.
However, the expression 'séparément, indépendamment de
l'épiscopat' had been concocted by Dupanloup, and it can be
argued that, by the repetition of similar terms, he had come
to suggest the idea of scission between the Pope and the episcopate, if not of opposition.

Dupanloup ended his letter to Manning with a defence of
the Gallican Church, which the Popes had praised innumerable times, and which was truly devoted to the Holy See. To
claim that Gallicanism was more dangerous than Anglicanism
was unjust, an insult made more poignant by a comparison
which harnessed together Bossuet and Cranmer, Louis XIV
and Henry VIII!

Mgr. Dechamps had also written a response to Dupanloup's
letter of 11 November: 'you have undoubtedly touched upon
the final issue, and enveloped it in mists ... It is a mist, Monseigneur, this term, *new dogma* ... A mist again, Monseigneur,
these terms of *personal* and *separate* infallibility of the Sovereign
Pontiff.'[83] It could be said that Manning also came in for
some criticism from Dechamps, although he would probably
not have recognized it as such. The latter referred to those
who spoke of 'separate infallibility', saying that if by that

---

[81] Ibid.   [82] Ibid. 7.
[83] V. Dechamps, *A Letter to Monseigneur Dupanloup, Bishop of Orléans* (London,
1870), 7–9. The letter was dated 30 Nov. 1869.

'they mean that, to establish tradition, the Pope has no need always to convoke Councils, or even to consult the Bishops, they mean what is true, but they express it badly'.[84]

The Council had already started its sessions when Dupanloup published his *Réponse*. Manning wrote to him once again. He acknowledged the fact that Dupanloup had cleared him of maintaining the possibility of opposition or schism between the Pope and the bishops. In the letter he reformulated his central thesis: that the Roman Pontiff, when he speaks *ex cathedra*, is infallible, without consulting the Episcopal Body. He did not want to continue the discussion; it was not appropriate in the circumstances. And he ended by expressing his sorrow at disagreeing with a brother in the episcopate for whom he had had for many years profound admiration.[85] Ullathorne summed up well the controversy in his letter of 28 December: 'The Archbishop tells me he has sent another note to Orléans, still holding that Orléans does not fairly translate him. I told Dr. Manning I had read his pastoral nearly in the same sense, and that others had done so. People certainly imagined that by *apart from* the Episcopate, he meant isolated, and *not* merely acting apart although in union with them. However it is a petty quarrel which has damaged both combatants.'[86] Manning could perhaps have argued: why did you not say so when correcting the 1867 pastoral before its publication?

The Council had now started. Manning's words in his 1869 pastoral expressed the general feeling of the Fathers:

If the Council should decide contrary to their previous judgment, they would rejoice to be corrected by its unerring guidance; if it should refrain from pronouncing on matters on which they previously believed a decision to be opportune or even necessary, they would with their whole heart submit their judgment, and believe that such a decision would be not only not necessary, but not even opportune. In this sense of perfect submission, springing from faith in the perpetual and infallible assistance of the Holy Spirit, all Catholics will await the final result of the first Council of the Vatican.[87]

[84] V. Dechamps, *A Letter to Monseigneur Dupanloup*, 10.
[85] Cf. Manning MSS Pitts, box 7, folder 7, vol. viii, letter dated 20 Dec. 1869.
[86] Quoted in Butler, *Vatican Council*, 155.
[87] *Privilegium*, ii. 26.

VII

The First Vatican Council

The Council was solemnly opened by Pius IX on 8 December 1869, the feast of the Immaculate Conception. The first General Congregation took place two days later, and in it were announced the names of those Council Fathers appointed by the Pope to the congregation *De Postulatis*.[1] Their task, according to the Reglament of the Council, was to consider the bishops' proposals on new topics to be introduced in the Council, and to report them, with their opinion, to the Pope, on whom the final decision rested. The congregation had an all-important role to play, given that, as decided during the preparatory work of the Council, the introduction of the subject of the Pope's infallibility had been left to the initiative of the Council Fathers. The actual list of twenty-six members of the congregation included a wide spectrum of shades of opinion on the infallibility of the Roman Pontiff, as represented in the Council. Among their number were three of the main promoters of the definition: Archbishop Victor Dechamps of Malines, Archbishop Manning, and Conrad Martin, Bishop of Paderborn.

The next item on the agenda of the Council was the election of the special deputations. These were to have great influence in the actual work of the Council. Upon the particular deputations fell the greatest share of the work of shaping the material to be studied and voted on by the Council; they also had to deal with the amendments presented by the Fathers to the documents under study. Thus, the election of the deputation *De Fide* would see infallibilists and inopportunists exerting themselves to the utmost to influence its outcome. 'Everybody feels', wrote Ullathorne on 16 December, 'that on the twenty four [members of the Deputation] much will depend when *the question* comes on'.[2] Before the election, the Fathers were pre-

---

[1] The Segretaria di Stato had notified Manning of his appointment on the 7 Dec. (Manning MSS Pitts, box 7, folder 7).   [2] Quoted in Butler, *Vatican Council*, 140.

sented with lists prepared by the committees on both sides of
the argument about 'the question'. The list of the infallibilist
group did not include any bishop who was thought to oppose
the definition, while the inopportunists' one had some supporters of the definition among its names. Passions were running
high, and each party charged the other with intrigue and un-
derhand tactics. In the end, the election returned the names of
all those included in the infallibilist list. The lack of representa-
tion of the minority in the deputation was to be one of its
main grievances. Many considered their exclusion a tactical
mistake, to be laid at Manning's door. Still, an inopportunist
found his way on to the list put forward by the infallibilist
grouping: Archbishop Simor, Primate of Hungary. The pastoral he had issued before the Council gave to understand that
he was in favour of the definition, but on his arrival in Rome
he joined the ranks of the inopportunist party, and he absented
himself from the meetings of the deputation when it discussed
the primacy and infallibility of the Pope.

Manning's possibilities for influence in the running of the
Council were quite considerable, as a member of the congregation *De Postulatis* and of the deputation *De Fide*.[3] His sphere of
activity, though, was not confined to the work of the commissions. He was tireless in his efforts to bring about the definition
of infallibility by, among other things, canvassing support for
the petition to introduce the subject into the Council and
bring forward its discussion. Within and without the deputation *De Fide*, Manning worked very closely with Ignaz von Senestréy, Bishop of Ratisbon.[4] At times, in the meetings of the
deputation, they would find themselves unable to get their

---

[3] He was also well prepared for the work of the Council. On 10 Jan. 1869, the
directing Congregation of the preparatory work for the Council had approved a resolution, subsequently confirmed by the Pope, giving Manning access to the work of
the preparatory commissions (*M* xlix, cols. 513D–514A). On his return to London,
Manning took with him many of the votes of the experts, preparatory drafts, etc.,
particularly those of the Theological Commission. These texts can now be found
among Manning's papers at Pitts Theological Library, Emory University.

[4] Manning had regular contact and assistance from the Jesuit theologian Clement
Schrader. There was substantial agreement among them on their general views of
the Church and the Roman Pontiff. Schrader, after reading *The Temporal Mission of
the Holy Ghost*, had remarked how pleased he was to see that Manning's principles
were the same as those he had been teaching at Vienna in 1867 (Schrader to Man-

points of view accepted by other members. There, the opinions of Dechamps and Martin, more conciliatory in their approach to the objections of the minority, had great weight, and tended to prevail with Cardinal Bilio, president of the deputation. Manning described the situation in his manuscript 'Reminiscences of the Vatican Council': 'In the *deputatio de fide* he [Bilio] was overborne by Malines and Paderborn, and had a fear of French Bishops, who beset him in private. Ratisbon has given the history.'[5] Manning, on some of those occasions, would restrain himself from arguing a point further, considering that it would be to little avail, and would serve only to generate friction within the deputation.[6] However, that did not mean that he had given up promoting it; with the help of Senestréy and others, he continued looking for ways to advance the principle in question in another forum. Manning was aware of the animosity which his incessant activity generated even among supporters of the definition, and, to avoid increasing it, he at times passed ideas and even written texts to other Fathers, for them to bring to the Council's attention. It would be difficult to trace these contacts in detail, but some speeches in the General Congregations, and some written amendments or suggestions made by the Fathers could probably be identified as having originated with Manning.

A. THE CONSTITUTION ON CATHOLIC FAITH

On 10 December the Fathers received the draft schema of the Constitution on Catholic Faith and Rationalism. The text was distributed in eighteen chapters, preceded by an introduction. The first two condemned materialism, pantheism, and ration-

ning, letter dated 19 Jan. 1869, Manning MSS Pitts, box 7, folder 7). Senestréy and Manning also relied heavily on Canon Maier, the personal theologian of the Bishop of Ratisbon.

[5] Quoted in *P* ii. 454; for Senestréy's Diary see *M* liii, cols. 276C–286B.

[6] Schrader, in his correspondence with Manning during the month of February, insisted on the importance of preserving unity among those who were agreed on fundamental points, avoiding disputes over minor questions (Manning MSS Pitts, box 7, folder 7).

alism, arguing that such errors had their origin in the Reformation. They were followed by three chapters on the nature and sources of divine revelation and the mysterious character of revealed truth, transcending human reason. Chapters 6–11, which interested Manning particularly, dealt at length with the nature of faith and its relationship to the human sciences. Finally, the schema referred to those errors which affected particular truths of faith.

The General Congregation of 28 December initiated the discussion of the proposed draft schema. The general feeling expressed by the Fathers was that the schema was too long, too polemical, touching on very specialized errors—and far removed from the needs of the faithful; its tone was more that of a dogmatic treatise than of a conciliar document. The schema was sent to the deputation *De Fide* to be redrafted. Manning's perception of the schema was somewhat different from that of the majority of the Fathers who spoke in the General Congregations. 'The original *schema*', he wrote a few years later, 'was one of the grandest of theological documents, cast in the traditional form of conciliar decrees, taking its shape, as they did, from the errors which required condemnation.' He admitted that it was somewhat archaic in language; still, it was 'worthy to rank with the decrees of the Councils of Toledo or of Lateran'.[7] His praise for the schema is particularly significant when one considers how economical Manning would be in his praise of the first schema *De Ecclesia*, which, being based entirely on the doctrine of the Mystical Body of Christ, should have been close to his heart. The fact is that the need for a proper understanding of the nature of the act of faith was second to none in Manning's mind. Semi-rationalism was for him the great enemy of the Church at the time, and he could not but welcome as clear a denunciation as possible of that pernicious error, the fountain from which sprang innumerable others. Besides, he felt that the progress of the natural and historical sciences made it imperative to have a clear concept of the relationship between science and faith.

When Franzelin, the main author of the schema rejected by the Fathers, defended it before the deputation *De Fide* on 11

---

[7] *True*, 93.

January, he must have found a sympathetic hearer in Manning. The schema, Franzelin said, followed an 'essential' order. It dealt first, briefly, with absolute rationalism and its denial of a supernatural revelation. The second section, the main body of the schema, was devoted to refuting the errors of semi-rationalism about the nature of Christian knowledge. It also considered the formal aspects of faith: the object, nature, and sources of divine revelation, together with the supernatural character of the act of faith. After that, it went on to deal with the differences and connections between faith and science. In this respect, the schema pointed out that faith and science have different formal objects, although the unity of truth meant that there were many connections between these two fields of knowledge, and that they could never contradict each other. The final chapters dealt with errors concerning particular truths of faith which followed from mistaken conceptions about the nature of revelation or of faith.

The decision of the deputation *De Fide* was to maintain the substance of the original schema while dramatically remodelling it. The work of revision was entrusted to a commission of three bishop-members of the deputation with the assistance of some theologians. By the end of the revision work, the schema had been reduced from eighteen to nine chapters, and these had been divided in two separate schemata. The first was made up of four chapters: chapter 1 dealt with the natural knowledge of God, as Creator, through his creatures (natural revelation); chapters 2–4 were concerned with God's supernatural revelation, including the nature of the knowledge of faith and the relationship between faith and science. This schema, once studied and reformed by the Council, was to become the First Constitution on Catholic Faith, *Dei Filius*. The second schema *De Fide*, which would not be discussed in the Council, was concerned with the condemnation of particular errors against individual truths of faith.

The beginning of the proemium of the schema *De Fide* referred to the innumerable benefits and good results derived from the holding of Ecumenical Councils, as far as the preservation and formulation of the Faith was concerned. During its study by the deputation it was suggested that a reference to the role of the Holy See in combatting error be introduced in the same place. The deputation, on Martin's advice, decided unanimously on 2 March not to add another reference to the magisterium of the Pope in the opening lines of the proemium, as he was already mentioned in a similar context at the end of it. The matter, though, would not rest there. Manning's notes tell of a meeting he held, with four other bishops, some time before the start of the debate on the proemium in the General Congregation. In that meeting, they prepared three amendments asking for the proemium to mention the magisterium of the Pope where it spoke on that of the Councils. Manning left a record of the reasons for the proposed emendations:

Silence on the Roman pontiff in this place in the introduction, especially after the many papal condemnations made in the preceding three centuries, would not pass unnoticed; such silence would certainly cause *admiratio* among the faithful. An omission of this sort would be more conspicuous since mention was made of the councils; the text would seem to insinuate that the supreme rule and magisterium of the Church was exercised only in ecumenical councils. Precaution ought to be taken lest this omission, alongside a later mention of the bishops as judges, seem to favour in some way the 'theories of pseudo-Catholics' on these matters.

Manning's notes show that he also tried to anticipate and answer those who might argue against the proposal that it seemed 'to prejudice the discussion of papal infallibility that would come with the second dogmatic schema'. His reply to this objection was that the 'intention here was simply to recognize the Church's supreme magisterium as it was already held by all the faithful'.[8] The amendments were put forward in the General Congregations of the 22 and 23 March by three of the bishops who attended Manning's meeting: Dreux-Brézé of Moulins; the Bishop of Seo de Urgel, Caixal y Estradé; and Magnasco, a titular bishop. The reasons adduced were similar to those used by Manning. The suggestions did not prosper, the amendments being dismissed by the deputation.

During the study by the deputation of chapter 2, on revelation, Manning proposed a change to its fifth paragraph, which contained a reaffirmation of Trent's teaching on the authority of the Church as interpreter of Holy

---

[8] Cwiekowski, *English Bishops*, 194–5.

Scripture.[9] Manning thought that the suggested wording could give the impression that the unanimous consent of the Fathers, when interpreting Holy Scripture, was on a level with the interpretation of the Church, as a sort of parallel norm of faith. Thus, the present text would seem to offer some support to the claims of those who appealed from the teaching of the living Church to the unanimous consent of the Ancient Fathers, as Anglicans did. The deputation accepted Manning's suggestion, and the reference to the Fathers of the Church was omitted in the text presented to the Council Fathers for study. The omission did not pass unnoticed, and some of the bishops later remarked upon it during the debates of the General Congregation. These comments prompted Manning to intervene in the debate, on 28 March, in order to explain to the General Congregation the reasons for the exclusion. He spoke of how the apologists of the Anglican schism, from Jewel to Pusey, had justified the separation from Rome on the grounds that the Roman Church had departed from the original purity of the Faith, and that the Anglican Reformers' only aim had been to restore it by going to the uncontaminated fountains of primitive Christianity and the Fathers of the Church. Manning quoted from Pusey's third *Eirenicon* to illustrate the point in question.[10] His intervention was not wholly unsuccessful. At the insistence of the Fathers, the full text was later on reintroduced, but it now contained a clause making clear that it was the task of the Church not only to interpret Holy Scripture but also to judge of the consent of the Fathers.[11]

Manning's quotation of Pusey did more than illustrate the Anglican appeal to the Fathers. It also described the theory of the three branches of the Church, as used by Pusey to refuse submission to the definitions of Trent on the basis that only the dogmatic decisions of the universal Church—of which the

---

[9] 'Quia vero, quae sancta Tridentina synodus de interpretatione divinae Scripturae, ad coercenda petulantia ingenia, salubriter decrevit, a quibusdam hominibus prave exponuntur, idem decretum hoc approbante concilio renovantes, hanc eius mentem esse definimus, ut in rebus fidei et morum, is pro vero Scripturae sensu habendus sit, quem tenuit et tenet sancta mater ecclesia, *aut quem sanctorum patrum consensus unanimis attestatur*' (*M* liii, col. 166B, my emphasis).

[10] *M* li, cols. 165B–166B.

[11] *M* li, cols. 287D–288D; this clause had been requested by several Council Fathers as early as January.

Roman was but a branch—could demand acceptance as matters of necessary belief. With this quotation, which did not
quite relate to the point in question, Manning seems to have
lent indirect support to Ullathorne's proposal of 24 March to
change the opening words of chapter 1 from *Sancta Romana catholica ecclesia* to *catholica atque romana ecclesia*, on the basis that
the original wording, Ullathorne argued, could offer some
ground to the Anglican claims.[12] The deputation decided to
reject Ullathorne's suggestion on 27 March; Manning spoke
in the General Congregation the day after. This ruling of the
deputation seems to have been the reason for the *placet juxta
modum* votes of a good number of American and English
bishops on 12 April. In the end, the deputation was to reverse
its own vote—and that of the General Congregation—in
order to include Ullathorne's suggestion.

When it came to the study of chapter 3, on faith, Manning
took Senestréy's side in the deputation. In the meetings of 5
and 9 March, Senestréy had suggested that mention should be
made of the fact that the object of faith was not confined to
the solemn dogmatic definitions of the Church, but also included those truths taught by the ordinary magisterium. He
proposed a possible text, plus the corresponding canon and
anathema, to be incorporated into chapter 3.[13] Manning felt
deeply the need to defend this fundamental principle. In his
pastoral on the centenary of the martyrdom of St Peter and St
Paul he had written: 'many truths of Divine revelation have
not been defined. All that is defined is indeed *de fide*, but not
all that is *de fide* has been defined.'[14]

The deputation, while acknowledging the importance of the
matter, decided that the topic belonged more fittingly to the
study of the infallibility of the Church. Manning made no objection to the deputation's decision, 'not, indeed, from assent,
"sed pro reverentia erga Em[minentissimum] Praesidem" '.[15]
His notes recorded his hope that Senestréy's suggestion would

---

[12] *M* li, cols. 105A–106B.
[13] *M* liii, cols. 188BC and 192C. Senestréy was a determined opponent of the opinions of the Munich school, and, like Manning, an ardent defender of the authority
of the ordinary magisterium.
[14] *Privilegium*, i. 66.
[15] Cwiekowski, *English Bishops*, 192.

be introduced eventually; it was necessary to correct a German error which had some influence in England, and, in particular, to make clear that the Christian was to believe the whole of revealed truth, not just what had been defined. Their insistence was partly rewarded. The text presented to the Council Fathers on 14 March, and the final one, includes a clause stating that 'all those things are to be believed with divine and Catholic faith which are contained in the Word of God, written or handed down, and which the Church, either by a solemn judgment, *or by her ordinary and universal magisterium*, proposes for belief as having been divinely revealed'.[16] This positive obligation was to be complemented by a negative one in the final paragraph of the Constitution: 'it is not sufficient to shun heretical pravity, unless those errors also be diligently avoided which more or less nearly approach it',[17] and which had been condemned by the Holy See.

There was also an attempt to reinforce, with a canon and an anathema, the obligatoriness of accepting the teaching of the ordinary magisterium. The schema, as presented to the Council Fathers on 14 March, included a canon condemning those who maintained the licitness of upholding doctrines condemned as erroneous by the Church but not defined as heretical.[18] That did not seem sufficient to some of the Fathers. While the schema was being discussed, new suggestions were made. The *Emendationes* to chapter 3 contain a proposal from Monzón y Martín, Archbishop of Granada, and another one from Meurin, Bishop of Ascalon, to introduce a canon and anathema imposing on all the faithful the obligation to believe with divine faith all those things contained in Holy Scripture and Tradition, and which are taught by the solemn or ordinary magisterium. Manning's copy of the *Emendationes* shows

[16] *M* li, col. 432C; Manning's trans. in *Privilegium*, iii. 198, emphasis added. The word 'universal' was introduced at the request of some Fathers who felt that, otherwise, it would be thought that the sentence referred only to the Pope's magisterium.

[17] *M* li, col. 436A; trans. by Manning in *Privilegium*, iii. 203. Gasser would later defend this sentence before the General Congregation by saying that no reference had been made in the text of the Constitution or in its canons to the role of the Holy See in the defence of the Faith; it was necessary to do so in view of the circumstances of the time.

[18] See canon 3 of chapter 4 (*M* li, col. 38B). This canon was not included in the final text of the Constitution.

his concern regarding the need to clarify the status of the ordinary magisterium.[19] His marginal notes, probably intended for
use in the meetings of the deputation, contain alternatives to
the wording of Monzón y Martín's canon. It is interesting to
note that, where Monzón had spoken of the obligation to believe with divine faith the teachings of the ordinary magisterium, Manning's text stressed the connection of that teaching
to divine revelation, and how the truths so taught should be received as part of it.[20] The emendations were rejected by the deputation, the argument used being the same as that used in
declining Senestréy's proposal.

Manning also took an active part in introducing a new
canon among those of chapter 3, on faith. In the meeting of
the deputation of 6 March he suggested restoring in canon 6,
with some slight alterations, the wording of the canon corresponding to chapter 9 of the original schema. The deputation
accepted his proposal. The newly worded canon rejected the
claim of those who thought that it would be legitimate for
Catholics to doubt, 'with suspended assent, the faith which
they have already received under the magisterium of the
Church, until they shall have obtained a scientific demonstration of the credibility and truth of their faith'.[21] The canon
had the primary objective of condemning Hermesian doubt as
a method claiming that an adult faith and theology required,
as a first step, doubting one's faith in order to build it up afterwards on a rational basis. However, it was also, in Manning's
eyes, an explicit rejection of the claims advanced by those
who, on the basis of the new scientific theories or the findings
of the so-called school of historical criticism, felt justified in
questioning the faith of the Church and the recent pronouncements of the magisterium.

In *The True Story of the Vatican Council* (1877), when explaining the new Constitution, Manning wrote that, although very
different from the original schema, it was 'full of condensed
doctrine', and that the whole of it had 'a singular beauty and

---

[19] *M* li, col. 311C.
[20] Manning MSS Pitts, box 6, folder 23; 'Emendationes ... propositae ad Caput
III', 40.
[21] *M* li, col. 435D; Manning's trans. in *Privilegium*, iii. 202.

splendour of divine truth impressed upon it'.[22] He strongly approved where Strossmayer, Bishop of Bosnia, had complained of a lack of irenicism in the proemium, where the Reformation was charged with having as its natural offsprings rationalism and naturalism.[23] Manning had said as much in his writings before the Council. The final text toned down those expressions without sacrificing the connection between the Reformation and modern error.

When the time came to explain the Constitution, Manning maintained that *Dei Filius* taught that the first cause of all the evils which had followed the Reformation was 'the rejection of the divine, and therefore infallible, authority of the Church. The inevitable consequence of this rejection was to leave all matters of religion to be decided by the judgment of individuals; from this, again, has followed the multiplication of sects conflicting with each other.' The faith of many Christians had been shipwrecked in the ensuing confusion. Three hundred years before, the Reformers had claimed Holy Scripture to be the sole foundation of Christian faith; but the Holy Scriptures were now rejected as myths by many who had followed in the footsteps of the early Protestants. The rejection of divine authority had generated in time two main principles of error: 'the one, Rationalism, which makes the human reason to be the test, the measure, or the source of all truth itself; the other, Naturalism, which denies altogether the existence of a supernatural order of grace and truth'.[24] Pantheism, atheism, materialism, and, in politics, the 'lawless spirit of revolution' followed in their train.

Philosophy had trodden a parallel path and reached similar conclusions. The Reformation, Manning thought, had 'revolted against both the scholastic theology and the scholastic philosophy';[25] the end result had been rationalism, scepticism, pantheism, atheism, naturalism. In summary, the Reformation, and the ideologies born of it, had closed both the natural and the supernatural paths of access to God. The Council, by

---

[22] *True*, 93.

[23] In the printed text of Franzelin's defence Manning marked in pencil the phrase where the Jesuit theologian had made this very point (cf. Manning MSS Pitts, box 6, folder 23).

[24] *True*, 124.   [25] Ibid. 129.

contrast, had reaffirmed the existence of these two orders of knowledge, and defined that human reason can prove the existence of God. This was of fundamental importance to Manning:

This certainty of our natural reason may be called the infallibility of the natural order. ... This infallible certainty is the foundation of the moral life of man. St. Paul says that they who know not God, by the things which are made, are inexcusable. But they would not be inexcusable if God could not be known by the light of reason. And if in this knowledge the reason could be deceived—that is, if it were not certain—then there could be no moral obligation upon the conscience to believe. The atheist, pantheist, and sceptic, would all be excused for their doubt and unbelief. But if the existence and moral character of God be doubtful, the basis of all morals is doubtful too. *Lex dubia non obligat*.[26]

Having affirmed the possibility of gaining knowledge of God through natural reason, the Constitution had gone on to say that the communication of supernatural truth to man by means of a supernatural revelation is not only possible, it is also necessary, for two reasons: 'first, that man may attain to the knowledge of truths above and beyond the order of nature, and, secondly, that by such revelation man may be raised to a higher order of knowledge and perfection'.[27]

Manning considered chapter 3, on faith, as particularly relevant for the times; it might 'be truly said', he wrote, 'that in this chapter every word is directed against some intellectual aberration of this century'.[28] It taught 'that inasmuch as God reveals to man truths of the supernatural order, man is bound to believe that revelation by reason of the authority or veracity of God, who can neither deceive nor be deceived. The infallibility of God is the motive of faith', and the act of believing the supreme act of reason, '[f]or no act of the reason can be more in harmony with its nature than to believe the Word of God. ... It is also an act not of necessity but of perfect freedom.' Although reasonable, he would add, the act of faith is an act not 'of the natural order, but of the supernatural, and springs from the preventing grace of the Holy Spirit, Who illuminates the intelligence and moves the will'. It embraces, as its object, the whole of God's revelation: 'Whatsoever God has

[26] *True*, 131–2.   [27] Ibid. 133.   [28] *Privilegium*, iii. 46.

revealed, man, when he knows it, is bound to believe.' And God had 'made provision that man should know His revelation, because He has committed it to His Church as the guardian and teacher of truth'. Thus, we are bound to believe all that the Church proposes to our belief, 'whether by its ordinary and universal teaching, or by its solemn judgment and definition'.[29] Significantly, Manning gives precedence to the ordinary teaching of the Church over the solemn teaching, changing the order in which they appear in the Constitution. The reason behind this change was his concept of the ordinary and universal teaching of the Church as the means she uses to communicate the Faith generation after generation. The ordinary magisterium contains all the truths to be believed, while the solemn dogmatic definitions, because of their origin and nature, cover a much narrower spectrum of revealed truth.

Once the character of the knowledge of faith had been clarified, the Constitution, in its fourth chapter, went on to define the relationship between faith and natural knowledge. Manning, when explaining the Constitution, would carefully develop this point, as he felt that this was the area where the errors of rationalism grew thicker, and where the seeds of confusion had been sown in plenty, even among Catholics. *Dei Filius*, Manning wrote, had clearly taught three things: 'first, that there are two orders of knowledge; secondly, that they differ as to their object; thirdly, that they differ as to their methods of procedure'.[30] The Constitution affirmed that human reason was not the sole fountain, measure, and judge of truth; there was a truth which no man could reach on his own, but to which he must submit, once it was made known to him. Absolute rationalism and semi-rationalism obliterated this distinction: the first, by its denial of any supernatural truth; the second, by maintaining that 'although without revelation many truths would not have been known to man, yet when once revealed they may be adequately comprehended and proved by reason, so that they become objects not only of faith but of science'.[31] The Constitution was primarily concerned with the rationalist errors of Günther and Hermes— and with Bautain's fideism, at the other end of the spectrum.

---

[29] Ibid. 46–7.   [30] Ibid. 48.   [31] *True*, 135.

Still, their condemnation also covered the errors of Anglicanism, given that, as Manning saw it, they all shared a common vision of the act of faith as originating in a human act and a human authority.

Faith and reason 'move on different planes', different levels of truth, between which there is no continuity or opposition. Their objects and methods of procedure are different: 'in the order of nature the instrument of knowledge is discovery; in the supernatural order, it is faith, and the intellectual processes which spring from faith'.[32] Thus, science and faith can never be in real contradiction; 'the conflict can only be apparent and transient, and while it seems to exist we are bound even by reason, which assures us of the certainty of faith, to believe the conflict to be not real, but only apparent'.[33] It could spring, Manning thought, either 'from error as to the doctrine of the Church, or error in the assumptions of science. Every assertion, therefore, contrary to the truth of an illuminated faith, is false.'[34] The Church had always promoted and encouraged the cultivation of the human arts and sciences; on the other hand, as the Council had pointed out, it has the right and the duty—together with the divine assistance to implement them—to correct the false sciences which 'by going beyond their own limits ... enter upon and disturb the things which are of faith'.[35] The Church, Manning said, did not claim jurisdiction over the development of philosophy and science; the 'only judgment it pronounces regards the conformity or variance of such processes of the human intelligence with the deposit of faith, and the principles of revealed morality'.[36]

In the final paragraphs of the constitution, the Roman Pontiff, by his supreme authority, commanded all the faithful—pastors and people—to drive away errors contrary to faith, whether solemnly condemned as heretical or denounced as more or less close to it by the Holy See. Manning felt that if the 'Vatican Council had met and parted without any act beyond this one decree, it would have applied a direct and

---

[32] *Privilegium*, iii. 49.   [33] *True*, 137.   [34] *Privilegium*, iii. 49.
[35] *M* li, col. 434B; Manning's trans. in *True*, 137.
[36] *Privilegium*, iii. 77–8.

searching remedy to the intellectual aberrations of the nine-teenth century'.[37] No Council, in his estimation, had defined so explicitly the divine and infallible authority of the Church in declaring and defending the deposit of revelation.[38] He thought that the importance of the Constitution could not be overestimated, and that at the time, because of its great breadth, its full significance might 'not as yet be fully perceived'.[39]

The Constitution, as far as Manning was concerned, was the best introduction to the definition of the infallibility of the Pope: 'It begins with God and His revelation; it closes with the witness and office of the Visible Church, and with the su-preme authority of its Head. The next truth demanded by the intrinsic relations of doctrine was the divine endowment of in-fallibility. And when treated, this doctrine was, contrary to all expectation, and to all likelihood, presented first to the Coun-cil, and by the Council to the world, in the person and office of the Head of the Church.'[40]

B. THE PATH TO THE DEFINITION OF PAPAL INFALLIBILITY

I. *The Introduction of the Subject in the Council*

1. *Petitions for its Inclusion in the Schema* De Ecclesia

The infallibility of the Pope had been the subject of public debate from the very moment the Council had been sum-moned. Once the Council was under way, the unceasing activ-ity of those advocating its definition and of those who opposed it shaped the whole progress of the Council; moves and counter-moves followed in each other's steps: petitions to bring in the topic and counter-petitions to delay its introduc-tion, reasons which made the definition imperative and argu-ments that showed the harm that would come from it, efforts

---

[37] *True*, 137.
[38] Cf. *Privilegium*, iii. 50; 'fidei doctrina, quam Deus revelavit, ... tamquam divi-num depositum Christi sponsa tradita, fideliter custodienda et infallibiliter declar-anda' (ch. 4).
[39] Ibid. 49.   [40] Ibid. 51.

to talk out the definition and counter-manœuvres to put an
end to the debates, appeals to the Powers to put pressure on
the Council, exaggerations to raise fears. The partial blindness
of mind, and the distortions generated by the heat of controversy, go some way to explain certain actions of the main pro-
tagonists of the infallibility debate, which, at a distance, look
less than praiseworthy for the individuals concerned.

The lines were drawn, and the first skirmishes had already
been fought, by the time the Council Fathers received the text
of the schema *De Ecclesia* on 21 January 1870.[41] The draft submitted for their study contained fifteen chapters covering the
nature and mystery of the Church: its divine origin and properties (such as unity, immutable constitution, and infallibility),
the hierarchical character of the Church and the primacy of
the Roman Pontiff, and finally, the relations between Church
and State. Central to the schema was the presentation of the
Church as the Mystical Body of Christ, a perspective which
marked a clear progress from the too juridical ecclesiology predominant at the time.[42] Manning could not but welcome that
treatment of the Church, and he expressed his opinion on the
schema in the notes he wrote during the Council, which were
probably intended as points to bring up in the public sessions
of the Council or in the meetings of the deputation *De Fide*.
His notes praised the schema as a whole because

it treated the creed's article on the Church at length and in an or-
derly way. Trent was so preoccupied with explicit heresies ... that
in the last analysis it was scarcely able to see the source and principle of the Protestant error: the rejection of the Church and its prerogatives. In rejecting the infallible authority of the teaching
Church, Protestantism rejected the ordinary means instituted by
God to lead men to the faith. It was altogether necessary that this

---

[41]   *M* li, cols. 539A–553A.

[42]   The treatment of the Church as the Mystical Body of Christ was criticized by
many of the Council Fathers. Schrader was very anxious to defend chapter 1, 'De
Corpore Christi Mystici', and he sent Manning a summary of the reasons for its preservation, and some advice on how to proceed (2 Feb. 1870). Maier may have also
seen the letter, and added some of the marginal comments. One of them, probably
by Manning, says 'lege et age' (Manning MSS Pitts, box 7, folder 7). It is difficult
to know whether Manning did anything along the above lines. The effort to promote
the introduction of the infallibility of the Pope may have absorbed the best part of
his energy at the time.

council solemnly define the Church's teaching on the institution and prerogatives of the Church. [43]

He considered that the definition of the Church's infallibility, founded on the perpetual living presence of the Holy Spirit within it, was particularly necessary for those countries where Catholics and non-Catholics lived side by side: 'Non-Catholics accepted the authority of a revealing God ... but they questioned the means by which revealed truth was given to men.'[44] Protestants and Anglicans had in common the emphasis on private judgement, and they both rejected the infallibility of the living Church.

Manning added another reason for praising the schema: its treatment of the principle 'extra ecclesiam nulla salus'. This was a question which had exercised his mind even before becoming a Catholic, and which he had considered at length in his fourth volume of Anglican sermons. Manning felt that there was a great ignorance on the subject, among both Catholics and non-Catholics: 'Catholics despaired of the salvation of non-Catholics and non-Catholics rejected the Catholic doctrine as incompatible with divine mercy and justice. This misunderstanding was a great obstacle to conversions, Manning complained, and his efforts to clarify the Church's position were met with the charge that he was mitigating the Church's doctrine without proper authority. [45]

This schema, *De Ecclesia Christi*, was never to be discussed in the Council, however. The main reason for this was that, although it affirmed in clear terms the infallibility of the Church, there was no reference in it to the infallibility of the Roman Pontiff.

As soon as the Council started, the wheels had been set in motion to introduce the study of the infallibility of the Pope, or to prevent its insertion, into the proceedings of the Council. Cardinal Rauscher, Archbishop of Vienna, and Dupanloup opened fire for the opposition, but the infallibilists did not remain silent for very long. Manning, Senestréy, Dechamps, Martin, and some others met on 23 December to prepare the

---

[43] Quoted in Cwiekowski, *English Bishops*, 219.
[44] Ibid.   [45] Ibid. 220.

text of a petition asking for the subject to be introduced.[46] They later attached to the petition a statement of the reasons for the opportuneness of the definition, needed in order to win the support of many of the Fathers, and an appendix containing some recent decisions of provincial synods touching upon the matter. The petition was ready by the 28th, and it was circulated with a covering letter to all the bishops, 'omitting', according to Manning, 'only those whose known opposition made it a duty of delicacy and of respect not even to seem to obtrude upon them'.[47] The signing of the petition went on for most of January. 'I remember our anxiety', Manning wrote years later, 'while the signatures were coming in, hindered and delayed by intrigue and misrepresentation.'[48] Some 380 bishops signed the petition. Its text,[49] however, did not satisfy all those in favour of definition: some thought that it was too extensive; others, while wanting to preserve the substance of the definition, preferred different wordings. As a result, there were several other petitions in favour of the definition, one of them attracting sixty-eight signatures. On the inopportunist side, petitions against the introduction of papal infallibility in the Council were signed by 136 Council Fathers,[50] the main *Postulatum* against the introduction of the subject in the Council being that of the forty-six bishops headed by Schwarzenberg, Cardinal-Archbishop of Prague, and vehement against the definition.[51]

Ullathorne, who did not sign any of the petitions, pro-

---

[46] Manning, in his copy of the petition, wrote that the text had been drawn up by the bishops of Ratisbon (Senestréy), Paderborn (Martin), Luxemburg (Adames), Hebron (Mermillod), and Westminster (Manning MSS Pitts, box 7, folder 7). Manning may have meant Dechamps when he wrote 'Luxemburg'.

[47] *True*, 115–16; for Ullathorne's comments see Butler, *Vatican Council*, 184.

[48] Quoted in *P* ii. 453.

[49] *M* li, cols. 646C–650A.

[50] Text in *M* li, cols. 677C–679A.

[51] It called forth some typical comments from Manning. His copy of the *Postulatum* has some marginal notes remarking on the vagueness of the text. Where it said that the Council cannot exist without the Pope, Manning wrote: 'sed extra Concilio, et inter Concilia?' Was infallibility dormant? The *Postulatum* added that Florence had already spoken about the Pope. Manning acknowledged the fact, but remarked '*Quo sensu?*'. The language of the *Postulatum* was also ambiguous when speaking about obeying the Pope's decrees (*mandatis*); it did not clarify whether these included doctrinal decrees, or whether they were due internal or only external obedience (cf. Manning MSS Pitts, box 7, folder 4; *Postulatum*, 5–6).

nounced that Manning's formula—which he misquoted—'did not incorporate the doctrine of infallibility at all. The *suprema ideoque irreversibilis auctoritas* was just our own constitutional doctrine: there being no tribunal above him, the King can do no wrong.'[52] The actual wording of the petition was: 'that the authority of the Roman Pontiff is supreme, and, therefore, exempt from error [*supremam, ideoque ab errorem immunem*], when in matters of faith and morals he declares and defines what is to be believed and held, and what to be rejected and condemned, by all the faithful'.[53] In another place it said: 'the judgments of the Roman Pontiff in matters of faith and morals are irreformable'.[54] It is hard to see how the wording of the petition—or the English Constitution, for that matter—could support Ullathorne's interpretation. Wiseman would have recognized in those words the main thrust of his attack against the Anglican rule of faith.

This petition was the first conciliar text to attempt to put into words the doctrine of the infallibility of the Pope. It insisted on the connection between primacy and infallibility: Sacred Scripture plainly taught 'the Primacy of jurisdiction of the Roman Pontiff, the Successor of St. Peter, over the whole Church of Christ, and, therefore, also his Primacy of supreme teaching authority'.[55] That the supreme judge in doctrine must be infallible, and his judgements irreformable, had been obvious to Manning from his late Anglican days; were this not so, it would be left to private judgement to decide whether the Pope had judged correctly in matters of doctrine.

The Congregation *De Postulatis*, in its meeting of 9 February, decided to send the petition to the Pope, accompanied by its favourable opinion.

2. *The New Chapter on the Pope's Infallibility*

From the very beginning of the Council, those opposed to the definition of the Pope's infallibility were on the alert to prevent any wording of the conciliar documents that could affirm it

---

[52] Quoted in Butler, *Vatican Council*, 184–5, my emphasis.

[53] *M* li, col. 646C, also 650A; Manning's trans. in *Privilegium*, iii.167.

[54] *M* li, col. 646D: 'Romani Pontificis iudicia de fidei morumque doctrina irreformabilia esse'; Manning's translation in *Privilegium*, iii. 167.

[55] *M* li, col. 646CD; Manning's trans. in *Privilegium*, iii. 167.

by implication. This was the reason why some of the Fathers objected to the final paragraphs of the Constitution *Dei Filius*. In them, the Roman Pontiff, by his supreme authority, commanded all the faithful, and particularly the pastors, to ward off and eliminate the errors described and condemned in the Constitution. Then he added: 'And since it is not sufficient to shun heretical pravity, unless those errors also be diligently avoided which more or less nearly approach it, We admonish all men of the further duty of observing those constitutions and decrees by which such erroneous opinions as are not here specifically enumerated, have been proscribed and condemned by this Holy See.'[56] The paragraphs in question were originally to be found at the end of the reformed schema *De Fide*, after the canons attached to chapter 9;[57] once the schema had been divided in two, they were included at the end of what became the first Constitution *De Fide*. These sentences aroused the suspicion of the inopportunist Fathers, who saw in them a veiled reference to the Pope's infallibility. They argued, at first, that the words should be reserved for the end of the second Constitution on faith. Later on, after the eighty-three *placets juxta modum* in the vote of 12 April, forty-four Fathers signed a memorandum asking for the suppression of the paragraphs in question, adding that this change would help achieve unanimity in the final vote.[58] The request was rejected. Gasser, Bishop of Brixen (Austria), on behalf of the deputation *De Fide*, would explain that the character of the Pope's previous pronouncements was not modified by the concluding paragraphs; that is, infallibility was not touched upon in them.[59]

The inopportunists' objection could have been considered somewhat far-fetched, but Manning, when presenting the Council to the faithful of his diocese, seemed to substantiate it by giving particular prominence to that precise text. He

---

[56] *M* li, 436AB; Manning's trans. in *Privilegium*, iii. 203.

[57] *M* liii, col. 177B.

[58] *M* li, cols. 411B–412C.

[59] Cf. *M* li, 424BD; Odo Russell, writing to Clarendon on 25 April, would bring to his attention the last paragraph of the decree: 'To my mind this paragraph is the first step taken by the Council towards the dogmatization of Papal Infallibility' (quoted in N. Blackinstone (ed.), *The Roman Question* (London, 1962), 426; see also 433).

seemed to have been less than candid in saying that when 'these words were written, it was not foreseen that they were a preparation, unconsciously made, for the definition of the Infallibility of the Roman Pontiff'.[60]

The first schema *De Ecclesia* dealt with the infallibility of the Church in chapter 9, entitled 'De ecclesiae infallibilitate'.[61] It affirmed that infallibility had been revealed as a permanent prerogative of the Church, a consequence of the perpetual presence and action of the Holy Spirit in it; that immunity from error was an essential property of the Church, absolutely necessary for the fulfilment of her mission as pillar of truth in the world. The schema went on to say that the Church's infallibility extended to all the things contained in God's revelation; within its realm were also those truths necessary to preserve revelation intact, propose and explain it without error, and defend it against the claims of 'false science'. Consequently, as enunciated in canon 9 of the same schema,[62] the scope of infallibility also embraced those truths which, although not contained in divine revelation, were required to preserve the integrity of the deposit.

Having received the text of the schema *De Ecclesia*, the Council waited several weeks for the decision of the Pope on whether to grant permission for the introduction of the infallibility of the Roman Pontiff. In the meantime, the study of the schema and the preparation of suggestions and amendments by the Fathers proceeded apace. Manning was not idle either. On 15 February he presented a petition to the congregation *De Postulatis* in which he tried to introduce into the schema, as it stood, the infallibility of the Pope, independently of whether permission were to be granted to discuss it on its own.[63] The *Postulatum* tried to do so in a somewhat indirect way. It asked, among other things, for a new canon to be inserted after canon 16. This did not contain the word 'infallibility'; its main thrust was to define the irreformable character of the decrees on faith and morals promulgated by the Roman Pontiff as supreme pastor and doctor of the universal Church. The connection between irreformable decrees and infallibility

---

[60] *Privilegium*, iii. 51.   [61] *M* li, cols. 542D–543B.   [62] *M* li, col. 552A.
[63] *M* liii, cols. 519D–520B.

had already been established in the text of the petition: the decrees of the Pope were irreformable not because they emanated from a supreme tribunal, from which there was no appeal, but because they necessarily conformed to truth.[64] In the final instance, by declaring, with the assistance of the Holy Spirit, that a particular doctrine was revealed, those decrees were anchored in God's truthfulness and omniscience.

On 1 March, Pius IX gave his approval, and the decision was communicated to the Council Fathers five days later. They received at the same time a new additional chapter on the Pope's infallibility, to be included after chapter 11 of the schema *De Ecclesia*, which dealt with the Pope's primacy of jurisdiction. The granting by Pius IX of the petition for the introduction of the infallibility of the Pope in the Council made Manning's *Postulatum* redundant. The new chapter, entitled 'Romanum Pontificem in rebus fidei et morum definiendis errare non posse', was based on the texts of definition proposed by Manning and Dechamps, and it had been re-elaborated by Cardinal Bilio.[65] The introduction referred to the foundation of the privilege of infallibility on the divine will; adding how the primacy of the Pope made him supreme judge in matters of faith, to defend it and to judge in the controversies about the faith. The definition then followed:

hinc, sacro approbante concilio, docemus et tamquam fidei dogma definimus, per divinam assistentiam fieri, ut Romanus pontifex ... cum supremi omnium christianorum doctoris munere fungens pro auctoritate definit, quid in rebus fidei et morum ab universa ecclesia tenendum sit, errare non possit; et hanc Romani pontificis inerrantiae seu infallibilitatis praerogativam ad idem obiectum porrigi, ad quod infallibilitas ecclesiae extenditur.[66]

---

[64] The same supreme tribunal could have reformed any of its own decrees. Mgr. Gasser elaborated later on the distinction between the decrees emanating from a supreme authority, without appeal, and infallible decrees (cf. *M* lii, cols. 1225C and 1316AB).

[65] Several formulas of definition had been presented at different times to the cardinals presiding over the Council. They had them printed to facilitate their study (*M* li, cols. 697A–699B). Manning's formula was the result of his work with Schrader, and it seems that it was ready by 7 February. Schrader in his letter to Manning of 14 Feb. 1870 spoke of 'our formula', and Manning acknowledged its double authorship in his copy of the printed formulas by adding in pencil Schrader's name and his own at the side of the text (cf. Manning MSS Pitts, box 7, folder 7). There are indications that Maier may have been consulted about it.

[66] *M* li, cols. 701D–702A.

therefore, the Sacred Council approving, we teach and define that it is a dogma of faith that the Roman Pontiff ... cannot fall into error when, in the exercise of his office as supreme teacher of all Christians, he defines that which is to be held by the universal Church in matters of faith and morals; the object of this prerogative of inerrancy or infallibility of the Roman Pontiff reaches out as far as the object covered by the infallibility of the Church.

The word 'infallibility' was used; its object was very widely defined, while the conditions of its exercise were left rather vague. The classical *ex cathedra* clause, traditionally employed to describe the infallible utterances of the Roman Pontiff, was not part of the text. The suggested formula, in its place, inserted a descriptive sentence: 'cum supremi omnium christianorum doctoris munere fungens pro auctoritate definit, quid in rebus fidei et morum ab universa ecclesia tenendum sit'. It is quite likely that the exclusion of the *ex cathedra* formula might have been an attempt to bypass the problems arising from the claims, made by opponents to the definition, about the difficulty of agreeing what *ex cathedra* actually meant.

The text of definition presented to the Fathers was substantially that of Dechamps[67], Manning's formula[68] contributing a couple of phrases to the proposed definition. The first, 'et tamquam dogma fidei', qualified the character of the doctrine being defined; the second made reference to the object of the infallibility of the Pope, and said that it was coextensive with the infallibility of the Church. This last had been taken from the draft on the Pope's infallibility prepared by the Theological Commission, to which Manning had had access, and which was never presented to the Fathers. As it happened, the expression had been criticized by some of the members of the preparatory Theological Commission, and it was to encounter similar criticisms in the Council, both in the deputation and in the debates of the General Congregations.

The Fathers were given until 25 March to study it and to submit their comments and amendments to chapter 11 and the new one on infallibility. Numerous observations were made on both chapters, the one on infallibility receiving the greater number. The commentators ranged from those who thought the definition inopportune, or even impossible, to those who, while favouring definition, wanted to improve its wording and the general presentation of the doctrine.

The observations of Cardinal Rauscher of Vienna and of Archbishop Kenrick of St Louis conjured back to life some of Manning's old expressions. The cardinal and the bishop seemed to imply that Scripture and Tradition, plus the consent of the Church, were enough to judge and condemn the new errors that might arise against the truths of faith.[69] Manning was generous with his marginal notes: 'Quo judice et qua certitudine[?]', 'Quo interprete?', 'Quo judice?', 'Et quis et de Ecclesiae consentium testes, et si ex dubium judex?' Who is to judge the consent of the Church and determine whether it exists in case of doubt? Manning did not let pass either the cardinal's reference to Councils having infallible authority, Nicaea having been the first Council of the Church. 'Sed quod antea? Et antea nemo?'[70] Was there no infallibility or infallible tribunal in the Church before the year 325?

3. *Moves to Change the Order of the Debates*

During the end of March and the first weeks of April, the energies of the Fathers were not wholly absorbed by the study of the chapters on the Roman Pontiff or the discussion of the text of the Constitution *Dei Filius*. A number of petitions had been presented asking for a change in the order of the debates, and suggesting that the study of the infallibility of the Pope be introduced immediately after the discussion and final vote on the First Constitution *De Fide*.[71] The bishops of the minority opposed this move, asking for the order of the chapters to be preserved; some of them went as far as petitioning that the chapters on the relationship between Church and State be studied before those on the primacy.[72]

Manning described the reasons in favour of a change in the order of procedure: first, the need for the definition itself, and,

---

[69] *M* li, cols. 974B–975D and cols. 1065AC.

[70] Manning MSS Pitts, box 7, folder 2, 'Synopsis Analitica Observationum', 7, 10, 228, 229.

[71] *M* li, cols. 703D–711A.

[72] *M* li, cols. 719D–722A.

secondly, the importance of discussing it while the majority of the Fathers were still resident in Rome. Those in the inner circle of infallibilists saw clearly that the absence of many members of the Council from the debates and the vote on infallibility would reinforce the claims—already made before the Council—that the infallibility of the Pope would be introduced surreptitiously. The adversaries of the definition would be able to claim that the matter had been kept under wraps until its main opponents had left Rome; then, the small number of Fathers left behind could be easily manipulated or overawed into acquiescence. The question was of such importance, and the discrepancy so public, that it seemed imperative that the matter be discussed and decided 'by the largest possible assembly of the Catholic Episcopate. All other questions, on which little divergence of opinion existed, might well be left to a smaller number of Bishops. But a doctrine which for centuries had divided both Pastors and people, the defining of which was contested by a numerous and organised opposition, needed to be treated and affirmed by the most extensive deliberation of the Bishops of the Catholic Church.'[73] The uncertainty as to the future of the Council, because of the threat of impending war between Germany and France, added urgency to the demands of the majority.

Adhering to the established order of debates implied that, before addressing the primacy and infallibility of the Pope, the Fathers would have to study the second schema *De Fide* and the first ten or so chapters of the schema *De Ecclesia*. This meant that the subject, on a conservative estimate, would not come up for debate before the General Congregation of the Council until some time well into 1871. The situation was too uncertain, and the matter too important, to wait so long to bring it up. The Fathers of the majority also felt that there was no point in studying aspects of the doctrines of the Trinity or the Church which had already been clearly taught and defined, and were held without dispute by the faithful. What was really urgent was to study and define, in Manning's words, 'such truths as at this time are both especially contradicted and vitally necessary to the very foundations of the

[73] *Privilegium*, iii. 53–4.

faith'.[74] The rest might safely be deferred. The schema on the Church, in Manning's estimate, 'was prolix and multifarious. . . . Much of its contents had been already implicitly or even explicitly defined. Its chief points, as, for instance, the infallibility of the Church, have never been denied or even doubted by any Catholic.'[75] That was not the case with the infallibility of the Pope. Therefore, the majority of the Fathers considered that it would be wise 'to define first the truths which had been denied, to declare that which had been contradicted, to settle that which had been in controversy, before treating of those things in which all men were agreed'.[76]

The minority's weightiest argument was the need to treat of the Church before dealing with the Pope and to study the infallibility of the Church before defining the Pope's infallibility. Manning would have partly conceded the point, although he would have argued that the infallibility of the Church was common doctrine, not assailed by any Catholic, and thus not in need of study or definition. The Constitution *Dei Filius* had made clear that the assent of faith was due not only to dogmatically defined doctrines but also to those handed down by the Church's ordinary and universal magisterium. Consequently, the doctrine of the infallibility of the Church, as taught by the ordinary magisterium and held by all the faithful, could be used as a foundation for the discussion of the Pope's infallibility.

In his speech to the Council on 25 May, Manning went even further, using the words of *Dei Filius* to support his contention that the infallibility of the Pope was 'doctrina catholica fidei divina et catholica credenda':[77] it had been taught by the ordinary and universal magisterium of the Church; it had been proclaimed—at least implicitly—by several Ecumenical Councils; it was common doctrine among theologians; and it had been believed and accepted, always and everywhere, by the faithful. As far as Manning was concerned, it bore more than enough marks to identify it as a revealed doctrine to be believed with divine faith, even before it had been the object of a dogmatic definition. A definition was now necessary, not to

---

[74] *True*, 194.   [75] Ibid. 195.   [76] Ibid.
[77] *M* lii, col. 251B.

make the Pope's infallibility into a doctrine of faith but in order
to defend a doctrine of faith, against those who assailed it.
The infallibility of the Pope was not a matter for free opinion
among Catholics; those who, speaking about this subject,
quoted the dictum 'In necesariis unitas, in dubiis libertas' laboured under a misconception.[78]

The reluctance of the presidents of the Council to change the
order of the debates led some members of the deputation *De
Fide* to meet together at Manning's residence during Holy
Week (10–16 April), to decide on a plan of campaign to
achieve their end.[79] The result of their deliberations was to
accept the suggestions put forward by the theologians Maier
and Schrader, the main one being to prepare a separate constitution on the Roman Pontiff, made up of the chapters on the
primacy and infallibility. They also agreed on not changing
the formula of the definition proposed on 6 March and, in
order to speed up the proceedings within the deputation *De
Fide*, they committed themselves to abstain from proposing
modifications to that text in its meetings. But their approach
to Bilio—and, later on, to the First President of the Council,
Cardinal de Angelis—did not produce the desired effect. The
cardinals adhered to the original order of debates. There was
no appeal left, except to go directly to the Pope, and to him
they went. Senestréy and Manning had an audience with Pius
IX on the morning of the 19th, at the end of which they
thought that the Pope would act in the direction of their desires. Business within the Council, however, proceeded as
usual in the following days. The members of Manning's group
grew impatient, wondering whether the advice of those intent
on preserving the previous order of debates had prevailed
with the Pope. On the 22nd they decided not to wait any
longer, and in a meeting in the residence of Roullet de La
Bouillerie, Bishop of Carcassonne, they drew up a formal petition asking the Holy Father to bring forward the schema on
the Roman Pontiff.[80] Eighty-four bishops had signed it by the
23rd, when the petition was presented to the Pope. On the

---

[78] *M* lii, col. 252A.
[79] See Senestréy's diary; *M* liii, cols. 279C–280A.
[80] *M* li, cols. 722B–724A.

27th, the deputation *De Fide* received the news that the schema *De Romano Pontifice* was to be brought in at once, and they started work on it that same day. The Fathers of the Council were notified on the 29th. Gratitude and disappointment at the Pope's decision found expression in different documents, the most relevant of which was perhaps the one signed by some seventy bishops putting forward reasons—theological and pastoral—against the change of order.[81]

II.   *The Definition*[82]

1. *The Minority's Fears*

The new schema was ready for the Council Fathers to study by 8 May. The deputation *De Fide* had been working from 2 to 8 May on a text presented by Maier and Schrader. It was entitled *Constitutio Dogmatica Prima de Ecclesia Christi*, suggesting that it did not exhaust the study of the Church that the Council intended to carry out. Maier and Schrader had distributed the subject-matter in four chapters; the first three dealt with the primacy of the Roman Pontiff, the fourth with his infallible magisterium. The revision of the first three chapters did not occupy the deputation for long, and it afforded few substantial amendments. The discussion of chapter 4, as was to be expected, was more extensive and took them from 5 to 8 May.

The bishops of the minority, particularly the French bishops, had expressed before the Council their fears of a definition which would declare what they called the 'personal, separate and absolute infallibility of the Pope', fears which seemed to have found confirmation in the verbal excesses of some French supporters of the definition. Maret, in his book, had given definite, clear conceptual expression to those fears, coining the formula that the minority would use, time and time again, in the conciliar debates. He also defined the meaning of the terms which made it up. The Ultramontane school, to Maret's mind, did 'not conceive infallibility as attached "to the

---

[81]   *M* li, cols. 727B–732B.

[82]   For a study of the debates and of the suggestions which shaped the formula of definition see U. Betti, *La Constituzione Dommatica 'Pastor Aeternus' del Concilio Vaticano I* (Rome, 1961), and G. Thils, *Primauté et infaillibilité du Pontife Romain au Vatican I et autres études d'ecclésiologie* (Leuven, 1989).

human person". Rather, infallibility as attached "to the pontifical person, to the pontiff, becomes, in this sense, personal".
By *absolute*, this school means "without condition, or rather
with conditions which no one can or should verify". . . . By *sepa-*
rate, this school means "the attribution of this divine privilege
to the pope, exclusive of any agreement of the bishops in pontifical decisions, either this agreement be antecedent, concomitant, or subsequent; whether it be expressed or tacit".[83]
Dupanloup, in his correspondence with Dechamps, expressed
himself in similar terms about personal infallibility: 'You say:
"It is not to a *private* but to a *public* person that infallibility
was promised". The personal infallibility of which I spoke is
the infallibility of the public person of the pope.'[84] At first,
most minority bishops seem to have concentrated their attention on the 'separate infallibility', but it seems that they soon
came to view the three aspects as closely connected, each one
of them logically demanding the other two.[85] Unfortunately,
the terms—personal, separate, and absolute—were equivocal
even to Council Fathers: they suggested more than the precise
meaning given to them by Maret and Dupanloup; for the
public outside the Council, they were grotesque, and provided
plentiful ammunition for those who wished to caricature its
proceedings and the bishops supporting the definition.

Manning's pastoral of 1869, particularly his appendix about
Maret's book, was viewed and judged by Dupanloup in the
French context. Manning's use of the expression '*apart from* the
bishops', when speaking of papal infallible pronouncements,
had, in many minds, set Manning's name firmly at the head
of the list of proponents of a personal, separate, and absolute
infallibility. His disclaimers availed him little. After the Council he would dwell on this expression, consecrated by repeated
use, to disprove those who had attributed it to him.

The frequency and confidence with which this formula was repeated, as if taken from the writings of the promoters of the
Definition, made it not unnatural to examine into the origin, history, and meaning of the formula itself. I therefore set myself to

[83] M. O'Gara, *Triumph in Defeat: Infallibility, Vatican I, and the French Minority
Bishops* (Washington, 1988), 84.
[84] Letter dated 1 Mar. 1870, quoted in O'Gara, *Triumph in Defeat*, 84.
[85] Cf. O'Gara, *Triumph in Defeat*, 78.

search it out; and I employed others to do the same. As it had been ascribed to myself, our first examination was turned to anything I might have written. After repeated search, not only was the formula as a whole nowhere to be discovered, but the words of which it is composed were, with the exception of the word 'independent', equally nowhere to be found.[86]

For those who used the formula, though, Manning's admission of an 'independent' infallibility would justify attributing to him the expression in its entirety. As a matter of fact, after Manning's correspondence with Dupanloup on the subject, the opponents of the definition would speak at times of a 'personal, separate, independent, and absolute infallibility'.

The deputation *De Fide* had, therefore, a twofold task. On the one hand, it had to hammer out a precise and accurate formula of definition. At the same time, it had to try to assuage the fears—genuine or tactical—of those who opposed the definition on the above grounds. It was no easy task: Cardinal Guidi of Bologna, as late as 18 June, was still raising the issue of a personal, separate, independent, and absolute infallibility. He was answered the following day by d'Avanzo, Bishop of Calvi, speaking in the name of the deputation. His explanations, though, did not seem to satisfy some of the Fathers; and Bishop Moriarty, of Kerry, ploughed the same furrow of a personal, separate, and absolute infallibility on the 28th. Manning did not intervene in the debates on this point, although his notes have many references to it. It was left to Mgr. Gasser, in his long defence of the definition of 11 July, to explain how the proposed formula did not put forward a personal, separate, independent, and absolute infallibility.

2. *A Personal Infallibility?*

The title of chapter 4 of the Constitution *Dei Filius*, devoted to the infallibility of the Roman Pontiff, went through several revisions in the course of its history. It started, as the additional chapter to the general schema *De Ecclesia*, as 'Romanum Pontificem in rebus fidei et morum definiendis errare non posse'; the subsequent first schema of the Constitution on the Roman Pontiff was rather more vague and general: 'De Romani Ponti-

---

[86] *Privilegium*, iii. 93.

ficis infallibilitate'; it became, in the definitive version, 'De Romani Pontificis infallibili magisterio'. Manning would later say that 'the reason of this change was not only for greater accuracy, but because even the title of the decree excludes at once the figment of a *personal* infallibility'.[87] The first paragraphs of the chapter reinforced that idea.

Manning, when commenting later on the decrees of the Council, pointed out how the first words of chapter 4 established the clear connection between primacy and infallibility: 'the supreme power of teaching is also included in the Apostolic primacy'.[88] 'The supreme ruler is also supreme teacher', he would say elsewhere. As he explained: '[t]he primacy contains two things, the fullness of jurisdiction, and a special assistance in the exercise of it'. And, 'under jurisdiction is contained the office of teaching'. He rounded off the argument by saying that the 'assistance of infallible guidance is attached to the *magisterium* or teaching office, and the *magisterium* is contained in the primacy'.[89] He described the nature of this privilege as 'a supernatural grace, or *charisma*, attached to the primacy in order to its proper exercise'.[90] Manning added that by using the word 'charisma' the Council had once again excluded the notion of a 'personal' infallibility. A charism is not a grace granted by God to make the person who receives it acceptable in his sight; it is rather 'a *gratia gratis data*, or a grace the benefit of which is for *others*'. The nature of this type of grace also clarified another misconception: 'that if Popes are infallible they are therefore impeccable; that if they cannot err in faith, they cannot sin in morals; that if their intelligence be guided by divine light, their will must be necessarily conformed to divine grace'.[91] Infallibility, he would say, is not a 'quality inherent in the person, but an assistance inseparable

---

[87] *True*, 173. Manning seems to have championed the final title. The words are written, in what appears to be his own hand, in one of the printed working papers of the deputation *De Fide* (cf. Manning MSS Pitts, box 7, folder 2).

[88] *M* lii, col. 1333B; Manning's trans. in *Privilegium*, iii. 216.

[89] *True*, 173–4.

[90] *Privilegium*, iii. 97.

[91] *True*, 185. Maret, in the book he published before the Council, established, from a different point of view, the connection between holiness and infallibility: infallibility could be the prerogative only of a person endowed with an extraordinary degree of holiness. Manning viewed this opinion as some sort of intellectual quasi-Donatism.

from the office. It is therefore not personal, but official. It is personal only so far as the primacy is borne by a person', not by a commission; it 'is personal, therefore, only in the sense that the successor of S. Peter is a man and not a body of men'.[92] The Roman Pontiff is not infallible as a 'private person, or a private doctor, or as a local Bishop, or as sovereign of a state ... In all these acts the Pontiff may be subject to error. In one and only capacity he is exempt from error; that is, when, as teacher of the whole Church, he teaches the whole Church in things of faith and morals.'[93] The Council 'does not even say that it is an abiding assistance present always, but only never absent in the discharge of their supreme office.'[94]

Manning, in his personal notes taken during the Council, had tried to place the privilege of infallibility within the distinction between personal, real, or mixed types of privileges. A privilege was *personal*, he said, when it 'looked not to a thing or to an office but to a person; it was *real* when it was ascribed to a thing or to a place, or to an office; and it was *mixed* when it belonged to a college or to a community of persons'. He concluded that the 'privilege of infallibility was real in so far as it belonged to the primacy and personal because it was ascribed to the person enjoying the primacy, but it was not mixed in the sense that it belonged to the pontiff only if he were united with the episcopate'.[95] In his pastoral on the Council, Manning touched on another possible legitimate use of the adjective 'personal' when referring to the Pope's infallibility. He quoted authors like Ballerini and Toletus, who claimed that by 'personal' they understood a privilege which could not be communicated to another, and which did not require the help or association of others for its exercise.

Gasser, in his speech to the General Congregation on 11 July, pointed out that the infallibility of the Pope could also be called personal in order to exclude the Gallican distinction between the Roman Church and the Roman Pontiff, the Sede and the one who sat in it; a distinction which would reserve in-

---

[92] *True*, 174.   [93] *Privilegium*, iii. 58.   [94] *True*, 186.
[95] Cwiekowski, *English Bishops*, 263. He seems to have owed this distinction to the Jesuit canonist Tarquini, who wrote Manning a long letter on the subject (27 May 1870; Manning MSS Pitts, box 7, folder 7).

fallibility for the first element of each of these binomials, the second being fallible. The prerogative, Gasser added, belonged to each and all of the Roman Pontiffs, not, as some had claimed, to the series of the Roman Pontiffs as a whole.[96]

The definition of papal infallibility would make clear that this special assistance of the Holy Spirit—the origin and foundation of his infallibility—was granted to the Pope only in the exercise of his office as supreme pastor and doctor of the Church; even here, the definition did not affirm that all his acts were guaranteed by the charism of infallibility, but just his *ex cathedra* pronouncements. The Council, Manning said later, had adopted a terminology which had become classical in that context. It had also fixed its meaning: the Pope is infallible when '*loquens ex cathedra*; that is, [when] speaking from the Seat, or place, or with the authority of the supreme teacher of all Christians, and binding the assent of the Universal Church'.[97] In the same pastoral, he also invoked more general definitions of the formula: the 'Pontiff speaks *ex cathedra* when, and only when, he speaks as the Pastor and Doctor of all Christians'.[98] Manning's conclusion was that 'the whole *magisterium* or doctrinal authority of the Pontiff as the supreme Doctor of all Christians, is included in the definition of his infallibility. ... The Definition, then, limits the infallibility of the Pontiff to his supreme acts *ex cathedra* in faith and morals, but extends his infallibility to all acts in the fullest exercise of his supreme *magisterium* or doctrinal authority.'[99]

Some of Manning's expressions seem to obscure one of the constitutive elements of an *ex cathedra* pronouncement: the act of defining a doctrine as divinely revealed, to be believed as such by all. It can safely be said that the mind of the Council Fathers was in harmony with the statement made by Gasser in his speech to the Council of 11 July: an *ex cathedra* act is one in which the Pope not only proposes a doctrine as supreme doctor and pastor of the Church, but one in which he has a clear intention of defining a doctrine of faith or morals by passing a definitive sentence.[100] This clarification was of para-

---

[96] *M* lii, col. 1212CD.   [97] *Privilegium*, iii. 57.   [98] Ibid. 58.
[99] Ibid. 89–90.
[100] *M* lii, cols. 1225C and 1316AB.

mount importance, given that the Pope's ordinary teaching is also an exercise of his supreme magisterium and demands interior assent of the faithful, even though he may not be teaching infallibly.

Manning did not ignore the above, and in his pastoral he referred to what definition and defining meant in the Constitution. By the word 'definition', Manning said, the Council signified the precise judgement or sentence in which any revealed truth on faith or morals traditionally handed down in the Church may be authoritatively formulated. He also described the act of defining as 'an authoritative termination of questions which had been in doubt and debate, and therefore of the judgment or sentence thence resulting. ... *Definire* is *finem imponere*, or *finaliter iudicare*. It is therefore equivalent to *determinare*, or *finaliter determinare* ... It is in this sense that the Vatican Council uses the word *definienda*. It signifies the final decision by which any matter of faith and morals is put into a doctrinal form.'[101]

It has been claimed that Manning seemed to have a juridical understanding of infallibility.[102] This interpretation, beside its terminological ambiguity, fails to take into account that Manning, when speaking of the power of teaching as judicial, was setting it in contrast with a legislative power, able to create law: the Church cannot create the law of faith, she can only proclaim and apply the law of truth promulgated by God. As an Anglican he realized that he had found the true rule of faith—Scripture and antiquity—but not the judge to apply it in order to find the true Faith. He had finally concluded that

---

[101] *Privilegium*, iii. 87–8. When explaining the Council's decrees, he affirmed that the Church taught the doctrine of faith positively, and also in a negative way; to 'define doctrines of faith, and to condemn the contradictions of heresy, is almost one and the same act' (*Privilegium*, iii. 73). She was infallible in both cases.

[102] J. T. Ford thinks that Manning 'seems to understand it [the act of defining] as a juridical process ... [thus] one should not be completely surprised that Manning describes infallibility as a charism of juridical discernment' ('Different Models of Infallibility', *Proceedings of the Catholic Theological Society of America*, xxxv (1980), 225). In a previous article, he had spoken of a certain ambiguity in the conciliar fathers' ideas about the concept of magisterium: 'one suspects that some participants considered magisterium as basically a teaching power which invites the response of faith, while others construed magisterium as essentially a law-making power which requires the response of obedience' ('Infallibility', 287–8). He seemed to include Manning in the second group. See pp. 113–14 above.

an infallible judge was needed as foundation of supernatural faith, given that this demands certainty in the object and certainty in the believer. Manning saw the primacy, or power of supreme jurisdiction, as containing within it the supreme doctrinal authority or supreme doctrinal jurisdiction: 'under jurisdiction is contained', he would say, 'the office of teaching', adding that to 'deliver the law is to teach'.[103] He would also say that infallibility 'is a quality of the doctrinal jurisdiction of the Pontiff in faith and morals'.[104] The above, though, did not confine the exercise of infallibility to passing sentence on controversial questions regarding faith and morals. The definition, Manning would say, 'speaks of the doctrinal authority of the Pontiff in general; and therefore both of what may be called pacific definitions like that of the Immaculate Conception, and of controversial definitions like those of St. Innocent against the Pelagians'.[105] Thus, 'jurisdiction' also meant that the Pontiffs are 'witnesses, teachers, and judges of the revelation already given to the Church; and in guarding, expounding, and defending that revelation, their witness, teaching, and judgment, is by Divine assistance preserved from error'.[106]

The assistance of the Holy Spirit preserved from error those acts of the Pope performed in the exercise of his supreme magisterium. This sentence, as it stood, was in need of further qualification. Were all the acts of the Pope in the exercise of his supreme magisterium infallible? The pro-infallibilist majority in the Council was divided on the issue of how much should be defined in the present circumstances, rather than on basic principles. These differences of opinion exercised the minds of the members of the deputation *De Fide* and, more than once, nerves became frayed in their discussions on the subject. In the process, the new chapter of 6 March, defining the Pope's infallibility, was to be dramatically changed by the deputation while preparing the schema of the First Constitution *De Ecclesia*.

Cardinal Bilio, the cardinal-president, to the surprise of the members of the deputation, opened fire by criticizing the for-

---

[103] *True*, 174.   [104] *Privilegium*, iii. 97.
[105] Ibid. 88; Gasser had explicitly excluded the restrictive interpretation (*M* lii, col. 1316AB).
[106] *Privilegium*, iii. 85.

mula of 6 March, which he himself had prepared. The difficulty arose, in his opinion, from dealing with the infallibility of the Pope before carrying out a detailed study of the Church, and of her infallibility. In Senestréy's diary he is reported as saying: 'No more can be defined concerning the infallibility of the Pope than has been defined concerning the infallibility of the Church; but of the Church this only is of faith, that she is infallible in dogmatic definitions strictly taken; therefore the question arises whether in the proposed formula the infallibility of the Pope be not too widely extended.'[107] He thought it inappropriate to define the infallibility of the Pope as reaching beyond the defined infallibility of the Church, and suggested including Martin's qualification—'ab universa ecclesia fide catholica credendum sit' (those things to be believed by the whole Church as of Catholic faith)[108]—in the formula of definition. On the other hand, Cardinal Bilio was of the opinion that the sentence which defined the object of the Pope's infallibility by making it coextensive with the object of the infallibility of the Church should be preserved. Franzelin then produced a new formula along the lines suggested by Bilio; it was presented to the Fathers of the deputation that same evening.[109]

It was here that the dividing line was drawn within the infallibilist camp. Dechamps and Martin were content with defining the infallibility of the Pope when proposing dogmatic definitions. Cardinal Bilio shared their point of view. Manning and Senestréy, on the other hand, were unhappy with this restrictive definition, particularly if it gave to understand that the Pope was infallible only in those cases. Senestréy's diary records that, in reply to Bilio's arguments, it was contended that it was true that 'the infallibility of the Church had never been defined; even so, it was evident to all that the infallibility of

---

[107] M liii, cols. 281D–282A; trans. Butler, *Vatican Council*, 376.

[108] M liii, col. 249CD. The Archbishop of San Francisco also made a similar restrictive suggestion: 'de questionibus fidei et morum iudicans, de iis definit, quid ab universali ecclesia sub haeresis censura credendum vel reiiciendum sit, errare non possit' (M liii, cols. 249D–250A).

[109] M liii, col. 250D: 'in rebus fidei et morum ab universa ecclesia fide divina credendum tenendumve vel reiiciendum sit, errare non possit; et hanc Romani pontificis infallibilitatis praerogativam ad idem obiectum porrigi, ad quod infallibilitas ecclesiae extenditur'.

the Church was a dogma and that it was a fundamental dogma, as all Catholics in proffering the act of faith confessed: "Credo quod Deus revelavit et ecclesia catolica credendum proponit." As, therefore, it is of faith that the Church is infallible, let the same be defined of the Pope.'[110] Senestréy does not say who it was who uttered these words, but they reflected well Manning's thought.[111] Senestréy and Manning felt that the new formula represented a serious set-back: the ground which had been gained recently with the Munich Brief and with the final paragraph of *Dei Filius*, was now being surrendered.

Manning's notes registered the objections he found to the new wording of the definition: it restricted the number of truths to be believed to those which had been defined as dogmas; infallibility would not guarantee other truths taught by the Pope or those errors condemned by him with a censure below that of heresy; on top of all that, as the object of the infallibility of the Church had not been defined, it could not be used—on the above basis—to define the object of the infallibility of the Pope. Besides, looking beyond the question in hand, Manning considered that the present restriction in defining the infallibility of the Pope would prejudice the future definition of the infallibility of the Church, which was to be subsequently studied by the Council.[112]

The arguments were put forward in the meetings of 5–7 May. The discussion became rather heated at times. Two of the Fathers—probably Manning and Senestréy—asked for a monitum to be added after the canons to avoid restricting the object of faith to dogmatic definitions, in accordance with the letter of Pius IX to the Archbishop of Munich, as it had been done in the Constitution *Dei Filius*;[113] several Fathers of the deputation reiterated this petition, unsuccessfully, on 7 May. The text finally passed by the deputation had it as: 'quid in

---

[110] *M* liii, col. 282AB; my trans.

[111] In *The True History of the Vatican Council* Manning wrote: 'no one who denies it [the Church's infallibility] is a Catholic. Whosoever doubts it ceases to be a Catholic. But this doctrine has never been defined. It needs no definition' (*True*, 190). The new dogma 'defined that the head of the Church is infallible, and it is assumed as certain that the Church is also infallible' (ibid. 191).

[112] Cf. Cwiekowski, *English Bishops*, 238.

[113] *M* liii, col. 252AB.

rebus fidei et morum ab universa ecclesia tamquam de fide tenendum vel tamquam fidei contrarium reiiciendum sit'. [114] The formula went some way towards answering the requests of those who thought like Manning and Senestréy, but it did not satisfy them.

When the schema was distributed to the Council Fathers, many felt, Senestréy reports in his diary, that these changes had deformed rather than reformed the text, and, in the debates of the General Congregations, the object of papal infallibility attracted the greatest number of criticisms and amendments. Many Council Fathers pointed out that the new formula restricted infallibility to definitions of faith, leaving out the dogmatic facts, the censures below heresy, the canonization of saints, etc., which had traditionally been considered as covered by the infallibility of the Church. Meanwhile, a group of bishops—Manning and Senestréy among them—started meeting together to study ways of bringing back the original formula of definition of 6 March. It is quite likely that Senestréy's *emendatio* was one of the fruits of those meetings. In it he suggested a new wording for the clause on the object of infallibility: 'quid in rebus fidei et morum ad ecclesiam universalem spectantibus tenendum aut reiciendum sit'. [115] This was a subtle but far-reaching change.

As it happened, the insistence of the Council Fathers would bring about the omission of any reference to the infallibility of the Pope being confined to what was to be believed as 'de fide Catholica'—dogmatic definitions—or have attached to it the censure of heresy. The final formula of the definition described the object of papal infallibility in words closer to those used in the text of 6 March: 'cum .... doctrinam de fide vel moribus ab universa ecclesia tenendum definit'. The intentional vagueness of the formula used left open the path to different possible interpretations about the extension of the object of papal infallibility, restricting or enlarging the number of papal pronouncements to be considered *ex cathedra*. It was certain that the Pope was infallible when proclaiming a dogma or when censuring an error as heretical; but, many thought that papal infallibility also embraced other doctrinal definitions or minor censures.

[114] *M* lii, col. 7B.   [115] *M* lii, col. 1152B.

The Fathers' objections to the restrictive wording of the definition, and the consequent changes effected in it, suggest that it
was the intention of the Council not to exclude—explicitly or
implicitly—from the range of papal infallibility a wider range
of pontifical acts. The question was left open.[116]

Manning argued that the Church's infallibility also covered
the proscribing of errors condemned with a note below heresy,
the so-called minor censures: 'In like manner, the detection
and condemnation of propositions at variance with theological
certainty is a function of the same discernment by which theological certainty is known. But the Church has an infallible discernment of truths which are theologically certain; that is, of
conclusions resulting from two premises of which one is revealed and the other evident by the light of nature. In these
two kinds of censures, at least, it is therefore of faith that the
Church is infallible.'[117] These other censures—temerarious,
scandalous, or offensive to pious ears—were more related, according to Manning, to the moral character of propositions.
'If the Church be infallible in faith and morals, it is not to be
believed that it can err in passing these moral judgments on
the ethical character of propositions.'[118] Manning, though,
with Gasser, would not qualify as heresy the denial of the infallibility of the Pope when he condemned a proposition with
a censure below heresy. Some theologians judged these papal
pronouncements as being infallibly true, others qualified them
as theologically certain; both groups agreed on considering
their denial as theological error rather than heresy. Besides
the doctrinal definitions and censures, Manning thought that
the Pope was also infallible in 'all legislative or judicial acts,
so far as they are inseparably connected with his doctrinal
authority; as, for instance, all judgments, sentences, and decisions, which contain the motives of such acts as derived from
faith and morals'—like laws of discipline, canonization of
saints, approval of religious orders; 'all of which intrinsically

---

[116] This seems to be the opinion of most of the commentators (see Betti, *La Constituzione Dommatica*, 640 ff.).

[117] *Privilegium*, iii. 73–4. Gasser, when clarifying how the deputation understood
the term 'definivit', did not confine its use to dogmatic definitions or heresy censures
(*M* lii, col. 1616AB).

[118] *Privilegium*, iii. 74.

contain the truths and principles of faith, morals, and piety'.[119]
Some of these, like the canonization of saints or the approval
of religious orders, were generally admitted to be infallible.[120]

Although he had clear and definite ideas on the subject, on
the few occasions when, after the Council, he asked somebody
to subscribe to its decrees, Manning did not demand total
assent to his explanation of them. He was well aware that Fessler's interpretation of the definition, in his answer to the distortions of Dr Schulte, had been well received in Rome.
Manning would not ask for more, as his contacts with William
Maskell on the subject showed.[121] However, this did not detract from his conviction that his interpretation was more in
accordance with Catholic doctrine than Fessler's.

3. *The Object of Faith and the Object of Infallibility*

Gasser's speech had insisted repeatedly on the need to keep
always in mind that, whatever was said about the object of
the infallibility of the Church, was to be predicated also of the
infallibility of the Pope: infallibility was one and the same in
both cases, and for the same end. Chapter 9 of the general
schema *De Ecclesia*, and the canon attached to it, made clear
that the end of the privilege of infallibility is the safeguarding
of the deposit of faith. Its object extends to the whole of divine
revelation, and to all those non-revealed truths without which
it would not be possible to preserve, propose, explain, or
defend the deposit. Infallibility, therefore, has a double object:
revealed truth and non-revealed truth closely connected with
truths revealed. The difficulty of drawing precise boundaries
to the secondary object of infallibility showed in the debates
about the wording of the definition; this section attracted a
good deal of criticism and numerous amendments from the
Council Fathers, although the doctrine itself was generally accepted. Gasser's speech of 11 July, when explaining the mind

---

[119] *Privilegium*, iii. 89.
[120] Newman, in the preface to the third edition of his *Lectures on the Prophetical Office of the Church*, affirmed the infallibility of canonizations, using an argument to support it which others applied also to the approval of religious orders (cf. V *M* i., p. lxxxiv).
[121] I owe this information on William Maskell to Dr D. W. Maskell. This seems to contradict Ford's assertion that Manning 'was never so indiscreet as to acknowledge the legitimacy of interpretations more moderate than his own' ('Infallibility', 297).

of the deputation *De Fide* with respect to the object of infallibility, followed those lines. It undoubtedly embraced, he said, all those things contained *per se* in the deposit of revelation: truths capable of dogmatic definition and imposed under censure of heresy; as far as truths not directly contained in the deposit but necessary for its custody, transmission, and defence (dogmatic facts, etc.), it was the unanimous consent of theologians that the Church was infallible when defining them, and that it would be a serious error to deny this infallibility. There was a diversity of opinions, though, about whether this was a truth *de fide* or *theologice certa*, and the deputation had seen it prudent not to decide this particular matter.[122]

In his pastoral after the Council Manning described the object of infallibility by saying that 'the definition limits the range, or, to speak exactly, the object of infallibility, to the doctrine of faith and morals. It excludes therefore all other matter whatsoever.'[123] He pointed out that there still was an unanswered question; the Constitution *Pastor Aeternus* had declared that the Pope's infallibility—and that of the Church— 'extends to all matters of faith and morals, but it is not defined where the limits of faith and morals are to be fixed'.[124] 'The infallibility is defined but not its extent', he wrote to Aubrey de Vere; and to William Maskell: 'The extension of his Infallibility is a matter of theology. The Council intended not to touch the extension of his Infallibility. You are therefore free, *debita reverentia*, to regard this as a matter of theology.'[125] He was far from saying, however, that it was an open theological question.

In the months following the definition, that state of indefiniteness was viewed with apprehension by both 'infallibilists' and 'inopportunists'. The latter were afraid of any further definition; the former felt that, as things stood, the Council had left behind an unnecessarily open question. Newman expressed his fear that 'the tyrant minority is still aiming at enlarging the *province* of Infallibility'.[126] The definition had declared papal infallibility to be coextensive with the infallibility of the

---

[122] *M* lii, col. 1226AC.   [123] *Privilegium*, iii. 59.   [124] *True*, 191.
[125] Quoted in Leslie, *Henry Edward Manning*, 231.
[126] Letter dated 21 Aug. 1870, *LD* xxv. 192.

Church, and Newman was afraid of this clause. Even before the Council, he had pointed out that those 'who deny the Pope's Infallibility and lodge the gift in the Church, *enlarge the subject matter*. Ultramontanes, who uphold the Pope's Infallibility, *contract* the subject matter. Ward burns the candle at both ends—upholding the Pope's Infallibility *and* enlarging the subject matter.'[127] He saw clearly the corollaries which necessarily followed from the connection between the infallibility of the Church and that of the Pope. In a letter to Hope-Scott, in January 1870, he remarked: 'you cannot make a division in the Pope's divine gift, and say he is infallible *only in part* of the things in which the *Church* is infallible, to pass a decree that the Pope is infallible in matters *de fide* is to say that in all matters *not* de fide, there is *no where* any gift of infallibility—but this is contrary to the Gallican notion, which, lodging the gift in the Church, *not* the Pope, *enlarges* the subject matter of the gift, taking in, for instance, infallible condemnations of *books*'.[128] The definition seemed to have consecrated Ward's view. The Council had defined the Pope to be infallible, with an infallibility coextensive with that of the Church. The borders of the Church's infallibility were not yet firmly fixed by a dogmatic definition. Were the Council to continue, it would treat next of the Church and her infallibility, and make precise what was still open to discussion. Newman, in that context, expressed the fervent desire that the Pope would be driven from Rome, and would not continue the Council, as the only way of preventing the definition of the object of the Church's infallibility.[129] This time, his desire was, in the main, granted.

Manning, as we have already seen, when explaining the conciliar decrees, tried to map those regions still unexplored by the Council. In doing so, he did not always make clear where the limit between what was generally admitted by theologians and his more personal opinions stood, and he gave no indication of the theological weight of his different assertions relative

---

[127] Letter to W. Monsell dated 3 Sept. 1869, *LD* xxiv. 327.

[128] Letter dated 16 Jan. 1870, *LD* xxv. 9–10. See also letter to A. St John, 14 Jan. 1870 (cf. ibid. 8). Newman's idea of the *pomeria* of faith led to a similar answer to that given by the Ultramontanes. He did not want it defined, though, and would complain of those who kept trying to extend the object of infallibility.

[129] Letter dated 21 Aug. 1870, *LD* xxv. 192.

to one another. This could not but give rise to misunderstandings. He was not alone in this. Many wrote at this time about
the 'true concept of infallibility', claiming for their 'theological'
interpretation the exclusive title of 'authentic'. Even before
the Council, some had contributed to creating a considerable
degree of confusion by referring to the infallibility of the Pope
as a 'theological opinion' or, in most cases, simply as an 'opinion'. In so doing, they had used a technical term, part of a re-
fined and complex system of qualifying and weighing
theological propositions, which in normal language conveyed
the impression of an idea held on the basis of emotion, prejudice, or unstable logical grounds; thus, by implication, they
suggested that the doctrine could be ignored or dismissed as
an irrelevance.

Manning drew his arguments about the object of the Pope's
infallibility from the chapter on the infallibility of the Church
in the original schema *De Ecclesia*. From there he proceeded
by successive steps to clarify what 'doctrine of faith and
morals' stood for. As was his custom, he did this by marshalling
a long series of quotations from Popes, Councils, and theologians. The expression 'faith and morals', Manning said, 'signifies the whole revelation of faith; the whole way of salvation
through faith; or the whole supernatural order, with all that is
essential to the sanctification and salvation of man through
Jesus Christ'.[130] The authorities quoted, he went on to say, affirmed more or less explicitly,

that the Church has an infallible guidance in treating of all matters
of faith, morals, piety, and the general good of the Church. The
object of infallibility, then, is the whole revealed Word of God, and
all that is so in contact with revealed truth, that without treating
of it, the Word of God could not be guarded, expounded, and defended. . . . Further, it is clear that the Church has an infallible guidance, not only in all matters that are revealed, but also in all
matters which are opposed to revelation. For the Church could not
discharge its office as the Teacher of all nations, unless it were able
with infallible certainty to proscribe doctrines at variance with the
word of God.[131]

[130] *Privilegium*, iii. 60.   [131] Ibid. 66.

This included, as the fourth chapter of the Constitution *Dei Filius* had declared, the proscribing of the errors of false philosophies and false science. Thus, the promulgation, explanation, and defence of revelation requires the Church to be infallible in some matters which belong to the natural sciences, like the existence of substance, or to philosophical knowledge, like the immateriality of the soul. It also embraced truths of history—that Peter was Bishop of Rome, that the Council of Trent was ecumenical, etc.—and the interpretation of the literal and doctrinal meaning of scriptural texts, judgements about the orthodoxy of human writings, and so on.

Manning ended up by saying—somewhat to his reader's surprise—that he did not want to enumerate the subject-matters that fell under the infallibility of the Church; it was for the Church to do so. 'Hitherto it has not done so except by its acts, and from the practice of the Church we may infer to what matter its infallible discernment extends.' The Vatican Council had some unfinished work to do: 'By the definition of the Vatican Council, what is traditionally believed by all the faithful in respect to the Church is expressly declared of the Roman Pontiff. But the definition of the extent of that infallibility, and of the certainty on which it rests, in matters not revealed, has not been treated as yet, but is left for the second part of the "Schema De Ecclesia".'[132]

4. An 'Absolute' and 'Separate' Infallibility?

Gasser, in the name of the deputation *De Fide*, had clearly rejected the interpretation claiming that the formula of definition affirmed the *absolute* infallibility of the Pope. Only God, he said, has absolute infallibility: he is infallible always and in everything. Any participated infallibility would be limited—in its exercise and object—by the end for which it is communicated. The infallibility of the Pope is limited by reason of the subject: the Pope is infallible only in the exercise of his office. It is also restricted by reason of the object, as it is concerned only with matters of faith and morals. And it was further confined by reason of the act itself, as only those acts which define

---

[132] *Privilegium*, iii. 78–9.

what is to be believed or to be rejected by all the faithful are guaranteed by the privilege of infallibility.[133]

In view of these comments, Manning's references, after the Council, to the legitimate use of the term 'absolute', when referring to the Pope's infallibility, seem somewhat misjudged and likely to create confusion or resentment, even when the use of the word was carefully qualified, along the lines of Gasser's explanations: 'It is *absolute*, in as much as it can be circumscribed by no human or ecclesiastical law; it is not absolute, in that it is circumscribed by the office of guarding, expounding, and defending the deposit of revelation.'[134] Unfortunately, the use of the word on other occasions, within the same pastoral, was not so nuanced, as when he wrote: 'that what is circumscribed by no condition is absolute'.[135] He had not used the word 'absolute' before the Council, and to use it after the definition was as unnecessary as it was provoking.

It was different when it came to the question of a *separate* infallibility. The Archbishop of Westminster had been on the receiving end of some of the first shots fired against it. Dupanloup had preyed on his 'apart from', taking it as implying a separate infallibility. Although Manning had tried to dissociate himself from that interpretation, by claiming that 'apart from' meant not *separate* but *independent*, this, as we have seen, did not help his case in the eyes of the minority. They contended that the Roman Pontiff could not be separated from the Church: it was absurd to think of a headless body or a bodiless head. Manning, for his part, confessed that he found it hard to believe that serious men could have drawn that conclusion from his words, even less from the texts concerning the Pope's infallibility proposed to the Fathers: 'such a monstrous sense includes at least six heresies; and I could hardly think that any Catholic would fail to know this, or, knowing it, would impute it to Catholics, still less to Bishops of the Church'.[136] The infallibility of the Pope is '*separate* in no sense, nor can be, nor can so be called, without manifold heresy, unless the word be taken to mean *distinct*'.[137]

The fears of the minority sprang from the absence of any re-

---

[133] *M* lii, col. 1214AB.   [134] *Privilegium*, iii. 113.   [135] Ibid. 97.
[136] Ibid. 105.   [137] Ibid. 113

ference to the need for the Pope to consult the bishops, as a normal means to arrive at a right judgement. The deputation tried to clarify the issue through the explanations given by some of its members. Gasser said that it was legitimate to speak of a *separate*, or, better, a *distinct* infallibility: the infallibility of the Roman Pontiff was founded on a special assistance of the Holy Spirit, distinct from that which is granted by the same Spirit to the whole teaching Church united to its head. But this is no *separate* infallibility, separating the Pope from the Church; the Pope is infallible only (*solummodo*) when exercising his office of supreme doctor of all the faithful; that is, when, representing the whole Church, he defines what is to be believed or rejected as contrary to the faith of the Church.[138]
The difference between the position of the deputation and that of the minority seemed to consist in the fact that the minority felt that the only way to avoid separating the Pope from the Church when speaking *ex cathedra* was to introduce into the definition some reference to the need to consult the bishops before its publication or to obtain their subsequent consent. They viewed this previous consultation or *post factum* assent as an essential element of any infallible pronouncement. The deputation denied this to be the case, although, in the normal course of events, the Pope would probably consult some or all bishops, and also use other means to ascertain revealed truth. This co-operation was not excluded by the definition, given that infallibility was not inspiration or revelation; the Constitution itself described different means available to the Pope for that purpose. The Pope was morally bound to use the appropriate means to ascertain the truth of revelation, but it was part of the charism of infallibility to know which ones he should use in any particular case.[139]

Manning's notes registered his thoughts on the matter during the sessions of the Council: the indwelling of the Holy Spirit in the Church makes it impossible that the Head be separated from the Body or that they be in opposition. This *separation* was a mere ghost, invented to frighten the bishops

---

[138] *M* lii, col. 1213BC; he pointed out that the Roman Pontiff manifests the mind of the Church and speaks 'universalem ecclesiam representans'.
[139] *M* lii, cols. 1213D and 1215CD.

away from the definition.[140] He developed these ideas in his pastoral on the Council, where he described the indissoluble union of the Head and the Body in the Church in three points:

1 It is *de fide*, or matter of faith, that the head of the Church, as such, can never be separated, either from the *Ecclesia docens*, or the *Ecclesia discens*; that is, either from the Episcopate or from the faithful.

  To suppose this, would be to deny the perpetual indwelling office of the Holy Ghost in the Church, by which the mystical body is knit together ... On this unity all the properties and endowments of the Church depend; indefectibility, unity, infallibility. As the Church can never be separated from its invisible Head, so never from its visible head.

2 Secondly, it is matter of faith that the *Ecclesia docens* or the Episcopate, to which together with Peter, and as it were, in one person with him, the assistance of the Holy Ghost was promised, can never be dissolved; but it would be dissolved if it were separated from its head. Such separation would destroy the infallibility of the Church itself. The *Ecclesia docens* would cease to exist; but this is impossible, and without heresy cannot be supposed.

3 Thirdly, it is also matter of faith that not only no separation of communion, but even no disunion of doctrine and faith between the Head and the Body, that is, between the *Ecclesia docens* and *discens* can ever exist. Both are infallible; the one actively, in teaching, the other passively, in believing; and both are therefore inseparably, because necessarily, united in one faith.[141]

Manning turned the tables on the opponents of the definition of infallibility: they were the ones who really presumed that a separation could exist. The reason for this

inseparable union [of the Head and the Body] is precisely the infallibility of its head. Because its head can never err, it, as a body, can never err. How many soever, as individuals, should err and fall away from the truth, the Episcopate would remain, and therefore

---

[140] Cf. Cwiekowski, *English Bishops*, 261 ff.

[141] *Privilegium*, iii. 105–7; see also Gasser's speech in *M* lii, cols. 1213D–1214A. In his notes Manning mentioned two ideas which had a long tradition in his thought: 'unity as *sacramentum veritatis*', and the reference to the Mystical Body of Christ as *unus homo* (cf. Cwiekowski, *English Bishops*, 264).

never be disunited from its head in teaching or believing. ... They, therefore, and they only, teach the possibility of such a separation, who assert that the Pontiff may fall into error. But they who deny his infallibility do expressly assert the possibility of such a separation.[142]

Infallibility was a power aimed at uniting the Church, not at dividing it:

1 It is *de fide* that the plenitude of jurisdiction was given to Peter and his successors; and that its exercise over the whole body, pastors and people, import no separation or disunion from the Body. How then should the exercise of infallibility, which is attached to that jurisdiction, import separation?

2 Again, it is *de fide* that this supreme jurisdiction and infallibility was given to maintain and perpetuate the unity of the Church. How then can its exercise produce separation, which it is divinely ordained to prevent?

3 Lastly, it is *de fide* that in the assistance promised to Peter and his successors, all the means necessary for its due exercise are contained. An infallible office fallibly exercised is a contradiction in terms. The infallibility of the head consists in this, that he is guided both as to the means and as to the end. ... It is a part of the promise, that, in the selection of the means of its exercise, the successor of Peter will not err.[143]

The Pope's infallibility is *independent*, he would add, 'inasmuch as it does not depend upon either the *Ecclesia docens* or the *Ecclesia discens*; but it is not independent, in that it depends in all things upon the Divine Head of the Church, upon the institution of the primacy by Him, and upon the assistance of the Holy Ghost'.[144]

Manning wanted to prevent the introduction of any form of conditional clause in the definition. He thought, for example, that to make the infallibility of the Pope's pronouncements dependent on the assent—concomitant or subsequent—of the bishops would amount to Gallicanism; it would also nullify the effect of the definition, and leave the Church in worse con-

---

[142] *Privilegium*, iii. 107.
[143] Ibid. 108. Manning had mentioned the last point in his speech to the Council on 25 May (cf. *M* lii, col. 253B). The Constitution also made a passing reference to it.
[144] *Privilegium*, iii. 113.

dition than before. Who would be the judge of whether those conditions had been properly fulfilled?[145] Again, if 'the consent of the Universal Church is to be obtained before a doctrine is certain, how is it to be done? Is it to be the consent of the bishops only, or of the priests also, or of theologians, or of the faithful, or of all together? And from what age? If the *ecclesia discens* is to confirm the *ecclesia docens*,' Manning added, 'no member of it ought to be disfranchised ... If the consent of the Church is to be obtained, it must be waited for. ... And how long is it to be waited for, and in the meanwhile in what state are the doctrines defined? Are they of faith or not of faith?'[146]

Manning's mind revolted against such ideas, both on the basis of Christian revelation and on purely logical grounds. He felt that the role of the *Ecclesia discens* could not be to confirm the faith of the *Ecclesia docens*; that would mean a total inversion of Christ's injunction to Peter to confirm his brothers in the faith. The role of Peter would consequently become vague and unreal: 'If the certainty of the teaching depends upon the assent of the taught, what becomes of the teacher?'[147]

A related question was the concept of *moral unanimity* put forward by the minority. Their ideas on the subject were clearly expressed in a pamphlet on the subject published during the Council.[148] It affirmed that a dogmatic definition could not be passed on a simple majority; moral unanimity was necessary for the definitions of faith. Disciplinary laws could be passed by mere majority, but for the valid election of a Pope two-thirds of the votes of the cardinals were required; a much greater unanimity was 'absolutely essential' when dogmatic definitions were in question. This was particularly necessary in a

---

[145] Pusey, in his third *Eirenicon*, had remarked how an infallible authority would be needed to determine if the conditions had been fulfilled in each particular case (cf. E. B. Pusey, *Is Healthy Reunion Impossible?* (London, 1870), 306). One would find oneself in a similar situation to that of Anglicans with respect to Article 21: the Church is the judge regarding the controversies about the Faith, but she should not be followed if her judgement is against Holy Scripture. Who would determine whether that is the case? *Quo judice?*

[146] *True*, 193–4; Gasser had used similar arguments, see *M* lii, cols. 1215A and 1216A.

[147] *True*, 193.

[148] *De l'unanimité morale nécessaire dans les conciles pour les définitions dogmatiques: Mémoire présenté aux Pères du Concile du Vatican* (Paris, 1870).

Council where the minority was made up of bishops of such important dioceses, eminent in doctrine and character, while, on the other hand, the ranks of the majority were swollen by numerous Italians and titular bishops, and their assent vitiated by pressures. The Protest signed by the minority bishops would include these ideas, plus a thinly veiled threat that a definition without moral unanimity would be null and void.[149]

What the supporters of *moral unanimity* did not say, Manning remarked, was that the majority of the minority bishops were opposed not to the truth of the doctrine but to the opportuneness of its definition. Was the principle of *moral unanimity* applicable to decisions about the opportuneness of defining a doctrine, or only to judgements as to whether a particular doctrine was true or not? Manning did not have much time for the whole argument:

About a tenth part [as signified by the final vote] of the Council endeavoured by argument, reason, influence, and the powers given to them by the order or procedure of the Council, to prevail upon the vast majority of their brethren, which was, morally, indeed, the episcopate of the Church, to follow their guidance. ... The minority were not wronged because the majority would not swerve. What injury was done to them if the Council declined to yield to the judgment or will of those who were only a tenth of its number?[150]

The same difficulties *vis-à-vis* the universal consent presented themselves when trying to determine what constitutes moral unanimity. Where should the line of moral unanimity be drawn? Should the minority have held the Council to ransom against the wishes of the majority of the Fathers? Acton, for one, saw in moral unanimity an instrument to nullify infallibility. Everything depended, he wrote to Döllinger, on the question of majority rule. If Rome conceded the point of moral unanimity, she surrendered herself. 'An infallibility which is

---

[149] *M* li, col. 27AD. Lord Acton had been very active in promoting these ideas among the minority bishops. He would write to Gladstone (10 Mar. 1870): 'In Chapter VIII and IX the Protest affirms the principle that no dogma can be proclaimed which does not command a moral unanimity among the bishops representing the Churches ... The last paragraph of IX, where the bishops say that the claim to make dogmas in spite of the minority endangers the authority, liberty and oecumenicity of the Council, was inserted by me' (*Selections from the Correspondence of the First Lord Acton*, ed. J. N. Figgis and R. V. Laurence (London, 1917), i. 107).

[150] *True*, 162–3.

subject to the veto of the minority of bishops ceases to be infallibility; the condition of moral unanimity in the Episcopate excludes it.'[151]

During the discussions of the deputation Manning strove to
introduce into the definition a clear indication of how *ex cathedra* definitions of the Roman Pontiff did not require the concurrence of the bishops—whether before, during or after their
study and publication—to be infallible. On 5 May he asked
that the word 'irreformabile' be added when speaking of the
decrees and judgements of the Roman Pontiff on faith and
morals; in this request he was supported by Steins, Vicar Apostolic of Calcutta.[152] The word 'irreformabile' was commonly
used in that context by theologians, and could be found in the
Vota of the Consultors preparing the draft schemata before the
Council; it had also been requested by several Fathers,[153] who
wanted clearly stated by the Council that the Pope was infallible *per se*, independently of the consent or concurrence of the
bishops. The deputation incorporated the word into the new
paragraph added to the definition of infallibility: 'et eiusmodi
decreta sive iudicia, per se irreformabilia, a quovis christiano,
ut primum ei innotuerint, pleno fidei obsequio excipienda et te-
nenda esse'.[154]

The formula 'per se irreformabilia' would be slightly modified and reinforced in the new text of the schema presented for
the study of the deputation on 19 June. The new wording was
'ex sese irreformabilia esse',[155] a precision long used by the
theologians. This, in turn, was to become 'esse ex sese
irreformabiles',[156] in the text hammered out after the debates
in the General Congregations and put to the vote of the Council Fathers on 13 July. All seemed to suggest that this would
be the final version of that clause.

The above wording did not satisfy all the Fathers of the majority, though, and many references were made in the debates
to the need to include in the Constitution some explicit mention of the fact that the antecedent, concomitant, or subsequent
consent of the Church was not necessary to consider as

---

[151] Quirinus, *Letters from Rome on the Council* (London, 1870), 410.
[152] *M* liii, col. 248AB.
[153] Cf. Betti, *La Constituzione Dommatica*, 139–41 and 177.
[154] *M* liii, col. 255CD.   [155] *M* liii, col. 266A.   [156] *M* lii, col. 1235B.

infallible an *ex cathedra* definition. Maier put forward such a request on 27 April, during the discussions of the deputation, and Senestréy did likewise in the canon he included in his *Postulatum*.[157] Manning, for his part, used similar words in the proposal of definition, and accompanying canon, presented for the study of the deputation on 24 June: 'Si quis dixerit ... non esse irreformabilia, antequam consensus ecclesiae accesserit; anathema sit.'[158] The deputation considered that the formula of definition, as it stood, was clear enough, and that it did not need any further precision.

Moves were afoot, however, outside the deputation, not to leave matters as they then stood. On 14 July, Mgr. Freppel, Bishop of Angers, and some other French bishops wrote to Pius IX to express their concern over the formula of definition as it stood after the last vote by the Council. They felt that it still left the door open to a Gallican interpretation, and that it was necessary to qualify it even further, adding a reference to the fact that the *consensus episcoporum* (whether antecedent, concomitant, or subsequent) was not necessary. Pius IX passed the letter to Bilio, president of the deputation *De Fide*, with his favourable opinion.[159] That same night, the deputation added to the definition the words 'non autem ex consensu ecclesiae', which until then it had rejected as unnecessary.

The minority was also active in its attempts to introduce some last-minute changes softening the effect of the Constitution. Their efforts arrived too late, and they were bound to produce, if anything, the opposite effect to the one intended. On 15 July, representatives of the minority had a meeting with Pius IX, during which they asked the Pope, among other things, whether in the definition some mention should be made of the union of the Pope with the Church on those occasions. At the request of Pius IX, Darboy, Archbishop of Paris, put in writing, the following day, some of their suggestions. There were several possible ways, Darboy would say, of expressing the above union, as, for example, the expressions 'testimo-

---

[157] *M* liii, col. 238C and *M* lii, col. 1152C. The Theological Commission preparing the draft schemata before the Council had also considered that it would be necessary to include this clarification (cf. *M* xlix, col. 712A).

[158] *M* liii, col. 267C; see also his notes in Cwiekowski, *English Bishops*, 271.

[159] *M* lii, col. 1262AD.

nio ecclesiarum innixus', 'et mediis quae semper in ecclesia catholica usurpata fuerunt adhibitis', or 'non exclusis episcopis'.[160] It was clearly said in the letter that these, and some other minor changes, would secure the unanimous *placet*s of those who until then had been voting against the definition. They were too late: the Pope had been forewarned about the ambiguity of the formula of definition as it stood, and viewed the suggestions in that light; the new addition had already been made by the deputation, and it was to be put to the vote of the General Congregation the day Darboy's letter was dated. The new text approved by the Fathers now read: 'Romani Pontifices definitiones ex sese, non autem ex consensu ecclesiae, irreformabiles esse'. Dupanloup wrote in support of Darboy, after the vote had taken place, and complained of how new words had been added to the definition—'probably without informing His Holiness'—reinforcing the absolute and separate character of the Pope's infallibility.[161]

Manning could not but welcome this addition, as buttressing the meaning of the original formula. He would stress the importance of the clause when writing about the Council: 'it is affirmed that the doctrinal declarations of the Pontiff are infallible in and *of themselves*, and not from the consent of the Church. That is to say, they are infallible by divine assistance, and not by the assent or acceptance of the Church to which they are addressed. ... The motive for these words is obvious. They were the critical difference between what must be called once more by names which now have lost both meaning and reality, the Ultramontane and the Gallican doctrines.'[162] Those words 'precluded all ambiguity by which for two hundred years the promise of our Lord to Peter and his successors has in some minds been obscured'.[163]

* * *

The path to the formula for the definition of infallibility had been a long and laborious one for the Council and, in particular, for the deputation *De Fide*. Their efforts had repeatedly run aground in the drifting sands of the innumerable proposals

---

[160] *M* lii, col. 1322CD; see also Senestréy's Diary, *M* liii, cols. 285D–286A.
[161] *M* lii, cols. 1321B–1322B.   [162] *True*, 192–3.   [163] *Privilegium*, iii. 92.

presented by the Council Fathers. A clear way forward did not appear until 18 June, when Cullen, Archbishop of Dublin, presented, at the suggestion of Bilio, a formula which was to serve as the basis of the one approved by the Council. On the 19th, Bilio proposed it to the deputation, and it was favourably received by its members. Its study was postponed until after the deputation had finished considering the amendments suggested in the General Congregations to chapter 3 of *Pastor Aeternus*. In the meantime, Bilio introduced to the deputation another proposal of definition with its accompanying canon, the work of Manning and Franchi, titular Bishop of Thessalonica. It seems that this was the first formula, among those put forward for the study of the deputation, which included the *ex cathedra* clause.

On the 26th, the deputation started the study of the different formulas of definition which had been suggested to date by the Council Fathers. Most of its members seem to have been in favour of Cullen's formula, but there was no general agreement: some wanted to introduce changes in it, while others still preferred the formula included in the schema. Given the inconclusive outcome of their discussions, the deputation decided not to present a new formula to the Council Fathers, but to wait till the end of the debates on the subject, in order to take into consideration all the comments made. Only then, having in view the opinions of the Council, would the deputation decide which of the formulas was the most appropriate. Meanwhile, the deputation's search for the right wording of the definition was not abandoned. Its members discussed the subject again on 3 July. On this occasion Manning presented yet another formula, which preserved the *ex cathedra* expression avoiding this time the link established between the infallibility of the Church and that of the Pope, given that, as it had been pointed out, its wording could be misinterpreted. The deputation dealt with the same problem in the Congregations of 7 and 8 July, when a new wording was devised to express that correlation.

On the basis of those discussions, the theologians Kleutgen and Franzelin prepared the new formula. It was presented on 8 July to the deputation, which approved it that same day. With slight modifications of style, and addition of the clause 'non autem ex consensu ecclesiae', it was passed by the Council as the definition of papal infallibility on 16 July. It read:

Itaque nos traditioni a fidei christianae exordio perceptae fideliter inhaerendo, ad Dei Salvatoris nostri gloriam, religionis catholicae exaltationem et christianorum populorum salutem, sacro approbante concilio, docemus et divinitus revelatum dogma esse definimus: Romanum pontificem, cum ex cathedra loquitur, id est, cum omnium christianorum pastoris et doctoris munere fungens, pro suprema sua apostolica auctoritate doctrinam de fide vel moribus ab universa ecclesia tenendam definit, per assistentiam divinam, ipsi in beato Petro promissam, ea infallibilitate pollere, qua divinus Redemptor ecclesiam suam in definienda doctrina de fide vel moribus instructam esse voluit; ideoque eiusmodi Romani pontificis definitiones ex sese, non autem ex consensu ecclesiae, irreformabiles esse.[164]

Therefore faithfully adhering to the tradition received from the beginning of the Christian faith, for the glory of God Our Saviour, the exaltation of the Catholic Religion, and the salvation of Christian people, the Sacred Council approving. We teach and define that it is a dogma divinely revealed: that the Roman Pontiff, when he speaks *ex cathedra*, that is, when in discharge of the office of Pastor and Doctor of all Christians, by virtue of his supreme Apostolic authority he defines a doctrine regarding faith or morals to be held by the Universal Church, by the divine assistance promised to him in blessed Peter, is possessed of that infallibility with which the divine Redeemer willed that His Church should be endowed for defining doctrine regarding faith or morals: and that therefore such definitions of the Roman Pontiff are irreformable of themselves, and not from the consent of the Church.[165]

The solemn proclamation of the dogma of papal infallibility took place in the midst of the storm so dramatically described by Tom Mozley: 'The storm, which had been threatening all the morning, burst now with the utmost violence ... And so the "placets" of the Fathers struggled through the storm, while the thunder pealed above and the lightning flashed in at every window ... "Placet", shouted his Eminence or his Grace, and a loud clap of thunder followed in response.'[166]

---

[164] *M* lii, col. 1334CD.
[165] Manning's translation, in *Privilegium*, iii. 218.
[166] Quoted by Butler, *Vatican Council*, 413.

Newman saw in the storm a sign of God's displeasure at the proceedings of the Council; Manning would view it in a different light: 'critics saw in this thunderstorm an articulate voice of divine indignation against the definition. They forgot Sinai and the Ten Commandments.'[167]

[167]   *True*, 147.

Conclusion

Gladstone always considered Manning a man of principle in action. Intellectually, Manning was a man of first principles. Pastoral needs, his own temperament, and the circumstances of the times all conspired to channel his study and interest in that direction. He was involved in some of the major social and religious events of his time, and always brought first principles to bear upon the case in question. Sometimes they lay just beneath the surface of the argument, but on most occasions they emerged into broad daylight. He felt there was a need for clear exposition and defence of first principles, and this belief did not diminish with the progress of the century. On the contrary, the advances made in the natural and historical sciences opened new fronts against basic principles or the traditional assumptions of faith and religion, and made it ever more urgent. Old certainties and assumptions could no longer be accepted on trust. New questions had arisen, and they were urgently in need of answers.

The Church claimed to be the teacher of truth, and she required acquiescence in her doctrines. This was an empty claim and an unjust demand if she were not in possession of the truth she professed to hand on. In the early 1830s, Manning embarked on a journey in search of the rule by which divine truth might be ascertained with certainty. Theologically, the Anglican Manning was very much a self-taught man, something not uncommon at the time. He had no teacher to direct his steps, nor did he look for one. His ideas were not shaped in the hotbed of intellectual intercourse that was Tractarian Oxford; rather, they germinated and grew up in Lavington, the fruit of study and silent contemplation. There, echoes of the agitation at Oxford and elsewhere reached him, muted by distance and by the peaceful atmosphere of the South Downs countryside. In so far, however, as the Oxford Movement was trying to breathe new life into fundamental theological principles within the Church of England, as a reaction against latitudinarianism, Manning could not fail to identify with their general aims and to co-operate, from a distance, in their efforts.

In his search for solid religious principles, Manning found shelter, for a while, in High Church doctrines about the rule of faith and the unity of the Church. It was to be but a short-lived resting-place. His confidence in High Church principles was shaken by the crisis of the Oxford Movement and, in particular, by Newman's *Essay on the Development of Christian Doctrine*. The latter helped him to discover that the Anglican rule of faith was incomplete: he had found the rule, but not the judge to apply it. The anxious time that followed was a prelude to what he called his 'illumination': the discovery of the permanent presence and teaching action of the Holy Spirit in the Church, and her consequent infallibility. He also came to see that only an infallible Church could preserve and transmit the truth revealed by God in its purity and integrity. Rome was the end of his pilgrimage.

The fundamental principle which he discovered in his journey from Lavington to Rome was a light which Manning, after his conversion, did not intend to keep under a bushel. It was also in need of reassertion within the Catholic Church, where recent scientific progress had similarly challenged doctrine. As he saw it, the problem was compounded by the fact that some Catholic minds lacked a firm grasp of first principles and were not fully acquainted with the nature, basis, and sources of the Faith. Thus, they were particularly ill-equipped to weigh and judge the discoveries of the new sciences, and to evaluate how they impinged on the basic truths of the Faith. His Catholic years, up to First Vatican Council, were marked by a growing realization that the educational and formative force of the truth he had seen so clearly would not achieve its potential fruitfulness and shine in all its splendour—within and without the Catholic Church—until it was enshrined among the defined dogmas. Only then, he thought, would it exert its full educative and forming influence on minds and hearts. He had always claimed that faith did not depend on the definitions of Councils, being independent of them and existing prior to their occurrence. He believed, none the less, that the circumstances of the times demanded the conciliar definition of the infallibility of the Church and of papal infallibility, the latter being, as Manning saw it, the foundation-stone on which the infallibility of the Church rested. It was not just a matter of defending a particular truth against those who assailed it; the very existence of the Faith was at stake.

At the end of the Council, Manning felt at peace. As he wrote in a later 'Note': 'On my return from the Council I wrote a Pastoral which recorded all I thought was necessary. This done, I have never named Council or Definition or Infallibility. The Day was won and the Truth was safe, like it was after the Council of Nic[a]ea. We had no need to talk about it.'[1] He was aware of the difficulties which had followed Nicaea, and he knew that the dogmatic definition of papal infallibility would also encounter opposition. He felt, however, that the defined dogma would, in time, work its way into the consciousness of the whole Church, and develop its full corollaries.

The questions which had dominated his mind for so long seemed, in good measure, settled. There were, however, some matters very close to Manning's heart which still remained unanswered at the end of Vatican I. The object of papal infallibility had been defined by the Council as coextensive with that of the infallibility of the Church, but the suspension of the Council, because of the Piedmontese invasion of Rome, did not allow the Fathers to define the object of the Church's infallibility, the next point on their agenda. Again, the infallibility of the ordinary magisterium had been touched upon, but it had not been fully developed by the Council. Vatican I had addressed those points, although not as clearly and fully as Manning had desired. He was particularly concerned about the infallibility of the ordinary magisterium of the Church and of the Popes, because only this contained and transmitted the entire faith of the Church. So important for him was the Pope's ordinary magisterium, on which the Council had said but little, that he appeared to include most of it under the *ex cathedra* umbrella.

---

[1] Quoted in *P* ii. 458.

The subject, as Manning had foreseen, was to become of paramount importance after Vatican I. Schatz has pointed out that the Popes, particularly since Leo XIII, have published numerous encyclicals, and that their ordinary magisterium has not confined itself to the condemnation of erroneous doctrines but has also treated doctrine in a positive way. These documents, Schatz says, have been surrounded with 'un nimbe d'infaillibilité',[2] whose precise nature is not yet clearly defined. This, in a sense, has achieved most of what a good number of those among the majority in the Council wanted but could not accomplish. The subject is still under discussion. Newman, as we have seen, in dealing with the question of the ordinary magisterium of the Pope before Vatican I, had used the flexible concept of *pietas fidei*, a theological concept which seems to have been largely ignored by Newman scholars. In recent times, the Second Vatican Council (*Lumen Gentium*, 25) has expounded some general principles for the proper understanding of the teaching authority of bishops dispersed throughout the world, and of the authority enjoyed by the ordinary papal magisterium. Still, as some reactions to the recent apostolic letter *Ordinatio Sacerdotalis* (May 1994), reserving ordination to men, have shown, the questions surrounding the status of the ordinary magisterium remain in need of further clarification.

The charge of superficiality against Manning does not stand up to detailed examination. Cwiekowski seemingly contradicts himself when, after repeating it, he goes on to add that Manning, 'by his emphasis on the Holy Spirit in his explanation of papal infallibility', avoided the 'most serious shortcoming of so much of nineteenth-century ecclesiology, that the Church was seen more as a perfect society than as a supernatural mystery'. He considers, however, that 'the breadth of Manning's outlook became constricted in the agitation surrounding the council's debates'.[3] This evaluation is largely untenable in the light of a detailed study of Manning's thought. The texts and amendments he proposed—indeed, his very actions during the Council—show clear continuity with his previous utterances on the

---

[2] Cf. K. Schatz, *Le Primauté du Pape: Son histoire des origenes à nos jours* (Paris, 1992), 245.

[3] Cwiekowski, *English Bishops*, 318–19.

subject of the Church and its infallibility. Manning's theology of the Mystical Body of Christ and of the act of faith, and of the corollaries which follow from both, was always the foundation of his interventions in the Council.

It might be suggested that Manning, while essentially coherent in his ideas, lacked moderation in promoting them. The charge that he lacked restraint was already old by the time of the Council. It was not long after his conversion that people began to remark on what they saw as a change in him. While in the Anglican Church, Manning had been regarded as over-moderate, slow to advance, cautious to excess, and over-English. However, according to his critics, once a Catholic, he had metamorphosed into a violent Ultramontane, the ultra of ultras, violent and unreasoning, bitter in his animus against the Church of England.[4] References to Manning as moderate or violent are equivocal, since these qualifications may refer either to the moral quality of the individual or to his principles. Palmer of Worcester was probably the first to place Manning among the safe and trustworthy supporters of High Church principles. W. G. Ward, soon after Palmer, included Manning's name among the moderate promoters of Catholic principles in the Church of England, as opposed to the more advanced wing of the Tractarian Party which he himself represented.[5] However, moderation of principle did not smother Manning's passionate nature. This showed itself publicly, before he became a Catholic, in his letters to the *British Magazine* against Wiseman in 1836, and in his reaction to the excesses, as he saw them at the time, of the *British Critic* in 1842 and 1843. He was defending fundamental High Church principles, yet his friends upbraided him for the tone in which he did so. That he was earnest and indefatigable in the pursuit of his objectives for Church reform, Anglican education, and many other causes dear to his heart while a member of the Church of England was acknowledged by all. It was the very same passion that he put into promoting papal infallibility,

---

[4] Cf. H. C. G. Matthew (ed.), *The Gladstone Diaries, with Cabinet Minutes and Prime-Ministerial Correspondence*, vii (Oxford, 1982), 202; Pusey, *Case as to Legal Force*, 3–4, 5, 17, 21; Manning, *Workings*, 38 ff.

[5] Cf. W. G. Ward, *Ideal of a Christian Church*, 101.

Catholic education, and improving the condition of the lowest in society.

Manning would answer these charges by asking whether the statements his critics found offensive contained hard truths or epithets. He had never intended to be violent or offensive, and he was ready to withdraw any such statements if they were pointed out to him. On the other hand, if it was to hard truths they objected to, he could not withdraw them. He was ready, however, to express them in more moderate words if such could be found.[6] Manning pointed out that those who judged him moderate or extreme did so from the positions they occupied at the time. Pusey had drifted backwards from his old moorings on Catholic principles, while Manning had moved ever onwards, first to reach Pusey's original stance, then beyond it.

During the Council, too, Manning was charged with lack of moderation. There is little doubt that some resented Manning's incessant activity, but the same could be said of Dupanloup and his inopportunist group. Both parties were defending positions and truths which they felt vital for the life of the Church, and both used all the means at their disposal. When the minority found itself unable to move the majority, it did not refrain from putting pressure on the Council through foreign governments and the press. The contest was indeed unequal, but the majority can hardly be blamed for having had the weight of numbers on their side. In any case, what is taken as virtue in Dupanloup should not be used to condemn Manning. As to his principles, it could be said with justice that many shared a good number of them, albeit without Manning's determination to bring them into the Council documents.

The claim that Manning was not an original thinker is also misleading. It is generally accepted that he was a man who thought and acted by himself, that he had a mind of his own. Those who deny Manning's originality of thought do so mainly on the grounds of his not having opened new grounds of theological enquiry. It could be said, in answer, that although Manning certainly spent much time seeking the al-

---

[6] Cf. *Workings*, 40 ff.

ready well-charted doctrine of the infallibility of the Church, the voyage of discovery was all his own. For this very reason, he came to have a remarkable grasp of the principles involved and of the corollaries which followed from them. He had discovered those principles for himself, after long enquiry, and he had tried them long and hard before making them his own.

On the other hand, his doctrine of the Mystical Body of Christ, developed in good measure while he was still an Anglican, was far in advance of contemporary thought, even within Catholic theology. His pneumatological concept of the Church, as acknowledged by Cruz and Cwiekowski, was in striking contrast to the more institutional and juridical vision then prevalent. Manning's ideas were not fully appreciated in his time. Some of the concepts he touched upon did not engage the attention of theologians until well into the twentieth century. He played little part in this development, which did not build on his work. His fourth volume of Anglican sermons, perhaps the most original of his works, was confined to a theological limbo by his conversion to Catholicism a year after its publication. Anglicans shunned it, while Catholics ignored it as the work of an Anglican. When Manning looked into the possibility of republishing some of his Anglican works, he was discouraged from doing so. Dr Bernard Smith advised against publication, saying: 'Recollect these were the works of Dr. Manning, a Protestant. They were the fruits of the Anglican not of the Catholic Church.'[7] That decided the issue of republication. Manning, when writing later about the abandoned project of reprinting his volumes of Anglican sermons, was to say: 'I wished my past, while I was in the twilight, to lie dead to me, and I to it.'[8]

The influence of his ideas was also conditioned by the style of his works. They were not the writings of a professional theologian. Rather, they were conceived and written in the midst of unceasing administrative and pastoral work. The expression of his thought suffered, with regard to clarity and completeness, from the fragmented way in which he presented it and

---

[7] Letter dated 18 Mar. 1865, quoted in *P* ii. 723.

[8] Note dated 1882, quoted in *P* ii. 722. F. Sheed went as far as saying that it had been Robert Hugh Benson who had introduced the doctrine of the Mystical Body of Christ to the English-speaking world (cf. *The Church and I* (London, 1975), 28).

from the hurried composition of his writings. He could, no doubt, see in his mind all the connections of the ideas he was putting forward, but in presenting them, he sometimes presumed that his readers were as familiar with them as he was himself. As a result, it often happens that sentences and concepts contained in a particular work can only be properly understood in the context of his other writings. When taken in isolation from the whole corpus of his work, they leave the door open to misunderstanding. That difficulty is compounded by Manning's occasional rhetorical excesses. These might have gone down well on a public platform, but in his published works they often served to obscure his thought, deforming the public appearance of his ideas and detracting from the force of the argument, while offering an easy handle to the critic or the satirist. While Manning cannot be said to have created a school, the numerous editions of his works testify to his deep and lasting influence on English Catholicism.

Manning's position in Catholic theology may not be as exalted as that bestowed on him by John Hungerford Pollen, who depicted Manning on the ceiling of Merton College chapel as Daniel, prophet of doctrine, alongside Pusey as Jeremiah, prophet of the captivity. Still, he had a theological mind, a deeper mind than many have given him credit for. Peter Erb has said that Manning was 'a fine theologian', although his works had primarily a pastoral end in mind.[9] E. Hocedez, for his part, has remarked on how Manning put dogma at the service of the spiritual life, saying that his ascetical works were 'imprégnés de théologie'.[10] That stood to reason: for Manning, every light which revealed God's nature and love to man should lead towards conversion. Dogmatic principles were sterile by themselves if the power of truth did not transform the human mind and heart that perceived them.[11]

Manning, while vigorously defending the dogmatic principle in religion, was remarkably free from the dogmas of class, party, economic theory, and the like, which fettered many of

---

[9] Cf. Erb, *Question of Sovereignty*, 6.
[10] Hocedez, *Histoire de la Théologie*, ii. 223.
[11] Cf. *ASer* iv. 67–8.

his contemporaries; his theology helped him to escape the narrow councils of prejudice and of public opinion. 'Manning's religion was the driving force of his humanitarianism, he did not owe any fundamental debt to the Christian Socialists or to the Positivists. The material end was the same, perhaps, but Manning's policy was invigorated by a highly personal sense of religion, of practical Christianity.'[12] The problems of Ireland, of the working class, and of the lack of education for children, the social problems in Europe and elsewhere, were issues a Christian should attend to: the Holy Spirit spoke through them, and called on Christian justice and charity to respond.

Many were surprised at Manning's involvement in social ventures promoted by non-Catholics. Sheridan Gilley has described his reasons for getting involved. His pneumatological theology, while leading him to recognize the Catholic Church as Christ's Church, in all the exclusiveness of her claims, enunciated also 'a dynamic ecclesiology which is far more impressive than its rather grim model of self-expression'. Manning thought that the Holy Spirit works all over the world: among Christians as well as among the heathen. He worked in the world even before Christ's Incarnation. The Holy Spirit, Manning added, acts in a special way among those who confess faith in Christ, even though separated from his true Church. The doctrine of the universal office of the Holy Spirit 'inspired Manning to recognise its presence wherever it was to be found, whether among the Nonconformist Joseph Arch's agricultural labourers or the philanthropy and preaching of the Salvation Army. The paradox was that the very exclusiveness of his Spirit ecclesiology was part and parcel of his own practical universalism. In defending Russian Jews against pogroms, in consorting with trade unionists who were championing the poor, he was acting with those who did the Spirit's work even if they knew it not themselves.'[13]

One final point needs to be clearly stated. The identification of absolutist monarchical principles as the key to understanding the minds of those who supported the doctrine of papal infallibility, if valid at all, is certainly not applicable to

---

[12] McClelland, *Cardinal Manning*, 215.

[13] S. Gilley, 'Manning: The Catholic Writings', in McClelland, *By Whose Authority?*, 250–1.

Manning. As we have seen, he would not force the analogy of the natural realm on to supernatural reality; neither would he abuse analogy the other way round. Faith and science had different objects and were ruled by different laws, although both were concerned with truth. Likewise, the Church and human society were founded on different principles, although both had as their end man's good. The divine structure of the Church need not necessarily be the ideal model for human society, but neither was human society the ideal model for the Church.

Manning loved peace; still, he treasured truth above peace, holding firmly to the conviction that peace could only be built upon truth. As a man of action, he valued expediency; on the other hand, as a man of deep faith and deep thought, he held that only actions rooted in sound principles were truly expedient. He tried to live by these convictions.

Bibliography

Manuscript Sources

British Library, London: Gladstone Papers (Add. MSS 44247–50, 44709).

Bodleian Library, Oxford: Manning Papers (MSS Eng. Lett. b. 37, c. 651–64, d. 526–7; MSS Eng. Misc. c. 873–6, d. 1278–80, e. 1393–9, g. 355), Wilberforce Papers.

Pusey House, Oxford: Pusey Papers, Copeland Papers.

Ushaw College, Durham: Wiseman Papers, Wilberforce Papers, Gillow Papers.

Westminster Diocesan Archive, London: Wiseman Papers, Manning Papers.

Venerable English College Archive, Rome: Talbot Papers.

Birmingham Oratory Archive: Newman Papers (particularly his correspondence with H. E. Manning), Ryder Papers.

Archives of the Sacred Congregation of Propaganda Fidei (SCPF), Rome: Scritture Riferite nei Congresi, Anglia.

Pitts Theology Library, Emory University, Atlanta: Manning Papers (MSS 002, boxes 1–12).

St Andrews University Library, Ward Papers (V. Miscellaneous papers, letters and notes; VI. Letters from Ward to different correspondents; VII. Letters to Ward).

Published Works by Manning

The English Church: Its Succession and Witness for Christ (London, 1835).

Catena Patrum no. III: Testimony of Writers in the Later English Church to the Duty of Maintaining, quod semper, quod ubique, quod ab omnibus traditum est, Tracts for the Times, lxxviii (new edn., London, 1839). With C. Marriot.

National Education: A Sermon Preached in the Cathedral Church of Chichester in Behalf of the Chichester Central Schools (London, 1838).

The Principle of the Ecclesiastical Commission Examined, in a Letter to the Right Revd. Lord Bishop of Chichester (London, 1838).

The Rule of Faith (London, 1838).

The Rule of Faith: Appendix to a Sermon (London, 1838).

The Mind of Christ the Perfection and Bond of the Church (Chichester, 1841).

A Charge Delivered at the Ordinary Visitation of the Archdeaconry of Chichester, in July 1841 (London, 1841).

The Moral Design of the Apostolic Ministry (London, 1841).

A Charge Delivered at the Ordinary Visitation of the Archdeaconry of Chichester, in July 1842 (London, 1842).

The Unity of the Church (London, 1842).

A Charge Delivered at the Ordinary Visitation of the Archdeaconry of Chichester, in July 1843 (London, 1843).

Sermons Preached before the University of Oxford (Oxford, 1844).

A Charge Delivered at the Ordinary Visitation of the Archdeaconry of Chichester, in July 1845 (London, 1845).

A Charge Delivered at the Ordinary Visitation of the Archdeaconry of Chichester, in July 1846 (London, 1846).

A Charge Delivered at the Ordinary Visitation of the Archdeaconry of Chichester, in July 1848 (London, 1848).

A Charge Delivered at the Ordinary Visitation of the Archdeaconry of Chichester, in July 1849 (London, 1849).

Sermons (4 vols., London, 1842–50).

The Appellate Jurisdiction of the Crown in Matters Spiritual: A Letter to the Right Reverend Ashurst-Turner, Bishop of Chichester (London, 1850).

The Grounds of Faith (2nd edn., London, 1856) (1st edn. 1852).

The Office of the Holy Ghost under the Gospel (London, 1857).

The Temporal Power of the Vicar of Jesus Christ (2nd edn., London, 1862) (1st edn. 1860 as *Temporal Sovereignty of the Popes*).

The Crown in Council, on the 'Essays and Reviews' (London, 1864).

The Workings of the Holy Spirit in the Church of England (London, 1864).

The Temporal Mission of the Holy Ghost (6th edn., London, 1909) (1st edn. 1865).

The Reunion of Christendom: A Pastoral Letter (London, 1866).

England and Christendom (London, 1867).

Denominational Education: A Pastoral Letter (London, 1869).

Petri Privilegium: Three Pastorals (London, 1871).

Sermons on Ecclesiastical Subjects. i (Dublin, 1863); ii (London, 1872); iii (London, 1873).

The Four Great Evils of the Day (8th edn., London, n.d.) (1st edn. 1871).

The Fourfold Sovereignty of God (London, 1871).

Sin and its Consequences (London, n.d.) (1st edn. 1874).

The Vatican Decrees in their Bearing on Civil Allegiance (London, 1875).

The Internal Mission of the Holy Ghost (9th edn., London, n.d.) (1st edn. 1875).

The Glories of the Sacred Heart (London, 1876).

The True Story of the Vatican Council (2nd edn., London, n.d.) (1st edn. 1877).

The Independence of the Holy See (London, 1877).

Miscellanies (3 vols., London, 1877–88).

The Pastoral Office (Printed for private use only, 1883).

The Office of the Church in Higher Catholic Education: A Pastoral Letter (London, 1885).

Religio Viatoris (5th edn., London, n.d.) (1st edn. 1887).

A Pastoral Letter on Education (London, 1889).

National Education (London, 1889).

Pastime Papers, ed. W. Meynell (London, n.d.).

Contemporary Periodicals

British Critic
British Magazine
Dublin Review
Home and Foreign Review
Rambler
Tablet
Union Review
Westminster Gazette

Other Works Consulted

Acton, J. E., *The Correspondence of Lord Acton and Richard Simpson*, ed. J. L. Altholz, D. McElrath and J. C. Holland (3 vols., Cambridge, 1971–5).

——*The History of Freedom and Other Essays*, ed. J. N. Figgis and R. V. Laurence (London, 1909).

——*Selections from the Correspondence of the First Lord Acton*, ed. J. N. Figgis and R. V. Laurence (London, 1917).

Allchin, A. M., *Participation in God: A Forgotten Strand in Anglican Tradition* (London, 1988).

Allies, M., *Thomas William Allies* (London, 1907).

Allies, T. W., *Per Crucem ad Lucem* (2 vols., London, 1879).

Altholz, J. L., *Anatomy of a Controversy: The Debate over Essays and Reviews, 1860–1864* (Aldershot, 1994).

——*The Liberal Catholic Movement in England* (London, 1962).

Aubert, R., *Le Problème de l'acte de foi* (3rd edn., Louvain, 1958).

——*Vatican I* (Paris, 1964).

Barnes, A. S., *The Catholic Schools in England* (London, 1926).

Beck, G. A., *The English Catholics, 1850–1950* (London, 1950).

Bellamy, *La Théologie Catholique au XIXe siècle* (3rd. edn., Paris, 1904).

Bellasis, E., *Memorials of Mr. Serjeant Bellasis* (2nd edn., London, 1895).

Betti, U., *La Constituzione Dommatica 'Pastor Aeternus' del Concilio Vaticano I* (Rome, 1961).

Biemer, G., *Newman on Tradition* (Freiburg, 1967).

Blackinston, N. (ed.), *The Roman Question: Extracts from the Despatches of Odo Russell from Rome, 1858–1870* (London, 1962).

Bodley, J. E. C., *Cardinal Manning: The Decay of Idealism in France: The Institute of France* (London, 1912).

Bossy, J., *The English Catholic Community, 1570–1850* (London, 1975).

Bradley, I., *The Call to Seriousness* (London, 1976).

Brandreth, H. R. T., *The Oecumenical Ideals of the Oxford Movement* (London, 1947).

Bremond, H., *The Mystery of Newman* (London, 1907).

Brendon, P., *Hurrel Froude and the Oxford Movement* (London, 1974).

Brilioth, Y., *The Anglican Revival: Studies in the Oxford Movement* (London, 1925).

Brown, F. K., *Fathers of the Victorians: The Age of Wilberforce* (Cambridge, 1961).

Burgess, H. J., *Enterprise in Education: The Story of the Work of the Established Church in the Education of the People prior to 1870* (London, 1958).

Butler, C., *The Life and Times of Bishop Ullathorne, 1806–1889* (2 vols., London, 1926).

——*The Vatican Council, 1869–1870* (new edn. London, 1962).

Butler, P. A., *Gladstone: Church, State and Tractarianism: A Study of his Religious Ideas and Attitudes, 1809–1859* (Oxford, 1982).

——(ed.) *Pusey Rediscovered* (London, 1983).

Caudron, M., 'Magistère ordinaire et infaillibilité pontificale d'après la constitution "Dei Filius" ', *Ephemerides Theologicae Lovaniensis*, xxxvi (1960), 393–431.

Chadwick, O., *Catholicism and History* (Cambridge, 1978).

——*The Spirit of the Oxford Movement: Tractarian Essays* (Cambridge, 1990).

——*The Victorian Church* (3rd edn., 2 vols., London, 1987).

Chapeau, A., 'Manning the Anglican', in J. Fitzsimons (ed.), *Manning: Anglican and Catholic* (London, 1951), 1–39.

Chapman, R., *Father Faber* (London, 1961).

Chinnici, J. P., *The English Catholic Enlightment: John Lingard and the Cisalpine Movement, 1780–1850* (Shepherdstown, 1980).

Church, R. W., *The Oxford Movement* (London, 1891).

Clark, J. C. D., *English Society, 1688–1832: Ideology, Social Structure and Political Practice during the* Ancien Règime (Cambridge, 1985).

Congar, Y., 'L'Ecclésiologie de la Révolution Française au Concile du Vatican sous le signe de l'affirmation de l'autorité', *Unam Sanctam*, xxxiv (Paris, 1960), 77–114.

Conzemius, V., 'Lord Acton and the First Vatican Council', *Journal of Ecclesiastical History*, xx (Oct. 1969), 267–94.

Cruickshank, M., *Church and State in English Education: 1870 to the Present Day* (London, 1963).

Crumb, L. N., *The Oxford Movement and its Leaders: A Bibliography of Secondary and Lesser Primary Sources* (Metuchen, NJ, 1988).

Cruz, F. L., *Spiritus in Ecclesia: Las relaciones entre el Espíritu Santo y la Iglesia según el Cardenal Manning* (Pamplona, 1977).

Cunliffe, C. J. (ed.), *Joseph Butler's Moral and Religious Thought* (Oxford, 1992).

Cwiekowski, F. J., *The English Bishops and the First Vatican Council* (Louvain, 1971).

Dawson, C., *The Spirit of the Oxford Movement* (London, 1933).

Dechamps, Mgr., *L'Infaillibilité et le Concile Général* (2nd edn., Paris, 1869).

——*A Letter to Monseigneur Dupanloup, Bishop of Orléans* (London, 1870).

De l'unanimité morale nécessaire dans les conciles pour les définitions dogmatiques: Mémoire présenté aux Pères du Concile du Vatican (Paris, 1970).

Dessain, C. S., *John Henry Newman* (London, 1966).

—— 'What Newman Taught in Manning's Church', in *Infallibility in the Church* (London, 1968), 59–80.

Dewan, W. F., 'Preparation of the Vatican Council's Schema on the Power and Nature of the Primacy', *Ephemerides Theologicae Lovanienses*, xxxvi (1960), 23–56.

Dibble, R. A., *John Henry Newman: The Concept of Infallible Doctrinal Authority* (Washington, 1955).

Döllinger, I. von, see Janus and Quirinus.

Dupanloup, Mgr. F., *The Future Oecumenical Council: A Letter by the Bishop of Orléans to the Clergy of his Diocese* (London, 1869).

——*Lettre de Mgr. l'Évêque d'Orléans au clergé de son diocèse relativement à la définition de l'infaillibilité au prochain concile* (2nd edn., Paris, 1869).

——*Réponse de Mgr. l'Évêque d'Orléans à Mgr. Manning* (Paris, 1869).

——*Réponse de Mgr. l'Évêque d'Orléans à Monseigneur Dechamps, Archévêque de Malines* (Paris, 1870).

Earnest, J. D. and Tracey, J., *John Henry Newman: An Annotated Bibliography of his Tract and Pamphlet Collection* (New York, 1984).

Erb, P. C., *A Question of Sovereignty: The Politics of Manning's Conversion* (Atlanta, 1996).

Fessler, J., *The True and False Infallibility of the Popes: A Controversial Reply to Dr. Schulte* (London, 1875).

Fitzsimons, J. (ed.), *Manning: Anglican and Catholic* (London, 1951).

Ford, J. T., 'Different Models of Infallibility', *Proceedings of the Catholic Theological Society of America*, xxxv (1980), 217–33.

——'Infallibility: A Review of Recent Studies', *Theological Studies*, xl (1979), 273–305.

Forrester, D., *Young Doctor Pusey* (London, 1989).

Fothergill, B., *Nicholas Wiseman* (London, 1963).

Froude, R. H., *The Remains of Richard Hurrell Froude*, ed. J. Keble and J. H. Newman, Part I (2 vols., London, 1838); Part II (2 vols., Derby, 1839).

Gasquet, A. (ed.), *Lord Acton and his Circle* (London, 1906).

——'Unpublished Letters of Cardinal Wiseman and Dr. Manning', *Dublin Review*, clxix (Oct.–Dec. 1921), 161–91; clxxii (Jan.–Mar. 1923), 106–29.

Gilley, S., 'John Keble and the Victorian Churching of Romanticism', in J. R. Watson (ed.), *An Infinite Complexity: Essays in Romanticism* (Edinburgh, 1983), 226–39.

——'Manning: The Catholic Writings', in V. A. McClelland (ed.), *By Whose Authority? Newman, Manning and the Magisterium* (Bath, 1996), 244–58.

——'New Light on an Old Scandal', in A. Bellenger (ed.) *Opening the Scrolls: Essays in Catholic History in Honour of Godfrey Anstruther* (Bath, 1987), 166–98.

——*Newman and his Age* (London, 1990)

Gillow, J., *A Literary and Biographical Dictionary of the English Catholics from the Breach with Rome in 1534 to the Present Time* (5 vols. (London, 1885–1902).

Gladstone, W. E., *Studies Subsidiary to the Works of Bishop Butler* (Oxford, 1896).

——*The Vatican Decrees in their Bearing on Civil Allegiance* (London, 1874).

Gomez-Hera, J. M., *Temas dogmaticos del Concilio Vaticano I* (Vitoria, 1971).

Gray, R., *Cardinal Manning: A Biography* (London, 1985).

Greenfield, R. H., 'The Attitude of the Tractarians to the Roman

Catholic Church, 1833–1850' (unpub. D.Phil. thesis, Oxford, 1956).

Griffin, J., 'L'Eirenicon du Dr Pusey de 1865: une interpretation', *Revue d'histoire ecclésiastique*, lxxxii/2 (Apr.–June 1987), 281–90.

Gwyn, D. *The Second Spring, 1818–1852: A Study of the Catholic Revival in England* (London, 1942).

Härdelin, A., *The Tractarian Understanding of the Eucharist* (Uppsala, 1965).

Hasler, A. B., *How the Pope became Infallible* (New York, 1981).

Hilton, B., *The Age of Atonement* (Oxford, 1988).

Hocedez, E., *Histoire de la Théologie au XIXe siècle*, (3 vols., Brussels and Paris, 1947–52).

Holmes, J. D., *More Roman than Rome: English Catholicism in the Nineteenth Century* (London, 1978).

——'Newman, History and Theology', *Irish Theological Quarterly*, xxxvi/1 (Jan. 1969), 34–45.

Hutton, A. W., *Cardinal Manning* (London, 1892).

Hylson-Smith, K., *High Churchmanship in the Church of England from the Sixteenth Century to the Present Century* (Edinburgh, 1993).

Imberg, R. *In Quest of Authority: the 'Tracts for the Times' and the Development of the Tractarian Leaders, 1833–1841* (Lund, 1987).

Ippolito, R., 'Archbishop Manning's Championship of Papal Infallibility, 1867–1872', *Ampleforth Journal*, lxxii/2 (Summer 1972), 31–9.

Jagger, P. J. (ed.) *Gladstone, Politics and Religion* (London, 1985).

Jaki, S., *Les Tendences nouvelles de l'écclésiologie* (Rome, 1957).

Janus (Döllinger), *The Pope and the Council* (2nd edn., London, 1869).

Keble, J., *Sermons Academical and Occasional* (Oxford, 1847).

Ker, I., *John Henry Newman: A Biography* (Oxford, 1990).

Kerkvoorde, A., 'La Théologie du "Corps Mystique" au dix-neuvième siècle', *Nouvelle Revue Théologique*, lxvii (Sept.–Oct. 1945), 417–30, 1025–38.

Knight, M., 'The Sacramental Theology of Robert Isaac Wilberforce' (unpub. M.A. thesis, Durham, 1979).

Knox, T. F., *When Does the Church Speak Infallibly; or the Nature and Scope of the Church's Teaching Office* (2nd edn., London, 1870).

Lathbury, D. C. (ed.), *Correspondence on Church and Religion of W. E. Gladstone* (2 vols., London, 1910).

Leslie, S., *Henry Edward Manning: His Life and Labours* (2nd edn., London, 1921).

Liddon, H. P., *Life of Edward Bouverie Pusey* (4 vols., London, 1893–7).

Macaulay, T. B., '*The state in its relations with the Church* by W. E.

Gladstone' (review article), *Edinburgh Review*, lxix/139 (Apr. 1839), pp. 231–80.

McClelland, V. A., *Cardinal Manning: His Public Life and Influence 1865–1892* (London, 1962).

——'Corporate Reunion: A Nineteenth Century Dilemma', *Theological Studies*, Vol. xliii/1 (Mar., 1982), 3–29.

——*English Roman Catholics and Higher Education (1830–1903)* (Oxford, 1973).

——'The "Free Schools" Issue and the General Election of 1885: A Denominational Response', *History of Education*, v/2 (1976), 141–54.

——(ed.) *By Whose Authority? Newman, Manning and the Magisterium* (Bath, 1996).

——(ed.) Henry Edward Manning (1808–1892), *Recusant History*, xxi/2 (Oct. 1992).

McCool, G. A., *Catholic Theology in the Nineteenth Century: The Quest for a Unitary Method* (New York, 1977).

McElrath, D., *Lord Acton: The Decisive Decade, 1864–1874* (Louvain, 1970).

——*The Syllabus of Pius IX: Some Reactions in England* (Louvain, 1964).

Madoz, J., 'La Iglesia Cuerpo Místico de Cristo según el primer esquema "De Ecclesia" en el Concilio Vaticano', *Revista Española de Teologia*, iii (1943), 159-181.

Mansi, J. D. (ed.), *Sacrorum Conciliorum nova et amplissima collection*, vols. xlix–liii (Arnhem and Leipzig, 1923–7).

Maret, H., *Du Concile générale et de la paix religieuse* (2 vols., Paris, 1869).

Maskell, W., *What is the Meaning of the Late Definition on the Infallibility of the Pope?* (London, 1871).

Mathew, D., *Lord Acton and His Times* (London, 1968).

Mathew, H. C. G., *Gladstone, 1809–1874* (Oxford, 1986).

——(ed.) *The Gladstone Diaries, with Cabinet Minutes and Prime-Ministerial Correspondence*, vii (Oxford, 1982).

Mersch, E., *The Whole Christ: The Historical Development of the Doctrine of the Mystical Body in Scripture and Tradition* (London, 1938).

Misner, P., 'Newman and the Tradition concerning the Papal Antichrist', *Church History*, xlii (1973), 375–88.

——*Papacy and Development: Newman and the Primacy of the Pope* (Leiden, 1976).

Möhler, J. A., *Symbolism: or Exposition of the Doctrinal Differences between Catholic and Protestants, as Evidenced by their Symbolical Writings* (2 vols., London, 1843).

——*Unity in the Church, or The Principle of Catholicism*, (ed.) P. C. Erb (Washington, 1996).

Mozley, T., *Reminiscences: Chiefly of Oriel College and the Oxford Movement* (2 vols., 2nd edn., London, 1882).

Murphy, J. *Church, State and Schools in Britain, 1800–1970* (London, 1970).

——*The Education Act 1870* (Newton Abbot, 1972).

Newman, J. H., *An Essay on the Development of Christian Doctrine* (London, 1906).

——*Apologia pro Vita Sua* (Oxford, 1913).

——*Certain Difficulties felt by Anglicans in Catholic Teaching* (new edn., 2 vols., London, 1897–8).

——*Correspondence of John Henry Newman with John Keble and Others, 1839–1845*, ed. J. Bacchus (London, 1917).

——*Discussions and Arguments on Various Subjects* (London, 1891).

——*The Idea of a University* (new edn., London, 1907).

——*On Consulting the Faithful in Matters of Doctrine*, ed. J. Coulson (London,1961).

——*The Theological Papers of John Henry Newman on Biblical Inspiration and on Infallibility*, ed. J. D. Holmes (Oxford, 1979).

Newsome, D.,*The Convert Cardinals: John Henry Newman and Henry Edward Manning* (London, 1993).

——*The Parting of Friends: A Study of the Wilberforces and Henry Manning* (London, 1966).

Nockles, P., 'Continuity and Change in Anglican High Churchmanship in Britain 1792–1850', (D.Phil. thesis, 2 vols., Oxford, 1982).

——*The Oxford Movement in Context* (Cambridge, 1994).

Norman, E., *Anti-Catholicism in Victorian England* (London, 1968).

——*The English Catholic Church in the Nineteenth Century* (Oxford, 1985).

O'Gara, M., *Triumph in Defeat: Infallibility, Vatican I, and the French Minority Bishops* (Washington, 1988).

O'Gorman, C., 'A History of Henry Manning's Religious Opinions 1808–1832', *Recusant History*, xxi/2 (Oct. 1992), 152–66.

Ollivier, É., *L'Église et l'État au Concile du Vatican* (2 vols., Paris, 1879).

O'Meara, Kathleen, *Thomas Grant, First Bishop of Southwark* (2nd edn., London, 1886).

Ornsby, R., *Memoirs of James Hope-Scott* (2 vols., London, 1884).

Page, J. R., *What Will Dr. Newman Do? John Henry Newman and Papal Infallibility 1865–1875* (Collegeville, Minn., 1994).

Palmer, W., *A Narrative of Events Connected with the Publication of the*

Tracts for the Times, with Reflections on Existing Tendencies to Romanism (2nd edn., Oxford, 1843).

Palmer, W., *A Treatise on the Church of Christ* (3rd edn., 2 vols., London, 1842; 1st edn., 1838).

Pawley, M., *Faith and Family: The Life and Circle of Ambrose Phillipps de Lisle* (Norwich, 1993).

Paz, D. G., *Popular Anti-Catholicism in Mid-Victorian England* (Stanford, 1992).

Penelhum, T., *Butler* (London, 1985).

——'Butler and Human Ignorance', in C. J. Cunliffe (ed.), *Joseph Butler's Moral and Religious Thought* (Oxford ,1992), 117–39.

Prickett, S., *Romanticism and Religion: The Tradition of Coleridge and Wordsworth in the Victorian Church* (Cambridge, 1976).

Purcell, E. S., *Life and Letters of Ambrose Phillipps De Lisle* (2 vols., London, 1900).

——*Life of Cardinal Manning* (2 vols., London, 1896).

Pusey, E. B., *Case as to the Legal Force of the Judgment of the Privy Council in re Fendall v Wilson* (London, 1864).

——*An Eirenicon: In a Letter to the Author of 'The Christian Year'* (London, 1865).

——*Is Healthy Reunion Impossible? A Second Letter to the Very Rev. J. H. Newman, DD* (London, 1870).

Quinn, D., 'Manning as Politician', *Recusant History*, xxi/2 (Oct. 1992), 267–86.

——*Patronage and Piety: The Politics of English Roman Catholicism, 1850–1900* (Basingstoke, 1993).

'Quirinus' (Döllinger), *Letters from Rome on the Council*, repr. from the *Allgemeine Zeitung* (London, 1870).

Reardon, B., *From Coleridge to Gore: A Century of Religious Thought in Britain* (London, 1971).

Rowell, G., 'Remember Lot's Wife—Manning's Anglican Sermons', *Recusant History*, xxi/2 (Oct. 1992), 167–79.

——(ed.) *Tradition Renewed* (London, 1986).

——*The Vision Glorious* (Oxford, 1983).

Ryder, H. I. D., *Catholic Controversy: A Reply to Dr Littledale's 'Plain Reasons'* (London, 1881).

——*Idealism in Theology: A Review of Dr Ward's Scheme of Dogmatic Authority* (London, 1867).

——*A Letter to William George Ward, Esq., D.Ph., on his Theory of Infallible Instruction* (London, 1868).

——*Postcriptum to Letter to W. G. Ward, Esq., D.Ph.* (London, 1868).

Schatz, K., *Le Primauté du Pape: Son histoire des origenes à nos jours* (Paris, 1992).

——*Vaticanum I, 1869–1870* (3 vols., Paderborn, 1992–4).

Schiefen, R. J., *Nicholas Wiseman and the Transformation of English Catholicism* (Sheperdstown, 1984).

Schrader, C., *De Unitate Romana* (Friburgi Brisgovia, 1862).

Sheed, F., *The Church and I* (London, 1975).

Snead-Cox, J. G., *The Life of Cardinal Vaughan* (2 vols., London, 1910).

Strachey, L., *Eminent Victorians: Cardinal Manning, Florence Nightingale, Dr Arnold, General Gordon* (London, 1918).

Stuart, E. B., 'Roman Catholic Reactions to the Oxford Movement and Anglican Schemes for Reunion, from 1833 to the Condemnation of Anglican Orders in 1896' (unpub. D.Phil thesis, Oxford, 1987).

Thils, G., *Primauté et infaillibilité du Pontife Romain au Vatican I et autres études d'ecclésiologie* (Leuven, 1989).

Ullathorne, W. B., *Letters*, ed. by the nuns of St Dominic Convent, Stone (London, 1892).

——*Notes on the Education Question* (London, 1857).

——*The Anglican Theory of Union as Maintained in the Appeal to Rome and Dr Pusey's 'Eirenicon': A Second Letter* (London, 1866).

Van Ackeren, G. (ed.), *The Church Teaches* (Rockford, Ill., 1973).

von Arx, J. P., 'Archbishop Manning and the Kulturkampf', *Recusant History*, xxi/2 (Oct. 1992), 254–66.

——'Manning's Ultramontanism and the Catholic Church in British Politics', *Recusant History*, xix/3 (1989), 332–47.

Walsh, J., Haydon, C., and Taylor, S. (eds.), *The Church of England c. 1689–c. 1833* (Cambridge, 1993).

Ward, B., *The Eve of Catholic Emancipation* (3 vols., London, 1911).

—— *The Sequel of Catholic Emancipation* (2 vols., London, 1915).

Ward, W., *The Life and Times of Cardinal Wiseman* (new edn., 2 vols., London, 1912).

——*The Life of John Henry, Cardinal Newman* (2 vols., London, 1912).

——*Ten Personal Studies* (London, 1908).

——*William George Ward and the Catholic Revival* (London, 1893).

Ward, W. G., *The Authority of Doctrinal Decisions which are not Definitions of Faith* (London, 1866).

——*A Brief Summary of the Recent Controversy on Infallibility; Being a Reply to Re Fr. Ryder on his Postscrip* (London, 1868).

——*De Infallibilitatis extensione: Theses quasdam et quaestiones theologorum judicio subjicit Gulielmus Georgius Ward* (London, 1869).

——*The Ideal of a Christian Church Considered in Comparison with Existing Practice* (London, 1844).

——*A Letter [to] the Revd. Fr. Ryder on his Recent Pamphlet* (London, 1867).

——*A Second Letter to the Revd. Father Ryder* (London, 1868).

Webb, C. C. J., *Religious Thought in the Oxford Movement* (London, 1928).

Wilberforce, R. I., *The Doctrine of the Incarnation of our Lord Jesus Christ, in its Relation to Mankind and to the Church* (London, 1848).

Wiseman, N., *Essays on Various Subjects* (2 vols., London, 1853).

——*Lectures on the Principal Doctrines and Practices of the Catholic Church* (2 vols., London, 1836).

Woodward, E. I., *The Age of Reform, 1850–1870* (new edn., Oxford, 1949).

Index